SHATTERED PAST

SHATTERED PAST

Reconstructing
German Histories

Konrad H. Jarausch
and
Michael Geyer

PRINCETON UNIVERSITY PRESS
Princeton and Oxford

In the United Kingdom: Princeton University Press, 3 Market Place,
Woodstock, Oxfordshire OX20 1SY

Library of Congress Cataloging-in-Publication Data
Jarausch, Konrad Hugo.
Shattered past : reconstructing German histories / Konrad H. Jarausch and
Michael Geyer.
p. cm.
Includes bibliographical references and index.
ISBN 0-691-05935-7 (alk. paper)—ISBN 0-691-05936-5 (pbk. : alk. paper)
1. Historiography—German—History—20th Century. 2. History—Philosophy.
3. Nationalism—German—History—20th Century. 4. Holocaust, Jewish
(1939–1945)—Historiography. 5. Germany—Social conditions—20th century.
I. Geyer, Michael, 1947 — II. Title.
DD86 .J253 2003
943.08'07'2043—dc21   2002016933

This book has been composed in Palatino

Text design by Carmina Alvarez-Gaffin

The paper used in this publication meets the minimum requirements of ANSI/
NISO Z39.48-1992 (R 1997)
(Permanence of Paper)

www.pupress.princeton.edu

Printed in the United States of America

10 9 8 7 6 5 4 3 2 1

Contents

Preface

Broken glass, twisted beams, piles of debris—these are the early memories of the "children of the rubble," who grew up amid the ruins left by the Third Reich. Only by traveling to regions spared from destruction did those of us born in Germany during or after World War II learn that houses were supposed to have roofs; windows, panes; and families, fathers. To our insistent questions about the reasons for this devastation we received only evasive answers from harassed adults, preoccupied with surviving the hunger, cold, and uncertainty of the postwar years. Either anonymous enemy airmen with their bombs or evil "Nazis," with whom nobody claimed to have had anything to do, were supposed to have been responsible for all that destruction. In contrast to the proud heritage of the victorious occupiers, the German past seemed literally shattered, covering the present with shame and burdening the future with its detritus. It had become a history of "the German catastrophe."

More than five decades later, German youths live in manicured suburbs and stroll across prosperous pedestrian malls, looking back at a surprisingly successful rebuilding of their country into a civil society. As the soaring cupola on top of a refurbished but shell-scarred Reichstag building suggests, the Federal Republic has magically transformed a tarnished legacy into a gleaming modernity. The run-down eastern cities that still bear the marks of Communist mismanagement are gradually recovering as well, even if they are not exactly the "flourishing landscapes" promised during unification. Current reconsiderations of

German history, therefore, must also take into account the sense of achievement that comes with an astounding recovery of material wealth and cultural creativity. The <u>tension between the experience of the second half of the twentieth century and the memory of the first half</u> begs to be explored. This sharp contrast often seems mind boggling—it runs through individual life experiences as much as through the collective history of the age.

This history is not for the Germans alone, since Hitler's war at home and abroad has injected a German presence into the world. As professional historians in the United States, the authors have often encountered questions from older Americans about why their fathers or siblings had to die on the European continent twice in the twentieth century. To our young students, the unspeakable horror of the Holocaust continues to awaken interest in German history. They tend to conceive the Holocaust as the exemplary "other" to western traditions, sufficiently close to be held up to these standards and yet unimaginably distant in its deviance from civilized norms. In either case, the direct involvement of German history in other people's life histories has sustained a passionate interest in the German past that has not yet abated. Several generations of scholars have elaborated a series of explanations for this history that returns time and again to the difference of German development. Professional shorthand calls this the *Sonderweg* thesis—the idea that Germany's course into and through the twentieth century has been exceptional and, hence, has "made" history.

At the beginning of the twenty-first century, a new examination of the meaning of this perplexing past is not only possible but overdue. Over fifty years have elapsed since the collapse of Hitler's Reich, surely enough time to cool the immediate passions of the events and provide a longer perspective on their causes and consequences. By the same token, after 1945 the Federal Republic of Germany has become a model of stability, peacefulness, and prosperity—almost the exact reverse of its predecessors. Preoccupied with the unspeakable horrors of the former, scholarly and public opinion on both sides of the Atlantic is reluctant to give the constructive development of the latter its due. Since the catastrophe has become synonymous with German history, the implications of success have yet to be fully realized. Without a framework to guide them, many historians fall back on uncovering the secret history of an age they thought they knew—nowhere is this more evident than in the history of the GDR. But one still wonders what kind of history the so-called postwar years represent. Is it the long aftermath of war and genocide, or is it an alternative development that picked up on traditions repressed and submerged in the years of tyranny? Is it the history, perhaps, of a conversion—the rebirth of a nation in a Europe yet to be constituted? How does the German past look with 2000 as its pivot rather than 1945?

The reappraisal of German history in this century is also motivated by a shift in intellectual perspectives and modes of inquiry. Whereas a wartime generation of scholars probed with the help of a predominantly political history the collapse of the Weimar Republic, the Nazi seizure of power, and the unleashing of World War Two, their postwar successors in the 1960s turned, for the most part, to social history, looking for causes of "the German problem" in social structures or in everyday habits and conveniences. These latter approaches were remarkably successful because they corresponded to the democratizing impulse of the postwar experience. Nonetheless, they preferred to treat people as "social forces" rather than conscious agents of their destiny, and were reluctant to grant them thought, speech, or image. Whatever the people did in making their history, they were mute, deaf, and blind in doing it. German historians also tended to think of themselves primarily as caretakers of facts, viewing "history" as a set of physical remains, archival traces, or collective memories to be measured, weighed, and assembled—with or without a framing theory. The quest for factuality, in other words, was part and parcel of the postwar experience.

Not by chance has postmodern theory barely made a dent in the writing of German history, for in that past, the draperies of conventional interpretations or benevolent assumptions that might elsewhere hide the historians and their history-making are in notoriously short supply. Preciously little accrued wisdom serves as a customary method for reading it or as a foil to be deconstructed. In contrast to their French or American colleagues, German historians had no room for play since there were lies to be revealed and traditions to be salvaged. The impulse of German historians was to recover a lost past and to hold a disastrous one at bay. Hence, they fiercely resisted the withering critique of "good" traditions or the probing of "bad" symbolic practices, and tended to hide behind facts where shared customs of interpretation were not readily available. In a different intellectual climate, marked by the linguistic turn, the new challenge is to write a more reflexive history that is aware of the artifice we historians create to give the past a voice and an imagination. To be sure, this voice and this imagination should be truthful. But the assemblage of facts alone, while creating a reliable chronicle, does not constitute the history of a troubled century.

Our joint effort is the result of a decade-long intellectual collaboration. Almost by accident, we coorganized a conference on the implications of the linguistic turn for German historiography at the University of Chicago in 1990, the papers of which were published in a special issue of *Central European History* (22 [1989]: 227–459). Kenneth Barkin's attack on this initiative and our reply in *German Studies Review* (18 [1995]: 241–73), as well as the ensuing controversy on the H-German network, convinced us that we needed to elaborate our ideas in a more extensive treatment to prevent further misunderstandings and to draw out the full implications of our initial suggestions. *Shattered Past* is, therefore, the product of a long discussion process, propelled by the incisive queries and reactions of our graduate students. Offering three different angles of entry, it begins with a review of the current historiographical situation, characterized by the eclipse of the dominant national, Marxist, and progressive master narratives. The text then proceeds to examine seven important themes that offer substantive examples of how new kinds of German histories might be written. Finally, it concludes with a dual reflection on the German role in this century—from below and above, as it were.

Contrary to initial plans, our labor had to be divided less equally than we had hoped. The preface, introduction, and concluding chapter were written jointly. Because of inadvertent circumstances, Michael Geyer's contributions were limited to the chapter on war and genocide (chapter 4) and that on consumption (chapter 10), and to offering suggestions for the other texts. Konrad Jarausch has therefore drafted the historiographical chapters as well as the essays on dictatorship, power, migration, identity, women, and memory. Needless to say, we gave each other support and plenty of criticism. By combining our distinctive backgrounds, generational outlooks, and institutional perspectives, we hope the arguments have been pushed further than either of us might have done alone. Our final revisions were also aided by the incisive questions of Rudy Koshar and Peter Fritzsche, for which we are grateful.

The aim of this book is nothing less than a reconsideration of the German past in the twentieth century. There is no single master narrative to be told, no *Weltgeist* to be discovered, no national character to be indicted or, at long last, absolved. But there are fascinating stories to be told, revolving around a central problem—fundamentally, the extraordinary difficulty of an emergent nation in finding a way of living together, in generating a civic culture to unite a diverse society, and in developing viable forms of participatory and peaceful politics, and thus, to modulate and negotiate popular activism. This frailty of sociability was the source of catastrophe. And yet it was also the impetus for a persistent effort to overcome the fissures that separate people and make strangers into enemies—an effort that, one might hope, has borne some fruit since 1945. Germans have come to repudiate the heritage of illiberalism and have quite successfully democratized society, culture, and political life. The struggle over how to constitute a whole nation from its parts is surely not exclusively a German issue, but its extremes make the German case worth pondering. For the coming generation of scholars, the challenge, therefore, consists of constructing a new kind of cultural history of German politics.

An American perspective on the transformation from catastrophe to civility will enlighten this history, if it manages to abandon its preceptorial tone. In the postwar period, American academics helped provide the assurance of stability and the possibility of a post-catastrophe future. With the reemergence of a unified and sovereign Germany, however, this mentoring role is no longer appropriate for an outside observer. But neither should the German past fall back into the purview of Germans alone, as if Germans had once again come into their rightful inheritance. Germany is too much part of American history and identity and the presence of the United States in Germany is too strong for either scholarly community to shut out the other. Hence, we think that any such history will have to be informed by the grand competition over modern ways of life that has shaped the relations between Germany and the United States. A great deal can be learned from the intertwinement and the competition of the two histories. The main benefit of this "inter-national" perspective derives from the difference entailed in thinking about the German past in both the United States and Germany. Conceived and written on two continents, it is a history that can use the transatlantic distance and imbrication critically to reflect on and better to understand each other.

Konrad H. Jarausch and Michael Geyer
Chapel Hill and Chicago

SHATTERED
PAST

Twentieth-Century Germany: Rethinking a Shattered Past

The electoral defeat of Communist rule in Poland (1989), the unification of the two Germanys (1990), the collapse of the Soviet Union (1991), and the civil war in Yugoslavia (1992/95) have pushed Europe into a new age. These events had their origins in the particular circumstances of eastern Europe, but they affected the entire continent and reflected a general European condition.[1] They may not have been quite the revolutions that they were meant to be, but they were moments of transition—rites of passage with all the carnivals and risks that accompany them.[2] As far as Europe is concerned, the twentieth century has thereby become history.

In the most immediate sense, these four events have brought to an end a long postwar truce that had provided a semblance of order after a devastating period of war—stability by default, put into place in the wake of the unconditional surrender of a twice-defeated Germany.

---

[1] Charles S. Maier, "The Collapse of Communism: Approaches for a Future History," *History Workshop* 31 (Spring, 1991): 34–59. Cf. Konrad H. Jarausch and Martin Sabrow, eds., *Weg in den Untergang. Der innere Zerfall der DDR* (Göttingen, 1999).

[2] Timothy Garton Ash, *The Magic Lantern: The Revolution of '89 Witnessed in Warsaw, Budapest, Berlin, and Prague* (New York, 1990).

This provisional armistice incrementally grew amidst recriminations and an arms race that pitted two hostile intercontinental blocks against each other and cut the continent in half. The Cold War could hardly be called "peace," but it was a kind of stability that had eluded Europe since the turn of the last century. Also, this period of uneasy deterrence shared with both the early years of the century and the restoration of order in the aftermath of the Napoleonic Wars, an unequal, but altogether dizzying spread of industry and prosperity and an efflorescence of civil life. The postwar history was both expression and consequence of Europe's tumultuous modernity.

Thus, the turn of 1989/92 may well be said to have completed a long cycle of one hundred or even two hundred years. But Europe is no longer what it once was, since the notion of a "catch-up revolution" for Eastern Europe is as deceptive as it is deficient.[3] The nineteenth century is long gone, notwithstanding its bourgeois attractions, which historians in Europe and the United States had come to portray ever more lovingly.[4] No amount of enlightening ardor can skip a century or even half a century as if it were an interregnum, a fact to which eastern Europeans will attest after initial hopes to the contrary. Although imagining the revolutions of 1989/90 as a "springtime of people" made sense, it was but a metaphor, perhaps even hyperbole.[5] This was neither 1848 nor 1918. It was 1990.

More importantly, the *res gestae* of the twentieth century have left their indelible traces. As the twentieth century recedes, it cannot be repeated, not even with the intent of getting it right a second time. To be sure, the artifacts and ideas of this century can be reproduced, lived in, and put on display, but they are ornaments of a different age—bitter-sweet memories, perhaps, of how good the twentieth century was or could have been. Yet the continent and its people have been transformed, not only by the revolutions at the end of the century, but also by the very regimes against which these upheavals were directed. National Socialism and Fascism have been defeated. Bolshevism has collapsed. While the consequences of their deeds and of the utopias that have informed them remain deeply imbricated in what Europe has become, Europe is moving on. The past, we rediscover, as did the histori-

---

[3] Jürgen Habermas, *Die nachholende Revolution. Kleine politische Schriften VII* (Frankfurt/Main, 1990).

[4] Thomas Nipperdey, *Deutsche Geschichte 1860–1866. Bürgerwelt und starker Staat* (Munich, 1987), and *Deutsche Geschichte 1866–1918. Arbeitswelt und Bürgergeist* (Munich, 1990); and Peter Gay, *The Bourgeois Experience, Victoria to Freud*, vol. 2: *The Tender Passion* (New York, 1986).

[5] Timothy Garton Ash, "Eastern Europe: Après le déluge, nous," *New York Review of Books* 37, no. 13 (1990).

ans in the aftermath of the French Revolution, cannot be recaptured, let alone be reenacted.[6] It can only be written down as history. That is, it can be rethought and retold in a critical assessment of where Europe has come from in order to ascertain where it might go.

Such a stock-taking is all the more important since the pieces are not falling neatly into place. Instead of establishing a "new world order," the 1990s have exhibited, if anything, a distressing kind of chaos, for instance, in the ethnic cleansing of the Balkans. Saddled with a highly ambivalent legacy, Europe is once again confronted with the task that it had failed to accomplish the first time: to constitute from within and on its own an order that provides security and a modicum of well being for all; to establish relations with the rest of the world based on tolerance and exchange rather than a presumption of superiority. The events of 1989/92 have left Europe in an awkward position because they have undone the postwar order without replacing it with a discernable design. The challenge is immense in view of the past. Under changed and changing circumstances Europe is reconstituting itself from the effects of a shattered past that outlasted the removal of physical ruins by several decades. For better or worse, Europeans are poised to give themselves a new constitution—not necessarily as a single document, but as a set of arrangements that give shape and meaning to their manifold interactions.

Ironically, the very old and the very new meet in this condition. In 1795 Immanuel Kant had used the satirical inscription "To Eternal Peace" to wager that peace would come to Europe (and he thought of Europe as a universal condition) if constitutional government ruled supreme. He feared ridicule and, worse, persecution if this prediction were not taken as a "sweet dream," or so he said.[7] Two hundred years later Europe must decide whether to follow his vision. The debates over the future of Europe, the disenchantment over technocratic integration (*Maastricht*), and the quandaries of including eastern Europe are indications of the obstacles that lie ahead. Kant was well aware of the difficulties of practical politics. He insisted that peace is not a natural state, a *status naturalis*, but rather is to be constituted; *stiften*, to build foundations, is the venerable German term he used. But he also maintained that "eternal peace" is not an "empty idea." Even if always only approximated, a semblance of it might be made to work.[8]

---

[6] Peter Fritzsche, "Chateaubriand's Ruins: Loss and Memory after the French Revolution," *History and Memory* 10 (1998): 102–17.

[7] Immanuel Kant, "Zum ewigen Frieden. Ein philosophischer Entwurf [1795]," in *Werke in zehn Bänden*, vol. 9: *Schriften zur Anthropologie, Geschichtsphilosophie, Politik und Pädagogik*, ed. Wilhelm Weischedel (Darmstadt, 1964), 191–251.

[8] Ibid., 203, 251.

The success of creating a peaceful order depends on the ability to "think" Europe, and, given the continent's contentious development, this means to rethink and retell what it has become. This is what the phrase "the past is being constructed" as history means—not as a brazen act of invention, but as a deliberate venture to capture on the basis of the evidence what only a short while ago was an unselfconscious event and its effects in the flow of present time.[9] In this wider reconsideration, German developments occupy a central place, not only because of their geographical location, but also because of their powerful effects on the entire continent.

The Shattering of the German Past

The caesura of 1989/92 reveals how profoundly academic history and popular memory have been shaped by the effects of two disastrous wars that many Germans so desperately tried to leave behind. This tug-of-war between the impulses to forget and to remember, the popular memoirs and the academic analyses of the past, continues into the present.[10] Although a "western" liberalism and an "eastern" socialism put themselves forth as alternatives, much recollection remained centered on German traditions of thought that were not easily shaken off, even if they had evidently been tarnished by the Third Reich.[11] This past has now begun to recede, but the events of 1989/90 offer no escape, no guarantee that we do any better with history and memory. Rather it seems that unification might serve as an invitation to do worse—or nothing at all.[12] Proclamations of an "end of history" are not just premature, they are wrong-headed. Germany may be a "normal" country again, as the political mantra goes, but its twentieth-century history is not. The twentieth-century German past can be transformed into history, but it cannot be "normalized."

A judicious approach to the vicissitudes of the twentieth century entails, as a first step, an inquiry into the message of those overarching narratives of the past that suggest a pattern of historical development for the public as well as the scholar. This is not exactly what French

[9] Joan Scott, "Nach der Geschichte?" *GeschichtsWerkstatt* 17 (1997): 5–23.

[10] Dan Diner, *Kreisläufe: Nationalsozialismus und Gedächtnis* (Berlin, 1995).

[11] Götz Aly, *Macht, Geist, Wahn. Kontinuitäten deutschen Denkens* (Berlin, 1997); and Aleida Assmann and Ute Frevert, *Geschichtsvergessenheit, Geschichtsversessenheit. Vom Umgang mit deutschen Vergangenheiten nach 1945* (Stuttgart, 1999).

[12] Konrad H. Jarausch, "Normalisierung oder Re-Nationalisierung: Zur Umdeutung der deutschen Vergangenheit," *Geschichte und Gesellschaft* 21 (1995): 571–84.

intellectuals had in mind when they coined the notion of "master narratives;" they thought quite literally of the tales of colonial masters that silenced the stories of their slaves. But as the concept has assumed a metaphorical meaning, referring to any large-scale interpretative account, it might be useful in the German context to think of them in this way.[13] Historiographic self-questioning is inevitable because the various German masters of the twentieth century—such as nationalists, Marxists, and liberals—have developed profoundly different ways of telling the story of German past, selecting alternative incidents, emphasizing distinctive patterns of development, and drawing contrasting conclusions from them. Moreover, popular memory, or, in fact, memories, had their own dictates and did not necessarily follow those of their masters, as the East German case shows quite clearly.[14] Much like the German past itself, the representation of this past in historiography and memory is fractured.

Until 1945 the dominant version of presenting German development was the national master narrative, which sought to legitimize the existence of the nation state. Created by liberal leaders of the drive to unification, such as Heinrich von Treitschke, it was appropriated by advocates of imperialism during the Wilhelmian era, modified by defenders of a defeated nationality after Versailles, and pushed beyond recognition by Nazi zealots of racial hegemony over Europe.[15] Because of its undeniable complicity in the genocidal war and Holocaust, this nationalist story-line lost much of its intellectual credibility as well as its moral authority with the second defeat.[16] In the West, such neo-conservative scholars as Gerhard Ritter sought to rescue the chastened remnants of this legacy by purging it of its militarist and authoritarian excesses.[17] They argued that Prussian and national traditions had been debased by a populist nationalism and a plebiscitary politics unknown to conservatism and bourgeois patriotism alike—a claim theoretically

[13] Jean Francois Lyotard, *The Postmodern Condition: A Report on Knowledge* (Minneapolis, 1984). See also Konrad H. Jarausch and Martin Sabrow, eds., *Die historische Meistererzählung. Deutungslinien deutscher Nationalgeschichte nach 1945* (Göttingen, 2002).

[14] Lutz Niethammer, Alexander von Plato, and Dorothee Wierling, *Die volkseigene Erfahrung. Eeine Archäologie des Lebens in der Industrieprovinz der DDR: 30 biografische Eröffnungen* (Berlin, 1991).

[15] For a critical synopsis, see Georg G. Iggers, *The German Conception of History: The National Tradition of Historical Thought from Herder to the Present*, rev. ed. (Middletown, 1983).

[16] Peter Schöttler, ed., *Geschichtsschreibung als Legitimationswissenschaft 1918–1945* (Frankfurt am Main, 1997). Winfried Schulze, *Deutsche Geschichtswissenschaft nach 1945* (Munich, 1993). Rüdiger Hohls and Konrad Jarausch, eds. *Versäumte Fragen. Deutsche Historiker im Schatten des Nationalsozialismus* (Stuttgart, 2000).

[17] Winfried Schulze, *Deutsche Geschichtswissenschaft nach 1945* (Munich, 1993).

amplified in the notion of a "totalitarian democracy."[18] Some echoes of this kind of thinking can be found in the apologetic writings of an Ernst Nolte[19] or in the neo-liberal work of François Furet.[20] What unites the range of these conservative perspectives is their deep suspicion of a mass-democratic age, which they associate with tyranny and violence—and the end of German and, for that matter, European ascendancy.

GDR historiography

In the East, humanist antifascist scholars, as well as Communist historians, tried to substitute a Marxist counter-narrative focused not on the state but on the working class. This critique attacked nationalist rationalizations and pointed to the material bases of historical development to justify the building of a better Germany. Yet after an impressive intermezzo of discordant voices that reflected older left-liberal and Marxist traditions, a heavy-handed Stalinism put down these promising departures and, despite various thaws, never released East German historians from its grip. In its denunciation of pluralism, this official Marxism appeared authoritarian and anti-Western, paradoxically even resurrecting the anti-Socialist Bismarck as a Prussian culture-hero.[21] Even if younger GDR scholars broke the Stalinist mold, their writings remained part of an authoritarian "ruling discourse" that propped up the SED-dictatorship and thereby largely squandered the emancipatory and radical-democratic potential inherent in the Marxist tradition. In spite of some attention by intellectuals abroad, the Marxist counter-narrative had only a limited impact beyond East Germany.[22]

West German Gesellschafts-geschichte

Beginning in the 1960s, a younger generation of West German historians revived the progressive-liberal tradition anchored in the Weimar Republic. They took up a liberal critique of nationalism and Marxism, preserved and passed on by German émigrés, that set German authoritarianism and aggression against the promise of liberty and prosperity. This analysis suggested as the main cause for the descent into repression and murder the fierce opposition against the democratic project by an illiberal Prussian elite that fought hard to hang on to its premodern privileges and defended its antidemocratic, authoritarian hab-

---

[18] Jacob L. Talmon, *The History of Totalitarian Democracy* (London, 1952).

[19] Ernst Nolte, *Das Vergehen der Vergangenheit: Antwort an meine Kritiker im sogenannten Historikerstreit* (Berlin, 1989).

[20] François Furet, *Le passé d'une illusion: essai sur l'idée communiste au XXe siècle* (Paris, 1995).

[21] Ernst Engelberg, *Bismarck: Urpreusse und Reichsgründer* (Berlin, 1985).

[22] Georg G. Iggers, Konrad H. Jarausch, Matthias Middell, and Martin Sabrow, eds., *Die DDR-Geschichtswissenschaft als Forschungsproblem*, Historische Zeitschrift special issue 27 (1998). Cf. Alf Lüdtke, ed., *Was bleibt von marxistischen Perspektiven in der Geschichtsforschung?* (Göttingen, 1997).

its and mentalities at all costs. In particular, Fritz Fischer's taboo-break-
ing study of the war aims movement, which asserted German responsibility for the outbreak of World War I, prompted a wholesale
reassessment of the course of German history.[23] Partisans of a new and
more social-scientific approach to history, *Gesellschaftsgeschichte*, argued that the inadvertent rise of democratic forces, a reflection of the
ascent of society over the state, was blocked by the authoritarian structures of the state and conservative forces, producing "structural" tensions that led from smaller catastrophes to bigger ones—from the
threat of civil war to world war and on to genocide.[24] Politically, this
approach promoted the westernization of Germany, the cause of social
reform, and eventually an *Ostpolitik* of détente toward the eastern
bloc.[25] Intellectually, it amounted to a vindication of a functional and
rational technocratic modernity.

The communist and progressive strands of German historiography
were anchored in competing Marxist or Weberian modernization narratives, respectively. By focusing on the formation of the working class
or the emergence of the *Bürgertum*, twentieth-century Germany became the site for the battles and unfulfilled promises of the preceding
centuries.[26] They disagreed on the nature of the Third Reich, portraying
it either as hypertrophy of corporate capitalism or as departure from
western paths toward democracy, but otherwise left the study of a deviant, contemporary history to specialists whose main charge was to
discover exactly what happened. Only when a then-youngish group
of British historians challenged the entire notion of a German
Sonderweg—they found nothing peculiarly German about the defense
of class privilege and disliked the normative limitations of using
Anglo-American benchmarks of modernity—this began to change.[27]
Committed to a democratic history from below, their challenge triggered an avalanche of studies on such previously marginal subjects as
women and minorities. But their critique solved none of the problems
of catastrophe and recovery, thereby extending the scope of, but not
really replacing the framing of earlier master narratives.

---

[23] Fritz Fischer, *Griff nach der Weltmacht. Die Kriegszielpolitik des kaiserlichen Deutschland 1914/18* (Düsseldorf, 1961); and Gerhard A. Ritter, *The New Social History in the Federal Republic of Germany* (London, 1991).

[24] Jürgen Kocka, "Ursachen des Nationalsozialismus," *Aus Politik und Zeitgeschichte* (1980), Nr. 25: 3–15.

[25] Georg Iggers, *The Social History of Politics: Critical Perspectives in West German Histori-cal Writing since 1945* (Leamington Spa, 1985).

[26] Jürgen Kocka, ed., *Bürgertum im 19. Jahrhundert. Deutschland im europäischen Vergleich* (Munich, 1988).

[27] David Blackbourn and Geoff Eley, *The Peculiarities of German History: Bourgeois Soci-ety and Politics in Nineteenth-Century Germany* (New York, 1984).

popular historical
consciousness
↓
memory

Largely irrespective of academic debates, the historical consciousness of the population followed a different trajectory that revolved
around an embattled politics of memory. Initially, the public harbored
rather positive images of the Third Reich as a time of order and prosperity, superior to the turn of the century because of the modern and
popular nature of the regime. The war, particularly the attack against
the Soviet Union, and the persecution of the Jews were considered a
"mistake," an unfortunate and disastrous flaw of the regime. Instead
of speaking of Nazi crimes, Germans preferred to dwell on their own
suffering at the front and during bombardment at home, and on their
expulsion from the eastern parts of the Reich.[28] These experiences fed
a widespread sentiment that saw ordinary people as a victim of politics, betrayed by outside forces beyond their control. Many people
blamed Hitler and the Nazis for leading the nation into a war that they
could not possibly win, or the Allied decision to fight to unconditional
surrender, rendering pointless the heroism of common men and
women.[29] This appeal to overwhelming calamity initially proved to be
impervious to any kind of consciousness-raising, let alone scholarly
argument.

It took until the 1960s for this numbness to give way to a searching
encounter with the causes and consequences of the Nazi regime. The
establishment of a central prosecutor's office in Ludwigsburg, the
media coverage of the Eichmann indictment in Jerusalem as well as
the Auschwitz and other trials in Germany, and the debate about extending the deadline for persecutions in the Bundestag, insistently
raised the question of legal responsibility. A group of exceptionally talented writers—Heinrich Böll, Günter Grass, Rolf Hochhut, and Peter
Weiss, among them—not only portrayed the sufferings of the World
War but also asked probing questions about the role of the ordinary
Germans in supporting Hitler's crimes. The East German government
continued to release "brown books" with damning material on such
leading West German politicians as Chancellor Kurt-Georg Kiesinger,
and a restive younger generation was ready to accuse parental authority as fascist. Finally, a growing number of television documentaries
and a series of impressive films dramatized complicity and made ordinary Germans visible as both perpetrators and victims reminding Ger-

[28] Robert G. Moeller, *War Stories: The Search for a Usable Past in the Federal Republic of
Germany* (Berkeley, 2001).
[29] Robert Moeller, "War Stories: The Search for a Usable Past in the Federal Republic
of Germany," *American Historical Review* 101 (1996): 1008–48; and Mary Fulbrook, *German
National Identity after the Holocaust* (Cambridge, UK, 1999).

mans of their own presence in what was universally called "the past," thereby initiating a more critical turn in memory culture.[30]

By the 1970s, this growing historical self-awareness began to cross the boundaries of stereotypes about Jews, Poles, or Russians that lingered long after the romance of the Third Reich. The shift from self-victimization to empathy with Nazi victims entailed a difficult leap of imagination since it breached a cultural barrier of a deep-seated anti-Semitism and of a racial, anti-Slavic prejudice. For the older generation, it proved immensely difficult to re-encounter former Jewish neighbors and Polish and Russian coworkers, or to acknowledge their absence, while the younger generation rather awkwardly suffused past distress into their own adolescent angst. Still, by agonizing over the pain inflicted not only on "victims" but also on actual people—by giving them a voice, even if not always their own, and investing them with symbolic presence—many Germans began to extricate themselves from the armor that had hardened them against the pain they had inflicted.[31] The consequences were far reaching and always remained embattled.[32] Effectively, many Germans were undergoing something akin to a conversion, a remaking of a sense of themselves, of body and soul. Germany was becoming a different country.   GDR?

Popular reactions to evidence of complicity, however, reveal how difficult it remained for Germans to encounter themselves in the past, prompting new strategies of distancing. The difference between the favorable reception of Daniel Goldhagen's indictment of Germans as "willing executioners"[33] and the concurrent outcry over an exhibition concerning the crimes of the Wehrmacht is a striking example.[34] Though Goldhagen boldly indicted all "ordinary Germans" for the crimes of the Third Reich, his figures were so stereotypically Nazi, so grimly determined to do their job, so solidly part of a by-gone age, that they might as well have lived on a different planet. In contrast, the Wehrmacht exhibition showed grandfathers, fathers, and brothers who

---

[30] Konrad H. Jarausch, "Critical Memory and Civil Society: The Impact of the Sixties on German Debates about the Past" (MS, Berlin, 2001). See also Harold Marcuse, *Legacies of Dachau: The Uses and Abuses of a Concentration Camp, 1933–2000* (Cambridge, 2001).

[31] Peter Reichel, *Vergangenheitsbewältigung in Deutschland. Die Auseinandersetzung mit der NS-Diktatur von 1945 bis heute* (Munich, 2001); and Y. Michal Bodemann, *Gedächtnistheater. Die jüdische Gemeinschaft und ihre deutsche Erfindung* (Hamburg, 1996).

[32] Jane Kramer, *The Politics of Memory: Looking for Germany in the New Germany* (New ✗ York, 1996).

[33] Daniel Jonah Goldhagen, *Hitler's Willing Executioners: Ordinary Germans and the Holocaust* (New York, 1996).

[34] Hannes Heer and Klaus Naumann, eds., *Vernichtungskrieg. Verbrechen der Wehrmacht 1941–1944* (Hamburg, 1995).

resembled present-day family members laughing and clowning while presenting themselves in pictures of abominable crimes. These images were troubling precisely because they were so familiar, especially for an MTV generation just encountering the genocide in Bosnia. The message, in any case, was clear. In distancing themselves from earlier crimes with great emotional effort, the Germans wanted to make sure that their past remained past. They could deal with stereotypical Germans of an earlier age but not with people like themselves being implicated in a past that looked like the present.

The opposing postwar positions on the politics of memory had in common a highly emotional relationship to the past. Many people desperately attempted to rescue a piece of tradition and developed a "salvage approach" to prove the relative innocence of a particular social group, political idea, or interest vis-à-vis the Third Reich. Still attached to the nation, the churches or their own sense of integrity, ordinary people went to great lengths to extricate themselves through sometimes quite elaborate operations. Even antifascist historians sought to show that workers and peasants had heroically resisted and that the fault lay elsewhere. In contrast, far fewer commentators called for collective acts of contrition, portraying all Germans as implicated in war and genocide, thereby evoking obdurate resentment. This "contrition approach" viewed the entire past as deeply flawed, pointing inevitably to the Nazi seizure of power and the subsequent war as well as the Holocaust.[35] Such self-incrimination called for a radical break between past and present, a rupture of identity, and the reconstruction of a new collective self. As Günter Grass came to suggest, the division of Germany was the just price for the crime of Auschwitz.[36] But Grass spoke for a minority.

The caesura of 1989 facilitated a different reconciliation with the past by reinforcing the growing temporal distance from the Third Reich. Much ridicule has been heaped on ex-Chancellor Helmut Kohl's claim of "the benefit of late birth," but his rhetoric of admitting the potential guilt of many Germans in earlier times and of highlighting the "temptation" of Nazi rule has been a resounding success.[37] Instead of either salvage attempts or protestations of contrition, the solution of the 1990s consisted of separating an evil past from a better present. Ironically, the argument ran thus: the more evil the past, the more clearly distinct

[35] Jeffrey Herf, *Divided Memory: The Nazi Past in the Two Germanys* (Cambridge, Mass., 1997).

[36] Dagmar Barnouw, "Time, Memory and the Uses of Remembrance," *Alexander von Humboldt-Stiftung Magazin* 73 (1999): 3–10.

[37] The notion of "temptation" hails from Fritz Stern, *Dreams and Delusions: The Drama of German History* (New York, 1987).

a humdrum present. By extension, the "two dictatorships" of the Third Reich and of the communist GDR are now quite routinely set apart as the abject history of Germany in contradistinction to the paradigmatic success of West Germany, regardless of whether the latter is interpreted as a national or post-national entity.[38] By the end of the 1990s, Germans had developed two twentieth-century histories, and public memory happily concurred in keeping them apart. Even some historians have started to step out of their postwar narratives' degeneration into catastrophe, and to think of the past century as split.

two 20th-century histories?

Both history and memory reflect the fundamental shattering of a past, evident in the difficulty of reconciling in a single record the indelible stigma of earlier murder and genocide with later recovery and rehabilitation. As a result, there is a surfeit of memories as well as of histories but little sense of the shape and structure of the twentieth century.[39] Each in its own way, history and memory appear fractured along the seams of destruction on one hand and the good life on the other. An emerging consensus sets apart an earlier period of abjection from a later time of vindication at the risk of ignoring their vital interrelationship. Instead, a more convincing and altogether more compelling interpretation would acknowledge both the extent of these ruptures and the fracturing of the nation into incommensurate parts to then comprehend the frantic efforts to restore continuity and community—not as "before" (1945) and "after" (1945/89) snap-shots, but as simultaneous processes of the making and unmaking of the German nation.

Is this a sensible way to look at the course of twentieth-century German history? Surely many advances in science, technology, or consumption incrementally continued irrespective of all catastrophes. Social structures and milieus also changed piecemeal, and people lived on through the upheavals, whether scandalously hiding their past or picking up the pieces to start anew. If international peace, material prosperity, and western-style democracy prevailed in the long run, should one not stress the successful march of progress rather than its temporal interruptions and ugly failures? Nonetheless, there are good reasons not to proceed in this fashion. First, ignoring the ruptures and fracturing would write out of history the widespread absences that are not just an intrinsic but also an essential aspect of the twentieth-cen-

---

[38] Günther Heydemann and Christopher Beckmann, "Zwei Diktaturen in Deutschland. Möglichkeiten und Grenzen des historischen Diktaturvergleichs," *Deutschland Archiv* 30 (1997): 12–40; and Günther Heydemann and Eckart Jesse, eds, *Diktaturvergleich als Herausforderung. Theorie und Praxis* (Berlin, 1998)

[39] Jürgen Habermas, "Learning By Disaster? A Diagnostic Look Back on the Short 20th Century," *Constellations* 5 (1998): 307–320.

tury German past. Without accounting for the human and cultural loss, Germans and, for that matter, Europeans will never be able to reconcile with one another and their troubling memories. Second, focusing on the long run average does not account for the intense fluctuations that mattered at a given time—the extraordinary upheavals that ripped apart a nation, and all the exertions required to allow a people to pull itself back together. These immense labors of undoing and belonging disappear when leveling out the extremes. For good and bad, these labors made history.

The manifold contradictions between ruptures and continuities, fracturing and restoring community, are therefore a central feature of German history in the twentieth century. The frightening truth of the matter is that the extremes cannot be separated from the mainstream since innocence and complicity are intertwined.[40] Neither at large nor *en détail* can German history be salvaged as if a redeeming feature could be defended and then recovered after defeat in a miraculous process of self-cleansing. There is no self-evident site of redemption. But the entirety of the German past does not just point to Hitler and cannot be subsumed as a pre-history of the Nazis. It is not just that there are other important lines of continuity and that many Germans lived on beyond the end of the Third Reich. Rather, what matters is the contentious nature of the process that got German history into one place and then into another.

The prevarications of historiography reflect disorientation in the face of a century that will remain known for its catastrophic violence as much as for its unprecedented prosperity and creativity. German and European history encompass both excruciating violence and pain and exquisite wealth and happiness. The incommensurability of simultaneous man-made life-worlds of utter privilege, wealth, and consumption and death-worlds of utter degradation, starvation, and brutal annihilation is the sign of twentieth-century German history. To think and retell both—and to reflect one in the other—is the challenge for scholarship. How could one happen along with the other? How could one happen after the other? How could one happen and be related to the other? The simultaneity of incommensurate worlds, of bonds of belonging having turned into deadly bondage and being forged anew, will have to concern historians as they look back at the twentieth century and begin to convert its passing present into history.

Perhaps the British gadfly A.J.P. Taylor was right after all when he scathingly claimed that this history was marked by an excess of contra-

[40] Theodore S. Hamerow, *On the Road to the Wolf's Lair; German Resistance to Hitler* (Cambridge, Mass., 1997).

dictions—a surplus that more conventional accounts try to gloss over.[41] But this larger-than-life quality is the main reason why German history will continue to be told. Inextricably linked to the world wars and the Holocaust, the German experience has come to function as a negative exemplar, as the ultimate warning against aggression, domination, and racial extermination. At the same time, the postwar development of the Federal Republic is an extraordinary success story, an unexpected collective recovery that can also serve as a model.[42] Neither of these contradictory images alone makes up twentieth-century German history, which holds both trajectories in a single lifetime. This paradox raises high the political, emotional, and intellectual stakes of interpreting the German past—it is an excessive past that escapes history or, in any case, conventional ways of retelling.

Sober recognition of the fractured character of this past can serve as a starting point for a reconstruction that puts squarely at the center what is memorable about twentieth-century Germany. In plain speech, the Germans got themselves into a murderous past and they got themselves out of it, not all by their own doing, but surely also a result of their thought and action. It is the history of a disastrous and wanton miscarriage of civility, of unprecedented destruction of bonds of human solidarity, of unspeakable collective acts that were thought impossible in a modern age. At the same time, it is also a record of the desperate effort to learn from the self-inflicted disaster and reconstruct a better polity based on a more equitable social order and the pursuit of a more peaceful foreign policy. It finds people and institutions straddling this divide, succumbing to hatred and prejudice, haughtily denying that it ever existed, and yet picking up the pieces, reforming themselves, and casting about for a livable present. If this was a "German century," it is not so because the Germans have "made good," as a certain hagiography suggests, but rather because this life-and-death struggle over what constitutes a humane community testifies to the fallibility and frailty of modern society. Perhaps this is a lesson that might have a wider resonance.

This basic ambivalence suggests the usefulness of a cultural approach to German history. Such a perspective does not primarily mean the study of culture as a discrete sphere or subsystem, such as the high *Kultur* of philosophy, literature, art, or music, or, for that matter, the popular culture of film, television, travel, and other kinds of leisure

---

[41] Alan John Percival Taylor, *The Course of German History: A Survey of the Development of Germany since 1815* (New York, 1962).

[42] Anthony J. Nicholls, *The Bonn Republic: West German Democracy, 1945–1990* (London, 1997).

cultural approach to German history

activities. Nor can it just be subsumed under an ethnographic look at the customs, symbols, and behaviors of continental natives, be they peasant lifestyles in danger of extinction, working-class subcultures threatened by commercialization, or patterns of consumption promoted by the media. Such a perspective must also grapple with the implications of the linguistic turn, which suggest that action does not translate into social effects without the intercession of language or thought, that "society" and the "state" are not mechanically existing structures to be plucked from the past by historians. It draws attention to public discourse, symbolic representation, and personal experience to recover dimensions of reflection and meaning, to become more sensitive to exclusions and silences in historical accounts, and to understand the dialogic nature of reconstructions of the past. Though some critics, such as Richard Evans, are still warning against a wholesale abandonment of "reality," which they identify with "deconstruction," this debate has largely run its course.[43] After the passing of postmodernism, the importance of the historicity of language and symbols as its mediating part has been recognized even by its detractors.

The particular challenge of a cultural approach to German history consists in the exploration of how a sense of self and bonds of belonging are formed, and when and why they are torn. According to the turn-of-the-century sociologist Georg Simmel, "culture" involves the many and contentious ways that social fabrics are put together.[44] He greatly emphasized the creative, or for that matter destructive, nature of making and unmaking societies, an activity called *Vergesellschaftung* in German. While the constant flux may seem unnerving, this perspective sees society not as a container that holds individuals or as a structure that can be coaxed into action, but rather as a process of becoming without resorting to organic metaphors.[45] Gender, class, and ethnicity are now commonly invoked as the test cases, but they only make historical sense as markings in networking or disintegrating communities. That this is a mediated and public process, in which the stage played as much of a role as the electronic media do today, and that it

---

[43] For echoes, see Wolfgang Hardtwig and Hans-Ulrich Wehler, eds., *Kulturgeschichte heute* (Göttingen, 1996), as well as Richard Evans, *In Defense of History* (London, 1997).

[44] Georg Simmel, *Soziologie: Untersuchungen über die Formen der Vergesellschaftung* (Frankfurt am Main, 1992). Less conclusive is David Frisby and Mike Featherstone, eds. *Simmel on Culture: Selected Writings* (London, 1997).

[45] In a different register, but with the same thrust, see William Sewell, "Three Temporalities: Toward an Eventful Sociology," in Terence J. McDonald, ed., *The Historic Turn in the Human Sciences* (Ann Arbor, 1996), 245–80, and "The Concept of Culture(s)," in Victoria E. Bonnell and Lynn Hunt, eds., *Beyond the Cultural Turn: New Directions in the Study of Society and Culture* (Berkeley, 1999), 35–60.

is a performative and enacted event, which has as much to do with body-cultures as with establishing moral authorities—all that may still need to be pointed out, but it should not distract from what matters. Cultural history explores the ways and means by which individual and social bodies constitute themselves, how they interact with each other, and how they rip themselves apart.[46]

This approach appears so suitable for an exploration of the twenti-eth-century German past because this past involves a society that broke apart in producing war and genocide. The networks of German society were torn, to the very core of personal existence, by the violence that they generated and suffered. Hence, their history cannot be reas-sembled as if brutality and savagery had not left any traces or could be separated out from the main course of long-term developments. By the same token, the assertion of life after genocide, in processes of leave-taking as much as in reconstituting bonds of civility and commu-nity, makes telling this history possible after all. It also makes for a permanently fractured history. As a record of the living generations, it is a history that cannot but be acutely cognizant of violent death and its effects.[47]

This kind of history is none the worse for being indebted to German traditions of enlightenment, for this is what a Lessing surmised to be the struggles of the modern age. It is such an emplotment of German history that Hannah Arendt suggested when she spoke lovingly about the unruly heritage of this enlightenment and its quintessential task to "construct" society after the rupture of traditions.[48] She set the chance and the challenge of a "new beginning" squarely against the "politics of antiquarian attachment,"[49] which try to salvage a mythical past (be it the Middle Ages, Prussian glory, or the Bismarckian Empire) to root an uncertain present. Her injunction also suggests that historical recon-struction must become aware of the temporality of memory regimes, such as Cold-War Liberalism, in which it is embedded. Instead of being driven by the sources or by current concerns alone, this history must attempt to fashion a conscious dialogue between the past and the pres-ent by a process of constant self-reflection.

[46] This is a conception of cultural history that goes beyond the recent collection by Thomas Mergel and Thomas Welskopp, eds., *Geschichte zwischen Kultur und Gesellschaft* (Munich, 1997).

[47] Michael Geyer, "Germany, or, The Twentieth Century as History," *South Atlantic Quarterly* 96 (1997): 663–702.

[48] Hannah Arendt, *Von der Menschlichkeit in finsteren Zeiten. Gedanken zu Lessing* (Munich, 1960).

[49] Katie Trumpener, *Bardic Nationalism: The Romantic Novel and the British Empire* (Princeton, 1997), 124.

Reconstructing German Histories

How can a historical narrative be forged from such disparate parts? This question invites philosophical answers. So much is at stake; so daunting is the challenge; so intimidating is the stretch from the utter destruction of the *shoah* to the surplus of well-being of the *Wirtschaftswunder*. But even grand answers hinge on a deceptively simple concern: What happens to the narratives of German history if we bring into stereoscopic view the first half of the twentieth century with the second half—neither diminishing the crimes of the first nor denying the good life of the second? While the immediate postwar period can still be understood as a working-out of the consequences of the world wars, the decades of development thereafter produced a very different and more hopeful pattern that cannot be subsumed any longer under the framework of a catastrophic history. The processes of conversion that helped bring about this reversal need to be more fully incorporated and will have to be viewed against the background of the initial and disastrous entry into the twentieth century.

There is surprisingly little debate on this issue, although there is a great deal of jockeying for a new narrative of German modernity.[50] The straightforward procedure of adding fifty years of a divided history—disregarding Austria and, thus, sealing the division of 1866—means, in effect, making room for a vast amount of new development. The tidal wave of German postwar historiography that emphasizes the successful transformation of the country has barely reached the American shores but is bound to submerge much of the older history. Whichever way one turns, the subject and the subjects of German history are bound to change with what seem to be altogether pragmatic adjustments.

Just adding the second half to the first will be of little help, since the res gestae of twentieth-century German history do not yield very easily to a chronological approach. While American and, for that matter, British historians may get away with adding yet another episode or administration to their long histories, this procedure does not work for continental Europe. In the German case, it makes little sense to say or imply that Adenauer and Ulbricht "followed" Hitler after a brief interregnum of occupation, and that Helmut Kohl followed both. It

---

[50] Detlev Peukert *Die Weimarer Republik. Krisenjahre der klassischen Moderne* (Frankfurt/Main, 1987).

takes a tremendous amount of explanation to get from one end of the century to the other. The kind of linear continuity, typical of other national histories, falters in the face of the ruptures of German twentieth-century experience. In stark contrast to the myth of national stability, nothing was more transient than territorial, governmental, and social arrangements in central Europe. Joining the second half of the century to the first therefore requires more fundamental deconstructions and reconstructions.

A conventional way of telling this transient history would be to emphasize the alternating instances of rupture and periods of stability. From the perspective of politics, at least four major regime changes during the twentieth century, in 1918, 1933, 1945, and 1989, changed not just governments but entire constitutions, elites, and ideologies.[51] An economic vantage point would emphasize different ruptures, such as 1923, 1929, 1948, and 1990, highlighting inflations, depressions, and currency reforms instead of system transformations. Yet between such moments of crisis, periods of normalcy allowed people to get on with the business of living, marrying, having children, and dying, as if nothing ever could or would change. Much of the history that is written uses the ruptures as bookends, focusing instead on the functioning of the different systems, such as the Second Empire or the Third Reich, as if they were eternal fixtures, monads in the flux of time.[52]

An alternative approach, better suited to the shattered nature of this past, would start with the recognition of the very instability of the German condition and make it the pivotal concern of historical reconstruction. To reflect this point in the form of its presentation, such an approach needs to break through the crust of a single narrative to recover the multiple subjects that make up a national history. Dissolving the single overarching story of the nation into multiple histories permits the recovery of a sense of the nation's fractures and of the labors in joining and orchestrating them. Such a perspective means asking where Germany was (for the territory shifts), who the Germans were (for the people change), and what these diverse German subjects did in putting society together and breaking it apart (for this is the difference entailed in war and murder). The question about how these many subjects fared puts the nation back into the center, not as a self-evident fact or normative given, but as an embattled construct of forces contending for its

---

[51] Dietrich Papenfuß and Wolfgang Schieder, eds., *Deutsche Umbrüche im 20. Jahrhundert* (Cologne, 2000), 3–29.

[52] The periodization of major survey series, like the Siedler Verlag's volumes on *Die Deutschen und Ihre Nation* (Berlin, 1989–2002), follows this pattern.

control. It requires a history transformed by telling of the labors of belonging and contemplating with sadness when and where they failed.

THEMES

Seven major themes that cut across politics, economy, society, and culture may serve as guideposts in deciphering the shifting map of territories and people that make up the twentieth-century German past. The chapters on dictatorship and democracy as well as on Germany's changing place in Europe address traditional definitions of "the German problem" in a somewhat different way.[53] Other chapters on the Holocaust, identity, migration, gendering, or consumption pick up more recent themes of discussion that are missing from the older pictures. Our selections do not imply that other topics, such as the development of the economy or technological innovation, are unimportant. Instead, they are meant to provide examples of how one might go about reassembling the fragments of a central European past into new patterns and intended to stimulate discussion on which themes ought to be considered crucial for shifting the narrative frame from a history of Germany as a state to the histories of Germans as a people.

1) war genocide

While beginning with war and genocide raises a basic conundrum of twentieth-century German history, there is some doubt whether this history is currently being written in an appropriate way. Clearly, the savagery of German war and genocide reverberates in memory and will incite the imagination of generations to come, since World War II and its combination of savagery and genocide may well be Germany's world historical moment. But pulp fiction and film pay far too much attention to the virtuosity of the German killing machine, which has entered Anglo-American consciousness and exerts a lurid fascination far beyond the right-radical scene. A more significant hesitation concerns the reduction of German history to war, killing, and dying as the end-all of the past—as if it were a history of the dead and defeated. There was life after catastrophe, and German history exists only because it is written by the living, suggesting a process of overcoming, a process necessary to any history of war and genocide worth its name.

Historicizing war and genocide means squarely facing the history of a disastrous miscarriage of civility as well as of the faltering and desperate defense of decency. It requires an exploration both of the destruction of bonds of human solidarity that hold societies together and of the good life in search of a public culture and constitution to sustain it. It finds people and institutions straddling the divide, succumbing to hatred and prejudice, haughtily denying that it ever existed, and

[53] David Calleo, *The German Problem Reconsidered: Germany and World Politics, 1870 to the Present* (Cambridge, UK, 1979). Cf. also Dirk Verheyen, *The German Question: A Cultural, Historical and Geopolitical Exploration*, 2nd ed. (Boulder, 1999).

yet picking up the pieces, transforming and reforming themselves and casting about for a livable present. Such a history of catastrophe starts from the recognition that war and violence do not arise accidentally and do not simply disappear. Military historians (but also historians of genocide and the Holocaust) tend to point out that "their" violence follows a distinct and unique logic. Yet the physical reality of violence builds on social and cultural conditions that generate it and which need to be understood.

Mass murder leaves marks on people and societies that are only ← slowly and hesitantly, if ever, overcome. Wounds and traumas may be healed, but the destruction of entire societies and cultures is not easily, if ever, undone. Still, bonds of belonging begin to rupture long before the killing sets in, and, if the tear of violence is ever mended, it happens long after the fact. These labors of civility, lost and destroyed at a crucial juncture in German history and tentatively and hesitantly recovered after catastrophe, are the subject of a German history that give catastrophe—war, genocide, and the Holocaust—its proper and, one might say, rightful place as one of the grand caesurae of modern history and one of the significant and, indeed, signifying events of the twentieth century. But it is also a history that makes evident that, even in the face of deliberate murder, history does not end.

A second major theme of twentieth-century history is the contested *2) state institutions governance* nature of German governance, that is, the permutability both of the state and its institutions. The cliché of German authoritarianism misses the protracted struggles over participation and citizenship rights within the boundaries of the state. Not only in central Europe did turning subjects into citizens prove to be an immensely challenging task. Mass democracy was a provocation for autocrats as much as for the notables of liberal constitutionalism who gave way only reluctantly. Battles over empowering excluded and marginalized groups, a majority of citizens, over when and where they could vote, mark this century. The lines of conflict were redrawn time and again. Should women have the vote? Should equal rights extend beyond ethnic, religious, social, and sexual boundaries? Should rights entail entitlements? Even when these questions were resolved in principle, they led to persistent tensions and conflagrations in practice. The implementation of self-determination of citizens and the conversion of citizenship rights into personal or group entitlements were primary zones of a conflict which continues well into the present.

Far from catching up from backwardness to modernity, the German reconstruction of politics championed both the expansion of the state sphere and claims to citizenship rights. Universal suffrage for men and women was extended in 1871 and 1918, respectively, ahead of much

of Europe. The resulting struggles over participation and welfare provision mark the key turn from the nineteenth to the twentieth century.
The contest over how mass politics could be instituted, what constraints and limits applied, runs through the entire course of the twentieth century, all the way from the Second Empire to the Federal Republic.[54] From Bismarck's *Sozialpolitik* on, the development of the
welfare state was an attempt to respond to popular wishes, seeking to
gain loyalty for such embattled regimes as the Weimar Republic. The
Third Reich's bargain of social protection in exchange for hard work
and political docility was repeated by the *Fürsorgediktatur* of the SED
under different ideological auspices, suggesting the need for more analytical comparisons of the question of legitimacy of both dictatorships.[55]

The ultimate winner of the triangular ideological contest nonetheless
turned out to be democracy. The negative experiences of war and persecution under Fascism, and of material deprivation as well as political
repression under Communism, helped cure the population of normative utopias. But the phenomenal success of the social market economy,
as a compromise between market capitalism and a "security state,"
also provided positive arguments for the superiority of representative
government. Compared to the depth and sophistication of work on the
dictatorships, the cultural process of conversion to democracy, the
transformation of values or lifestyles, and the emotional attachment to
human rights, remain under-researched and under-theorized. Conventional success stories are unable to explain why the Germans should,
after such aggressiveness and authoritarianism, suddenly have turned
into pacifist democrats.[56]

A third significant theme concerns the classic question of fitting a
German national state into the European order. Was it excess size and
economic potential that made the Second Reich so restless? Was it the
unsettled style of foreign policy that created exaggerated fears abroad,
or was it the lack of experience among the elites that inspired attempts
at outright domination?[57] Perhaps Ludwig Dehio was correct in seeing

---

[54] James Retallack and Larry E. Jones, eds., *Elections, Mass Politics and Social Change in Modern Germany* (Cambridge, UK, 1992).

[55] Konrad H. Jarausch, ed., *Dictatorship as Experience: Towards a Socio-Cultural History of the GDR* (New York, 1999); and Joachim Hirsch, *Der Sicherheitsstaat. Das 'Modell Deutschland', seine Krise und die neuen sozialen Bewegungen* (Frankfurt/Main, 1986).

[56] The leading account, by Dennis L. Bark and David R. Gress, *A History of West Germany* 2 vols., 2nd ed. (Oxford, 1993), is stronger on narrative exposition than on analysis.

[57] Gerhard Weinberg, "National Style in Diplomacy," in Erich Angermann and Marie-Louise Frings, eds., *Oceans Apart? Comparing Germany and the United States* (Stuttgart, 1981), 146–60.

the world wars as attempts at a forceful resolution of this dilemma through successive bids for German hegemony over the European continent.[58] While there may be some lingering disagreement about the share of the German guilt for the outbreak of the First World War, there is no such doubt about Nazi culpability for the Second.[59] The causes of these bids for control have much to do with an antiquated agrarian definition of power that required territory, instrumentalized its inhabitants, and failed to provide a European vision that might inspire non-Germans to follow it. The consequence of these wars was an extraordinary shifting of territories, increasing the size of the German state during victory and shrinking as well as partitioning it during defeat.

Since German power rested to a large degree upon the successful organization of the economy, this dimension needs to be integrated more clearly into twentieth-century histories. During the Wilhelmian Empire, the late but rapid industrialization, facilitated by state involvement, industrial banking, technological innovation, and large-scale concentration, has been called "organized capitalism." Cooperation between the growing trade unions movement and employers' association managed to weather even the hyperinflation until it foundered on the Great Depression. The Third Reich shifted the balance toward business, but its deficit financing required military conquest to balance the books, a process in which entrepreneurs collaborated with enthusiasm since they could dispossess racial and national victims. Only the GDR effort at state socialism foundered, whereas the corporatist consensus of the social market economy was one of the big reasons for the success of the western FRG.[60]

Bonn's postwar commitment to European integration is one of the most important indicators of a difficult process of learning from catastrophe. Pushed by the Marshall Plan and by cooperative neighbors such as Robert Schumann and Jean Monnet, the Federal Republic under Adenauer's leadership understood that cooperation was the road to recovery. In the construction of the Common Market in 1957, German economic potential was used constructively as industrial locomotive to propel the process of European integration. Similarly, NATO membership anchored FRG defense forces in the western alliance and transformed occupation troops into friendly allies in the Cold War confrontation. The cultural dimension of this process was a westernization

[58] Ludwig Dehio, *Germany and World Politics in the Twentieth Century* (New York, 1959).

[59] Konrad H. Jarausch, "From the Second to the Third Reich: The Problem of Continuity in Nazi Foreign Policy," *Central European History* 12 (1979): 68–82.

[60] Karl Hardach, *The Political Economy of Germany in the Twentieth Century* (Berkeley, 1980).

that embraced Anglo-American popular culture and consumption patterns while affecting a political reconciliation with France.[61] One of the
great postwar surprises was therefore the taming of a German power
that had once frightened the world.

4) migration mobility

The fourth theme of a twentieth-century German history is unsettlement and resettlement of Germans in a homogeneous homeland.
This topic is rehearsed by an impressive literature, which suggests that
throughout its modern existence Germany has been a nation of migrants.[62] But German history continues to be told in textbooks as if it
were entirely undisturbed and untouched by the spatial and social mobility of the people that constitute it. The societal and cultural consequences in severing, as well as reconstituting, bonds of belonging and
engendering a heightened fear of both mobility and migrants (as well
as those, like Jews, who were made in their image) have rarely been
incorporated into the understanding of national history. Even the issue
of mobility has been rather sidestepped, although it might be interpreted as breaking down national boundaries and creating, within limits,
equality of opportunity.[63] Such migration, therefore, is an important
constituent of twentieth century German and European society.

An optimistic history of European-wide mobility, however, elides
the catastrophic experiences of population movements in the twentieth
century, the unsettlement and extirpation produced by genocidal war.
These widespread, ideologically induced uprootings reappear in the
second half of the century as the global calamity of refugees and asy-
lum-seekers.[64] The forced shifting of populations in Europe is now
commonly understood as an effect of the dissolution of empires.[65] As
a result of the recent Balkan wars, such policies have come to be seen
as deliberate acts of ethnic cleansing in which newly constituted nation
states purged themselves of all those whom they considered enemies.
Beyond the history of war, they also should be related to the emergent
welfare-state and its entitlement programs, which led to the search for
cheap and un-entitled labor—not simply a second-class citizen, but a
non-citizen and, indeed, a non-person.

---

[61] Anselm Doering-Manteuffel, *Wie westlich sind die Deutschen? Amerikanisierung und Westernisierung im 20. Jahrhundert* (Göttingen, 1999).

[62] Klaus Bade, *Deutsche im Ausland—Fremde in Deutschland* (Munich, 1992).

[63] Hartmut Kaelble, *Auf dem Weg zu einer europäischen Gesellschaft. Eine Sozialgeschichte Westeuropas, 1880–1980* (Munich, 1987).

[64] Demetrios G. Papademetriou, *Coming Together or Pulling Apart? The European Union's Struggle with Immigration and Asylum* (Washington, D.C., 1996).

[65] Rogers Brubaker, *Nationalism Reframed: Nationhood and the National Question in the New Europe* (Cambridge, 1996); and Karen Barkey and Mark von Hagen, eds., *After Em-*

These forced population movements might be conceptualized as part and parcel of a process of nation-building by expelling presumed deviants. They coincided and overlapped with the pursuit of intra-social mobility and cannot be separated from it. The former defined the body social, whereas the latter settled the body politic in what effectively became a homogeneous German *Volksstaat*, divided into two. They reinforced each other, constituting the kind of uniform nation state, which, in turn, was the prerequisite for the extraordinary mobilization of wealth and privilege that ensued in the second half of the twentieth century. Ethnic resettlers and GDR refugees fueled the economic miracle until the arrival of so-called "guest-workers," the influx of "strangers who were to stay," brought people from a variety of countries, cultures, and ethnic origin.[66] As a target for asylum seekers, Germany has become, once again, a multicultural society but has also begun to fortify itself against real and imagined "waves of migration" as the new site of a global "civil war."[67]

The fifth theme concerns the struggle over German identities among different groups that tried to shape the emergent nation in their own image as part of a process of "becoming national."[68] The origins of German identity reach considerably back in time, whether one wants to see them in the constitution of a self-conscious language (the *Muttersprache*) or in the rise of an anti-French and anti-revolutionary nationalism of the early nineteenth century.[69] Captured in a distinctly bourgeois cultural memory, this identity was embedded in a rich associational life and entrenched in state institutions, particularly those of higher learning.[70] But having a national identity and building a nation—nationalization—are two quite different things. The notion of being German was, throughout the nineteenth century, linked to a local or, at best, regional conception of society that was highly particularist since the army was state-based and Protestantism consisted of state churches with jealously guarded autonomy. And this is to say nothing about the

---

pire: *Multiethnic Societies and Nation-Building: The Soviet Union and the Russian, Ottoman, and Habsburg Empires* (Boulder, 1997)

[66] Georg Simmel, *Soziologie: Untersuchungen über die Formen der Vergesellschaftung* (Frankfurt/Main, 1992), 764.

[67] Hans Magnus Enzensberger, *Aussichten auf den Bürgerkrieg* (Frankfurt/Main, 1993).

[68] Geoff Eley and Ronald G. Suny, eds., *Becoming National: A Reader* (New York, 1996).

[69] Michael Townson, *Mother-Tongue and Fatherland: Language and Politics in Germany* (Manchester, N.Y., 1992); and Michael Jeismann, *Das Vaterland der Feinde. Studien zum nationalen Feindbegriff und Selbstverständnis in Deutschland und Frankreich, 1792–1918* (Stuttgart, 1992).

[70] Aleida Assmann, *Arbeit am nationalen Gedächtnis. Eine kurze Geschichte der deutschen Bildungsidee* (Frankfurt/Main, 1993).

powers of ethnicity and their connotations with *Heimat*, which were amalgamated into a strong Länder tradition.[71]

The German process of nationalization was carried forward by competing mass-movements that sought to impose a minority vision upon the entire society. The initially cultural and then gradually political agenda of the nationalist movement was mostly promoted by educated middle-class men of the younger generation, searching to invent a wider, translocal community in the student movement of the *Burschenschaft*. It took several generations before their message, relayed in gymnastic clubs, singing societies, and literary groups, reached the business people as well as members of the working class. Ironically, Socialism and Catholicism also sought to transcend the particularist proclivities of local elites and to organize on a nationwide level, notwithstanding their internationalist or ultramontane stances. They took advantage of universal (male) suffrage in building transregional mass-political parties and associated social and cultural movements. All three movements propagated competing visions of community that overlapped in their national focus but clashed in terms of lifestyle and life-expectations.[72]

The process of constructing a national identity was, therefore, a struggle over who would define the nation and which of the competing visions would control the state. With the failure of the authoritarian empire and the lack of popular bonding to the Weimar Republic as a pale copy of the Second Reich, the nationalist project radicalized into a racial dictatorship under Hitler. Because of the enormous suffering in war and genocide, this hypertrophic nationalism collapsed in total defeat in 1945, never to recover. The slow unmaking of the nationalists' hold on both postwar Germanys was by no means automatic, posing instead one of the major challenges for contemporary historians. Ironically, the discrediting of the nationalists allowed the Catholic and Socialist alternatives to define the destinies of the two postwar Germanys for the second half of the twentieth century, until unification created a single state in which both traditions must coexist.

c) gender

The sixth theme, therefore, concerns the gendering of German history through competing definitions of womanhood and, by contradistinction, contrasting visions of manhood. In spite of the rapid development of women's history, the results of such research appear to be even less integrated into the existing master narratives than the work on

---

[71] Alon Confino, "The Nation as a Local Metaphor: *Heimat*, National Memory and the German Empire, 1871–1918," *History and Memory* 5 (1993): 42–86.

[72] See also the discussion of the historical background essay in Konrad H. Jarausch, ed., *After Unity: Reconfiguring German Identities* (Providence, 1997).

migration.[73] The German debate has focused on the seemingly self-evident notion of maternalism, since the women's movement used the rhetoric of "spiritual motherhood" to expand female rights to education and work. Yet during the Weimar Republic this notion was extended into "voluntary mothering," which combined greater emphasis on individual rights with an expansion of welfare provisions to ease the burdens of maternity. The negative connotations of the term, therefore, derive largely from the celebration of maternalism in the Third Reich—which was, however, limited to Aryan women, since Nazi racial policy was anything but motherly toward Jews, Gypsies, the handicapped, and so on.[74] Instead of condemning the language of motherhood by reflex, historians need to take a closer look at its actual uses at any given time.

Only in the postwar period did the values of egalitarianism and individualism gradually begin to dominate the debate on women's issues. In both successor states, the population disaster of World War II led to the reaffirmation of family priorities and a frantic search for normalcy of gender roles during the late 1940s. The East German state pushed women into the industrial workforce out of a mixture of ideological motives of Socialist equality and such practical concerns as meeting the labor shortage. In contrast, the Federal Republic, through legislation and propaganda, tried to restore the male-breadwinner model, although the burgeoning economy pulled women into service jobs.[75] As a result of lifestyle changes, the new feminism of the 1970s began to repudiate the maternalist legacy and insist upon individual equality in the West. After unification, the estranged sisters in East and West had much difficulty in finding common ground because of their different practical versus theoretical experiences with independence.[76]

The attendant gendering of the German nation is a more complicated issue than western stereotypes of the "fatherland" as the home of unreconstructed patriarchy would suggest. No doubt, a strong element of male bonding in nationalist, militarist, and racist rhetoric lends cre-

---

[73] Kathleen Canning, "Feminist History after the Linguistic Turn: Historicizing Discourse and Experience," *Signs* (Winter 1994): 368–400.

[74] Ann Taylor Allen, "Feminism and Motherhood in Germany and in International Perspective, 1800–1914," in Patricia Herminghouse and Magda Mueller, eds., *Gender and Germanness: Cultural Productions of Nation* (Providence, 1997), 113 ff.

[75] Robert Moeller, *Protecting Motherhood: Women and the Family in the Politics of Postwar Germany* (Berkeley, 1993); and Elizabeth Heineman, "The Hour of the Woman: Memories of Germany's 'Crisis Years' and West German National Identity," *American Historical Review* 101 (1996): 354–95.

[76] Hanna Schissler, "Women in West Germany from 1945 to the Present," in Michael G. Huelshoff, Andrei S. Markovits, and Simon Reich, eds., *From Bundesrepublik to Deutschland: German Politics after Unification* (Ann Arbor, 1993), 117–36.

dence to indictments of a tradition of male chauvinism. But women were also heavily involved in the national project, both as objects of symbolic signification (as various Germanias) and as subjects of practical participation in patriotic societies or factory-labor during war time. Moreover, women possessed considerable rights of education and work and even achieved the vote a whole generation earlier than their French counterparts! Ultimately, the gradual transformation of gender roles, as a result of the New Social Movements of the 1970s, has produced a surprising degree of sexual freedom and more permissive post-material and post-national definitions of the family. In a remarkable reversal of Wilhelmian patterns, this shift, therefore, suggests a gradual feminization of the most recent incarnation of the German nation.

The final theme addresses the issue of mass consumption and popular culture, which is beginning to emerge as a new narrative of continuous progress across the caesuras of the twentieth century. While historians of consumer society may be right about the long-run advancement of prosperity, disruptions of living standards mattered intensely in the short run since successive regimes tried to base their legitimacy on ideologically colored versions of the good life, and experiences of material deprivation strongly influenced the later craving for ostentatious consumption. These linkages are especially evident in the often neglected but fundamental question of food provision, since the repeated crises of hunger and starvation during and after the two world wars have left deep scars on the collective psyche of the Germans. For the longest time, dreams of affluence and the striving to render it secure against market fluctuations were a product of the nightmares of intense want.[77]

Another striking aspect of German development is the intense effort to shape consumption and culture according to ideological preconceptions so as to prove superior a particular system. During the hothouse climate of the Weimar Republic, theoretical debates about the problems of an emerging popular culture largely outstripped the modest advances in mass consumption since the uneven distribution of wealth actually created a crisis of underconsumption. In contrast, the Nazis made strenuous efforts to provide their own Aryanized variety of prosperity and entertainment based on full employment and state-organized leisure in the KdF to buttress their power by pacifying social strife. Even the unpopular SED-dictatorship sought to create an alter-

---

[77] Belinda Davis, *Home Fires Burning: Food, Politics, and Everyday Life in World War I Berlin* (Chapel Hill, 2000); and Michael Wildt, *Am Beginn der 'Konsumgesellschaft'. Mangelerfahrung, Lebenshaltung, Wohlstandshoffnung in Westdeutschland in den fünfziger Jahren* (Hamburg, 1994).

native version of a modest socialist consumerism to fulfill working class aspirations for the good life and compete with the aggressively successful *Wohlstandsgesellschaft* of the West.[78] What mattered in an unstable political context was less how much was actually consumed or how people were diverted than how living conditions and dreamworlds could be presented to reinforce political claims.

The long delayed advent of high consumption in West Germany during the 1960s and 1970s proved both gratifying and unsettling because it could be seen as recompense for earlier suffering, but it also threatened established self-conceptions. The dominant interpretation of the *Wirtschaftswunder* credited the secondary virtues of hard work, a neo-corporate pattern of labor relations, and the compromises of a social market economy as roots of widespread prosperity, thereby associating democracy with the good life. But at the same time, the arrival of widespread prosperity also brought with it Americanized styles of popular culture that advanced a process of westernization, embraced by youth but viewed with much skepticism by their elders.[79] The ensuing cultural struggles between the generations and proponents of different value systems left many Germans unsure of who they actually were beyond affluent consumers and world-champion travelers, since memories of scarcity lingered and self-gratification remained suspect as an end in itself. Among the different political currents, the Green Party continues to exhibit this fundamental ambivalence particularly strongly, since it is itself a product of the shift to postmaterial values; at the same time it criticizes the excesses of consumer society.

By offering distinctive but complementary perspectives, these seven themes address some of the key issues of German history in the twentieth century. These partial chronological narratives intersect in the multiple contests over constituting a German nation in the domestic realm and in the international state system. Focusing on these contentions— both in public and in private—over what kind of community Germany might be, over who belonged and who did not, and over where in Europe or the world Germany might be located, helps to unlock the course of twentieth-century history. The contending efforts to put together a society from disparate parts, the disasters and successes of

---

[78] Siegfried Kracauer, *The Mass Ornament: Weimar Essays* (Cambridge, Mass., 1995); Ronald Smelser, *Robert Ley: Hitler's Labor Front Leader* (Oxford, 1988); and Stephane Merl, "Sowjetisierung in der Welt des Konsums," in Konrad H. Jarausch and Hannes Siegrist, eds., *Amerikanisierung und Sowjetisierung in Deutschland 1945–1970* (Frankfurt, 1997), 167–194.

[79] Anthony J.Nicholls, *Freedom with Responsibility: The Social Market Economy in Germany 1918–1963* (Oxford, 1994); and Anselm Doering-Manteuffel, *Wie westlich sind die Deutschen? Amerikanisierung und Westernisierung im 20. Jahrhundert* (Göttingen, 1999).

these labors, constitute the signature of the age. What is impressive is the deliberateness of the efforts to mold a society and inscribe different versions of Germanness on the nation's subjects and on Europe—a process that did not stop in 1945 or in 1990.

By going through cycles of de- and re-civilizing, the contentious process of constituting a German nation within Europe has challenged the very foundations of civility.[80] *Pace* Norbert Elias, it is not necessary to attach any particular teleology to this existential, life-and-death confrontation. In view of similar processes in central and eastern Europe and in terms of experiences in former Yugoslavia, the challenge of "civilizing" no longer appears as uniquely German but as the very key to the formation of national societies.[81] Though in the German context this process seemed to end in disaster and moral depravity, it nonetheless had a surprisingly "happy ending." The severity of the deviation and the nature of the ending are somewhat diminished if we think of them as predestined to end in the West.[82] An unspecified reference to westernization is all too frequently used as a sleight of hand to efface what matters: the formation of a cultural code or, really, a succession of codes that put and hold together a texture of belonging in a deeply fractured society. Some aspects of this process might be captured in a sociological tradition that has the notion of societalization (*Vergesellschaftung*) at its center.

In the twentieth century, the constitution and severance of bonds of belonging were intimately tied to contestations over power, and these in turn were enmeshed in conflicts over worldviews. This was not at all a specialty of totalitarianism, although it gave these contestations a deadly turn.[83] The centrality of national or international power, and the quickness with which these contestations could turn to lethal violence, caution against a tendency to neutralize culture, be it in the spirit of anthropological inquiry or in the more recent pursuit of a history of consumerism. Indubitable merits mark both enterprises, but each one in its own way is oddly hesitant to acknowledge how much of a struggle was entailed in making and unmaking cultures and how closely involved cultural processes of societalization remained with life and death choices. As the nineteenth-century project of creating a national culture was beholden to its literature and music, its twentieth-century

---

[80] Georg Simmel, *Soziologie. Untersuchungen über die Formen der Vergesellschaftung* (Frankfurt/Main, 1992), 764.

[81] Isabel V. Hull, *Sexuality, State, and Civil Society in Germany, 1700–1815* (Ithaca, 1996), makes a convincing case.

[82] Norbert Elias, *The Civilizing Process* (New York, 1978).

[83] Michael Burleigh, *The Third Reich: A New History* (New York, 2000).

continuation was full of competing schemes in medicine or architecture, which were meant to better society and save the country. Each in its own way aimed to form a nation that remained constitutionally unstable, territorially unsettled, and socially fractured.

Narrating Nightmares and Reawakenings

More than their European neighbors, Germans of a certain age contend with troubled memories that, though put aside as a pop song has it in favor of "advancing the GNP," resurface at unexpected moments.[84] Private conversations with people over fifty years old are replete with recollections from World War II or the immediate postwar era, telling tales of survival through catastrophe but largely evading the question of responsibility. Occasionally these stories do touch upon agency, but they offer incidents of imprisonment and persecution, scraps with the Gestapo, or stints in a penal division—altogether not as unusual an occurrence as one might think. Survivors of the Holocaust or former slave-laborers have become omnipresent on television but are rarely encountered in everyday situations as neighbors. Layered over these remembrances are public commemorations, which tend to be painful and sometimes embarrassing. Instead of being a source of pride, German history is treated as a burden. For the wartime and, surely, for the postwar generation, the German past has come to function as a negative foil for current definitions of identity.[85]

What should historians do with these old men's and women's tales? Should they take them as authentic testimony for a past that must not return, put them into museums as mementos of a shipwreck, or ignore them in favor of more scholarly reconstructions? Instead of being dismissed as incomplete and unreliable, these stories need to be put squarely into a history of the twentieth century and made the outspoken record of the labors with which people pasted together their ruptured lives, of how they maintained and recreated social bonds and values, and of what kinds of passions moved them. For all their obvious inadequacies, such individual or collective recollections can serve as signposts along the crooked paths that the Germans—including those who have been German but no longer are and those who may yet become German but are still treated as foreigners who have

---

[84] This is unadulterated "deutsch rock" from the Ruhr, ca. 1984: "Jetzt wird wieder in die Hände gespuckt, wir steigern das Bruttosozialprodukt."

[85] Marc Fischer, *Germany, the Germans and the Burdens of History* (New York, 1995).

stayed—took to get from one end of the century to the other.[86] Such a perspective takes seriously that the making and unmaking of nations is a process that is, indeed, thought about, talked through, and put down in symbols and images.

Personal anecdotes and collective stories are also a reminder of the powerful role of narration in turning recollections of the past into history. Though some skeptics, such as Richard Evans, still argue that historians ought to stick only to analysis, the public craves narratives, and many scholars, perhaps against their professional conscience, resort to stories as they search for truth and recover past reality.[87] In the German case the penchant for storytelling is a response to the psychological problem of dealing with an incomprehensible catastrophe, of exploring the human aspects of inexplicable suffering. When looking for the truth about the past, historians stare war and genocide in the face. But when they steer around war and genocide, they risk erasing a central part of German reality. If these nightmares have receded, it is not because of the innocence of historians who have never sought anything but the truth, but it is for the stories of all those who have faced the truth and have not despaired. With due acknowledgment of the subterfuges that such plots provide, German historiography and public memory could not have faced their ghosts without recourse to some very powerful narratives.

The genres suggested by the philosopher Hayden White offer interesting but somewhat inadequate emplotments of the course of twentieth-century German history. If "Romance is fundamentally a drama of self-identification symbolized by the hero's transcendence of the world of experience, his victory over it, and his final liberation from it," the German story must be shorn of much of its self-inflicted terror to be read as a Dickensian triumph over adversity.[88] The related framing of the *Bildungsroman* as narrative of becoming, used by nationalists, seems hardly more appropriate for a nation or perpetrators.[89] Instead, critical historians prefer to turn to Tragedy as "intimation[s] of [terrible] states of division among men, . . . the fall of protagonists and the shaking of the world he inhabits" to tell a cautionary tale of the inevitable disaster of a misguided protagonist. Some optimistic scholars also resort to Comedy, seen as "reconciliations of men with men, of men with their

---

[86] Konrad H. Jarausch and Martin Sabrow, eds., *Verletztes Gedächtnis. Zeitgeschichte und Erinnerung im Konflikt* (Frankfurt, 2002).

[87] Richard J. Evans, *In Defense of History* (New York, 1999).

[88] Hayden White, *Metahistory: The Historical Imagination in Nineteenth-Century Europe* (Baltimore, 1973), 8–9.

[89] Aleida Assmann, *Arbeit am nationalen Gedächtnis. Eine kurze Geschichte der deutschen Bildungsidee* (Frankfurt am Main, 1993).

world and their society," which result in a "purer, saner, and healthier" condition of society.[90] Though perhaps too stylized, these distinctions may help explain some of the conflict between the older national academics, middling social science scholars and younger everyday historians during the course of the Federal Republic. While apologists tend toward Romance, critics are habitually tragedians, whereas some radicals ironically believe in the possibility of reconciliation.

Since it holds out hope, a redemptive emplotment in a Christian or psychological version has become popular among politicians and the general public. In their impressive syntheses the historian Heinrich August Winkler and the political scientist Peter Graf Kielmansegg have produced democratic narratives that seek to link the descent into catastrophe to the recovery of civility.[91] That emplotment reads like a tale with an initial stage of innocence (the pre-unification fragmentation of the nineteenth century), a twice repeated and each time more repulsive sin (the world wars and the Holocaust), a period of prolonged atonement (the postwar division), and an eventual redemption (the reunification of the FRG and GDR). The secular version of this narrative portrays the lifecycle of a nation as the arduous procession from youth to troubled adolescence, and on to maturity, which holds out the promise of an enlightened normalcy. Both versions are distinctly post-revolutionary, post-lapsarian tales, and if intellectuals still recoil from such a reading, it is for the most part because they do not trust human ability (or perhaps the Germans) to overcome catastrophe. Occasional missteps like Bitburg to the contrary, this redemptionist emplotment has also become the official self-representation of the Federal Republic as an answer to earlier disasters.[92]

At first glance, the framing of descent into darkness, followed by surprising recovery as a result of individual and collective learning processes, has much to recommend it. In terms of the themes discussed above, this perspective interprets the first half of the twentieth century as a negative spiral in which the experience of killing and death in World War I helped undercut the unloved Republic; Hitler's diatribes against the *Diktat* of Versailles promoted the Nazi cause; the expulsion from the East reinforced revanchist sentiment; the failure of authoritar-

[90] White, *Metahistory*, 9.

[91] Anselm Doering-Manteuffel, "Eine politische Nationalgeschichte für die Berliner Republik. Überlegungen zu Heinrich August Winklers 'Der lange Weg nach Westen'," *Geschichte und Gesellschaft* 27 (2001): 446–462; and Konrad H. Jarausch, "Die Geschichte der Deutschen diesseits der Katastrophe. Anmerkungen zu einem 'großen Werk'," *Potsdamer Bulletin für Zeithistorische Studien* (23-24 October, 2001): 16–18.

[92] Geoffrey Hartmann, ed., *Bitburg in Moral and Political Perspective* (Bloomington, 1986).

ian nationalism paved the way for a more radical, and racist, chauvinism; and population loss encouraged an instrumentalized and selective biopolitics.[93] In contrast, this view characterizes the second half of the century by the inverted image of a positive cycle in which negative experiences spurred benign developments that eventually reinforced one another: The murderous consequences of militarism engendered a deeply ingrained pacifism; the repression of dictatorship promoted a turn toward democratization; the double failure of hegemony encouraged an appreciation for the limitation of power; the suffering of mass flight spurred greater acceptance of immigration; and finally, the excesses of racist patriarchy encouraged more equality for women.[94] This reading sees the link between the two unequal halves of the century in the learning experiences that sought to prevent a repetition of the previous catastrophes.

For some intellectuals, this positive reading appears too pat a solution, smoothing out the jagged edges of the German past in a heartwarming story of transgression and redemption. They may feel more comfortable with the more ambiguous portrayals of such writers as Alfred Döblin, Uwe Johnson, or Christa Wolf and more recently Walter Kempowski, Alexander Kluge, or W. G. Sebald.[95] Their cunning fiction surely knows how to tell a tale, but their stories are made of the labors and the memories of their imaginary subjects in a multi-vocal and, indeed, discordant world in which German history stretches from New York to Stalingrad and Jerusalem and in which history is but the sum total of human endeavors. It is a fiction that tells both of the catastrophes and of the happinesses, and, as is so often the case, of the two being inextricably mixed. It also accounts for the ways that people come together and constitute themselves as community, as much as how they fight with and tear one another apart. And it jumps across the barrier of time, intermingling experiences in actual cataclysmic events with their later recollections. These are multi-layered and multi-

[93] Compare Henry Turner, *Hitler's Thirty Days to Power: January 1933* (Reading, Penn., 1996) to Peter Fritzsche, *Germans into Nazis* (Cambridge, Mass., 1998).

[94] See Peter Graf Kielmannsegg, *Nach der Katastrophe. Eine Geschichte des geteilten Deutschland* (Berlin, 2000).

[95] Alfred Döblin, *Berlin Alexanderplatz: The Story of Franz Biberkopf*, trans. Eugen Jolas (New York, 1983); Uwe Johnson, *Anniversaries: From the life of Gesine Cresspahl*, trans. Leila Vennewitz (New York, 1975); Christa Wolf, *A Model Childhood*, trans. Ursula Molinaro and Hedwig Rappelt (New York, 1980); Walter Kempowski, *Echolot* (Munich, 1993–1999); Alexander Kluge, *Chronik der Gefühle* (Frankfurt am Main, 2000); and W. G. Sebald, *The Rings of Saturn* (New York, 1998).

focal epics of the making and unmaking of individuals and nations that do not resort to a comforting telos of redemption.[96]

Finding appropriate modes of narrating the German nightmares and reawakenings of the twentieth century therefore remains a difficult challenge at the beginning of the twenty-first century. The master narratives of the postwar years sound curiously dated since the collapse of Communism has surprisingly reconstituted a shrunken and chastened German nation. Once again, their cautionary lessons—whether they were neo-national, Marxist, or liberal—were overtaken by the actual course of events from which they were drawn. If one so wishes, this is the "post-modern" moment in German history—not for any programmatic intent of replacing the modern, but for the actual working-through of a modern agenda, the fifty-year long effort at overcoming war and genocide and constituting a modern German society "after the fall." Because the modernization and westernization project has itself become history, perhaps it is only now that historians can begin to comprehend the twentieth-century past—writing "histories" as the Greek neologism has it—so that the labor of human beings may not be forgotten in the future.[97] For some skeptics, it may not appear to be a good omen that this call to preserve memory comes from an irrepressively fabulating, anthropologizing historian. But whatever else may be said about Herodotus, he made his inquiries and wrote as truthfully as he could, without providing a preconceived meaning by way of telling the story.

---

[96] For this reason Tadeusz Borowski, *This Way for the Gas, Ladies and Gentlemen and Other Stories* (New York, 1967), 180, also intended "to write a great, immortal epic" about his terrible experiences.

[97] Herodotus, *The Histories* (London, 1988), 7. The gently meliorating Penguin translation speaks of the goal "to preserve the memory of the past by putting down on record the astonishing achievements both of our own and of other people; and more particularly, to show how they came in conflict."

PART I

THE ECLIPSE
OF THE MASTER
NARRATIVES

1

A Return to National History? The Master Narrative and Beyond

The coincidence of political reunification with methodological shifts toward postmodernism raises the fundamental question: How should German history be told after the end of a century marked by its excesses? Once again the perplexing developments in central Europe leave scholars who approach history as an imaginative reconstruction of the past somewhat at a loss as to who the central actors are, what stories ought to be related, and which lessons they ought to impart.[1] Should historians return to a focus on the nation-state as the "natural" unit of analysis and narrate its rise, fall, and resurrection, focusing on international struggles for primacy and domestic conflicts for power? Or should they focus instead on alternate story lines such as the lives of ordinary people to suggest a more down-to-earth perspective that seeks to recapture their joy and suffering? At stake in the current debates, therefore, is the very framing of the German past as a narrative of national development, emphasizing political unity, or as a set of competing counter-stories, stressing social diversity.

[1] Gerhard A. Ritter, *Der Umbruch von 1989/91 und die Geschichtswissenschaft* (Munich, 1995).

The issue of how to narrate German history is not just a subject for academic speculation, but is a problem with profound political implications. As a dialogic enterprise that seeks to relate the past to the present, historical representation of prior events is always in tension with judgments about current developments.[2] The appalling collaboration of eminent nationalist historians in justifying the brutal racial expansionism of the Nazis in western and eastern Europe demonstrates that too uncritical an acceptance of political agendas of the present holds grave dangers for scholarly reflection.[3] Ironically, even the anti-fascist mobilization of progressive intellectuals in East Germany shows the perils of academic dedication to the service of another, albeit ideologically opposed, dictatorship.[4] The experience of such disastrous self-instrumentalization cautions German historians against political commitment, leaving them with the dilemma: Should they cling to wider post-national and European identities or should they participate in a "normalization" that would restore an assertively national history? Other scholars instead suggest, as a compromise, the construction of a new "democratic patriotism."[5]

From the perspective of the new cultural histories, this question revolves around the shape and content of the "master-narrative." This is a term that stems from the anthropological studies of Claude Levi-Strauss, who contrasted the written narrative of colonial masters with the oral stories of native slaves. The French linguist François Lyotard generalized the notion to cover *le grand récit marxiste*, extending it to canonized ideological explanations of the past that serve to legitimize certain power relationships. While local *petites histoires* seemed credible, he remained skeptical of large-scale hegemonial histories: "Strongly simplified, I define postmodernism as incredulity towards master narratives."[6] Some American historical theorists, such as Alan

---

[2] Ann Rigney, *The Rhetoric of Historical Representation: Three Narrative Histories of the French Revolution* (Chicago, 1990).

[3] Windried Schulze and Gerhard Oexle, eds., *Deutsche Historiker im Nationalsozialismus* (Frankfurt, 1999).

[4] Konrad H. Jarausch, Matthias Middell, and Martin Sabrow, "Störfall DDR-Geschichtswissenschaft. Problemfelder einer kritischen Historisierung," in Konrad H. Jarausch, Matthias Middell, Martin Sabrow, and Georg G. Iggers, eds., *Historische Zeitschrift*, special issue 27 (1998): 1–50.

[5] Stefan Berger, "Historians and Nation-Building in Germany After Reunification," *Past and Present*, no. 148 (1995): 187–222; and Konrad H. Jarausch, "Normalisierung oder Re-Nationalisierung? Zur Umdeutung der deutschen Vergangenheit?" *Geschichte und Gesellschaft* 21 (1995): 571–84.

[6] Kerwin Lee Klein, "In Search of Narrative Mastery: Postmodernism and the People Without History," *History and Theory* 34 (1995), 275 ff; and Alan Megill, "Grand Narrative

Megill, have imported the concept into historiography to distinguish meta-narratives, which offer grand accounts of the past ranging over long time-periods, including a wealth of different detail, and presenting a coherent interpretation of complex developments from more specific minor or counter-narratives that are generally regarded as subsets of a larger whole.[7] A narratological approach therefore poses the question of how the history of a people is to be emplotted, who its key agents are—the state, the workers, or society—and what broader meaning should be assigned to it.

In central Europe the most powerful of these master narratives centered on the creation and maintenance of the nation-state. During the mid-nineteenth century some liberal historians began to argue that Prussia's mission was to unify the German lands, supporting the nationalist cause with a novel interpretation that compared the glories of a unified past with the shame of a divided present. This "German conception of history" or "German model" stressed the necessity of thorough philological source criticism and intuitive hermeneutics, combining painstaking research with an imaginative understanding of the past on its own terms. This tradition of "historicism" also focused on high politics, wars, treaties, or revolutions, seeking to promote the creation and to describe the subsequent development of the nation-state as the highest form of political organization.[8] Even after Nazi atrocities had discredited such nationalism, the East German Marxists' refutation and the West German indictment of a German *Sonderweg* remained wedded to the national framework since they merely tried to reverse its affirmative connotation.[9] Only during the 1970s and 1980s did regional, social, feminist, and comparative critiques begin to dissolve the unitary mold so that multiple histories of different locales, religions, classes, and genders started to emerge.[10]

[handwritten margin notes: "German conception of history' → historicism → nation-state → high politics (1850s – 1970s)]

---

and the Discipline of History," in Frank Ankersmit and Hans Kellner, eds., *A New Philosophy of History* (Chicago, 1995), 151–73.

[7] Alan Megill, "Recounting the Past: 'Description,' Explanation, and Narrative in Historiography," *American Historical Review* 94 (1989), 627–54. Cf. also Konrad H. Jarausch and Martin Sabrow, eds., *Die historische Meistererzählung in Deutschland. Deutungslinien deutscher Nationalgeschichte nach 1945.*

[8] Hans-Ulrich Wehler, "Historiography in Germany Today," in Jürgen Habermas, ed., *Observations on the 'Spiritual Situation of the Age': Contemporary German Perspectives* (Cambridge, Mass., 1984), 221–59; Georg G. Iggers, *The German Conception of History: The National Tradition of Historical Thought from Herder to the Present*, rev. ed. (Middletown, 1982).

[9] Andreas Dorpalen, *German History in a Marxist Perspective: The East German Approach* (Detroit, 1985); and Georg G. Iggers, *The Social History of Politics: Critical Perspectives in West German Historical Writing Since 1945* (Leamington Spa, 1985).

[10] James J. Sheehan, *German History, 1770–1866* (New York, 1989).

Although older intellectuals may fear their postwar critiques threatened, a younger generation of scholars might see the conjuncture of reunification and postmodernism as an exciting opportunity for developing a new interpretative framework. While the traditional national master narrative that Gerhard Ritter sought to salvage across the disaster of 1945 sounds quaintly irrelevant half a century later, some of the often intensely negative counternarratives of American, or West or East German intellectuals also appear curiously antiquated in their telling of German history as cautionary tale, lest such terrors happen again.[11] A few historians are gradually beginning to realize that the contrast between the catastrophic and reconstructive halves of the twentieth century requires a rethinking of the German story, even if they are far from agreement on what such a different approach might look like. The following remarks explore this question by looking at the rise of the national paradigm, tracing some elements of the subsequent de-nationalization and commenting on the still ongoing normalization debate. Perhaps this brief reflection on the problematic development of German historiography might offer some clues to how a different framework could be found.

The National Paradigm

In the effort of romantic poets and publicists to transform the cultural nation into a political state, historians played a leading part by providing a scholarly justification for the national agenda as logical outgrowth of a common history. As *praeceptor Germaniae* Heinrich von Treitschke self-consciously set out to create a "national historical tradition common to all cultured persons" that would give the disparate Germans a feeling of belonging together, of sharing experiences through time. "It was my purpose to emphasize within the confusion of events those most important aspects and to stress the men, institutions, ideas and changes of fate, which have created the new unity of our people." This master narrative departed from a recollection of "the proudest kingdom of the Germans," personified by the mythical Emperor Frederick Barbarossa, who claimed "leadership over the civilized world." It went on to stress the humiliation of "the ugliest part of our history" because of the petty particularism of the territorial states, aggravated by the Protestant Reformation and the "terrible devastation" of the Thirty Years War. This story of a Golden Age, fall from grace,

---

[11] See the strong moralizing tone in Christian von Krockow, *Die Deutschen in ihrem Jahrhundert 1890–1990* (Hamburg, 1990), 342–43.

and eventual redemption concluded by celebrating "religious freedom and the Prussian state" as the wellsprings of a revival that would lead via the Wars of Liberation and the misshapen German Confederation to the triumphant recovery of unity under Bismarck's leadership.[12]

The lead text of the nationalist view, Treitschke's *German History in the Nineteenth Century,* offered the Germans a compelling vision of liberation and empowerment. First, unification would widen the political and cultural horizons beyond the borders of petty principalities to larger realms of communication, thereby throwing off confining local restraints. At the same time, the creation of a greater polity would make it possible to realize "the hopes for liberty" in a constitutional monarchy that allowed its subjects to participate in government and mature through assuming responsibility. Finally, the construction of a national state would satisfy the hitherto thwarted, but nonetheless "passionate and incitable national pride" by restoring sufficient German power to throw off foreign tutelage and participate in world affairs on an equal footing. This nationalist call resonated among the educated and propertied since it addressed not the rulers but the people and suggested a progressive mission of sweeping away the cobwebs of corporate society. The message was also appealing because it spoke with a great pathos "that feels the fatherland's fate as one's own sorrow or happiness, and endows historical narration with an inner truth."[13]

Rejecting the southern, Catholic, and Austrian alternative as divisive, north German Protestant historians such as Heinrich von Sybel gradually succeeded in anointing the rising state of Prussia as carrier of the national mission. This Borussian school labored to reconcile the undeniable military elements of the Hohenzollern heritage with the more attractive cultural impulses of the Stein-Hardenberg reforms and the liberal legacies of the western German states in a renewed, but federal Reich that might finally inspire "a delight in the fatherland" and obtain international respect.[14] These national-liberal scholars blended the disparate, discontinuous, and discouraging tales of the central Eu-

---

[12] Heinrich von Treitschke, *History of Germany in the Nineteenth Century,* vol. I, trans. Eden Paul and Cedar Paul (New York, 1915), xiii, and *Bilder aus der Deutschen Geschichte,* vol. I, 3rd ed. (Leipzig, 1909), 44 ff. See also Konrad H. Jarausch, Hinrich Seeba, and David Conradt, "The Presence of the Past: Culture, Opinion and Identity in Germany," in Konrad H. Jarausch, ed., *After Unity: Reconfiguring German Identities* (Providence, 1997).

[13] Treitschke, *History of Germany,* vol. V, v, 3 ff; and Konrad H. Jarausch, *Students, Society and Imperial Germany: The Rise of Academic Illiberalism* (Princeton, 1983), 208 ff.

[14] Treitschke, *History of Germany,* vol. I, xv; and Iggers, *German Conception of History,* 90–123.

ropean past into a cohesive master narrative that suggested a sense of common fate, focused political energies on the nation-state, commanded individual self-sacrifice for the greater whole, and rejected all foreign influences. By repetition in song, representation in painting, and celebration in ritual, this national vision gradually managed to redirect allegiances away from particularistic patriotism and inspire subsequent generations to feel as Germans across all differences of class, gender, or religion.[15] In effect, this new master narrative displaced older religious, dynastic, or regional histories, allowing them to exist only as subsidiary strands in a national tapestry.

The nationalist historians owed much of their success to the concurrent professionalization of their scholarship. Even if he praised Prussia, Leopold von Ranke, founder of the scientific method for historians, exemplified by the research seminar and the monograph, still belonged to an older world of state patriotism, preoccupied with dynastic intrigue and religious conflict. But his spiritual successor, Johann Gustav von Droysen, systematized the procedures of historical source criticism in his much cited text, called *Historik*, so as to transform history into a real *Wissenschaft* while at the same time promoting the national and liberal cause in his public stance.[16] This professionalization in method turned German historians into a group of well-trained archival researchers, while the nationalization in their values made them guardians of the state who saw the creation and preservation of the nation both as a scientific truth and a moral imperative. Basic to this combination of historicism with nationalism was the firm conviction, enunciated half a century later by the Pan-German Dietrich Schäfer, "that in historical writing the most scrupulous research can go hand in hand with enthusiastic and inspiring love of the fatherland."[17]

With the foundation of a united German state in 1871, this Prusso-centric version of history became the dominant narrative that legitimized the peculiar fusion of dynastic rule, state politics, and popular aspiration that constituted Bismarck's Second Reich. In the huge fresco that dominated the restored castle in Goslar, as well as in countless schoolbooks and official holidays, the Hohenzollerns invoked imperial traditions so as to suggest that the new state was merely the continuation of the old Holy Roman Empire. Academic historians, like Otto Hintze, played along with this historicizing self-representation by

---

[15] Matthew B. Levinger, *Enlightened Nationalism: The Transformation of Prussian Political Culture, 1806–1848* (New York, 2000).

[16] Leopold von Ranke, *Preussische Geschichte*, vols. I–V, and *Neue Briefe*, ed. Hans Herzfeld (Hamburg, 1949). Cf. Johann Gustav von Droysen, *Historik*, text edition of the first lecture in 1857 and the last printed copy of 1882 by Peter Leyh (Stuttgart, 1997).

[17] Dietrich Schäfer, *Deutsche Geschichte*, vol I., 9th rev. ed. (Jena, 1922), 13.

praising "the Hohenzollern and their work" as "five hundred years of patriotic history," thereby reconciling monarchist with popular themes.[18] Even if within the discipline Karl Lamprecht's cultural history and in the emergent social sciences Max Weber's sociological theorizing severely attacked the premises of historicism, the bulk of the Neo-Rankean historians remained firmly focused on political history, emphasizing the conflicts of international power-politics rather than domestic constitutional struggles.[19] While it shifted the focus away from power politics toward "outstanding thinkers," even Friedrich Meinecke's brilliant investigation into "the idea of the national state" that inspired the turn from cosmopolitanism to nationalism retained the nation-state as primary focus of historical thought.[20]

In the Weimar Republic the acrimonious controversies over the war-guilt clause and the stab-in-the-back legend polarized the debate about the past and effectively inhibited the democratization of the national paradigm. The majority of the educated public responded to Article 231 of the Treaty of Versailles, alleging "Germany's sole responsibility" for the outbreak of the war, with an angry incredulity that was fueled by Foreign Office support of the revisionist journal *Die Kriegsschuldfrage*.[21] In the much-publicized hearings on the responsibility for the German collapse, the Right also managed to cover its own faults and to saddle Democrats and Socialists with the responsibility for defeat, branding them as "November criminals."[22] A minority of professional historians became "republicans of reason," as did Hermann Oncken; explored the growth of democratic traditions in the 1848 revolution, as did Veit Valentin; or even started to examine the socio-structural sources of Wilhelmine hubris, as did Eckart Kehr.[23] But most of their

[18] Otto Hintze, *Die Hohenzollern und ihr Werk. Fünfhundert Jahre vaterländischer Geschichte* (Berlin, 1915).

[19] See Roger Chickering, *Karl Lamprecht: A German Academic Life, 1856–1915* (New Jersey, 1993); and Wolfgang J. Mommsen, *The Political and Social Theory of Max Weber: Collected Essays* (Chicago, 1989).

[20] Friedrich Meinecke, *Cosmopolitanism and the National State*, trans. Robert B. Kimber (Princeton, 1970), 9 ff.

[21] Ulrich Heinemann, *Die verdrängte Niederlage. Politische Öffentlichkeit und Kriegsschuldfrage in der Weimarer Republik* (Göttingen, 1983); and Wolfgang Jäger, *Historische Forschung und politische Kultur in Deutschland. Die Debatte 1914–1980 über den Ausbruch des Ersten Weltkrieges* (Göttingen, 1984).

[22] Eugen Fischer-Baling, "Der Untersuchungsausschuß für die Schuldfrage des ersten Weltkrieges," in Alfred Herrmann, ed., *Aus Geschichte und Politik* (Düsseldorf, 1954), 117–34.

[23] See the postwar introductions to Meinecke's *Cosmopolitanism and the National State*, 5–6; Veit Valentin, *Geschichte der deutschen Revolution 1848–1849* 2 vols. (Berlin, 1930); and Eckart Kehr, *Der Primat der Innenpolitik. Gesammelte Aufsätze zur Politik und Sozialgeschichte im 19. und 20. Jahrhundert*, ed. H.-U. Wehler (Berlin, 1965).

monarchist, neo-conservative, or volkish colleagues continued, like
Dietrich Schäfer, to focus "on the development of the German state"
in an avowedly "politically tendentious historiography" that merely
claimed to be inspired "by love of the fatherland and faith in its future."[24]

The Third Reich radically reasserted the national narrative by eliminating its critics, widened its methodological scope, and racialized its
interpretative thrust. Promoted by Nazi students, the "cleansing of the
universities" expelled democratic and Jewish scholars from their positions, silencing them professionally and forcing them into exile or condemning them to eventual death.[25] Even if some traditional research
continued and Walter Frank's new Reichsinstitut für deutsche Geschichte had only a limited impact, the nationalist majority of professors basically agreed with the sizable minority of Nazi sympathizers
on the restoration of German power, the rejection of Western democracy, and the dream of a new people's community.[26] More important
for the Nazification of the profession were the *Volksdeutsche Forschungsge-
meinschaften*, extra-university research groups that worked on ethnic
communities beyond the frontiers of the Third Reich, because they attracted a number of talented younger historians who developed a
more inclusive conception of *Volksgeschichte*. Integrally nationalist, this
approach shifted the emphasis from the state to the people, their dia-
lects, folk customs, or modes of production, thereby expanding the
methodological reach of historians to linguistics, ethnography, and
economics. Recent work has begun to uncover the appalling degree to
which such rising scholars as Theodor Schieder, Werner Conze, and
Franz Petri used this innovative research in service of Nazi expansionism and genocide.[27]

This brief sketch indicates the powerful hold of the national master
narrative on German historiography from the mid-nineteenth to the

[24] Schäfer, *Deutsche Geschichte*, vol. I, 12–13. See also Bernd Faulenbach, *Ideologie des
deutschen Weges. Die deutsche Geschichte in der Historiographie zwischen Kaiserreich und Nationalsozialismus* (Munich, 1980).

[25] Konrad H. Jarausch, "Die Vertreibung der jüdischen Studenten und Professoren von
der Berliner Universität unter dem NS-Regime," *Jahrbuch für Universitätsgeschichte* 1
(1998), 112–33; and Hartmut Lehmann and James J. Sheehan, eds., *An Interrupted Past:
German-Speaking Refugee Historians in the United States After 1933* (Cambridge, UK, 1991).

[26] Helmut Heiber, *Walter Frank und sein Reichsinstitut für Geschichte des neuen Deutschlands* (Stuttgart, 1966); and Ursula Wolf, *Litteris et Patriae. Das Janusgesicht der Historie*
(Stuttgart, 1996).

[27] Michael Burleigh, *Germany Turns Eastwards: A Study of Ostforschung in the Third Reich*
(Cambridge, UK, 1988); Karl Ditt, "Die Kulturraumforschung zwischen Wissenschaft
und Politik. Das Beispiel Franz Petri (1903–1993)," *Westfälische Forschungen* 46 (1996): 73–
176. Cf. Peter Schöttler, ed., *Geschichtsschreibung als Legitimationswissenschaft, 1918–1945*

mid-twentieth century. Its chief advantage was that it functioned largely as a self-referential discourse by excluding regional or transnational alternatives while leaving space for considerable dispute within its own borders: The national paradigm focused on a single actor, namely, the nation, whether construed as people, as state, or as dynasty; it proposed a clear telos, the creation, defense, and triumph of the nation against all challenges; it also emphasized a dramatic plot line, that is, the development of the nation-state in its internal form and external power; it measured events against an unambiguous standard, namely, their impact on the cohesion of the national community; it created identifiable enemy images against whom to rally, dividing the world into those who helped and hindered national success; and finally, it suggested a set of moralistic lessons, derived from past disasters, about how to act in the present so as to safeguard a shared future.[28] No wonder the national master narrative captured the allegiance of successive generations of German historians.

Unfortunately, this nationalist conception of history had a disastrous effect on the political development of modern Germany. Initially, liberal historians embraced the national cause since it promised to transcend partisan politics and overcome centuries of regional, religious, class, or ethnic division in a freer community. But Bismarck's successful wars of unification triggered a shift toward emphasizing the primacy of foreign policy and the necessity of military power to ensure the survival of a country without natural frontiers. Even such moderates as Otto Hintze remained skeptical of the divisiveness of parliamentary politics: "Due to our endangered middle position between the strongest powers of the continent, we have needed a different kind of constitution, namely a monarchical-military one which is chiefly the work of the Hohenzollerns."[29] With the rise of biopolitics after the turn of the century this emphasis on state, power, and authority increasingly identified Germaneness with the male gender and the Aryan race, thereby justifying the expulsion from the national community of all those who did not fit these preconceptions. Though the narrowing from liberal aspirations to racist chauvinism was more contested than is often remembered, this nationalist conception of history contributed greatly to the belligerent and annihilationist course of German politics.

(Frankfurt, 1997); and Jürgen Kocka's commentary on the papers of the 1998 Historikertag in *H-Soz-u-Kult*, October 16, 1998.

[28] Lloyd Kramer, *Nationalism: Political Cultures in Europe and America, 17756–1865* (New York, 1998). In contrast, see Christ Lorenz, "Postmoderne Herausforderungen an die Gesellschaftsgeschichte?" *Geschichte und Gesellschaft* 24 (1998): 617–32.

[29] Hintze, *Die Hohenzollern*, vi–vii. See also Richard Frankel, "Bismark's Shadow: The Iron Chacellor and the Crisis of German Leadership" (Ph.D. diss., Chapel Hill, 1999).

Repudiating the
National Narrative

The defeat of the Nazis in 1945 helped discredit the historical narrative that had supported the Third Reich. Scholars who were forced to flee Hitler's hordes were determined to "reeducate" the Germans by purging nationalism from their views of the past. In exile such luminaries as Fritz Epstein, Dietrich Gerhard, Felix Gilbert, Hajo Holborn, and Hans Rosenberg sought to create a democratic tradition, while their neglected counterparts such as Jürgen Kuczynski, Ernst Engelberg, or Walter Markov tried to establish a Marxist reading.[30] While these refugees rejected the simplifications of Allied war propaganda that constructed a straight line from Luther to Hitler, they also severely criticized the nationalist myth-making of those colleagues who had served the Third Reich. Although only a handful, for instance, the conservative Hans Rothfels and Hans-Joachim Schoeps, returned home, those who remained abroad inspired a serious study of central Europe in Anglo-American universities and thereby acted as an external conscience for German historiography. Through their support of exchange programs for young Germans, their own guest professorships, or their publications illustrating a different intellectual style, they supported innovative dissenters and helped nurture the democratization of the West German historical guild.[31]

In contrast to East German condemnations (discussed in chapter 2), West German historians were deeply divided on how to deal with the problematic national legacy after the war. Fueled by Allied reeducation efforts, the broad-ranging public debate about German responsibility for the immense suffering demanded clear answers from the professional guardians of the past.[32] The liberal octogenarian Friedrich Meinecke saw "the astonishing deviation" from the main lines of European development as an unmitigated "German catastrophe," resulting from the "intermingling of the nationalist and socialist waves" of au-

---

[30] Winfried Schulze, "Refugee Historians and German Academe, 1950–1970," in *An Interrupted Past*, 206–25; and Mario Keßler, *Exilerfahrungen in Wissenschaft und Politik. Remigierte Historiker in der frühen DDR* (Cologne, 2001).

[31] Winfried Schulze, *Deutsche Geschichtswissenschaft nach 1945* (Munich, 1989), underestimates this often intangible influence. See also Fritz Stern, "The German Past in American Perspective," *Central European History* 19 (1986): 131–63; and Konrad H. Jarausch, "German Social History—American Style," *Journal of Social History* 19 (1985): 349–60.

[32] Barbro Eberan, *Wer war an Hitler schuld? Die Debatte um die Schuldfrage 1945–1949*, 2nd. enlarg. ed. (Munich, 1985), 209 ff.

thoritarian mass politics.[33] More self-critically, the editor of the *Historische Zeitschrift*, Ludwig Dehio, who though partially Jewish survived as an archivist, called the world wars a failed bid for "European hegemony" since Germany lacked any constructive idea to inspire the support of others.[34] But Gerhard Ritter, a conservative close to the resistance and leader of the postwar profession, attempted to salvage a chastened national tradition by a "sober, thorough and unprejudiced revision of the conventional German understanding of history." His conclusions, that "Hitlerism was something fundamentally new" and that National Socialism was "a kind of romantic seizure," were comforting to patriotic academics since they made the Third Reich seem more an aberration than a logical outgrowth of earlier German development.[35]

It took the Fischer controversy in the 1960s to break the hold of the national paradigm over the historical profession in West Germany. The confrontation was triggered by a mild-mannered Hamburg scholar whose shocking encounter of boastful SS thugs in an internment camp made him abandon Protestant nationalism and consider the German past in a more critical light. For political reasons, the East Germans gave him access to a raft of sensational documents on the war-aims planning of the imperial government, which he published in 1961 in a massive volume, called *Griff nach der Weltmacht*. In its second chapter he broke with a long-standing nationalist taboo in an unprecedented admission of guilt: "Since Germany wanted, wished, and covered for the Austro-Serbian war, and, trusting in its own military superiority, consciously risked a conflict with Russia and France, the German imperial leadership bears a considerable part of the historical responsibility for the outbreak of a general war."[36] Though this statement may now seem innocuous, such traditionalists as Gerhard Ritter were outraged that Fischer was the first professional historian to concede what earlier patriots had fought so hard to reject. But younger intellectuals,

[33] Friedrich Meinecke, *The German Catastrophe: Reflections and Recollections* (Cambridge, Mass., 1950), 1–7.

[34] Ludwig Dehio, *Germany and World Politics in the Twentieth Century* (New York, 1967), 11–37.

[35] Gerhard Ritter, *Die Dämonie der Macht. Betrachtungen über Geschichte und Wesen des Machtproblems im politischen Denken der Neuzeit*, 6th rev. ed. with a new postwar preface (Munich, 1948), and *Europa und die deutsche Frage. Betrachtungen über die geschichtliche Eigenart des deutschen Staatsdenkens* (Munich, 1948), 193–206; and Christoph Cornelissen, *Gerhard Ritter* (Düsseldorf, 2001).

[36] Personal communications (1994) from Fritz Fischer and Joachim Petzold. See also Fritz Fischer, *Griff nach der Weltmacht. Die Kriegszielpolitik des kaiserlichen Deutschland 1914 / 18* (Düsseldorf, 1961), 97, as well as his *Krieg der Illusionen. Deutsche Politik von 1911 bis 1914* (Düsseldorf, 1969).

propelled by rising student unrest, welcomed the charge of structural continuity between the Second and the Third Reich as a liberating break with the national narrative.[37]

A new generation of scholars who embraced a different kind of *Gesellschaftsgeschichte* consolidated this attitudinal shift (elaborated further in chapter 4). Part of the international move toward social history, the German variant drew on the legacy of *Volkgsgeschichte*, renamed "structural history," but remained focused on questions of power, thereby creating "a social history of politics."[38] Led by charismatic figures such as Hans-Ulrich Wehler and Jürgen Kocka, this "Bielefeld school" elaborated a series of themes. First, in comparative studies, these scholars stressed the deviance of German developments from the western European pattern that constituted a *Sonderweg*, a peculiar path. Second, in terms of subject matter, they focused on social structures, organizations, and conflicts, assigning causative primacy to domestic rather than international politics. Third, through interdisciplinary reading of German classics and Anglo-Saxon theorists, they drew inspiration from the neighboring social sciences, and a few even explored the promise of quantitative methods. Fourth, in contrast to conservative objectivism, they were self-conscious partisans of the Enlightenment, striving to make history serve social reform and political democratization.[39] By an extraordinarily able strategy of fostering publications, founding new journals, and gaining appointments, this *Historische Sozialwissenschaft* succeeded in discrediting neo-historicism and transforming the outlook of the profession in the 1970s and 1980s.[40]

Though it failed to convince traditionalists, this critical view of the past was reinforced by a moralizing debate about German responsibil-

[37] Fritz Fischer, *Der Erste Weltkrieg und das deutsche Geschichtsbild. Beiträge zur Bewältigung eines historischen Tabus* (Düsseldorf, 1977). See also Konrad H. Jarausch, "World Power or Tragic Fate? The Kriegsschuldfrage as Historical Neurosis," *Central European History* 5 (1992): 72–92; John A. Moses, *The Politics of Illusion: The Fischer Controversy in German Historiography* (London, 1975).

[38] Iggers, *Social History of Politics*, 1–48. For an East German perspective, see also Gerhard Lozek and Hans Schleier, eds., *Geschichtsschreibung im 20. Jahrhundert. Neuzeit-Historiographie und Geschichtsdenken in Deutschland/BRD, Frankreich, Großbritannien, Italien, USA* (Berlin, 1990), 113 ff.

[39] For paradigmatic works, see Hans-Ulrich Wehler, *Das Deutsche Kaiserreich 1871–1918* (Göttingen, 1973); and Jürgen Kocka, *Sozialgeschichte* (Göttingen, 1977). As an introduction, see also Reinhard Rürup, ed., *Historische Sozialwissenschaft. Beiträge zur Einführung in die Forschungspraxis* (Göttingen, 1977).

[40] For examples, see Hans-Ulrich Wehler's edition of a series of readers, called *Neue Wissenschaftliche Bibliothek*, as well as bibliographies like *Bibliographie zur modernen deutschen Sozialgeschichte* (Göttingen, 1976), and such portraits of historians as *Deutsche Historiker* (Göttingen, 1971); and the multi-volume paperback series *Neue Historische Bibliothek*, with the Suhrkamp Verlag during the 1980s.

ity for the genocide of the Jews, Slavs, Gypsies, and homosexuals. Already, a minority of courageous politicians, churchmen, and writers such as Karl Jaspers had emphasized in the immediate postwar years the enormity of Nazi crimes. But in the restoration climate of the 1950s much of the public managed to evade the issue and concentrated on reintegrating Nazi accomplices, comforted by an official policy of restitution to Jewish victims and to the state of Israel.[41] Only with the Globke and Filbinger scandals, the Eichmann and Auschwitz trials, and the parliamentary debate on *Verjährung*, did the question return and produce personal contrition, which eventually changed school textbooks and media representations.[42] Buttressed by an impressive series of studies on the Nazi seizure of power and the functioning of the Third Reich that were sponsored by the Institut für Zeitgeschichte in Munich, this self-critical view became so dominant that it could not be dislodged even by repeated attempts to relativize German crimes.[43] According to Bernhard Giesen, the outcome of the *Historikerstreit* demonstrated that most intellectuals had come to define their identity through the shame of the Holocaust rather than through national pride.[44]

Only in the 1980s did the inverted paradigm of national guilt gradually begin to dissolve as a result of intellectual impulses associated with the new social movements and methodological expansions of the frontiers of social history. The rise of an everyday history that tried to capture the lives of ordinary people shifted attention to the local realm through numerous history workshops that traced the involvement of normal citizens in Nazi persecution or the war. Similarly, the turn to oral history sought to tap the memories of normal citizens across the various catastrophes and to provide an experiential perspective of life stories that often differed from textbook accounts of national affairs.[45]

[41] Jeffrey Herf, *Zweierlei Erinnerung. Die NS-Vergangenheit im geteilten Deutschland* (Berlin, 1998); and Norbert Frei, *Vergangenheitspolitik. Die Anfänge der Bundesrepublik und die NS-Vergangenheit* (Munich, 1996).

[42] Alf Lüdtke, " 'Coming to Terms with the Past': Illusions of Remembering, Ways of Forgetting Nazism in West Germany," *Journal of Modern History* 65 (1993): 542–72; Konrad H. Jarausch and Matin Sabrow, eds., *Verletztes Gedächtnis. Erinnerungskultur und Zeitgeschichte im Konflikt* (Frankfurt, 2002).

[43] Karl Dietrich Bracher, *The German Dictatorship: The Origins, Structure and Effects of National Socialism* (New York, 1970); and Martin Broszat, *The Hitler State: The Foundation and Development of the Internal Structure of the Third Reich* (London, 1981).

[44] Ernst Reinhard Piper, ed., *"Historikerstreit". Die Dokumentation der Kontroverse um die Einzigartigkeit der nationalsozialistischen Judenvernichtung* (Munich, 1987); and Bernhard Giesen, *Die Intellektuellen und die Nation. 2. Kollektive Identität* (Frankfurt, 1999).

[45] Alf Lüdtke, ed., *Alltagsgeschichte. Zur Rekonstruktion historischer Erfahrungen und Lebensweisen* (Frankfurt, 1989); and Lutz Niethammer, Alexander von Plato, and Dorothee

The gradual emergence of a women's history also shifted questions from the level of high politics to the more personal realm of gender relations within the workplace, the school, or the family.[46] Finally, an increasing awareness of the multicultural diversification of contemporary society also raised questions about the historical roots of immigration, and the role of minorities and xenophobia in earlier times.[47] The cumulative result of these shifts of interest was the erosion of the unified master narrative and its replacement with a more plural sense of German histories.

Normalization as Re-Nationalization?

The restoration of a reduced and chastened national state in 1990 suggested that the national master narrative no longer ended in 1945, followed by a post-script on division, but would receive a surprising continuation.[48] To those traditionalists who had long resented the cultural hegemony of the post-materialist Left, reunification seemed like a golden opportunity to reinstate a more positive view of German identity. For instance, the Bonn political scientist Hans-Peter Schwarz hoped that the healing of division would also mean the end of the endemic self-questioning through a gradual process of normalization: "After wandering astray for a long time, the country has finally returned to itself." While the outspoken wife of the former chancellor, Brigitte Seebacher-Brandt, railed against the "intellectual conformity" of the contrition-culture (*Betroffenheitskultur*), the literary critic Ulrich Greiner proclaimed the existence of a "post-89 generation," intent on overthrowing the intellectual dominance of its "68er" predecessor.[49] Even such respectable politicians as the CDU leader Wolfgang Schäu-

---

Wierling, *Die volkseigene Erfahrung. Eine Archäologie des Lebens in der Industrieprovinz der DDR* (Berlin, 1991).

[46] Isabel Hull, "Feminist and Gender History Through the Literary Looking Glass: German Historiography in Postmodern Times," *Central European History* 22 (1989): 279–300; and Ute Frevert, *Frauen-Geschichte zwischen bürgerlicher Verbesserung und neuer Weiblichkeit* (Frankfurt, 1986).

[47] Ulrich Herbert, *Hitler's Foreign Workers: Enforced Foreign Labor in Germany under the Third Reich* (Cambridge, 1997); and Klaus Bade, *Vom Auswanderungsland zum Einwanderungsland? Deutschland 1880–1980* (Berlin, 1983).

[48] Konrad H. Jarausch, *Die unverhoffte Einheit 1989–1990* (Frankfurt, 1995), 23 ff.

[49] Hans-Peter Schwarz, "Das Ende der Identitätsneurose," *Rheinischer Merkur*, 7 September 1990; Brigitte Seebacher-Brandt, "Strudel im Meinungsstrom. Gegen geistigen Konformismus," *Frankfurter Allgemeine Zeitung*, 18 April 1994. For other citations, see Jarausch, "Normalisierung oder Renationalisierung?" 571 f.

ble embraced the national dimension as a quasi-natural category: "The bond which holds such a community together and gives it identity is the nation."[50]

Not surprisingly, several scholars of the middle generation seized upon this shift in climate to advocate an emphatic return to the national master narrative. Unequivocally, the English historian Harold James denounced the "myths of critical history" proclaimed by the Bielefeld school and concluded: "The nation reappears as the main player on the historical stage." Equally polemically the Erlangen diplomatic specialist Gregor Schöllgen castigated *Gesellschaftsgeschichte* for its lack of attention to the issue of power and called for "stronger concentration on the urgent, central questions of today ... concerning the role of Germany in Europe and the world."[51] Similarly, Third Reich historian turned publicist Rainer Zitelmann suggested rehabilitating older self-identifications as "land of the middle" between East and West, questioning the one-sided western integration of the Federal Republic as "no longer capable of offering a reliable orientation" since it stemmed largely from "German self-hatred."[52] Finally, the neo-conservative high school teacher Karlheinz Weissmann flatly advocated a more affirmative view of the German past: "The strongest argument for the nation-state is that there is neither a practical nor a theoretical alternative" to it.[53]

Such pleas for a renationalization appealed to an obdurate segment of the public that had never quite warmed up to the self-critical history prevalent in the media and the universities. Though the proportion of opinion that held decidedly nationalist views kept shrinking with the passing of the older cohorts to less than one-tenth of the population, ugly outbreaks of xenophobic violence demonstrated that a minority of the young were also fascinated by power fantasies of the Second or Third Reich.[54] Behind such sentiments often lurked a deep resentment against foreign accusations of collective guilt and a longing for na-

---

[50] Ulrich Greiner, "Die Neunundachtziger," *Die Zeit*, 16 September 1994; Wolfgang Schäuble, *Und der Zukunft zugewandt* (Berlin, 1994). See also Heimo Schwilk und Ulrich Schacht, eds., *Die selbstbewußte Nation* (Frankfurt, 1994).

[51] Harold James, *Vom Historikerstreit zum Historikerschweigen* (Berlin, 1993); and Gregor Schöllgen, *Angst vor der Macht. Die Deutschen und ihre Außenpolitik* (Frankfurt 1993).

[52] Rainer Zitelmann, Karlheinz Weissmann, and Michael Grossheim, eds., *Westbindung. Chancen und Risiken für Deutschland* (Frankfurt, 1993); and Rainer Zitelmann, "Wiedervereinigung und deutscher Selbsthaß. Probleme mit dem eigenen Volk," in Werner Weidenfeld, ed., *Deutschland. Eine Nation—doppelte Geschichte* (Cologne, 1993), 235 ff.

[53] Karlheinz Weissmann, *Rückruf in die Geschichte. Die deutsche Herausforderung* (Frankfurt, 1992), and "Wiederkehr eines Totgesagten. Der Nationalstaat am Ende des 20. Jahrhunderts," *Aus Politik und Zeitgeschichte* (1993), no. 43: 3 ff.

[54] Hermann Kurthen, Werner Bergman, and Rainer Erb, eds., *Antisemitism and Xenophobia in Germany After Unification* (New York, 1998).

tional pride that could not be fulfilled by public rituals of contrition during the major anniversaries of Nazi crimes. Moreover, many people felt their own memories excluded from the official version of the German past, which insisted upon celebrating the "liberation" of 1945 when personal recollections suggested defeat, imprisonment, flight, hunger, and bereavement— that is, victimization.[55] Since advocates of normalization such as Jens Hacker could point to exaggerations in the self-critical postwar version,[56] some centrists, such as Hitler specialist Eberhard Jäckel, began to suggest a more upbeat reading of the German past as a success story.[57]

Alarmed by the resurfacing of nationalist currents, partisans of the Left warned of "new German dangers" to prevent a return of the old ghosts. The Bohemian-born Social Democrat Peter Glotz insisted that "the nationalization of Germany, as it occurred between 1890 and 1914, has to be avoided this time." In a searching essay, the Frankfurt social philosopher Jürgen Habermas labeled the attempt at normalization "the second founding lie of the Federal Republic." Belittling the new revisionism as "the third rehashing of ideas by a young conservative group," he suggested that instead of supporting "the dubious future of the nation state," it would be better to work toward the formation of new transnational entities.[58] Similarly, the doyen of the Bielefeld School, Hans-Ulrich Wehler, inveighed against the "new dreams of the intellectuals" of a "mystified nationalism" because the Holocaust had once and for all discredited the national master narrative. Afraid of losing their cultural hegemony, Leftist intellectuals and journalists crusaded with a touch of hysteria against the revival of national voices, ostensibly to prevent a relapse into the errors of a past that they had long thought overcome.[59]

[55] Robert Moeller, "War Stories: The Search for a Usable Past in the Federal Republic of Germany," *American Historical Review* 101 (1996): 1008–48; and Konrad H. Jarausch, "Zwischen Niederlage und Befreiung. Das Jahr 1945 und die Kontinuitäten deutscher Geschichte," *Gewerkschaftliche Monathefte* 46 (1995): 272–82.

[56] Jens Hacker, *Deutsche Irrtümer. Schönfärber und Helfershelfer der SED-Diktatur im Westen*, 2nd rev. ed. (Berlin, 1994).

[57] Eberhard Jäckel, *Das deutsche Jahrhundert. Eine historische Bilanz* (Stuttgart, 1996), 7–12, 71 ff, 108–10, 154–57, 196, 208 ff, 262, and passim. See also Hans-Ulrich Wehler, "Ein deutsches Säkulum? Eberhard Jäckels perspektivisch verengter Blick auf die letzten Hundert Jahre," *Die Zeit*, 8 November 1996.

[58] Peter Glotz, "Deutsche Gefahren," *Der Spiegel* (1997) Nr. 17, and, *Der Irrweg des Nationalstaats. Europäische Reden an ein deutsches Publikum* (Stuttgart, 1990); and Jürgen Habermas, "Wir sind wieder 'normal' geworden," *Die Zeit* 18 December 1992, and "Gelähmte Politik," *Der Spiegel* (1993) Nr. 28.

[59] Hans-Ulrich Wehler, "Gurus und Irrlichter. Die neuen Träume der Intellektuellen," *Frankfurter Allgemeine Zeitung*, 6 May 1994, and other essays in *Die Gegenwart als Geschichte* (Munich, 1995), 127 ff.

The reception of Daniel Goldhagen's indictment of German culture as matrix of "eliminationist" anti-Semitism helped reinforce critical self-perceptions. Ignoring the warning by established historians that the argument in *Hitler's Willing Executioners* was "ahistorical" or "monocausal," the public flocked to its readings and lionized the American author who insisted on something close to German collective guilt.[60] To the professional critics the many flaws of the overwritten social science theorizing that dismissed previous scholarship seemed self-evident, but intellectuals, especially of the younger generation, embraced it precisely for the comforting simplicity and rhetorical power of its central thesis of complicity. The timing of the accolades suggests that much of the book's success stemmed from its rejection of a liberal universalization of the Holocaust as consequence of modernity and its return to a "national narrative" that locates guilt with a clearly definable enemy, the German people.[61] The controversy about the Hamburg *Wehrmachtsausstellung*, which showed pictures of the army's complicity in racial murder in the East, similarly served to reassert the lesson of German guilt.[62]

Between the proponents of normalization and guardians of guilt, some moderates are attempting to establish the legitimacy of a democratic patriotism. Going beyond Dolf Sternberger's notion of "constitutional patriotism" the East German theologian and former SPD leader Richard Schröder has called for an attitude toward his "difficult fatherland" that is both critical of its past transgressions and affirmative of its democratic potential.[63] In his suggestive essays, the classical historian Christian Meier similarly mused about the Germans' reluctance to think of themselves as a nation and urged the creation of a new, western-style self-conception that includes a chastened version of the national dimension. Historian of the labor movement Heinrich August Winkler also argued that the unification of the disparate Eastern and Western states calls for a "new formation of the German nation"—not a continuation of discredited nationalism but rather a modernized

[60] Daniel J. Goldhagen, *Hitler's Willing Executioners: Ordinary Germans and the Holocaust* (New York, 1996); Julius H. Schoeps, *Ein Volk von Mördern? Die Dokumentation zur Goldhagen-Kontroverse um die Rolle der Deutschen im Holocaust* (Hamburg, 1996); and Michael Schneider, "Die 'Goldhagen-Debatte': Ein Historikerstreit in der Mediengesellschaft," *Archiv für Sozialgeschichte* 37 (1997), 67–88.

[61] A. Dirk Moses, "Structure and Agency in the Holocaust; Daniel J. Goldhagen and his Critics," *History and Theory* 37 (1998): 194–218.

[62] See the discussion between Klaus Vogel, Andreas Woell, and others on *H-Soz-u-Kult*, in February 1997.

[63] Dolf Sternberger, *Schriften*, vol. 10: *Verfassungspatriotismus* (Frankfurt, 1990), 11–38; and Richard Schröder, *Deutschland, schwierig Vaterland* (Freiburg, 1993), and "Warum sollen wir eine Nation sein?" *Die Zeit*, 2 May 1997.

sense of identity that is oriented toward Europe and anchored in Western values.[64] If successful, this attempt to provide a historical foundation for the emerging Berlin Republic may yet give the national story, albeit in a democratized and Europeanized form, another lease on life.[65]

Beyond the Master Narrative

To free themselves from the grip of the master narrative, historians need to make a conscious effort to confront their own role in its establishment and perpetuation. A first step in breaking out of this rhetorical regime could be its historicization, which would transform it from an authoritative framework into a historical problem. Instead of accepting the nation-centeredness of German historiography as self-evident, scholars ought to probe it as a product of the mid-nineteenth-century national movement that established as the professional ideal a combination of rigorous research and patriotic sentiment. A critical examination of the involvement of historians would trace the development of their agendas as they shifted from constitution to monarchy and from empire to ethnicity and race, thereby recapturing some of the protean character of the national vision. Such a perspective might also reveal the temporal limits of the ascendancy of the national paradigm as lasting about one century; the social boundaries of its support to the Protestant *Bildungsbürgertum*; and the political limitations of its appeal to the center-right, which gave it such a combative edge.[66]

Historicizing the national master narrative raises the question of whether this orientation of the German profession constituted in effect an historiographical *Sonderweg*. While some critics such as Stefan Berger emphasize such a negative exceptionalism, even a quick look at representative writings by such leading turn-of-the-century French or American historians as Ernest Lavisse or Henry Adams shows the universality of the nation as analytical category and of patriotism as reigning sentiment.[67] If positive presentations of a distinctive German path

---

[64] Christian Meier, "Die Republik denken," *Frankfurter Allgemeine Zeitung*, 29 April 1994, and *Die Nation, die keine sein will* (Munich, 1991). Cf. Heinrich August Winkler, "Nationalismus, Nationalstaat und nationale Frage in Deutschland seit 1945," *Aus Politik und Zeitgeschichte* (1991), no. 40: 12 ff.

[65] Heinrich August Winkler, *Der lange Weg nach Westen*, 2 vols. (Munich, 2000); and Peter Graf Kielmansegg, *Nach der Katastrophe. Eine Geschichte des geteilten Deutschland* (Berlin, 2000).

[66] Iggers, *German Conception of History*, passim; and Alter and Monteath, *Rewriting the German Past*, 8ff.

[67] Stefan Berger, *The Search for Normality. National Identity and Historical Consciousness in Germany since 1800* (Providence, 1997).

during the Empire were therefore part of a broader pattern, it was the ethnic and racial narrowing of narratives during the Weimar Republic and the Third Reich that set German historians apart since it radicalized the conception of the nation both internally and externally. An emerging *Volksgeschichte* sealed the break with the Enlightenment legacy by renouncing values like rationality, civil rights, and democracy, which occasionally checked bouts of Western chauvinism. More than traditional statism, such populist ethno-nationalism encouraged collaboration in the justification of Hitler's expansionism and genocide.[68]

A second strategy of cutting through the constraints of the national paradigm might be the problematizing of the nation as a cultural construct. Popular catchwords such as "imagined community" or "invention of tradition" highlight the importance of cultural innovation in creating the congeries of ideas that congealed in the ideology of "nationalism" and animated the movement in favor of the nation-state.[69] An investigation of nation building after 1871 ought to address the various nationalizing efforts that sought to transform Bavarians into Germans.[70] The Germanizing attempts in school, military service, public holidays, and so on, to foster allegiance to the new federal authority superior to the member states through a neo-medieval cult of the Hohenzollern dynasty as emperors have yet to be explored systematically.[71] Bismarck's nasty term *Reichsfeinde* suggests that Germans also defined themselves by "othering" internal as well as external enemies. Since religious, ethnic, and class divisions resisted normalizing, national circles warned incessantly against such divisive qualities as being Catholic, Jewish, or proletarian, and reinforced popular prejudices against threatening foreigners.[72]

---

[68] Contrast Haar, Oberkrome, and Schönwalder, in *Geschichtsschreibung als Legitimationswissenschaft*, 52–165, to Götz Aly, *Macht, Geist, Wahn. Kontinuitäten deutschen Denkens* (Berlin, 1997). Cf. Georg G. Iggers, "The German historians and the Burden of the Nazi Past," *Dimensions* 12 (1998): 21–28.

[69] Benedict Anderson, *Imagined Communities: Reflections on the Origin and Spread of Nationalism* (London, 1983); Eric Hobsbwam and Terence Ranger, eds., *The Invention of Tradition* (Cambridge, UK, 1983); and Geoff Eley and Roger Suny, eds., *Becoming National: A Reader* (New York, 1996), esp. 3–37.

[70] Norbert Mayr, "Particularism in Bavarian State Policy and Public Sentiment, 1806–1906" (PhD. dissertation, Chapel Hill, 1988); and Celia Applegate, *A Nation of Provincials: The German Idea of Heimat* (Berkeley, 1990).

[71] Alon Confino, *The Nation as Local Metaphor: Württemberg, Imperial Germany, and National Memory, 1871–1918* (Chapel Hill, 1997); and Siegfried Weichlein, "Nationsbildung und nach der Reichsgründung, Nationsbildung und Regionsbildung nach der Reichsgründing 1866–1890" (Habilitationsschrift, Berlin 2002) .

[72] See Jeff Peck, Mitchell G. Ash, and Christiane Lemke, "Natives, Strangers and Foreigners: Constituting Germans by Constructing Others," in Jarausch, ed., *After Unity*, for

A related problem is the ideological shift of nationalism from liberal constitutionalism to reactionary authoritarianism that associated it with the right-wing rejection of democracy in Central Europe.[73] Instead of treating Weimar's collapse as a foregone conclusion, it might be more productive to probe the various forms of nationalist opposition, from the Pan-Germans to the volkish fringe, from the neo-conservatives to the Nazis, against a republic that vainly promoted its own, more restrained brand of patriotism.[74] Moreover, it might be fruitful to take a critical look at the appropriateness of the Nazi description of the seizure of power in January 1933 as a "national revolution." Incessant propaganda about the creation of a *Volksgemeinschaft*, a national community, rhetorically covered up an unparalleled destruction of diversity by legal and physical exclusion of those people defined as "un-German," such as Leftist enemies, but also racial (anti-Semitic) and biopolitical (anti-gay, anti-handicapped) "inferiors."[75] Furthermore, the exaggeration of Hitler's international revisionism from German self-determination to military aggression, racial hegemony, and genocidal annihilation, expanded nationalist dreams beyond anything that could still vaguely be called "German,"[76] and provoked some older elites who believed in a more limited concept of the "national" into a desperate but futile resistance.[77]

After the disastrous defeat in 1945, the paradoxical existence of a nation without a state becomes the key explanatory issue. The enormity of the Nazi crimes had not only discredited chauvinism but also tarnished even more moderate versions of nationalism, therefore turning the majority of the intellectuals against the concept. At the same time, the division of the country kept some national questions alive in the campaign for "reunification" that only abated with the successful emergence of successor states and the change of generations without memory of prior unity. Instead of leading to another round of re-

---

the distinction between quasi-family, favorite foreigners, respected others, and inferior strangers.

[73] John L. Snell, *The Democratic Movement in Germany, 1789–1914* (Chapel Hill, 1976); and Jonathan Sperber, *Rhineland Radicals: The Democratic Movement in the Revolution of 1848–1849* (Princeton, 1991).

[74] Larry Eugene Jones and James Retallack, eds., *Between Reform, Reaction and Resistance: Studies in the History of German Conservatism from 1789 to 1914* (Oxford, 1993); and Joachim Petzold, *Franz von Papen. Ein deutsches Verhängnis* (Munich, 1995).

[75] Michael Kater, *Doctors under Hitler* (Chapel Hill, 1989); and Götz Aly, *Cleansing the Fatherland: Nazi Medicine and Racial Hygiene* (Baltimore, 1994).

[76] Gerhard L. Weinberg, *The Foreign Policy of Nazi Germany: Starting World War Two, 1937–1939* (Chicago, 1980).

[77] Theodore S. Hamerow, *On the Road to the Wolf's Lair: German Resistance to Hitler* (Harvard, 1997).

vanchism, the greater suffering of mass expulsion and flight, hunger, homelessness, and occupation after World War II, triggered a learning process, aided by allied reeducation efforts, that distanced most Germans from nationalist beliefs. The post-materialist shift, evident in the Western youth revolt of the 1960s and gradually also percolating into the East during the 1980s, reinforced this process of denationalization.[78] Yet some ethnic, cultural, or political sense of affinity remained, strong enough to direct the democratic awakening toward rejoining a united Germany instead of forming, like the Austrians, an independent state.[79]

A final way of escaping the traditional master narrative would be the rediscovery of vast areas of the central European past that lie below or beyond the national level. Because German statehood lasted only three-quarters of a century, and in a federal system politics revolved around local as well as regional issues, much history can and should be written without reference to the national perspective.[80] Moreover, industrialization studies have emphasized that the adoption of machine technology, the reorganization of industrial production, and the advent of mass marketing proceeded from islands of development to other, larger areas.[81] At the core of the new social histories is the "case study" method that investigates one particular village, such as Neckarshausen, or various "home towns" in depth to reconstruct the changes in a broader array of dimensions.[82] Arguing "that the German nation state is a relatively useless framework for examining German culture," intellectual historians have instead located their work in particular metropolitan spaces, such as Munich or Berlin, as exemplars of the dynamics of modernism.[83] Much of the innovative work of the last decades has simply ignored the national dimension.

---

[78] Konrad H. Jarausch, "Die Postnationale Nation. Zum Identitätswandel der Deutschen 1945–1995," *Historicum* (Spring 1995): 30–35.

[79] Gerhard Botz and Gerald Sprengnagel, eds., *Kontroversen um Österreichs Zeitgeschichte. Verdrängte Vergangenheit, Österreich-Identität, Waldheim und die Historiker* (Frankfurt, 1994); and Konrad H. Jarausch, "Nation ohne Staat. Von der Zweistaatlichkeit zur Vereinigung," *Praxis Geschichte* 13 (2000): 6–12.

[80] James J. Sheehan, "What is German History? Reflections on the Role of the *Nation* in German History and Historiography," *Journal of Modern History* 53 (1981): 1–23.

[81] Sidney Pollard, *Peaceful Conquest: The Industrialization of Europe, 1760–1970* (Oxford, 1981); and Joel Mokyr, ed., *The British Industrial Revolution: An Economic Perspective* (Boulder, 1993).

[82] David Sabean, *Property, Production and Family in Neckarshausen, 1600–1870* (Cambridge, 1990); and Mack Walker, *German Home Towns: Community, State and General Estate, 1648–1871* (Ithaca, 1971).

[83] Peter Jelavich, "Method? What Method? Confessions of a Failed Structuralist," *New German Critique* 95 (1995): 81 f.

At the same time, it might be useful to pay greater attention to the many significant developments that have transcended national borders. Have not political ideologies like Liberalism or Marxism spilled across frontiers, trading routes connected far-flung regions, cultural fashions and tastes spread from one great city to another, and even such social changes as the rise of the new middle class taken place simultaneously in different countries? While efforts to write transnational histories of Europe have rarely gotten beyond textbook-like syntheses, however well written,[84] some more systematic studies have sought to discern the outlines of a common continental society.[85] Much of the interest in comparative history has gone beyond the level of contrasting national cases to either more limited regional or local examples or to larger areas beyond nation-states.[86] Finally, the reformulation of traditional diplomatic history, which was based on the policy of nation-states, into an international history interested in cross-national relations among economies, cultures, and societies also strives to open wider interpretative horizons.[87] Greater flexibility in choosing the unit of analysis could, therefore, help diminish the dominance of national history.

What would such a more open-ended version of "German histories" look like? Since territorial shifts, constitutional changes, social conflicts, and ideological reversals in central Europe resist emplotment in a single narrative, a more plural approach of competing and intertwining stories would allow multiple voices to be heard. Perhaps the analogy of slave stories or subaltern studies might be helpful in suggesting ways of recovering dimensions that only appear as "problem areas" in the main narration, such as the Jewish issue, the women's question, or the social problem. No doubt these submerged histories are shaped to a considerable degree by the narrative of the masters, since the hegemonic groups that controlled the state, society, the economy, or culture also dominated the representation of their development. But the diverse experiences of such minorities in the partial compliance and partial resistance to the dictates of power also have an internal logic,

[84] For example, see the impressive series by Eric J. Hobsbawm, which includes *Age of Revolution, 1789–1848* (New York, 1962), *Age of Capital, 1848–1875* (New York, 1975), *Age of Empire, 1875–1914* (New York, 1987), and *Age of Extremes: The Short Twentieth Century* (London, 1994).

[85] Hartmut Kaelble, *A Social History of Western Europe, 1880–1980* (Dublin, 1989).

[86] Heinz-Gerhard Haupt and Jürgen Kocka, eds., *Geschichte und Vergleich. Ansätze und Ergebnisse international vergleichender Geschichtsschreibung* (Frankfurt, 1996).

[87] Charles S. Maier, "Marking Time: The Historiography of International Relations," in Michael Kammen, ed., *The Past Before Us: Contemporary Historical Writing in the United States* (Ithaca, 1980), 355–87.

agency, and dignity that need to be treated in their own right. Greater attention to these various counter-stories might reveal their paradoxical separateness from and interdependence with the national master narrative.[88]

A decentered account of the German past, written from the margins of national minorities, religious dissenters, feminist advocates, or labor organizers, would be quite different from the conventional state stories or nation narratives. Most importantly, it would communicate some sense of the enormous diversity of life stories and group experiences in central Europe lost in more homogenized representations. For instance, it might focus on the dogged *Eigen-Sinn* that pursued different visions in the face of normalizing pressures from the center, the partial accommodations to such demands, and the multiple forms of subversive practices.[89] Such a perspective would unmask the national project as a frantic effort to efface difference, in which aspiring elites invoked the nation to impose their own, rather limited set of North German, Protestant, authoritarian, or male values upon a reluctant population. It might also highlight the repeated efforts of Catholics, Socialists, Jews, and Ruhr Poles at inclusion in a broadened vision of the nation as well as the disastrous consequences of the figurative and literal expulsion of minorities from this community.

Any attempt at telling multiple stories that emphasize diversity, however, raises the question of the intellectual coherence of such "German histories." Would the dissolution of a unifying national master narrative into competing tales of different groups leave anything that might be particularly "German" about these accounts? Those accustomed to the linearity of the national paradigm might fear that an exclusive focus on difference might atomize the subject matter to such an extent that it would become difficult to tell any overarching story at all. But if one looked for the various intersections of different trajectories, an awareness of their complex interrelatedness might render it possible to reconcile the representation of a higher degree of diversity with a discussion of broader patterns of development. Perhaps a focus on the incessant struggles over those contested properties that contemporaries called "German" and on the negotiations between different ideologies, interests, and groups over their changing implications,

[88] For some of the difficulties, see Eckhardt Fuchs, "Remapping the German Past: Grand Narrative, Causality and Postmodernism," *Bulletin of the German Historical Institute* 22 (Spring 1998): 18–24.

[89] Alf Lüdtke, *Herrschaft als soziale Praxis. Historische und sozialanthropologische Studien* (Göttingen, 1991), and "Geschichte und Eigensinn," in Berliner Geschichtswerkstatt, ed., *Alltagskultur. Subjektivität und Geschichte* (Münster, 1994), 139–53.

might be able to do greater justice to the commonalties as well as the differences of the respective experiences associated with them.[90] The challenge for historians is, therefore, the construction of visions of the German past that more clearly represent its multiple aspirations and yet continue to recall some of its shared experiences.

[90] In contrast to Joan Scott, ed., *Feminism and History* (Oxford, 1996), it is not enough to emphasize diversity alone since one also needs to look for how particular differences interact with each other to constitute "German histories."

2

The Collapse of
the Counternarrative:
Coping with the
Remains of Socialism

The chief rival of the national paradigm was the Marxist attempt to preserve the memories of working-class struggles and to create an emancipatory history.[1] To hold out hope for the oppressed, this counternarrative had a rather Whiggish plot line, emphasizing across many setbacks the inexorable march of human progress as a kind of secular salvation story. By a determined rejection of religious, nationalist, or capitalist interpretations, socialist thinkers sought to construct an alternate view of the past that was inspired by central values of the Enlightenment, such as egalitarianism, cosmopolitanism, and by extension, feminism. Spearheaded by historically interested laymen from the labor movement, this effort to counter bourgeois conceptions on the basis of Karl Marx's dialectical materialism only gradually penetrated into the margins of academe before being entirely suppressed by Nazi

---

[1] Konrad H. Jarausch, "Die DDR-Geschichtswissenschaft als Meta-Erzählung," in Martin Sabrow, ed., *Verwaltete Vergangenheit. Geschichtskultur und Herrschaftslegitimation in der DDR* (Leipzig, 1997), 19 ff.

persecution.[2] In the antifascist resistance during exile and in the German underground, this oppositional reading of the past was sharpened into an uncompromising critique of monopoly capitalism, ready to point history into a different direction.

The victory of the Red Army offered the Marxist alternative the chance to become a master-narrative of its own, turning what remained an opposition critique in the West into a hegemonic discourse in the East.[3] To break with the racist chauvinism of the Third Reich, Communist intellectuals made rigorous efforts to repudiate the nationalist cast of bourgeois historiography and to instill an antifascist consciousness in the masses. In affirming the legitimacy of the newly founded GDR as the better Germany, the SED drew on a working-class vision, promoted by the labor movement, that hoped to end human exploitation with a social revolution, transforming East German society into socialism. This daunting task involved elaborating new interpretations, purging personnel, and replacing textbooks, as well as creating new infrastructures—in short a complete change in the content of historiography and the structure of the historical profession.[4] The result of such Stalinist restructuring was a curious hybrid of oppositional rhetoric and governmental apologetics, blending intense partisanship and professional practice, as well as working-class style and intellectual elitism.[5]

Ultimately, the socialist project of creating an alternative history failed because the Marxist narrative lost its critical thrust in the metamorphosis from radical challenge to Communist dogma. By serving a left wing dictatorship, this emancipatory effort became so discredited that the civic movement, unleashed by the democratic awakening of 1989, repudiated the SED experiment instead of merely reforming it.[6] Inevitably, the collapse of the second German state also brought Marxist scholarship down with it because attempts at self-renewal by throwing off academe's Stalinist distortions proved too little and came too

[2] Hans Schleier, *Geschichte der Geschichtswissenschaft. Grundlinien der bürgerlichen deutschen Geschichtsschreibung und Geschichtstheorien vor 1945* (Potsdam, 1983).

[3] Jeffrey Herf, *Divided Memory: The Nazi Past in the Two Germanys* (Cambridge, Mass., 1997), 13 ff.

[4] Martin Sabrow, "Geschichtskultur und Herrschaftslegitimation. Der Fall DDR," in *Verwaltete Vergangenheit*, 7 ff.

[5] Konrad H. Jarausch, Matthias Middell, and Martin Sabrow, "Störfall DDR," in Georg G. Iggers, Konrad H. Jarausch, Matthias Middell, and Martin Sabrow, eds., *Die DDR-Geschichtswissenschaft als Forschungsproblem*, *Historische Zeitschrift* special issue no. 27 (1998):1–50.

[6] Konrad H. Jarausch, *Die Unverhoffte Einheit 1989–1990* (Frankfurt, 1995); and Charles S. Maier, *Dissolution: The Crisis of Communism and the End of East Germany* (Princeton, 1997).

late.[7] When anticommunist dissidents accused GDR historians of incompetence, partisanship, or willful distortion, the intellectual credibility of the counternarrative evaporated and its institutional basis crumbled in the wake of the accession of the five new states to the FRG.[8] Nonetheless, some effects of Marxist indoctrination linger in many East German minds, displaced scholars are trying to continue the tradition outside the universities, and radical intellectuals are searching for a new basis for a critical counterhistory.

The double collapse of the GDR as state and scholarship has created an intense public and academic controversy over how to deal with the perplexing remains of socialism. On the one hand, internal dissidents and external opponents denounce East Germany as a totalitarian dictatorship, an illegitimate *Unrechtsstaat*. On the other hand, many of its former representatives and sympathetic commentators defend the SED regime as a genuine effort to break with fascist traditions. Finally, reformist intellectuals from the inside and dispassionate observers from the outside seek to paint a more nuanced picture of its many contradictions.[9] Echoing Cold War hostilities, these accusatory, apologetic, and differentiating discourses battle not only over the distribution of institutional spoils but also over fundamental political issues, such as the respective contribution of containment or *Ostpolitik* to the overthrow of the SED.[10] The stakes of this debate are high since they involve the shape of the historical memory of a united Germany: "The GDR may now be a closed chapter in strictly historical terms, but it is part of the postwar history of Germany, and the way we explain it to ourselves will have consequences for the way we judge and narrate Germany's relation to the present."[11]

Since the socialist rival has failed as disastrously as the national paradigm, any effort to renew critical perspectives must involve a rigor-

[7] For telling examples, see Rainer Eckert, Wolfgang Küttler, and Gustav Seeber, eds., *Krise—Umbruch—Neubeginn. Eine kritische und selbstkritische Dokumentation der DDR-Geschichtswissenschaft 1989/90* (Stuttgart,1992).

[8] Jürgen Kocka, *Vereinigungskrise. Zur Geschichte der Gegenwart* (Göttingen, 1995). See also KAI, ed., *Entwicklung einer Abwicklung. 3. 10. 1990 bis 31. 12. 1993* (Berlin, 1995).

[9] Mary Fulbrook, "Reckoning with the Past: Heroes, Victims, and Villains in the History of the German Democratic Republic," in Reinhard Alter and Peter Monteath, eds., *Rewriting the German Past: History and Identity in the New Germany* (Atlantic Highlands, N.J., 1997), 175–96.

[10] Timothy Garton Ash, *In Europe's Name: Germany and the Divided Continent* (New York, 1993); Konrad H. Jarausch, "Die DDR Denken. Narrative Strukturen und analytische Strategien," *Berliner Debatte. Initial* 4/5 (1995): 9–15.

[11] Marc Silberman, *What Remains? East German Culture and the Postwar Public* AICGS Research Report 5 (Washington, D.C. 1997), 2 ff.

ous examination of its disappointing development.[12] As a point of departure, such reflection might begin by tracing the emergence of alternate interpretations built upon the original Marxist formulations and later dreams of the labor movement. A brief reconsideration of the transformation of the opposition critique into a hegemonic story in the GDR could provide some clues on how its instrumentalization by state and party authorities ultimately eviscerated its emancipatory impulse. A closer look at the eclipse of the counternarrative might illustrate some of the ideological implications that the discrediting of the communist tradition after unification might have for the shaping of a post-wall German identity. Finally, a recapitulation of several key dimensions of the controversy over the East German past could yield suggestions for research strategies while clarifying its relationship to larger patterns of German histories. Perhaps such a reflection on the effect of the collapse of Communism on the counternarrative could also indicate some directions for the future of critical approaches to Central European history.[13]

Socialist Alternatives

From its inception in the *Communist Manifesto*, the Marxist dream rested on a revolutionary conception of history that sought to overthrow the liberal and national master narrative. Most clearly formulated in the 1859 preface to the *Kritik der Politischen Ökonomie*, this alternative view stressed the primacy of "forces of material production" as determinant of the "legal and political superstructure" in society: "It is not human consciousness which determines being, but on the contrary social being which determines consciousness." If during their development these "productive forces" come into contradiction with the arrangements of production and property, the economic basis transforms and "an epoch of social revolution begins," which eventually results in a new formation of society.[14] In the capitalist stage of production,

---

[12] Konrad H. Jarausch and Matthias Middell, "Die DDR als Geschichte. Verurteilung, Nostalgie oder Historisierung?" in Konrad H. Jarausch and Matthias Middell, eds., *Nach dem Erdbeben. (Re-)Konstruktionen ostdeutscher Geschichte und Geschichtswissenschaft* (Leipzig, 1993), 8–20.

[13] See the different positions in Gustavo Corni and Martin Sabrow, eds., *Die Mauern der Geschichte. Historiographie in Europa zwischen Diktatur und Demokratie* (Leipzig, 1996).

[14] Karl Marx, *The Communist Manifesto. An Annotated Edition*, ed. Frederic L. Bender (New York, 1988), and *Das Kapital. Kritik der politischen Ökonomie*, ed. Fred E. Schrader (Hildesheim, 1980). Cf. Wolfgang Kunkel, *Geschichte als Prozess? Historischer Materialismus oder Marxistische Geschichtstheorie* (Hamburg, 1987), 16 ff.

this dynamism leads to a class struggle between bourgeois owners and proletarian workers in which the latter eventually overthrow their masters and inaugurate a classless communist society. This post-Hegelian theory of history inverted liberal idealism through a dialectical materialism, but it also contained a paradoxical tension between the assertion of timeless historical laws and the appeal for individual revolutionary agency.[15]

The leftist journalist Franz Mehring made one of the first attempts at writing actual history from such a "Marxist" perspective in the last decade of the nineteenth century. Disillusioned with liberalism, this radical intellectual strove for a "critical dismemberment" of national myths, expressly attacking the Borussian school as a precondition for political change. Serialized in the theoretical journal *Neue Zeit*, his critique of the Lessing legend denounced the Prussian traditions as authoritarian compromises between crown and nobility, while interpreting the legacy of the classics as emancipatory humanism.[16] Even better known was his sweeping history of the German labor movement during the nineteenth century, which combined an analysis of the ideas of its leaders with attention to the role of the masses. Though criticized for Lasallean leanings, this monumental reconstruction of the evolution of working-class consciousness has become accepted as a seminal example of a nondogmatic Marxist history.[17] In editing socialist records, Mehring followed the standards of the historical discipline but broke with the bourgeois consensus by basing his counter-interpretation firmly on the outlook of "scientific communism."

In the more open climate of the Weimar Republic, the breadth and vitality of alternative historical voices strengthened noticeably. A talented group of democrats and socialists, for instance, Erich Eyck, George W. Hallgarten, Hedwig Hintze, Eckart Kehr, and Alfred Vagts, enunciated a clear critique of the national master narrative, attacking Bismarck's authoritarianism and William II's imperialism. Although they were willing to explore the usefulness of socioeconomic approaches, some of these younger scholars even succeeded in gaining academic positions.[18] Less influential, in contrast, were such orthodox communists as Jürgen Kuczynski and Albert Schreiber, who hailed the

---

[15] Wolfgang Küttler, ed., *Das geschichtswissenschaftliche Erbe von Karl Marx* (Vaduz, 1983), 1–54.

[16] Franz Mehring, *Die Lessing Legende* (Berlin, 1983). See also Glen R. McDougall, "Franz Mehring: Politics and History in the Making of Radical German Social Democracy, 1869–1903" (Ph.D. dissertation, New York, 1977).

[17] Franz Mehring, *Geschichte der deutschen Sozialdemokratie*, vol. I (Berlin, 1976), 3 ff, and *Aufsätze zur Geschichte der deutschen Arbeiterbewegung* (Berlin, 1980), 7 ff.

[18] Schleier, *Geschichte der Geschichtswissenschaft*, 156 ff.

Bolshevik Revolution as an epochal event and looked to international antecedents such as the Paris Commune or to indigenous legacies such as the Peasants' War for inspiration. While they remained virtually excluded from universities, these radicals created a collective memory for the KPD in popular articles or books and developed a historical justification for the necessity of a revolutionary seizure of power by the oppressed.[19]

The Nazis muffled any dissenting voices by intimidation, expulsion, and incarceration, but their disastrous policies ultimately proved the critics right. During the initial purges, about one dozen democratic historians, such as Martin Hobohm and Veit Valentin, were dismissed for political reasons and about twice that many, including Felix Gilbert or Hans Rosenberg, were expelled on racial grounds.[20] For many liberals, such as Hajo Holborn, Western emigration offered a chance to develop their own doubts into a sustained critique of the national narrative. But for such present or former Communists as Arthur Rosenberg, expatriation rendered the continuation of scholarship difficult, unless they could, as did Rudolf Lindau, Leo Stern, and Hanna Wolf, experience the exhilaration of Bolshevik rethinking firsthand in the Soviet Union. According to popular front policy, exiles in Britain, such as Jürgen Kuczynski and Alfred Meusel, advocated a democratic rebuilding of Germany, while émigrés in the United States, such as Albert Norden and Albert Schreiner, agitated with speeches and pamphlets for the Council for a Democratic Germany.[21] Although only a few scholars who remained behind were active in the resistance, critical historians continued the development of counternarratives during the Third Reich's darkest hours, albeit outside of Germany.

Already during the unquestioned ascendancy of the national master narrative, a multi-vocal rejection of its historicist methodology, preoccupation with politics, and nationalist orientation began to emerge. The most dangerous challenge came not from South German Catholic scholars or from foreign critics but from bourgeois liberals and Marxist radicals close to the growing labor movement whose priority was not the national issue but the social question. While they were divided into

---

[19] Klaus Kinner, *Marxistische deutsche Geschichtswissenschaft 1917 bis 1933. Geschichte und Politik im Kampf der KPD* (Berlin, 1982).

[20] Gerhard Lozek and Hans Schleier, eds., *Geschichtsschreibung im 20. Jahrhundert: Neuzeithistoriographie und Geschichtsdenken in Deutschland/BRD, Frankreich, Großbritannien, Italien, USA* (Berlin, 1990), 67 ff. Cf. Konrad H. Jarausch, "Die Vertreibung der jüdischen Studenten und Professoren von der Berliner Universität unter dem NS-Regime," *Jahrbuch für Universitätsgeschichte* 1 (1998), 112–33.

[21] Mario Keßler, *Exilerfahrung in Wissenschaft und Politik. Remigierte Historiker in der frühen DDR* (Cologne, 2001).

democrats, social democrats, and communists, the advocates of the counternarrative tried to write an emancipatory history interested in expanding human freedom and in alleviating suffering that shifted attention from leading statesmen to ordinary people. Though the nationalists succeeded in keeping most dissenting voices out of the guild, they could not prevent the formulation of alternative views of the past that stressed the importance of material conditions, celebrated advances of the labor movement, and demanded greater equality. When the Third Reich went down in flames, such Marxist intellectuals as Alexander Abusch and Paul Merker were ready to offer historical explanations for the disaster.[22]

Communist Hegemony

Turning an outsider's critique into a hegemonic narrative in the GDR was a daunting challenge for the small band of Marxist historians who had survived emigration and incarceration. On the one hand, breaking the dominance of "the reactionary bourgeois ideology of history" demanded the systematic discrediting of nationalist traditions, the replacement of scholarly personnel, and the establishment of new academic institutions. On the other hand, making "Marxism-Leninism the dominant theoretical foundation of historical scholarship" also required changing the philosophical outlook of historians to accept the "necessary succession of societal formations," emphasizing "the historical role of popular masses," paying more attention to "progressive and revolutionary traditions," and stressing the "class struggle as actual force of all historical changes."[23] Helped by the backing of Soviet scholars and the scientific aura of Marxism, fashioning a socialist interpretation implied the literal creation of a new historical narrative, an independent academic style, and a different conception of scholarship. Unfortunately, this attempt at a new departure was from the beginning blemished by the repressive aspects of Stalinism that forced moderate democratic or unorthodox socialist readings into the West.

As self-justification East German historiographers developed a detailed critique of bourgeois scholarship that rejected the philosophical

---

[22] Alexander Abusch, *Der Irrweg einer Nation. Ein Beitrag zum Verständnis deutscher Geschichte* (Berlin, 1949³); and Paul Merker, *Deutschland—Sein oder Nichtsein?*, 2 vols. (Mexico City, 1944).

[23] Walter Schmidt, "Zur Konstituierung der DDR-Geschichtswissenschaft in den fünfziger Jahren," in *Sitzungsberichte der Akademie der Wissenschaften der DDR* (Berlin 1984), 8 Gesellschaftswissenschaften: 6 ff. Cf. Ralph Jessen, *Akademische Elite und Kommunistische Diktatur. Die ostdeutsche Hochschullehrerschaft in der Ulbricht-Ära* (Göttingen, 1999).

assumptions, research priorities, and political consequences of the national master narrative. On the methodological level they objected to its "idealist historicism" that was preoccupied with the particular, neglected socioeconomic factors, lacked a concept of development, focused on "ideographic-individualized methods," and gave one-sided "primacy to political and intellectual history." In terms of content, GDR historians rejected any identification of "the nation [as] the typical form of historical life," opposed "the thesis that great men make history," and distanced themselves from "the incredible deification of the state" as well as the focus on foreign policy. Although they recognized that bourgeois views were not homogeneous, Marxist-Leninist historians deplored the profession's political subservience to the Prusso-German state, its support of *Weltpolitik*, and its adherence to the Nazi cause.[24] As a result, the East Germans considered the restoration of bourgeois historiography in the FRG a revival of the national master narrative that had to be fought with antifascist dedication, lest it lead again into catastrophe.

Since ideas require material support, the establishment of socialist historical scholarship in the GDR also had "a not-to-be-neglected institutional and organizational side." The strategic placement of committed activists, such as Walter Markov in Leipzig, or Alfred Meusel and Jürgen Kuczynski in Berlin, increased Marxist influence in the universities. Even more important was the creation of entirely new Marxist institutions, such as the party institutes for Marxism-Leninism (1949), or the institute for social sciences (1951), as well as the Museum for German History (1951), institutes for the history of the German people at the universities (1951), and the institute for history at the new Academy of Sciences (1956). East German scholars also established a spate of journals such as the *Zeitschrift für Geschichtswissenschaft*, reoriented publishing houses such as the Akademieverlag, and edited new textbooks for students. When they were unable to control professional associations, for instance, the Verband deutscher Historiker, GDR historians reluctantly founded their own alternatives such as the Historikergesellschaft der DDR (1958).[25] Within a decade, communist scholars succeeded in creating an entirely new infrastructure for the historical profession, free of the nationalist ballast of the past.

At the same time, East German historians had to develop authoritative texts to disseminate the counternarrative in the schools and uni-

[24] Schleier, *Geschichte der Geschichtswissenschaft*, 69 ff, 129 ff, and 181 ff. See also Wolfgang Herbst and Kurt Wernicke, *Museum für deutsche Geschichte* (Berlin, 1987).

[25] Schmidt, "Zur Konstituierung," 10 ff; Ilko-Sascha Kowalczuk, *Legitimation eines neuen Staates. Parteiarbeiter an der historischen Front. Geschichtswissenschaft in der SBZ/DDR*

versities and impart a Marxist conception of the past to the younger generation. In early 1951 the SED central committee therefore ordered the creation of "a comprehensive account of the history of the German people, written on the methodological basis of historical materialism and meeting scholarly standards." This collective effort to reach a consensus on a series of university textbooks struggled with shifting deadlines, personal disputes, and political dogmatism, but eventually produced enough volumes to guide teaching. The eight volume history of the labor movement, published in the mid-1960s, rested on firmer foundations,[26] and the multi-authored works of the 1970s on the history of the World Wars drew on solid research in sources that remained inaccessible in the West.[27] Finally, those volumes of a comprehensive German history that appeared toward the end of the GDR were sophisticated expositions that forced even skeptical observers to concede a growing professionalism of historiography in the East.[28]

The Marxist conception strove to present a different yet coherent picture of the past, focused not on the nation-state but on the class struggle. Instead of recounting the triumphs of the elite, it centered on other actors, namely, the long-suffering masses toiling in the factories and the farms. At the same time, it offered a separate periodization of historical development, which was governed by the evolution of the productive forces of society rather than by the succession of forms of political rule. It also followed a distinctive plot line of the trials of the progressive forces, which culminated in the formation of the labor movement and its political parties, largely ignoring affairs of state. Therefore, it attacked different enemies, namely, the feudal oppressors, bourgeois exploiters, and social-democratic rivals, rather than denouncing other countries as external threats. And finally, it taught other moral lessons of dedication to revolutionary goals and interna-

---

1945 bis 1961 (Berlin, 1997); and John Connelly, *Captive University: The Sovietization of East German, Czech, and Polish Higher Education* (Chapel Hill, 2000).

[26] See the many volumes of the *Hochschullehrbuch deutsche Geschichte* (Berlin, 1961 ff.); Institut für Marxismus-Leninismus, ed., *Geschichte der deutschen Arbeiterbewegung*, 8 vols. (Berlin 1966). Cf. Martin Sabrow, "Bauformen der nationalen Gegenerzählung in der DDR. Vom 'Lehrbuch der deutschen Geschichte' zur 'Deutschen Geschichte'," in *Die historische Meistererzählung in Deutschland*.

[27] Fritz Klein, ed., *Deutschland im Ersten Weltkrieg*, 2 vols. (Berlin, 1968); Wolfgang Schumann, ed., *Deutschland im Zweiten Weltkrieg* (Cologne, 1974); and Rolf Badstübner, ed., *Deutsche Geschichte*, vol. 9: *Die antifaschistisch-demokratische Umwälzung. Der Kampf gegen die Spaltung Deutschlands und die Entstehung der DDR von 1945 bis 1949* (Berlin, 1989).

[28] For example, Andreas Dorpalen, *German History in Marxist Perspective: The East German Approach* (Detroit, 1985); and Alexander Fischer and Günter Heydemann, eds., *Geschichtswissenschaft in der DDR*, 2 vols. (Berlin, 1988–1990).

tional class solidarity.[29] But in a divided country the impulse of thinking in terms of world revolution could not supplant the focus on national history, which was needed to contest control of the German past
with the West.[30]

As hegemonic discourse, the East German narrative also established
a separate, scholarly ideal that emphasized a notion of "partisan truth"
and effaced the difference between fact and fiction so as to fuse professionalism with partisanship on the basis of Marxist-Leninist theory.
According to the presentist maxim of "correct interpretation," the actual task of the researcher was "the recognition of the linkage between
the hierarchy of already known social laws and concrete historical
facts."[31] The GDR version of the past claimed total validity since its
historians thought of themselves as perpetually struggling with an
"objective opponent," namely those bourgeois nationalists who supported the allegedly revanchist policies of the FRG.[32] While more internal discussion about the implementation of party directives occurred
than remains evident in print, the shared assumptions about scholarship induced Marxist historians to support the regime and discipline
themselves without constant party intervention. GDR historiography,
therefore, represented a curious hybrid of normal scholarship and political engagement for the unpopular rule of the SED.

As a result, the products of East German scholarship had a style of
their own that made them immediately recognizable as a different
brand of historical writing. This distinctiveness had less to do with the
poor paper of the books and journals that were printed in the East or
with the tendency toward collective authorship in major works that
effaced individual contributions. Instead, it was their language—full
of Soviet imports, Marxist-Leninist phrases, SED-slogans, and East
German regionalisms—that seemed odd. Many of the concepts also
appeared unusual, referring to terms such as "monopoly-capitalism,"
which indicated a separate interpretative framework; at the same time,

---

[29] Heike Christa Mätzing, *Geschichte im Zeichen des historischen Materialismus. Untersuchungen zu Geschichtswissenschaft und Geschichtsunterricht in der DDR* (Hanover, 1999)

[30] Matthias Middell, "Jenseits unserer Genzen? Zur Trennung von deutscher und all-
gemeiner Geschichte in der Geschichtswissenschaft und Geschichtskultur der DDR," in
Konrad H. Jarausch and Matthias Middell, eds., *Nach dem Erdbeben. (Re-)Konstruktion ostdeutscher Geschichte und Geschichtswissenschaft* (Leipzig, 1994), 88–120.

[31] Martin Sabrow, *Das Diktat des Konsens. Geschichtswissenschaft in der DDR 1949–1969*
(Munich, 2001). Cf. Walther Eckermann and Hubert Mohr, eds., *Einführung in das Stu-
dium der Geschichte*, 3rd ed. (Berlin, 1979), 19–46, 215 ff.

[32] Martin Sabrow, "Der 'ehrliche Meinungsstreit' und die Grenzen der Kritik. Me-
chanismen der Diskurskontrolle in der Geschichtswissenschaft der DDR," in *Die Mauern
der Geschichte*, 79–117, and "Die Geschichtswissemschaft der DDR und ihr 'objektiver
Gegner'," in *DDR-Geschichtwissenschaft*, 53–92.

the topics, taken from labor history, comparative revolutions, or the communist world system, were unprecedented; finally, such interpretations as the explanation of the Reformation as "prebourgeois revolution" or of the Third Reich as "fascism" were quite different.[33] Buttressed by historical museums, public monuments, and anniversary celebrations, and promoted in film, radio, and literature, the Marxist counternarrative produced a distinctive socialist memory culture that stressed its separation from and superiority to its bourgeois rivals in the West.[34]

Despite its dominance, the counternarrative never quite succeeded in overcoming several basic deficits that ultimately proved fatal to its credibility. Chief among them was the question of national division, which could not simply be sidestepped by privileging "class" over nation in historical explanation. Hoping for a "national revolution," the GDR initially clung to a national rhetoric but eventually redefined itself as a "socialist nation," based on Marxist-Leninist ideology, to demarcate itself from the pervasive reunification rhetoric of the FRG. As legitimation for Honecker's course of *Abgrenzung*, such scholars as Walter Schmidt argued that the successor states in the East and the West were growing ever farther apart: "A national consciousness based on GDR socialism and a new historical identity are emerging."[35] During the 1980s the SED realized that such class arguments remained unconvincing and, therefore, allowed broader references to the "legacy and traditions" of German history, even invoking previously spurned figures like Luther, Frederic the Great, and Bismarck.[36] However clever, Honecker's resigned formula "nationality—German, state—GDR" ultimately failed to resolve the basic dilemma of social versus national identity for East German citizens.

Because of its negative fixation on overcoming the national paradigm, the Marxist-Leninist alternative history turned out to be less in-

[33] Konrad H. Jarausch, "Historische Texte der DDR aus der Perspektive des 'linguistic turn'," in *DDR-Geschichtswissenschaft*, 261–79.

[34] Essays by Simone Barck, Thomas Heimann, and Christoph Classen in Martin Sabrow, ed., *Geschichte als Herrschaftsdiskurs. Der Umgang mit der Vergangenheit in der DDR* (Cologne, 2000), 57–173; and the forthcoming dissertation on East German memory culture by Jon Berndt Olsen.

[35] Walter Schmidt, "Zum Begriff der 'deutschen Geschichte' in der Gegenwart," *Zeitschrift für Geschichtswissenschaft* 37 (1989): 5–19; and Klaus Erdmann, *Der gescheiterte Nationalstaat. Die Interdependenz von Nations- und Geschichtsverständnis im politischen Bedingungsgefüge der DDR* (Frankfurt, 1996).

[36] Helmut Meier and Walter Schmidt, eds., *Erbe und Tradition in der DDR. Die Diskussion der Historiker* (Berlin, 1988); and Herrman Brinks, *Die DDR-Geschichtswissenschaft auf dem Weg zur deutschen Einheit. Luther, Friedrich II und Bismarck als Paradigmen politischen Wandels* (Frankfurt, 1992).

novative than expected. Since Eastern historians spent much time in refuting Western interpretations through reviews and arguments, they continued to define themselves in contrast to bourgeois scholarship rather than exploring some of the new avenues suggested by their own ideology.[37] Though the shift away from high politics to the struggles of the working class was an important step in broadening the reach of historical interpretation, the leading East German texts remained preoccupied with political development and ideological disputes. Because of such conventional methods, social history and quantitative techniques arrived even later in the GDR than in the FRG and had to struggle longer for formal acceptance.[38] While a few daring scholars experimented with everyday history, virtually no-one took the linguistic turn or moved toward cultural history before 1989. As a result of such defensiveness, the intellectual provocation contained in the Marxist vision remained surprisingly limited in the actual works produced by East German historians.

Finally, the transformation into a hegemonic discourse that legitimized SED repression robbed the opposition narrative of much of its critical energy. The ethical appeal of the socialist alternative rested on its resolute rejection of war, exploitation, and genocide that was contained in the national paradigm. But by using antifascist rhetoric to explain away the injustices of expropriation, collectivization, persecution, and expulsion of another dictatorial regime, the counternarrative lost its moral force and engendered popular cynicism.[39] When East Germans compared their own memories of shelling, rape, flight, and plunder with official celebrations of "liberation" by the Red Army in 1945, the new version of the past appeared to hide as many aspects as it explained. Independent spirits encountered numerous taboos, called "blank spots," such as the secret protocol to the Nazi-Soviet Pact. Even if historians managed to bypass the new orthodoxy with such strategies as creative reinterpretation, withdrawal into empiricism, avoidance of conflict, and differentiation of cliches, they never dared chal-

[37] Gerhard Lozek, ed., *Zeitalter im Widerstreit. Grundprobleme der historischen Epoche seit 1917 in der Auseinandersetzung mit der bürgerlichen Geschichtsschreibung* (Berlin, 1982).

[38] Helga Schulz, "Ansätze zur Geschichte des sozialen Wandels in der DDR," in Konrad H. Jarausch, ed., *Zwischen Parteilichkeit und Professionalität. Bilanz der Geschichtswissenschaft der DDR* (Berlin, 1991), 77–90; and Georg Iggers, ed., *Ein anderer historischer Blick. Beispiele ostdeutscher Sozialgeschichte* (Frankfurt, 1991).

[39] Martin Sabrow, "Der staatssozialistische Geschichtsdiskurs im Spiegel seiner Gutachtenpraxis," in *Verwaltete Vergangenheit*, 35–65; and Konrad H. Jarausch, "The Failure of East German Anti-Fascism: Ironies of History as Politics," *German Studies Review* 14 (1991): 85–102.

lenge the dominance of the SED.[40] By creating a credibility gap between popular recollections and official histories that even tarnished the small band of Marxists in the West, such distortions helped erode the socialist alternative from within.

The Eclipse of
the Counternarrative

With the collapse of the GDR the Marxist narrative, which had prided itself upon explaining the laws of development, became an unexpected casualty of that very history. Confronted with a popular rising in the fall of 1989, most East German historians reacted with shock and disbelief, unable to understand their charges' emancipation from their own teachings. It took until November for the Leipzig social historian Hartmut Zwahr to confess that "the majority of historians has collaborated with the party administrative system of our country and its people's self-destruction, taken on the tasks set before it, and played its role. This truth is rather bitter." In early December Jürgen John, Wolfgang Küttler, and Walter Schmidt of the East German Academy of Sciences deplored "the reticence of professional historiography" and called for open engagement in the construction of "a democratic socialism." Some scholars who had been disciplined by the party also denounced the "double drug of Stalinism" as responsible for the self-censorship."[41] Since only a minority of liberal Communists was willing to examine its own complicity, all efforts to save the counternarrative by reforming the discipline from within were doomed because they were too belated and timid.

Impatient with the silence of leading scholars, Eastern dissenters and Western critics attacked "the failure of the historians." In January 1990 some younger and independent historians leveled a massive charge: "In the humanities the situation is deplorable. For decades an unpalatable stew of lies and half-truths smothered any free intellectual impulse. Ridiculous scholasticism and staid clichés were handed out as

[40] Hermann Weber, " 'Weiße Flecken' und die DDR-Geschichtswissenschaft," in *Zwischen Parteilichkeit und Professionalität*, 139–53. See Ralf Possekel, "Kuriositätenkabinett oder Wissenschaftsgeschichte? Zur Historisierung der DDR-Geschichtswissenschaft," *Geschichte und Gesellschaft* 24 (1998): 446–62.

[41] Hartmut Zwahr, "Zu einer beginnenden Diskussion. Administratives System und Gesellschaft, administratives System und Schule, Geschichtsschreibung usw"; Jürgen John, Wolfgang Küttler, and Walter Schmidt, "Für eine Erneuerung des Geschichtsverständnisses in de der DDR"; Wolfgang Ruge, "Die Doppeldroge. Zu den Wurzeln des Stalinismus," and other texts reprinted in *Krise—Umlruch—Neubeginn*.

'sole scientific Weltanschauung.' "[42] Conservative FRG commentators, who had long denounced Marxist historiography as pseudoscholarship, were delighted to join in this indictment, and even liberal observers were appalled by the extent of "crude partisanship, loss of reality, and neglect of sources" that indicated the need for a "radical cure."[43] This rising chorus of criticism stressed "the moral and political degeneration" of Eastern historical writing, and emphasized the responsibility of leading individuals for collaboration with the secret police. Based on a Neo-Rankean understanding of scholarly objectivity, these attacks sought to discredit the Marxist alternative by a thorough exposure of its many forms of academic duplicity.[44]

Disturbed by such assaults on their lifework, some established East German historians fought back to preserve the Marxist counternarrative in a united Germany. Claiming that "there was not only opportunism and stagnation," Kurt Pätzold emphasized "the considerable progress" of Marxist scholarship rather than dwelling on its "serious deficits."[45] This defensive perspective sought to differentiate between particularly deformed areas close to politics and other subjects less influenced by ideology. Apologists stressed the existence of lively internal debates that did not usually make their way into print, and pointed to an evident process of professionalization in published works, which had moved toward closer observance of universal standards that brought growing international recognition during the 1980s. They also argued that the influence of the SED on the writing of history was not always negative because the party had initially inspired new topics for investigation that proved fruitful. Finally, the defenders of East German scholarship warned against repeating the Nazi purge of Marxist historiography from the universities.[46]

---

[42] Armin Mitter and Stefan Wolle, "Aufruf zur Bildung einer Arbeitsgruppe unabhängiger Historiker in der DDR," in the extensive documentation compiled by Rainer Eckert, Ilko-Sascha Kowalczuk and Isolde Stark, eds., *Hure oder Muse? Klio in der DDR. Dokumente und Materialien des Unabhängigen Historiker-Verbandes* (Berlin, 1994), 22 ff.

[43] Winfried Schulze, "Das traurigste Los aber traf die Geschichtswissenschaft. Die DDR-Geschichtswissenschaft nach der 'deutschen Revolution';" and Christian Meier, "Im Zweifel lieber abwickeln," in *Krise—Umbruch—Neubeginn*, 213 ff., 258 ff.

[44] Konrad H. Jarausch, Matthias Middell, and Martin Sabrow, "Störfall DDR-Geschichtswissenschaft," *DDR-Geschichtswissenschaft*, 1–50.

[45] Kurt Pätzold, "Sich totstellen oder wehren?—das ist die entscheidende Frage," *Neues Deutschland*, 30 December 1990; and "Die Geschichtsschreibung in der Deutschen Demokratischen Republik," in *Mauern der Geschichte*, 187 ff.

[46] Walter Schmidt, "Geschichte zwischen Professionalität und Politik. Zu zentralen Leitungsstrukturen und -mechanismen in der DDR," in *Zeitschrift für Geschichtswissenschaft* 40 (1992): 1013 ff; and Wolfgang Küttler, "Geschichtstheorie und -methodologie in der DDR," *Zeitschrift für Geschichtswissenschaft* 42 (1994): 8–20.

Despite these arguments, most senior historians were fired after unification because of their earlier involvement in legitimizing the SED regime. In contrast to the wholesale dismissal of instructors in Marxism-Leninism, socialist economics, and law, only historical specialists in such overt ideological subjects as the evolution of the communist world system, were removed. The evaluation committees, comprising Western colleagues and Eastern dissidents, discovered a mixture of considerable competence coupled with appalling collaboration, though only a few individuals were outed as Stasi informants. The restructuring of curricula along Western lines eliminated some favorite GDR fields and promoted neglected areas, while the lack of financial resources compelled the dismissal of much mid-level teaching staff, now considered superfluous. In the rehiring process, West German competitors held better cards since they not only knew the members of the search committees but could also demonstrate the appropriate publishing credentials, methodological sophistication, and political affiliations. Consequently, only a handful of Easterners, for example Hartmut Zwahr, Jürgen John, and Helga Schulz, managed to survive, and most senior positions went to Westerners.[47]

The institutional restructuring of the historical discipline was, if anything, even more drastic. Since the East German Academy of Sciences was far too large to fit into the research structure of the FRG, the unification treaty stipulated that it be closed and only those parts that were evaluated positively would continue to exist. This decision spelled the end for the institutes concerned with German history, general history, and economic history, which had employed some three hundred scholars. While most older historians were sent into pre-retirement, those younger members judged to be doing promising work were reassigned to teaching in the universities, a plan that tended to founder on fiscal constraints. Another dozen historians were placed into a new research center on contemporary history (ZZF) located in Potsdam, where they worked together with an equal number of Western colleagues in a controversial intellectual laboratory. Other postunification institutions—the Hannah Arendt Institute in Dresden or the research branch of the Stasi archives in Berlin—also integrated some Eastern colleagues but hardly compensated for the closing of GDR structures.[48]

[47] Peer Pasternack, *Geisteswissenchaften in Ostdeutschland. Eine Inventur* (Leipzig, 1996), 242–87; and Konrad H. Jarausch, "Déstruction créatrice. Transformer le système universitaire est-allemend: le cas de l'histoire," *Sociétés contemporaines* no. 39 (2000): 39–60.

[48] Christoph Kleßmann and Martin Sabrow, "Zeitgeschichte in Deutschland nach 1945," *Aus Politik und Zeitgeschichte* (1996) Nr. 36: 3–14; and Konrad H. Jarausch, "The GDR as History in United Germany: Reflections on Public Debate and Academic Controversy," *German Politics and Society* 15 (1997): 33 ff.

The exchange of personnel and the collapse of infrastructure have virtually crushed the Marxist counternarrative in East Germany. Even the remaining channels of communication, such as the prominent journal *Zeitschrift für Geschichtswissenschaft*, have altered direction through changing editorship. Explicit advocates of dialectical materialism have, in effect, been displaced outside of academe, where some continue their work, albeit without much financial support or institutional help. Only the postcommunist PDS has sponsored a historical commission of its own, has organized various discussion groups, and offers publication outlets, used especially by the older cohort of retired but still active scholars who are trying to reflect on the reasons for the defeat of their glorious experiment.[49] In contrast, independent Marxists have founded a few new organs of debate such as *Berliner Debatte. Initial* or the historical journal *Comparativ* to discuss the intellectual implications of the collapse of East Germany for emancipatory views.[50] The painful soul-searching about the causes and implications of the defeat of the workers' and peasants' state has, therefore, barely begun.

The debacle of communism has ironically turned the once promising socialist alternative to the national paradigm into an arcane subject for historiographical analysis. Shocked by the complicity of historians in a leftist dictatorship, critics initially seized upon distressing evidence of collaboration and denounced flagrant examples of the violation of professional standards so as to distance the discipline from obvious transgressions. But the end of institutional restructuring in the East, the availability of more internal documentary evidence on the system, and the spread of poststructuralist methodologies are gradually moderating the tone and encouraging a more dispassionate analysis. Instead of getting clearer, the picture of the internal workings of the discipline in the GDR is becoming more complex and elusive because emancipatory aspirations and repressive practices seem to have been inextricably intertwined. So as to transcend moralizing condemnation, the subject calls for differentiating approaches that are attuned to nuances and ambivalences, and are willing to explore apparent contradictions.[51] The first step toward rehabilitating alternative histories would, therefore, be a thorough self-criticism of the deformation of the discipline in East Germany.

---

[49] See for example the texts in Rainer Eckert and Bernd Faulenbach, eds., *Halbherziger Revisionismus. Zum postkommunistischen Geschichtsbild* (Munich 1996).

[50] See the special issue on "Die DDR denken" of *Berliner Debatte. Initial*, 4–5 (1995); the section on "Wissenschaft in der DDR" in *Utopie kreativ*, 11–12 (1996); and the journal *Comparativ*, appearing in Leipzig since 1991.

[51] Karl Heinrich Pohl, ed., *Historiker in der DDR* (Göttingen, 1997); and Joachim Petzold, *Parteinahme wofür? DDR- Historiker im Spannungsfeld von Politik und Wissenschaft*, ed. Martin Sabrow (Cologne, 2000).

The GDR as History

The counternarrative was also discredited by its close association with a repressive state that became the subject of an intense public and academic controversy. Having experienced two dictatorships in the twentieth century, Germany confronts a "double burden" of the past, with the memory of coping with the first legacy influencing reactions to the second. In some ways, the situation after 1990 was reminiscent of that of 1945 since once again victims were clamoring for help, perpetrators needed to be punished, and the public to be enlightened about the crimes of the toppled regime.[52] But in other respects, conditions were rather different because the SED did not perpetrate a Holocaust and was overthrown from within rather than from without; therefore, there was no foreign occupation but rather a joining to a more successful state; moreover, this upheaval affected only one-third of the country rather than the whole nation, leaving the majority free to help reconstruct the rest. Finally, the ideological fronts were reversed, with the Left now on the defensive because its antifascism was being challenged by antitotalitarianism as the founding consensus of the united Germany.[53]

The public discussion has focused on Stasi-collaboration, with the media creating a lurid image of an oppressive state that was controlled by the secret police. The archiving of many documents, compiled by Mielke's zealous minions, in a new federal office for Stasi materials has provided an endless supply of shocking disclosures about collaboration, denunciation, and observation.[54] Controversy also involved the courts, which were confronted with thousands of accusations of injustices wrought by the SED regime. While well-documented shootings of people trying to flee across the Berlin Wall could be punished, other acts of despotism and chicanery proved difficult to prosecute since many had been "legal" by GDR standards, and prominent defendants

---

[52] Christoph Kleßmann, "Das Problem der doppelten 'Vergangenheitsbewältigung'," *Die Neue Gesellschaft*, 38 (1991): 1099–105; and Eberhard Jäckel, "Die doppelte Vergangenheit," *Spiegel* (1991) no. 52: 39 ff.

[53] Horst Möller, "Sind nationalsozialistische und kommunistische Diktaturen vergleichbar?" and Jürgen Kocka, "Nationalsozialismus und SED-Diktatur in vergleichender Perspektive," in *Potsdamer Bulletin für Zeithistorische Studien*, vol. 2 (Potsdam, 1994), 9–27.

[54] Joachim Gauck, *Die Stasi-Akten. Das Unheimliche Erbe der DDR* (Hamburg, 1991), and "Dealing with a Stasi Past," *Daedalus*, special issue 123 on "Germany in Transition" (1994): 277–84. Cf. Timothy Garton Ash, *Die Akte 'Romeo': Persönliche Geschichte* (Zurich, 1997).

invoked the procedural safeguards of a democratic *Rechtsstaat*.[55] More-over, the Bundestag "commission of inquiry" into "the history and the consequences of the dictatorship of the SED in Germany" produced much enlightening eyewitness testimony and 150 expert briefs on the inner workings of the GDR. But its final report, rushed to completion during the election campaign of 1994, achieved only limited credibility since it was dictated by a partisan majority of the Center Right.[56] As a result of such massive attacks on their erstwhile state, many East Germans began to cultivate a growing feeling of nostalgia, forgetting repression and bemoaning the loss of their former security.[57]

The academic debate has hardly been able to guide public sentiment in a more constructive direction because it was itself quite contentious and polarized. Though this scholarly contest moved on a more sophisticated level, it involved both material stakes, such as individual jobs or institutional prospects, and intangible intellectual matters, such as the power to interpret the past for the new Germany. Reflecting the divisions of the public discussion, three basic positions have crystallized, which function as reference system, arsenal of arguments, and identification of ideological affinity: Dominant in much of the media is an accusatory discourse that construes the GDR as a totalitarian dictatorship that ruthlessly oppressed its citizens; against this oversimplification argues an apologetic discourse that sees the East German state as a noble experiment that unfortunately did not quite live up to its billing; located between these extremes is a differentiating discourse that attempts to analyze the repressive as well as the emancipatory features of the SED regime. By accusing more discriminating views of being soft on Communism, the advocates of the Right are trying to use the evidence of GDR repression to regain their earlier academic ascendancy.[58]

As the permanent exhibition in the *Haus der Geschichte* in Bonn demonstrates, one bone of contention is the narrativization of GDR history, the way that this alternate story is to be included in representations of

[55] Richard Schöder, "Schwamm drüber? Das reicht nicht," *Die Zeit*, 29 August 1997. Cf. James McAdams, *Judging the Past in Unified Germany* (Cambridge, UK, 2001).

[56] Hermann Weber, "Rewriting the History of the GDR: The Work of the Commission of Inquiry," in *Rewriting the German Past*, 197 ff; and Deutscher Bundestag, *Bericht der Enquêtekommission Aufarbeitung von Geschichte und Folgen der SED-Diktatur in Deutschland* (Bonn, 1994). The various *Gutachten* were published in a multi-volume series by the Nomos Verlag (Baden-Baden, 1995).

[57] Christoph Dieckmann, "Das Hirn will Heimat," *Die Zeit*, 1 November 1996; Tom Peuckert, "Du bist ein widerlicher Bürger geworden!" *Tagesspiegel* 3 August 1997; and Joachim Gauck, "Noch lange fremd," *Spiegel* (1997) no. 40: 46 ff.

[58] Corey Ross, *The East German Dictatorship* (Oxford, 2002).

the FRG's past. Some Western anticommunists would just as soon take Stefan Heym's skeptical quip literally, that unification would reduce the GDR to a footnote of world history, treating it as a dead end to be passed over as soon as possible.[59] Fairer minds, like Hartmut Jäckel or Henry Ashby Turner, have been willing, in writing their textbooks, to allow that East Germany warrants a chapter of its own, but they use their limited discussion as a dark foil to make the successes of the Federal Republic shine all the more brightly.[60] Only a few perceptive scholars, like Christoph Kleßmann or Mary Fulbrook, have gone so far as to recognize the GDR as a text sui generis, requiring sustained treatment in its own right since not everything that was attempted in the East was necessarily inferior to the West. Journalist Peter Bender cautions appropriately that the multiple ways that Eastern and Western developments were connected to, comparable with, or independent of one another have yet to be worked out.[61]

Another focus of intense controversy is the conceptual approach, which ought to be used in dealing with the remains of real existing socialism. The unexpected collapse of Communism has led to a revival of the totalitarianism paradigm formulated by Central European émigrés during the 1950s to explain the surprising resemblance between the ideologically opposed dictatorships of the Right and the Left. The advantage of this perspective in public debate is its focus on the mechanisms of power and repression as well as its clear moral condemnation of unfreedom from a democratic point of view.[62] Critics with more favorable recollections of the East German system have denounced this picture of an *Unrechtsstaat* as a caricature that obliterates its emancipatory aspirations, oversimplifies its internal functioning, and misses its nonpolitical spaces. While outright condemnation might appeal to Eastern dissidents and Western anticommunists, they argue that it leaves out the positive memories of the majority of GDR citizens, not to mention its loyalists in the PDS. Insisting on the noble character of their experiment, apologists suggest, instead, that researchers ought to

---

[59] Haus der Geschichte der Bundesrepublik Deutschland, ed., *Erlebnis Geschichte. Das Buch zur Ausstellung* (Lübbe Verlag, n.p., n.d.). See also Stefan Heym and Werner Heiduczek, eds., *Die Sanfte Revolution* (Leipzig, 1990), 421–23.

[60] Eberhard Jäckel, *Das deutsche Jahrhundert. Eine historische Bilanz* (Stuttgart, 1996), 308–35; Henry Ashby Turner, *The Two Germanies since 1945* (New Haven, 1987).

[61] Christoph Kleßmann, *Zwei Staaten, eine Nation. Deutsche Geschichte 1955–1970*, 2nd ed. (Bonn, 1997); Mary Fulbrook, *The Divided Nation: A History of Germany, 1918–1990* (Oxford, 1992); and Peter Bender, *Episode oder Epoche? Zur Geschichte des geteilten Deutschland* (Munich, 1996).

[62] Eckhard Jesse, ed., *Totalitarismus im 20. Jahrhundert. Eine Bilanz der internationalen Forschung* (Baden Baden, 1996); and Klaus Schroeder, *Der SED-Staat. Partei, Staat und Gesellschaft 1949–1990* (Munich, 1998).

be going beyond appearances, distinguishing between shades of red and relativizing SED policies.[63]

More discriminating scholars are searching for a perspective that will reflect the contradictions inherent in the GDR as a historical object. Building on a revised version of the earlier *Systemvergleich* between East and West, these moderates compare the Nazi dictatorship with the Communist one, and contrast East Germany with the other Soviet satellites to establish commonalties as well as differences. For instance, Jürgen Kocka has suggested conceptualizing the GDR as a *durchherrschte Gesellschaft*, a society entirely permeated by politics, or as a "modern dictatorship" to emphasize its relative modernity along with its repression. Other commentators have, instead, looked at the limits of the SED's dictatorial power and investigated the survival of remnants of self-determined social life.[64] If one further explores this contradiction between emancipatory aims and repressive practices, one might classify the East German regime as an authoritarian form of the welfare state, representing a double radicalization of social democratic hopes for reform and participation into revolution and dictatorship. Because of the fundamental tensions typical of the GDR, the system would appear to be a kind of *Fürsorgediktatur*, a dictatorial version of the labor movement's aspirations for social provision.[65]

An approach to the East German experience that combines differentiating with evaluative strategies might, perhaps, be called a "critical historicization." Inspired by Martin Broszat's call for a *Historisierung* of the Third Reich, this perspective, to recover the otherness that needs explaining, would no longer treat its terrible events as if they were still part of the present. But this formula should also take into account Saul Friedländer's objection, that historicizing the NS system might open the door to an amoral revisionism bent upon discovering some "good sides" in it.[66] Applied to the GDR, such an explicitly critical historiciza-

---

[63] See the series *Ansichten zur Geschichte der DDR* (Bonn, 1995 ff), and the *hefte zur ddr-geschichte*. Cf. Rainer Eckert, "Strukturen, Umfeldorganisationen und Geschichtsbild der PDS," *Horch und Guck* 4, no. 15 (1995): 1 ff; and Stefan Wolle, *Die heile Welt der Diktatur. Alltag und Herrschaft in der DDR 1971–1989* (Berlin, 1998).

[64] Jürgen Kocka, "Ein deutscher Sonderweg. Überlegungen zur Sozialgeschichte der DDR," *Aus Politik und Zeitgeschichte* (1994) no. 40: 34–45; and Richard Bessel and Ralph Jessen, eds., *Grenzen der Diktatur. Staat und Gesellschaft in der DDR* (Göttingen, 1996).

[65] Konrad H. Jarausch, "Realer Sozialismus als Fürsorgediktatur. Zur begrifflichen Einordnung der DDR" *Aus Politik und Zeitgeschichte* (1998) Nr. 20: 33–46. See also Konrad H. Jarausch, ed., *Dictatorship as Experience: Towards a Socio-Cultural History of the GDR* (New York, 1999), as well as "Die gescheiterte Gegengesellschaft. Überlegungen zu einer Sozialgeschichte der DDR," *Archiv für Sozialgeschichte* 39 (1999): 1–17

[66] Compare Martin Broszat, "Plädoyer für eine Historisierung des Nationalsozialismus," in Hermann Graml and Klaus-Dietmar Henke, eds., *Nach Hitler. Der schwierige Umgang mit unserer Geschichte* (Munich, 1987), 159 ff, to Saul Friedländer, "Überlegungen

tion would treat the SED state as something past that should be analyzed dispassionately, but this approach could at the same time caution against blurring the distinctions between dictatorship and democracy. The key challenge appears to be the development of an analytical stance toward the regime that will clearly expose its dictatorial nature and yet do justice to the relative normalcy of people's lives within it, thereby problematizing their mutual relationship.[67] A second step toward the rehabilitation of alternative histories might therefore be the creation of an unflinching but differentiated approach to the contradictions inherent in GDR history.

Toward an Emancipatory History

What will finally be the future of the counternarrative after the collapse of Communism, its main ideological advocate, and its institutional carrier? Ironically, the political failure of this utopia has not so much liberated critical perspectives from the corset of party dogma as seriously damaged them by revealing the complicity of its advocates with a repressive system. A radical rethinking of the entire course of the revolutionary tradition within working-class history is, therefore, necessary, beginning with a reconsideration of its organization by the Communist Party that does not stop with denunciations of Stalinism or with recourse to the appealing figure of Rosa Luxemburg but goes back to the original ambivalence of Karl Marx's vision.[68] The collapse of the extremist version should also permit a reappraisal of the achievements and problems of moderate strands of the labor movement, as exemplified by Social Democracy, that, perhaps, lacks some of the radical chic but proves more constructive in improving people's lives.[69] Ultimately, the discrediting of Communism also ought to inspire a more serious look at the various anarchist and syndicalist strands of working-class

---

zur Historisierung des Nationalsozialismus," in Dan Diner, ed., *Ist der Nationalsozialismus Geschichte?* (Frankfurt, 1987), 34 ff.

[67] Konrad H. Jarausch, "Kritische Perspektiven zur deutschen Vergangenheit," in *Nach dem Erdbeben*, 21 ff.; and Martin Sabrow, "Schwierigkeiten mit der Historisierung. Die DDR-Geschichtswissenschaft als Forschungsgegenstand," in Martin Sabrow and Peter Walter, eds., *Historische Forschung und sozialistische Diktatur. Beiträge zur Geschichtwissenschaft der DDR* (Leipzig, 1995), 9 ff.

[68] See, e. g., Eric Weitz, *Creating German Communism: From Popular Protests to Communist State* (Princeton, 1997).

[69] For instance Heinrich August Winkler's magisterial trilogy on *Arbeiter und Arbeiterbewegung in der Weimarer Republik* (Berlin, 1984–1987).

politics that faintly echo in the New Social Movements of the 1970s
and the Green Party of the 1980s.[70]

Liberation from SED doctrine should allow for alternative histories
that more fully explore the complexities of working-class or other disadvantaged lives. The impulses of the new social history of the 1960s
have largely run their course; they produced an impressive literature
on the labor movement before shifting focus to the analysis of the middle class, the elusive *Besitz-* and *Bildungsbürgertum*.[71] The initiatives of
everyday historians have added another dimension of studies, focusing
on the seemingly mundane *Alltag* of wage earners and their often perplexing collaboration with or resistance to authority.[72] More recently,
attention has moved to working-class culture, to the language of labor,
the representations, symbols, and festivals that offer clues to the self-
definition of the masses, which had been largely overlooked. Although
it will not be able to supplant older studies of organization or industrial
conflict, this cultural shift is expanding the scope of labor history by
returning a sense of agency and reflexivity to its actors, a sense that
had often been lost in traditional party histories.[73] An entire realm of
other underclass struggles among landless laborers of the countryside
or the urban poor yet remains to find a sympathetic historian.

At the same time, the concept of "emancipatory history" ought to be
expanded to new subjects of discrimination beyond traditional labor
history. Since the national master narrative and its Marxist counterpart
have largely told male stories, one neglected area is the history of
women. In contrast to the political emphasis of Anglo-American feminism, the strategy of the German women's movement, focusing on
motherhood and the pursuit of educational opportunities, needs to be
explored more fully to appreciate its motives.[74] More systematic attention to the actual lives of different kinds of women would yield excit-

[70] Although they are perhaps too optimistic, see Andrei S. Markovits and Philip S.
Gorski, *The German Left: Red, Green and Beyond* (Oxford, 1993).

[71] Jürgen Kocka, ed., *Bürgertum im 19. Jahrhundert. Deutschland im europäischen Vergleich*, 3 vols. (Munich, 1988). See also Jonathan Sperber, "Bürger, Bürgertum, Bürgerlich-
keit, Bürgerliche Gesellschaft: Studies of the German (Upper) Middle Class and Its Socio-
cultural World," *Journal of Modern History* 69 (1997): 271 ff.

[72] Alf Lüdtke, ed., *Alltagsgeschichte. Zur Rekonstruktion historischer Erfahrungen und Le-
bensweisen* (Frankfurt, 1989); Geoff Eley, "Labor History, Social History, *Alltagsgeschichte*:
Experience, Culture and Politics of the Everyday—a New Direction for German Social
History?" *Journal of Modern History* 61 (1989): 297 ff.

[73] Vernon A. Lidtke, *The Alternative Culture: The Socialist Labor in Imperial Germany*
(New York, 1985); Thomas Mergel and Thomas Welskopp, eds., *Geschichte zwischen Kultur und Gesellschaft* (Munich, 1997).

[74] Ann Taylor Allen, *Feminism and Motherhood in Germany, 1800–1914* (New Brunswick,
1991); and James C. Albisetti, *Schooling German Girls and Women: Secondary and Higher
Education in the Ninetheenth Century* (Princeton, 1988).

ing new insights into the effect of gendering on individuals, as suggests the path-breaking work on women during and after World War II of Robert Moeller and Elisabeth Heineman[75] It might also be important to go beyond the dichotomy of construing women as victims or as perpetrators, a dichotomy that has dominated the debate about the Third Reich so as to get at the full complexity of roles and experiences under the Nazi dictatorship. At the same time, the question of the paradox of practical independence but theoretical lack of emancipation among women under real existing socialism clearly deserves another look.[76]

Another area of struggle for emancipation that requires closer scrutiny involves minorities of language, religion, and race. The homogenizing effects of the nation- or class-framing of the past have largely suppressed the memory of the amazing diversity of experiences in the German-speaking world. Because of the leadership of the Leo Baeck Institute, and a strange combination of filiopietist philanthropy and post-Holocaust guilt, the study of German Jewish history seems to be flourishing on both sides of the Atlantic.[77] Much less, however, is known about the fate of Polish speakers in Germany, not to mention various other ethnic minorities, such as the French, the Danes, or the Sorbs. While scholars have paid some attention to migration and slave labor, the more recent arrival and permanent residence of "guest-workers," especially Turks, has yet to inspire serious historical study.[78] Other nonmainstream groups such as homosexuals[79] or various religious sects that were openly persecuted by the Nazis also have yet to find sustained historical attention. The point is not just to add previously silenced voices to the general chorus but to rethink German histories from the margins to decenter received conceptions of what it meant to be German at a given time.

[75] Robert Moeller, *Protecting Motherhood: Women and the Family in the Politics of the New Germany* (Berkeley, 1993); and Elizabeth Heineman, *What Difference Does a Husband Make? Women and Marital Status in Nazi and Postwar Germany* (Berkeley, 1999).

[76] Gisela Bock, *Zwangssterilisation im Nationalsozialismus. Studien zur Rassenpolitik und Frauenpolitik* (Opladen, 1986); and Claudia Koonz, *Mothers in the Fatherland: Women, the Family and Nazi Policies* (New York, 1987). Cf. the essays by Leo Ansorg and Renate Hürtgen as well as Dagmar Langenhan and Sabine Ross in *Dictatorship as Experience*, 163–192.

[77] There are too many works too mention, we include only Monika Richarz, ed., *Jewish Life in Germany: Memoirs From Three Centuries* (Bloomington, 1991). See also issues of the *Leo Baeck Yearbook* (London, 1957-).

[78] Christoph Kleßmann, *Polnische Bergarbeiter im Ruhrgebiet, 1870–1918* (Göttingen, 1978); Klaus Bade, *Vom Auswandererland zum Einwandererland? Deutschland 1870–1980* (Berlin, 1983); and Ulrich Herbert, *Hitler's Foreign Workers: Enfored Labor in Germany under the Third Reich* (Cambridge, 1997).

[79] James D. Steakly, *The Homosexual Emancipation Movement in Germany* (New York, 1975).

A final field that should be included in a critical perspective is the history of the environment, or rather of its care or despoliation in Central Europe. Is it not curious that a culture that prides itself on its romantic sensitivity to nature and animals has paid so little attention to the development of this relationship over time? This neglect is a pity since a fascinating story waits to be told, as the innovative efforts of Ray Dominick and Sandra Chaney suggest.[80] In contrast to the American "use and throw away" attitude, the Germans have shown a greater concern for husbanding their limited natural resources and for maintaining a healthy environment. No doubt the gradual transformation from nature protection to ecological consciousness was a slow and contested process after 1945, but the strength of the Green Party indicates that this is a subject of considerable importance. Moreover, in the past, many of the champions of greater rights for labor, women, and minorities also campaigned for the protection of the environment, seeing them as interlocking causes of reform.

If anything, the victory of capitalism and the return of the nation-state have made the writing of counternarratives even more urgent. The danger of post–Cold War triumphalism is a myopic self-congratulation that assumes that the victorious Western system is perfect as it presently exists and that it no longer needs serious reform.[81] Yet mounting evidence of exploitation of minimum wage earners, gender discrimination, persistence of racial prejudice, continuation of ethnic wars, degradation of the environment, international terrorism, and so on, ought to encourage at least an occasional touch of doubt. The disappearance of the institutionalized antagonist has shifted this burden of critique to unattached intellectuals who, by keeping memories of injustices alive, can contribute to that public self-questioning necessary to develop capitalist democracy in a participatory and socially responsible direction. In their warnings, impulses of a less dogmatic Western Marxist tradition are likely to blend with newer feminist, minority, and ecological concerns. As long as they do not legitimize new forms of repression by becoming themselves hegemonic, such alternative histories will continue to be important as a source of essential criticism.[82]

---

[80] Raymond H. Dominick, *The Environmental Movement in Germany: Prophets and Protest, 1871–1971* (Bloomington, 1992); and Sandra Chaney, "Visions and Revisions of Nature: From Protection of Nature to the Invention of the Environment in the Federal Republic of Germany, 1945–1967" (Ph.D. dissertation, Chapel Hill, 1996).

[81] Charles S. Maier, "Gibt es einen Sieger der Geschichte? Geschichtswissenschaft und DDR Vergangenheit," *Zwischen Parteilichkeit und Professionalität*, 197 ff.

[82] Konrad H. Jarausch, "Towards a Postsocialist Politics? A Historical Postscript," in Christiane Lemke and Gary Marks, eds., *The Crisis of Socialism in Europe* (Durham, 1992), 116 ff. See also Klaus Hartung, "Was der Westblick im Osten übersieht," *Die Zeit*, 10 October 1997.

3

Modernization, German
Exceptionalism, and
Post-Modernity:
Transcending the Critical
History of Society

In West Germany the implicit master narrative of critical historians
has centered on the paradigm of modernization as the explanation of
social development. In a defeated, destroyed, and discredited country,
the notion of "modernity" appealed to intellectuals because it suggested a radical break with the Nazi past and the possibility of a fresh
beginning based on Western values and lifestyles.[1] In linguistic usage,
the adjective "modern" therefore came to mean not just "contemporary" but also "corresponding to the newest stage of social, scientific,
and technical development," thereby acquiring a liberating sense of the
innovative and international as in modern art or architecture.[2] Because
it was conflated with material prosperity, democratic self-government,

[1] Axel Schildt, *Moderne Zeiten. Freizeit, Massenmedien und "Zeitgeist" in der Bundesrepublik der 50er Jahre* (Hamburg, 1995), 16 ff, 441 ff.

[2] Compare Judy Pearsall and Bill Trimble, eds., *The Oxford Reference Dictionary* (Oxford, 1995), to *Brockhaus Enzyklopädie*, vol. 14, 19th ed. (Mannheim, 1991), 709 ff., and
Duden. Deutsches Universalwörterbuch, 2nd ed. (Mannheim, 1989), 1029.

and technological innovation, "modernity" assumed in postwar Germany the hallowed status of a "social myth," which prevented, as ecological critics have charged, criticism of industrial society and capitalist exploitation of the Third World.[3]

Although it may sound appealing, the concept of modernity has been a treacherous starting point for historical interpretation because of its relational and protean character. A look at the emergence of the idea suggests that in the Middle Ages, *modernus* meant to designate a time that was not *antiquus*, namely, a present that was different from something that had come before. Only in the Renaissance did the word "modernity" develop into a full-fledged notion of a historical epoch that could be separated from the previous periods, the ancient and the medieval. During the Enlightenment, the adjective "modern" assumed a positive connotation as a more rational and useful time that would be qualitatively superior to the past. But the continual extension of the present made it ever more difficult to call new developments modern, depriving the idea of specific content and making it signify a "fleeting moment" in contrast to the long duration of eternity.[4] The multiple meanings suggest that modernity is usually defined against an earlier stage and lacks an identifiable core of attributes beyond a self-proclaimed presentism. Yet it is precisely this chameleon-like quality that makes it popular, since it can be claimed by numerous competing currents.

In Germany programs of modernization have perhaps been more embattled during the last two centuries than elsewhere. Around 1900, advocates of modernity could, for instance, point to a growing corps of scientists and engineers whose advances in physics and chemistry were fueling the rapid growth of industry and won even Emperor William II's admiration. But already during the early stages of industrialization, some observers, such as Wilhelm Riehl and Richard Wagner, warned against the dangers of modernization, a critique that was continued by such cultural pessimists as Friedrich Nietzsche and Oswald Spengler, and fed into an anti-urban, anti-Semitic, anti-masses, and anti-industrial mindset.[5] The conflict was exacerbated by a self-proclaimed avant-

---

[3] Peter Wehling, *Die Moderne als Sozialmythos. Zur Kritik sozialwissenschaftlicher Modernisierungstheorien* (Frankfurt, 1992), 9 ff.

[4] Hans-Ulrich Gumbrecht, "Modern, Modernität, Moderne," in Otto Brunner, Werner Conze, and Reinhart Koselleck, eds., *Geschichtliche Grundbegriffe. Historisches Lexikon zur politisch-sozialen Sprache in Deutschland*, vol. 4 (Stuttgart, 1978), 93 ff.

[5] Cf. Frank Trommler, "Reformkultur oder *Progressivism*? Modernisierungskonzepte um 1900 in Deutschland und den USA," in Ragnild Fiebig von Hase and Jürgen Heideking, eds., *Zwei Wege in die Moderne. Aspekte der deutsch-amerikanischen Beziehungen 1900–1918* (Trier, 1998). Cf Thomas Rohkrämer, *Eine andere Moderne. Zivilisationskritik, Natur und Technik in Deutschland 1880–1933* (Paderborn, 1999).

garde of writers and especially painters who assembled under the banner of "modernism" to break with tradition and experiment in naturalist, impressionist, and expressionist directions. The campaign of the Roman Catholic Church against inroads of cultural experimentation and similar warnings by conservative Protestant divines contributed to making modernity into a sharply contested territory.[6]

Outside commentators also noted this ambivalence, praising the Second Empire's rapid technological progress, but wondering about its lagging political development. At the beginning of World War I, the American sociologist Thorstein Veblen, famous for his critique of the leisure class, formulated what became the classic indictment of this disparity in a volume eventually published under the title *Imperial Germany and the Industrial Revolution*. While recognizing that the breakneck speed of development in central Europe outstripped the British original, Veblen at the same time denounced the authoritarian structure of the dynastic government, the instability of the Kaiser, and the feudalistic spirit of the Prussian ruling class. Since he considered the discrepancy between the modernization of the economy and the inflexibility of the polity the cause of German imperialism, this shrewd observer implied that peace would return only once the Germans had learned the lessons of democracy.[7] Fitting neatly into wartime propaganda, this penetrating analysis reflected a reversal of academic opinion and provided the initial formulation for the perception of Germany as different from normal, that is, Anglo-American, development.

The modernization perspective is not just a "natural" way of looking at the German past but is also a critical construction with an ideological agenda that has largely gone unexamined. The contested background of the concept of modernity suggests that the program of *Gesellschaftsgeschichte*, imbued with this view, intended to break with the national master narrative to promote social reform in West Germany. At the same time, this approach purported to serve as an objective alternative to the Marxist counternarrative by offering greater accuracy and flexibility in interpreting historical development. The implication of German deviance from a standard model, advocated by the Bielefeld school, suggested the inversion of the traditional concept of a German *Sonderweg* into a critique of backwardness and difference. Since liberal

[6] Peter Paret, *The Berlin Secession: Modernism and its Enemies in Imperial Germany* (Cambridge, Mass., 1980); and Thomas Nipperdey, *Religion im Umbruch. Deutschland 1870–1918* (Munich, 1988).

[7] Thorstein Veblen, *Imperial Germany and the Industrial Revolution*, repr. (New York, 1954), 248 ff. Cf. Konrad H. Jarausch, "The University," in Joachim Remak and Jack Dukes, ed., *Another Germany: A Reconsideration of the Imperial Era* (Boulder, 1983), 181–206.

historians have generally been in sympathy with this critical history of
society, they have neglected to probe the analytical limits and political
pitfalls of the underlying modernization paradigm.[8] What were its intellectual origins, how did its arguments develop, and what were the
effects of the postmodern rupture on its explanatory power?

The Modernization
Perspective

Since the breakthrough of industry occurred in Great Britain, German
historians, under the spell of Leopold von Ranke, could long afford to
ignore its implications.[9] Only at the turn of the century did historical
economists confront the consequences of modernization, with such
conservative moralists as Adolph Wagner denouncing urban decadence, and such liberal thinkers as the economist Lujo Brentano touting
the social benefits of economic growth.[10] To gain a broader perspective,
the sociologist Max Weber probed the origins of the spirit of capitalism,
which he located in the realm of "the Protestant ethic" and explained
the advancement of social rationality as a consequence of the rise of
scientific inquiry and bureaucratic state administration. Though Weber
saw systematic scholarship as the method for promoting rationality, he
feared the irrational potential of aspirations for mass participation, and
hinted at certain dangers of modernity.[11] In contrast to Werner Som-
bart's optimistic portrayal of entrepreneurship, this ambivalent emphasis on the "iron cage" of modernity provided a state-centered view that
connected capitalist growth with bureaucratic organization, technological innovation, and individual self-discipline—in itself a reflection of
the somewhat different course of German development.

The positive sense of exceptionalism that emerged out of the propaganda battles of World War I, therefore, proclaimed a distinctive Ger-

---

[8] On this point, the self-representations, as well as the portrayals of others, are curiously mute. Cf. H.-U. Wehler, *Historische Sozialwissenschaft und Geschichtsschreibung. Studien zu Aufgaben und Traditionen deutscher Geschichtswissenschaft* (Göttingen, 1980); and
Georg G. Iggers, *The Social History of Politics in West German Historical Writing since 1945*
(Dover, N.H., 1985).

[9] For a partial exception, see Heinrich von Treitschke, *Deutsche Geschichte im 19. Jahrhundert*, vol. 5 (Leipzig, 1894), 433 ff.

[10] Kenneth Barkin, *The Controversy over German Industrialization, 1890–1902* (Chicago,
1970), 131 ff.

[11] Sam Whimster and Scott Lash, eds., *Max Weber, Rationality and Modernity* (London,
1987); and Detlev Peukert, *Max Webers Zeitdiagnose der Moderne* (Göttingen, 1989). See

man road to modernity. Repeated in patriotic speeches and professorial pamphlets, the conviction of the superiority of a profound, idealistic *Kultur* over a shallow, materialistic civilization found its classic formulation in Thomas Mann's diatribe, *Reflections of a Nonpolitical Man*.[12] This *Sonderbewußtsein* stressed the special geographic situation between the West and the East that made Germany part of neither and a bridge between both. It also emphasized the need for more governmental authority, domestic unity, and military strength since the country had few natural frontiers, many neighbors, and, it seemed, "a world of enemies." Claims for distinctiveness also centered on the impartiality and efficiency of an elaborate governmental bureaucracy that administered the German states, as well as on Bismarck's social policy, which sought to overcome class divisions through state welfare provisions for the working class. Though many mandarins continued to view the consequences of urbanization as problematic, German pride also involved a positive view of technological innovations and economic development, stressing the rise of industrial power and the spread of national prosperity.[13]

With defeat, perceptions of modernization grew more ambivalent because the triumph of social and cultural innovation became associated with economic crisis, domestic strife, and international conflict.[14] During the Weimar Republic, such left wing intellectuals as Walter Benjamin were both fascinated and repelled by modernity, while neoconservatives resentfully rejected Western democracy as well as modern artistic currents in general. After the so-called *Diktat* of Versailles, historians devoted much of their energy to refuting assertions of German responsibility for the outbreak of World War I, and methodologically clung to "the primacy of foreign policy." Some moderates (e.g., Hermann Oncken), Catholics (e.g., Franz Schnabel), and local historians (e.g., Rudolf Kötschke), began to refer to industrial society in their studies, but most deplored modernization as a source of the current crisis and as leading inevitably to social decay and cultural American-

---

also Andreas Anter, *Max Webers Theorie des modernen Staates. Herkunft, Struktur und Bedeutung* (Berlin, 1995), 160 ff., 203 ff.

[12] Thomas Mann, *Reflections of a Nonpolitical Man* (New York, 1983); and Fritz Fischer, *Griff nach der Weltmacht* (Düsseldorf, 1961).

[13] For a positive view by a historian, see Karl Lamprecht, *Zur jüngsten deutschen Vergangenheit*, the first half of the second supplement to his *Deutsche Geschichte* (Freiburg, 1903), 11 ff; and Louise Schorn-Schütte, *Karl Lamprecht. Kulturgeschichtsschreibung zwischen Wissenschaft und Politik* (Göttingen, 1984), 180 ff,

[14] Modris Eksteins, *Rites of Spring: The Great War and the Birth of the Modern Age* (Boston, 1989).

ization. Only a few younger, more original spirits, such as Eckhart Kehr, portrayed democratization and industrialization as positive paths toward modernity, and were willing to embrace the Republic as their somewhat problematic but nonetheless logical outgrowth.[15]

The "reactionary modernism" that characterized the Third Reich turned historians even more strongly in an antimodern direction, even if it did inspire some innovation in research methods. Traditional nationalists, cultural pessimists, or neoconservatives initially hoped to have their programs endorsed by the Nazis, but the racist ideologues of the Hitler state established a more murderous agenda of their own.[16] Instead, it was the development of *Volksgeschichte*, a curious combination of ethnic and populist history, that shifted attention away from statesmen and foreign policy toward such concepts as "people" and "space." As part of the anti-Versailles campaign of the Weimar Right, this radical nationalism drew upon cultural anthropology, sociology, and geography to defend German minorities in Eastern and Western Europe. Though methodologically innovative, such historians as Hermann Aubin and Hans Rothfels embraced an agrarian romanticism that loathed modernity as destructive of national health, and hatched settlement schemes to renew the body politic through contact with the land. As a result, some of the younger members of this *Ostforschung* provided some of the intellectual justification for ethnic cleansing and population transfers that were harbingers of the Final Solution.[17]

A democratic critique of German exceptionalism had to develop on the outside through the cooperation of American intellectuals and European émigrés during World War II. Among the former, such talented journalists as William Shirer, Edgar Mower, and Dorothy Thompson were the most notable, since their reports from Berlin drew vivid portraits of life in the Reich. More academic were the efforts of William McGovern to explain the differences in political development *From Luther to Hitler* or of Erik Erikson to plumb the depths of the authoritarian psyche. At the same time, such émigré publicists as Emil Ludwig and

---

[15] Bernd Faulenbach, *Die Ideologie des deutschen Weges. Die deutsche Geschichte in der Historiographie zwischen Kaiserreich und Nationalsozialismus* (Munich, 1980), 6 ff, 89 ff. Cf. Eckart Kehr, *Der Primat der Innenpolitik. Gesammelte Aufsätze zur preußisch-deutschen Sozialgeschichte im 19. und 20. Jahrhundert*, ed., Hans-Ulrich Wehler (Berlin, 1965); and Mary Nolan,*Visions of Modernity: American Business and the Modernization of Germany* (New York, 1994).

[16] Jeffrey Herf, *Reactionary Modernism: Technology, Culture and Politics in Weimar and the Third Reich* (Cambridge, 1984).

[17] Willi Oberkrome, *Volksgeschichte. Methodische Innovation und völkische Ideologisierung in der deutschen Geschichtswissenschaft 1918–1945* (Göttingen, 1993). See also Peter Schöttler, ed., *Geschichte als Legitimationswissenschaft 1933–1945* (Frankfurt, 1997).

Sebastian Haffner sought to inform American intellectuals of the reasons for the failure of democracy in Central Europe and to propose ways of fostering liberty in the future. Finally, such exiled historians as Hans Rosenberg, Hans Kohn, and Hajo Holborn provided interpretations of German peculiarity that highlighted the power of the landed elite, the strength of ethnic nationalism, and the otherworldliness of idealism. Despite their different approaches, these discussions, focused in the Office for Strategic Services, held up the Anglo-American pattern of democratic development as a standard and viewed German history as disastrous deviance from it.[18]

The concept of modernization as an economic perspective emerged only after 1945 in the context of decolonization and Cold War competition. Confronted with a plethora of newly independent states, policymakers tried to figure out how to provide a capitalist model of development that could compete with the communist form of industrialization in the Third World. "Modernization" became the catchword of this debate since it suggested a sweeping recipe for social change modeled on the Anglo-American experience of combining capitalism with democracy without explicitly referring to the West. Walter W. Rostow provided the most popular formulation in his treatise on "stages of economic growth," a stylized five-step model of industrialization that suggested a "theory about modern history as a whole." Eventually, sociologists expanded the concept of economic development into a broader notion of modernization that included a series of political, social, and cultural changes that would propel a country from a so-called traditional to a modern society.[19] Marxist thinkers, Georg Lukacs among them, also portrayed Germany as abnormal since, here, the bourgeoisie failed to break the hold of feudalism with a successful revolution.[20]

The *Sonderweg* Paradigm

It took a fundamental transformation of intellectual context for historians within Germany to accept the modernization perspective. The loss of national sovereignty and the division of the country in 1945 ren-

---

[18] See the rich material in Michaela Hönicke, " 'Know Your Enemy': American Interpretations of National Socialism, 1933–1945" (Ph.D. dissertation, Chapel Hill, 1998).

[19] W. W. Rostow, *The Stages of Economic Growth: A Non-Communist Manifesto* (London, 1960). Cf. Hanna Schissler, "Theorien des sozialen Wandels," *Neue Politische Literatur* 12 (1974): 155–89.

[20] Georg Lukacs, *Die Zerstörung der Vernunft. Der Weg des Irrationalismus von Schelling zu Hitler* (Berlin, 1955), 12.

dered an independent diplomacy impossible, thereby breaking the spell of nationalism and undercutting the primacy of foreign policy. At the same time, the drastic failure of a criminal Führer tarnished the authoritarian respect for leadership and cast doubt upon the "great men" theory of history. Postwar experiences in the Western zones instead suggested an alternate set of orientations: The surprising rapidity and extent of the material recovery transferred collective pride to the civilian achievements of the economy. The painful reconstruction of lives, families, and towns shifted the focus of public concern to societal processes. And the cultural hunger for catching up on the experimental painting, literature, and music that had been banned by Nazi censors created among intellectuals a veritable passion for modernity that came to seem like a progressive antidote to the murky volkish past.[21]

The total defeat of the Third Reich triggered a complicated questioning of the scholarly and ideological causes of the disaster. By dropping the content but extending the methods of *Volksgeschichte*, such former partisans as Theodor Schieder and Werner Conze began to call for a "structural history" that switched the focus of research from the state to society. Rediscovering Max Weber and open to theoretical impulses from the social, both looked beyond the historicist stress on particular events or individuals for generalized answers to the underlying social processes of change. While Schieder was more interested in the pattern of politics and the rise of nationalism, Conze, instead, focused on the labor movement, the industrial class system, and the problems of ethnic identity. Their linguistic switch from the incriminated terminus *Volk* to the abstract notion of "historical structures" prepared the more general turn toward social history.[22] Another important impulse was the critical scholarship of émigrés like Hans Rosenberg or Richard Löwenthal, who inspired an entire generation of American and German scholars to search for the reasons of the German catastrophe not just in political pathologies but also in economic problems, social disintegration, and cultural antimodernism.[23]

[21] Wolfgang Welsch, "Modernity and Postmodernity in Postwar Germany (1845–1995)," in Rainer Pommerin, ed., *Culture in the Federal Republic of Germany, 1945–1995* (Oxford, 1996), 109 ff.

[22] Oberkrome, *Volksgeschichte*, 222 ff. Cf. Theodor Schieder, *Staat und Gesellschaft im Wandel unserer Zeit* (Munich, 1958); and Werner Conze, *Gesellschaft—Staat—Nation. Gesammelte Aufsätze*, Ulrich Engelhardt, Reinhart Koselleck, and Wolfgang Schieder, eds. (Stuttgart, 1991).

[23] Konrad H. Jarausch, "Die Provokation des 'Anderen.' Amerikanische Perspektiven auf die deutsche Vergangenheitsbewältigung," in *Doppelte Zeitgeschichte*, 432 ff. See also Rüdiger Hohls and Konrad H. Jarausch, eds., *Versäumte Fragen. Deutsche Historiker im Schatten des Nationalsozialismus* (Stuttgart, 2000).

The modernization perspective caught the eye of the structural historians by suggesting explanations for the paradox of belated but rapid development in Central Europe. For instance, the economist Alexander Gerschenkron explained the deviance by the area's initial backwardness, which could be overcome only by the importation of up-to-date technology, the involvement of the banks, and the actions of the state. The macrosociologist Barrington Moore broadly compared the transition from feudalism to capitalism, identifying the lack of revolution, strength of bureaucracy, and manorial reaction as reasons for the turn to fascism rather than democracy or communism.[24] The sociologist Dietrich Rüschemeyer suggested, instead, the notion of a "partial modernization" that promoted change in some areas, such as the military or economy, to maintain antimodern structures in others, for instance, politics. In the FRG, the liberal sociologist Ralf Dahrendorf combined these various strands of criticism in his ringing indictment of the Germans' "structural incapacity for democracy" because of their penchant for consensus, obeisance to authority, and the like.[25] By focusing on the particular contradictions of German development, the global paradigm suggested social reasons of the catastrophe.

In the early 1970s innovative younger scholars at the new Bielefeld University formally adopted the modernization perspective as a tool for historical research. After Hanna Schissler subjected the diverse offerings to a careful review, Hans-Ulrich Wehler engaged modernization theory in a long essay that combined skepticism of American social science generalizations with curiosity for a broader explanation of social change. While exposing the dichotomy between "traditional" and "modern" society as oversimplification, he noted such processes as economic growth, structural differentiation, value change, social mobilization, public participation, and institutionalization of conflicts as interesting criteria for analysis. Though troubled by the normative ethnocentricity and economism of the modernization approach, Wehler was nonetheless fascinated by the theories of "political development," which suggested a model of overlapping crises of identity, legitimization, and participation as well as integration, penetration, and distribution. Reading Max Weber as modernization theorist seemed preferable to Marxist determinism because it offered a more

[24] Alexander Gerschenkron, *Economic Backwardness in Historical Perspective* (Cambridge, Mass., 1960), 5 ff; Barrington Moore, *Social Origins of Dictatorship and Democracy: Lord and Peasant in the Making of the Modern World* (Boston, 1966).

[25] Dietrich Rüschemeyer, "Partielle Modernisierung," in Wolfgang Zapf, ed., *Theorien des sozialen Wandels*, 3rd ed. (Cologne, 1971); and Ralf Dahrendorf, *Society and Democracy in Germany* (Garden City, N.Y., 1965).

multicausal and open-ended framework of social development that could be further specified by historians.[26]

By interpreting the German case not only as peculiar but rather as deviant, the modernization perspective suggested inverting the Wilhelmine notion of positive exceptionalism. As developed by Jürgen Kocka, the negative *Sonderweg* thesis sought to answer the question of "why Germany, in contrast to comparable countries in the West and the North, became perverted into fascism or totalitarianism during the general crisis of the interwar period." Explaining the failure of the Weimar Republic required probing long-range structural continuities of development across prior political ruptures, shifting attention from the acute difficulties of inter-war democracy to the more deep-seated problems of the Second Empire.[27] In this retrospective teleology, modern German history culminated in the Nazi seizure of power, the crimes of the SS and the disaster of 1945; that is, all the really important trajectories led to an inevitable catastrophe. Instead of belittling guilt, as had nationalist historians in the past, this self-critical view fiercely castigated the failure of German politics in the twentieth century. The explicit reference to a Western standard provided a comprehensive program of reforms that needed to be accomplished to democratize the country and prevent any dangerous relapse in the future.[28]

The substantive interpretations of negative exceptionalism, therefore, stressed various ways in which Germany failed to live up to the Anglo-American pattern of modernity. Compared to the West, the Germans were lagging in developing an industrial society, creating a nation-state, and producing a democratic form of government. Subsidiary arguments by other scholars, such as Heinrich August Winkler, stressed Bismarck's 1879 break with the liberals, which blocked parliamentary development. American commentators, such as Gordon Craig, liked to point to the ascendancy of militarism over the civilian government, which helped precipitate World War I and hampered the consolidation of the Weimar Republic. Cultural historians, such as

---

[26] Schissler, "Theorien des sozialen Wandels," 182 ff., and Hans-Ulrich Wehler, *Modernisierungstheorie und Geschichte* (Göttingen, 1975), 16 ff., 36 ff.

[27] This structural approach therefore tried to transcend the path-breaking but limited work of Karl Dietrich Bracher on *Die Auflösung der Weimarer Republik. Eine Studie zum Problem des Machtverfalls in der Demokratie*, 4th ed. (Villingen, 1960).

[28] Jürgen Kocka, "Nach dem Ende des Sonderwegs. Zur Tragfähigkeit eines Konzepts," in *Doppelte Zeitgeschichte*, 364 ff; and Helga Grebing, *Der deutsche Sonderweg in Europa 1806–1945. Eine Kritik* (Stuttgart, 1986), 196 ff. See also Thomas Welskopp, "Westbindung auf dem 'Sonderweg'. Die deutsche Sozialgeschichte vom Appendix der Wirtschaftsgeschichte zur Historischen Sozialwissenschaft," in Wolfgang Küttler, Jörn Rüsen, and Ernst Schulin, eds., *Geschichtsdiskurs*, vol. 5 (Frankfurt, 1999), 191–237.

George Mosse or Fritz Stern, fastened upon the emergence of a volkish radicalism on the Right and analyzed the broader pattern of illiberalism to explain the rejection of Western values. Scholars more interested in social history, such as Jürgen Kocka, talked about the weakness of the German *Bürgertum*, which proved unwilling and / or unable to overthrow the noble elites. In 1973 Hans-Ulrich Wehler finally combined many of these and other themes, like Bonapartism, negative integration, and so on, in a brilliant but tendentious indictment of the German Empire.[29]

The thesis of deviance from normal development produced a history in a new key, unlike any other that Germans had encountered before. First, these rather analytical writings stressed the need for comparison, seeking to break out of the national mold by contrasting the development of Central Europe with that of England and France. Second, many of these texts were self-consciously theoretical, freely borrowing hypotheses and interpretative models from sociology and political science, sometimes even employing statistical methods, as in the efforts of the QUANTUM group. Thirdly, the so-called Bielefeld school privileged collective processes over individual personalities, fastening upon impersonal forces, large-scale organizations, classes, or structures beyond personal control. Fourthly, the program of *Gesellschaftsgeschichte*, like the journal of that name, aimed at a comprehensive explanation of the past, not just supplementing politics with social elements but also integrating the various aspects of human existence in a vast and almost lawlike canvas of society. Finally, most of the actual works produced by the critical historians were politically engaged, starting from a left-liberal premise and evaluating the German past fearlessly by the standard of the present.[30]

This liberal alternative to the Marxist counternarrative could only overthrow the hold of the national master narrative through a series of fierce controversies. A brief recital of some of the major points will have to suffice: The first sally was the assertion of the primacy of domestic policy in the 1960s, which contradicted the conservative dogma of the priority of foreign affairs. For instance, the thesis of "social imperialism" claimed that the rush for empire was triggered by an effort to preserve the privileges of the elite rather than by international compe-

[29] For references to the other works mentioned, see Hans-Ulrich Wehler, *The German Empire, 1871–1918* (Leamington Spa, 1985).

[30] Iggers, *Social History of Politics*, passim. Cf. also Lutz Raphael, "Nationalzentrierte Sozialgeschichte in programmatischer Absicht: Die Zeitschrift 'Geschichte und Gesellschaft. Zeitschrift für Historische Sozialwissenschaft' in den ersten 25 Jahren ihres Bestehens," *Geschichte und Gesellschaft* 26 (2000): 5–37.

tition.[31] Another bone of contention was the relative weight of ideology and personality compared to the administrative chaos and polycracy of Nazi rule. While the "intentionalists" stressed the importance of Hitler's will, the "functionalists" emphasized the imperatives produced by the NS system.[32] Yet another focus of dispute was the degree of intended modernity of the Third Reich. While some conservative scholars argued that the Nazis advanced modernization by design, critical historians denied the Third Reich anything but a pretense of modernity because the term's positive emotional connotation did not fit a criminal regime.[33] Finally, in the infamous *Historikerstreit*, the historians of society largely succeeded in beating back the effort of various apologists to diminish the burden of German guilt.[34]

When the dust settled, the *Sonderweg* thesis inspired a number of syntheses that sought to provide a critical metanarrative of German history. The most ambitious was Hans-Ulrich Wehler's multivolume history of German society that aimed at "describing in its essential outlines . . . the two-hundred-year-long transformation process" from more than three hundred late feudal territories into a single capitalist and democratic society. Departing from a Weberian perspective, this immensely learned work focused on "economy, social hierarchy, political system, and culture" as "central axes of society" to trace the "irreversible acceleration of the modernization process" that led to the Nazi disaster and beyond. Its key explanatory concept was the notion of "defensive modernization," which tried, through partial reforms from above, to safeguard as much of the older economic, social, political, and cultural patterns as possible.[35] In his beautifully written volumes on the nineteenth century Thomas Nipperdey sought to provide a more positive, nuanced, and culturally sensitive alternative by highlighting also some positive accomplishments, especially in scholarship and urban reform. Similarly, the Anglo-American syntheses of James Sheehan and David Blackbourn, although stressing South German

---

[31] Hans-Ulrich Wehler, *Bismarck und der Imperialismus* (Cologne, 1969).

[32] Martin Broszat, *The Hitler State: The Foundation and Development of the Internal Structure of the Third Reich* (London, 1981); and Manfred Funke, *Starker oder schwacher Diktator? Hitlers Herrschaft und die Deutschen* (Düsseldorf, 1989).

[33] Michael Prinz and Rainer Zitelmann, eds., *Nationalsozialismus und Modernisierung*, 2nd rev. ed. (Wiesbaden, 1994), esp. 335 ff.

[34] Charles S. Maier, *The Unmasterable Past: History, the Holocaust and German National Identity* (Cambridge, Mass., 1988); and Konrad H. Jarausch, "Removing the Nazi Stain? The Quarrel of the German Historians," *German Studies Review* 11 (1988): 285 ff.

[35] Hans-Ulrich Wehler, *Deutsche Gesellschaftsgeschichte 1700–1815* (Munich, 1987), 5 ff, 531 ff. Cf. Jonathan Sperber, "Master Narratives of German History," *Central European History* 24 (1991): 69 ff, and "German Master Narratives: The Sequel," *Central European History* 29 (1996): 107 ff.

and Catholic developments, implicitly remained tied to a modernization view.[36]

Although its ascendancy could never be complete in a pluralist setting, the exceptionalism thesis gradually succeeded in creating a critical view of the German past that was shared by a wider intellectual public. While traditional Catholic and political versions of historiography continued to survive, the Bielefeld fusion of analytical argumentation, modernization theory, and Western orientation provided innovative impulses, intellectual coherence, and polemical vigor that proved well nigh irresistible. The generational rebellion and the reform climate of the social-liberal coalition also encouraged in the public a search for historical justifications for extending the benefits of the welfare state. Eventually, progressive journalists in *Die Zeit* or *Der Spiegel*, but also radio and TV commentators, were attracted to the paradigm of historical social science, giving it a currency beyond academe.[37] In due course, these efforts helped produce a Western-oriented, democratic memory culture in the FRG that took a remarkably self-critical view of the failures of the German past. Ironically, the *Sonderweg* thesis ultimately helped end German exceptionalism by serving as "an essential part of a new policy agenda, directed toward returning Germany to the circle of the civilized, free and peaceful nations."[38]

The Postmodernist Shift

During the 1980s unexpected economic transformations and cultural shifts appeared to announce the end of modernity as a distinctive, two-century long era. The oil shocks, high-tech developments, and the rise of the service sector eroded the patterns of high industrialism and moved toward what some sociologists came to call a "postindustrial

[36] Thomas Nipperdey, *Deutsche Geschichte 1800–1866: Bürgerwelt und starker Staat* (Munich, 1983), and *Deutsche Geschichte 1866–1918* (Munich, 1990). See also James J. Sheehan, *Germany 1770–1866* (New York, 1989); David Blackbourn, *The Long Nineteenth Century: A History of Germany, 1780–1918* (New York, 1998), and Wolfgang Hardtwig and Harm Hinrich Brandt, eds., *Deutschlands Weg in die Moderne. Politik, Gesellschaft und Kultur im 19. Jahrhundert* (Munich, 1993).

[37] Kocka, "Nach dem Ende des Sonderwegs," 373 ff. See Also Thomas Welskopp, "Identität ex negativo—Der 'deutsche Sonderweg' als Meistererzählung in der bundesdeutschen Geschichtswissenschaft nach 1945," forthcoming in *Die historische Meistererzählung in Deutschland*.

[38] Kurt Sontheimer, *Deutscher Sonderweg—Mythos oder Realität? Kolloquium des Instituts für Zeitgeschichte* (Munich, 1982), 30 ff. See also Bernd Faulenbach, "Überwindung des 'deutschen Sonderweges'? Zur politischen Kultur der Deutschen seit dem Zweiten Weltkrieg," *Aus Politik und Zeitgeschichte* (1998) no. 51: 11 ff.

society." At the same time, architects, filmmakers, and other creative spirits began to push beyond the functionalist taste of high modernism and experiment with fragments of style and collages from different epochs, developing a "postmodern" citationality. In philosophy and linguistic theory, such French thinkers as Foucault, Derrida, and Lyotard started to question canons, forms of representation, and standards of objectivity, dissolving rationalist consciousness into a poststructuralist uncertainty. Finally, in politics the New Social Movements began to criticize the ecological and human costs of science, seeing modernity not as the solution but rather as the source of the problem. In Germany, this multidimensional onslaught made less headway than in America since such leading thinkers as Jürgen Habermas defended the legacy of the Enlightenment as a source of social rationality, clinging to modernity as an "unfinished project."[39]

The first critique of the *Sonderweg* thesis came from an unlikely quarter—two young British historians who disagreed with the implied use of their country's past as positive standard. The critique of the idealization of the West by its own scholars, Geoff Eley and David Blackbourn, whose politics were clearly on the Left as well, caught the Bielefeld school completely off guard, provoking a furious defense of its negative exceptionalism. On the basis of examples from urban self-government to cultural history, these Gramsciite critics pointed out that the Central European *Bürgertum* was much more powerful than Wehler had allowed, and that one might talk about a bourgeoisification of the nobility instead. Behind Eley's and Blackbourn's objections lay a self-critical view of British history as repressive of the working class, the Celtic fringe in Ireland, and of other races in the worldwide British Empire, which made it a dubious point of reference. In a wider European perspective, German industrialization did not look nearly as exceptional as the first industrial breakthrough in England, since it seemed to follow an intermediary pattern of imported economic development, typical of countries on the continent.[40]

Another challenge to the structuralist school developed from an internal group of everyday historians, inspired by the environmentalist, pacifist, or feminist currents of the 1980s. Modeled on the British history workshop movement, these alternative *Geschichtswerkstätten* reached out to interested laymen who wanted to reconstruct popular

---

[39] Wolfgang Welsch, *Unsere postmoderne Moderne*, 4th printing (Berlin, 1993); and Wolfgang Welsch, ed., *Wege aus der Moderne. Schlüsseltexte der Postmoderne Diskussion* (Berlin, 1994).

[40] Thomas Nipperdey, "1933 und die Kontinuität der deutschen Geschichte," *Historische Zeitschrift* 227 (1978): 86–111. Cf. David Blackbourn and Geoff Eley, *The Peculiarities of German History: Bourgeois Society and Politics in 19th Century Germany* (Oxford, 1984).

lives, for example, under the Third Reich. In its more sophisticated variants this *Alltagsgeschichte*, headquartered at the Max Planck Institute for History in Göttingen, drew on French and American anthropological discussions in hoping to write a microhistory of ordinary people. Alf Lüdtke accused the reigning *Gesellschaftsgeschichte* of ignoring individual agency, overlooking the stubborn efforts of working people to determine their own lives, and not paying any attention to the shape of experiences that could only be recovered by oral history. The structuralists, in turn, charged their critics with pursuing "political activism," lacking broader interpretations, and romanticizing ordinary people. In the long run, the scholarly critique of the everyday historians, nonetheless, made considerable headway since it inspired successful exhibitions, city walks, and local histories.[41]

Influenced by Critical Theory, yet other intellectuals began to question the modernization perspective by pointing to dangerous pathologies of modernity. In his provocative overview of the Weimar Republic, Detlef Peukert explained the rise of the Nazis as backlash against the excesses of modernism, and pointed to inherent limits of attempts to provide participation and security, suggesting scientific sources of prejudice.[42] Similarly, the Polish philosopher Zygmund Baumann rejected the "exoticizing" of the Nazi's mass murder via anti-Semitism or German exceptionalism: "The Holocaust was conceived and implemented in the middle of a modern, rational society . . . and must, therefore, be considered as a problem of this society, civilization, and culture." Modernity was implicated through the scientific guise of racism, which justified the annihilation of inferior life; it was also present through the bureaucratic state, which provided the efficient organization of the killing; and it was instrumental in the use of advanced technology, such as poison gas, to implement the mass extermination.[43] This radical revision raised a disturbing question: If the Holocaust was a product of modernity, could that flawed project remain a standard for judging the failures of German historical development?

The gradual seepage of French theory across the Rhine further undermined the hegemony of historical social science as an approach to

---

[41] Thomas Lindenberger and Michael Wildt, "Radikale Pluralität: Geschichtswerkstätten als praktische Wissenschaftskritik," *Archiv für Sozialgeschichte* 29 (1989): 393–411. See also Alf Lüdtke, ed., *The History of Everyday Life: Reconstructing Historical Experiences and Ways of Life* (Princeton, 1995).

[42] Detlef Peukert, *The Weimar Republic: The Crisis of Classical Modernity* (New York, 1992), and *Max Webers Diagnose der Moderne*, 102 ff.

[43] Zygmund Baumann, *Dialektik der Ordnung. Die Moderne und der Holocaust* (Hamburg, 1992), 10 ff, and *Moderne und Ambivalenz. Das Ende der Eindeutigkeit* (Hamburg, 1992).

the past. While the story of the "linguistic turn" has been told else-where,[44] it is important to recall the solvent effect of deconstruction upon the structural realism of the Bielefeld school, since the questioning of referentiality imperiled the entire edifice of historical social science. The attack on metanarratives implicated a *Sonderweg* thesis that purported to offer a general account of German historical development during the last two hundred years. Finally, the critique of modernity as disciplining the individual and destructive of community also corroded the modernization perspective behind it. No wonder that progressive German historians and their American allies reacted with alarm, denounced such theorizing as neoromantic, and invoked the Holocaust as ultimate defense of objectivity in historical scholarship.[45] In contrast to the interest in poststructuralist impulses in the United States, where a pragmatic attitude toward their interpretative potential seemed to be developing, the representatives of historical social science in Germany reacted rather defensively.

The methodological shift toward the new cultural history has pushed beyond the limits of the Bielefeld approach. Influenced by Franco-American examples, younger historians during the 1990s turned to cultural topics, be they the high *Kultur* of the cultivated or the popular culture of the media. At the same time, venturesome spirits started to probe culture in an anthropological sense, looking at life-worlds, value structures, and forms of symbolic representation in the past to open up new subjects such as the gender dimension of the dueling code. Many scholars began reflecting on questions of meaning, patterns of experience, or shapes of memory to recover the subjective aspects of the past. The cultural turn finally encouraged greater attention to the issue of individual guilt[46] for NS-crimes or the need to address the silence of its own academic teachers which the structuralists had largely ignored.[47]

---

[44] See the special issue of *Central European History*, ed. Michael Geyer and Konrad H. Jarausch, on the postmodern challenge, volume 22 (1989); and Ute Daniel, "Clio unter Kulturschock. Zu den aktuellen Debatten der Geschichtswissenschaft," *Geschichte in Wissenschaft und Unterricht* 48 (1997): 195 ff, 259 ff.

[45] Kenneth Barkin, "Bismarck in a Postmodern Age," *German Studies Review* 18 (1995): 241 ff.; and Michael Geyer and Konrad Jarausch, "Great Men and Postmodern Ruptures: Overcoming the Belatedness of German Historiography," *German Studies Review* 18 (1995): 253 ff.

[46] Julius H. Schoeps, *Ein Volk von Mördern? Dokumentation zur Goldhagen Kontroverse um die Rolle der Deutschen im Holocaust* (Hamburg, 1996). Cf. Dirk A. Moses, "Structure and Agency in the Holocaust: Daniel J. Goldhagen and his Critics," *History and Theory* 37 (1998), 194 ff.

[47] See Winfried Schulze and Otto Gerhard Oexle, eds., *Deutsche Historiker im Nationalsozialismus* (Frankfurt, 1999); Hans-Ulrich Wehler, "In den Fußstapfen der kämpfenden Wissenschaft," *Frankfurter Allgemeine Zeitung*, 4 January 1999; and Götz Aly, "Stakkato der Vertreibung, Pizzikato der Entlastung," *Frankfurter Allgemeine Zeitung*, 3 February 1999.

In this process, some rediscovered the grand tradition of German cultural studies at the turn of the twentieth century, culminating in Aby Warburg and Ernst Cassirer before it was cut off by the Nazi hordes.[48] Such authorities as Hans-Ulrich Wehler responded by embracing some elements, such as Pierre Bourdieu's stress on mentality, while excluding more troubling thinkers such as Foucault.[49]

Finally, the unexpected collapse of Communism and the surprising unification of the German successor states also weakened the hold of the social history of politics. The dramatic democratic awakening during the fall of 1989 suggested that politics did matter, that events could develop with breathtaking speed, and that outcomes were far from predictable by a structural analysis that privileged continuities. The fierce ideological debate about whether conciliation toward or confrontation with Communism had contributed more to its demise, threatened the moral superiority of the Left's cooperation with the SED in the name of peace. The revelation of the extent of the economic and moral bankruptcy of the second German dictatorship tarnished the entire Marxist project as an alternative road to modernity and triggered a Western triumphalism that ignored the shortcomings of its own system. The return of unity, in effect, ended the postwar exceptionalism of the German division, turning the Federal Republic once again into a somewhat shrunken, but recognizable nation-state. As their conservative critics gleefully pointed out, many of the progressive structural historians were unprepared for this turn of events and had difficulty adjusting their worldview to its consequences.[50]

Transcending
Gesellschaftsgeschichte

Ironically, the modernization perspective is, therefore, gradually joining the national narrative and its Marxist alternative as yet another discredited metanarrative of German history. Whereas the dominant national framing was shattered by the total defeat of Hitler's Reich in

[48] Christoph Conrad and Martina Kessel, eds., *Geschichte Schreiben in der Postmoderne. Beiträge zur aktuellen Debatte* (Stuttgart, 1994), and *Kultur und Geschichte. Neue Einblicke in eine alte Beziehung* (Stuttgart, 1998). See also Ute Daniel, *Kompendium Kulturgeschichte. Theorien, Praxis, Schlüsselwörter* (Frankfurt, 2001).

[49] Thomas Mergel and Thomas Welskopp, eds., *Geschichte zwischen Kultur und Gesellschaft. Beiträge zur Theoriedebatte* (Munich, 1997); and Wolfgang Hartdwig and Hans-Ulrich Wehler, eds., *Kulturgeschichte heute* (Göttingen, 1996).

[50] Jens Hacker, *Deutsche Irrtümer. Schönfärber und Helfershelfer der SED-Diktatur im Westen* (Berlin, 1992); and Jürgen Kocka, *Vereinigungskrise. Zur Geschichte der Gegenwart* (Göttingen, 1995).

1945 and the Eastern Communist competitor fell to the civic revolution of 1989, the Western paradigm of exceptionalism became redundant by its very success. In contrast to the ossification of the Marxist laws of dialectical materialism and class struggle, the more open-ended emphasis of historical social science on modernization and deviance stimulated intellectual questions that called for answers beyond the limits of the original approach. Since it did not repudiate the productive forces of capitalism or the representative structures of democracy, the liberal thrust of *Gesellschaftsgeschichte*, which sought to tame both in a social-democratic synthesis of security and freedom, has encouraged numerous critics of its own shortcomings.[51] While the agenda of the Bielefeld school managed to dominate the Western intellectual scene for an entire generation, its brand of retrospective *Ideologiekritik* has started to look increasingly anachronistic, like a remnant from the old Federal Republic.

The evident breakdown of the master narratives of German history raises the question of how to write a progressive history after the end of the *Sonderweg*. Can the "hegemonic paradigm" of "a critical historical analysis of society with a political and pedagogical intent" be updated somehow, or is a more radical departure necessary? The primary response of the social historians of politics has been a defense of the "proven perspective of modernization theory," a selective cooptation of everyday history and other critics, a rediscovery of the neglected cultural component of Max Weber's work, and an effort to expand their scope to include ideology, mentality, and the like.[52] But one may doubt that stretching the societal approach or empirically refining the *Sonderweg* perspective will take care of the problem, since radical proponents of the culturalist challenge, feminist critique, or postcolonialist assault reject liberal inclusion into a paradigm that they see as fundamentally flawed.[53] At present this battle is still undecided among German historians, with age as well as position favoring the former, and youth as well as imagination the latter. Yet the debates in the journal *Geschichte und Gesellschaft* as well as the electronic network H-Soz-u-Kult suggest that cultural impetus has gone too far to be reined in any longer.

[51] This interdependence between the various metanarratives deserves to be explored further. Cf. Welskopp, "Westbindung auf dem 'Sonderweg'," 205 ff.

[52] Hans-Ulrich Wehler, *Die Herausforderung der Kulturgeschichte* (Munich, 1998), and "Endlich im Westen," *ZEIT Punkte* (Hamburg, 1999), 1: 64 ff.; and Kocka, "Nach dem Ende des Sonderwegs," 373 ff.

[53] For a salvage effort by the successor generation, see Thomas Welskopp, "Die Sozialgeschichte der Väter. Grenzen und Perspektiven der Historischen Sozialwissenschaft," *Geschichte und Gesellschaft* 23 (1997): 173–98

Precisely through some of its shortcomings, the social history of politics may still provide suggestions for developing a more flexible approach. First, the comparative method, initiated by *Gesellschafts-geschichte*, ought to be stripped of its judgmental ballast and applied equally in all directions. Instead of just looking West, comparisons also need point East or in other directions to recover Germany's transitional position in the geographical, as well as sociocultural center of Europe. Since the West "is a highly ideological construct," references to it have tended to serve the purpose of pointing to German shortcomings, indicating the many ways of failing to live up to an idealized version of democracy, capitalism, or good taste. One need not fall back into a muddled *Magic Mountain* syndrome to emphasize that this perspective is itself a Cold War product because it ignores the many historic relationships with Central and Eastern Europe. From the direction of Poland or the Ukraine, civil society, the *Bürgertum*, or self-government begin to look much stronger in the German lands. Such a broadening of comparative references does not have to diminish the historical disasters of the twentieth century, many of which occurred in the East to begin with, but it might indicate why, in the second half of the century, the Germans could make such a speedy recovery.[54]

Second, German historians ought to take more seriously the fundamental ruptures of the twentieth century so as to recover a multiplicity of contending continuities. The Bielefeld school's ubiquitous stress on continuity tends to cover up the profound breaks produced by the caesuras of 1918, 1933, 1945, and 1989 that overturned political systems and individual lives. As oral history projects point out, it is the repeated upheavals and catastrophes that dominate personal recollections.[55] A teleological fixation on 1933, which has, if anything, deepened with recent Holocaust concerns, produces a misleading picture of developmental linearity. No doubt the emphasis on the structural origins of the Nazi seizure of power, the unleashing of World War II, and the crimes of genocide was necessary to uncover the antecedents of these events. But an exclusive focus on the Third Reich fails to appreciate a wealth of other trajectories, such as labor struggles, periodic

---

[54] Contrast Hartmut Kaelble's *Auf dem Weg zu einer europäischen Gesellschaft. Eine Sozial-geschichte Europas* (Munich, 1987), to Jürgen Kocka, Manfred Hildemeier, and Christoph Conrad, eds., *Europäische Zivilgesellschaft in Ost und West. Begriff, Geschichte, Chancen* (Frankfurt, 2000). Cf. also Philipp Gassert, "Der Westen als nationaler Mythos der Berliner Republik," *Frankfurter Rundschau*, 19 September 2001.

[55] Lutz Niethammer, ed., *Lebensgeschichte und Sozialstruktur im Ruhrgebiet, 1938–1960* (Berlin, 1983); as well as Lutz Niethammer, Alexander von Plato, and Dorothee Wierling, eds., *Die Volkseigene Erfahrung. Eine Analyse aus der Industrieprovinz der DDR* (Berlin, 1991).

religious revivals, the persistence of scientific work, the expansion of the economy, the development of popular consumption, or the spread of mass tourism, which cut across that regime. The recent sesquicentennial of the revolution of 1848 has recalled that the existence of a minority tradition of democratic aspirations in Central Europe is curiously absent from public memory.[56]

Third, a more balanced and yet critical approach to the German past needs to draw upon a wider range of methods. After the linguistic turn, interdisciplinarity can no longer mean borrowing theory fragments and concepts only from the social sciences, but also requires engaging the complex debates about the construction and deconstruction of texts in what has come to be called cultural studies.[57] The new cultural historians have pointed out that even within structural constraints, consciousness remains important; that is, crucial questions revolve around how people experience a situation and what they do as a result of this reflection. Instead of fastening primarily upon such collective abstractions as the state, such institutions as the university, or such organizations as trade unions, historians ought to look at the people who constitute them and analyze individual agency within these constraints. The interesting work of everyday historians also points out that the relationship between micro and macro perspectives needs to be further worked out to clarify how the smaller context is related to the larger. Without suggesting premature closure, it seems likely that a middle ground may be emerging in the realization that the social approach needs the cultural dimension and vice versa.[58]

Fourth, a post-*Sonderweg* history ought not to view modernity as an obvious end in itself but rather as a Janus-faced problem that needs to be historicized. Recent attempts to pin down the elusive phenomenon of "cultural modernism" have had some difficulty finding an identifiable set of traits or styles of such movements beyond the claim to being avant-garde.[59] The comparative modernization discussion has also shown the process to be more complex than initially expected and has started to question the linkages between capitalism and democracy by pointing out instances of rapid economic development in authoritarian structures, such as among the Little Tigers or China.[60] Moreover, the

[56] Nipperdey, "1933 und die Kontinuität der deutschen Geschichte," passim; and Wolfgang J. Mommsen, ed., *1848: Die ungewollte Revolution* (Frankfurt, 1998).

[57] See Andrew Pickel's remarks on interdisciplinarity in the postscript to the volume *After Unity: Reconfiguring German Identities* (Providence, 1997), 701 ff.

[58] Mergel and Welskopp, *Geschichte zwischen Kultur und Gesellschaft*, passim

[59] See notes 4 and 5, above.

[60] Thomas Mergel, "Geht es weiterhin voran? Die Modernisierungstheorie auf dem Wege zu einer Theorie der Moderne," in *Geschichte zwischen Kultur und Gesellschaft*, 203

Holocaust debate, the peace movement, and ecological criticism have produced shocking evidence of the pathologies of modernity in the misuse of science for killing or the abuse of technology for environmental degradation, thereby casting a dark shadow on what was once a shining hope.[61] Instead of simply being an example of a lack of modernity, the German case illustrates a dangerous trajectory of modern possibilities from scientific discoveries to unspeakable crimes. Only a less deterministic and sanguine understanding of the meanings of "modern" can come to terms with the profoundly ambivalent consequences of the industrial era.

Finally, a new cultural history of politics also needs a broadened understanding of the Enlightenment legacy. The moral condemnation of German deviance by the historians of society was rooted in a rationalist understanding of the *Aufklärung* as a Habermasian project of public debate for the sake of human progress. Focused primarily on class inequalities, partisans of the Bielefeld school have claimed, in effect, that its brand of social history is the only method appropriate for an emancipatory history.[62] Some postmodernist historians criticize this understanding as being too narrow in substantive terms since during the past two centuries the practice of this purportedly universal vision has tended to be limited to white European males. Moreover, they maintain that linguistic and cultural approaches are essential to write the history of gender, minorities, and other forms of discrimination that may not just be only economic but also cultural. If one does not want to have the entire notion of human rights rejected as imperialist Western construction, it is necessary to reflect on the historical shortcomings of its practice and further to include hitherto neglected groups. A more self-critical understanding suggests that the Enlightenment impulse cannot be frozen into one particular political or methodological form but needs to continue to evolve to challenge new forms of injustice.[63]

Returning the debate to the fin-de-siècle uncertainties of a century ago, the eclipse of the grand narratives, nonetheless, presents an opportunity for a keener appreciation of the diversity of German pasts. With research interests moving beyond the nation-state, class, or soci-

---

ff. For another effort to defend the theory, see Johannes Berger, "Modernisierung und Modernisierungstheorie," as well as Wolfgang Zapf, "Die Modernisierungstheorie und unterschiedliche Pfade der gesellschaftlichen Entwicklung," in *Leviathan* 24 (1996): 7 ff.

[61] Contrast notes 38 and 39, above, to Ulrich Beck, *Risk Society: Towards a New Modernity* (London, 1992), and Volker Hildebrandt, *Epochenumbruch in der Moderne. Eine Kontroverse zwischen Robert Kurz und Ulrich Beck* (Münster, 1996).

[62] See Barkin, "Bismarck in a Postmodern Age," 241 ff.

[63] Jürgen Kocka, *Geschichte als Aufklärung. Aufsätze* (Göttingen, 1989). Cf. Lynn Hunt, *The French Revolution and Human Rights: A Brief Documentary History* (Boston, 1996).

ety as chief topics, an astounding multiplicity of individuals and groupings in Central Europe can return to the forefront of historical reconstruction. With a more balanced set of comparisons, the similarities as well as differences between the German case and Western or Eastern European patterns of development will become more apparent. With less emphasis on continuities, the enormity of the various system ruptures in the past century can come into focus so that the caesuras no longer serve as beginning or end, but are themselves subject to analysis. With a more plural set of methods, the dialectical interplay of structures and consciousness can become clearer and individual experience as well as agency be reclaimed from impersonal forces. With a more problematic sense of modernity, the process of modernization can once again become a subject of historical exploration in all of its troubling paradoxes. Instead of looking for new metanarratives such as European or global history, totalitarianism, or the Holocaust to put the various pieces back together, historians ought to follow Weber's injunction to face unsettlement and explore various directions for a while.[64]

The crumbling of the competing frameworks also calls for a new style of writing plural, interdependent narratives that acknowledges the fragmentation of the German past, a shattering that has been previously ignored.[65] Such a change of perspective would involve not just rebalancing the stress on negative continuities with the addition of more positive traditions, but also a realization of the multiplicity of lines of potential development and an analysis of their mutual entanglement.[66] Starting from the incoherence of the subject would mean stressing fracturing over wholeness, exploring subjectivity rather than structural determinants, and emphasizing difference instead of uniformity. In contrast to presuming a unified pattern, scholars ought to look more closely at the pieces of the German debris in order to figure out how they once fitted together and what broke them apart. The immense amount of suffering cries out for more sensitivity to people's

---

[64] Rainer Hudemann, Harmut Kaelble, and Klaus Schwabe, eds., *Europa im Blick der Historiker* (Munich 1995), Beiheft 25 of the *Historische Zeitschrift*; Charles Bright and Michael Geyer, "World History in a Global Age," *American Historical Review* 100 (1995), 1034–60; Eckhard Jesse, ed., *Totalitarismus im 20. Jahrhundert. Eine Bilanz der internationalen Forschung* (Baden-Baden, 1996); and Peter Novick, *The Holocaust in American Life* (Boston, 1999).

[65] Konrad H. Jarausch, "Die Krise der nationalen Meistererzählungen. Ein Plädoyer für plurale, interdependente Narrativen," in *Die historische Meistererzählung in Deutschland*. Cf. also Manfred Hettling, "Der Mythos des kurzen 20. Jahrhunderts," *Saeculum* 49 (1998), 327–45.

[66] Grebing, *Der deutsche Sonderweg*, 199 f.

experiences, their rationalizations, and nightmare memories. And the murderous effort to eradicate otherness compels greater scrutiny of the actual practice of the many forms of religious, sexual, regional, and ethnic diversity.[67] The result of such an effort need not be incoherence since these different histories intersect, conflict, and at times even converge on a shared, but distinctively interpreted sense of Germanness.

The shape of the German histories, written with dialogical reference to the Berlin Republic, remains indistinct because an overriding agenda, comparable to the cultural revolution of the late 1960s, has yet to emerge. If the pronouncements of the Schroeder-Fischer government of 1998 are any indication, its tenor is likely to be somewhat contradictory. On the one hand, there seems to be a greater willingness to acknowledge German crimes, pay restitution for economic exploitation or slave labor, and create a Holocaust memorial in Berlin. On the other hand, there is also a stronger sense of pride in postwar accomplishments, an impatience with foreign invocations of guilt, and more assertiveness in pursuit of German interests. How the popular desire for an end to self-incrimination, evident in Martin Walser's controversial speech on receiving the peace prize of German publishing, might be reconciled with the intellectual imperative of memory, which animated Ignatz Bubis' alarmist reply, remains to be seen.[68] Conservative attacks upon the proclivity to violence among the youthful rebels of the late 1960s have meanwhile initiated a media controversy about the history of the Federal Republic, adding a third dimension to debates about the past.[69]

The beginning of the new century, therefore, presents exciting opportunities as well as profound uncertainties to German historians because the master narratives have crumbled and no new pattern has yet taken their place. On the one hand, defenses of modernity, such as sociologist Ulrich Beck's revisionist proposal of "reflexive modernization," are likely to continue since modernity is such a cultural icon for German progressives.[70] On the other hand, the initial excitement about the post-

---

[67] Till van Rahden, "Juden und andere Breslauer" (Ph.D.dissertation, Bielefeld, 1999); and Robert Garris "Becoming German: Immigration, Conformity, and Identity Politics in Wilhelmian Berlin, 1880–1914" (Ph.D. dissertation, Chapel Hill, 1998).

[68] Martin Walser, "Erfahrungen beim Verfassen einer Sonntagsrede," *Börsenblatt des deutschen Buchhandels*, 13 October 1998, 17 ff. See also Karl Heinz Bohrer, "Schuldkultur oder Schamkultur," *Neue Züricher Zeitung*, 12 / 13 December 1998; and Reinhard Mohr, "Total normal?" *Der Spiegel* (1998) no. 49: 40 ff.

[69] Konrad H. Jarausch, "Critical Memory and Civil Society: The Impact of the Sixties on German Debates about the Past" (MS, Berlin, 2001).

[70] Ulrich Beck, *Reflexive Modernisierung* (Frankfurt, 1995), and *Risikogesellschaft. Auf dem Weg in eine andere Moderne* (Frankfurt, 1996).

modernist shift has dissipated, and some American intellectuals are wondering if they have not arrived at post-postmodernity. In a humorous fashion an anniversary performance, juxtaposing old cabaret programs of the West Berlin *Insulaner* and the East Berlin *Distel*, illustrates a playful distancing from such theory debates by irreverently juxtaposing slogans, scenes, and sequences from the various regimes. With the Holocaust serving as warning against an easy forgetting, the arguments over how to arrange the shattered pieces of the German past will, therefore, need to continue in a somewhat freer vein.[71]

---

[71] Sabine Zurmühl, ed., *'Man trifft sich.' Die Distel und die Insulaner* (Berlin, 1998); Norbert Frei, "Das Erbe der Mörder," *ZEIT Punkte*, vol. 1 (Hamburg, 1999), 68 ff.; and "Wir wollen mit uns ins reine kommen," interview with Lutz Niethammer in *Der Spiegel* (1999) no. 5: 64 ff.

PART II

RECONSTITUTING
GERMAN HISTORIES

4

War, Genocide,
Extermination: The War
against the Jews in an
Era of World Wars

Whatever else may be said about the Germans and their history,
they will be remembered for the ferocity with which they fought two
world wars and the depravity that led them to the premeditated attempt of murdering any and all Jews in their sphere of power. The
determination with which these wars were fought and the radical nature of the ambition to subordinate a continent, to enslave a good part
of its population, and to exterminate a people in its entirety mark the
twentieth century. We may close our eyes before the fury of the age or
hide its German mark. We may want to convince ourselves that an ill-
fated concatenation of circumstances or the delusion of fanatics
brought about the unhappy outcome. Moreover, looked at from a
greater distance, this particular "man-made mass death" may yet lose
its pungent sights and smells, its nightmarish memories.[1] It may yet
become another slaughter-bench in a human history that bursts with
unprecedented man-made catastrophe—each one unprecedented in

[1] Edith Wyschogrod, *Spirit in Ashes: Hegel, Heidegger, and Man-Made Mass Death* (New
Haven, 1985).

their time but recollected in a long history of human catastrophe. Still, the mark of having unleashed wars that challenge the very foundation of civility and the stain of having plotted the murder of every person of Jewish descent will not disappear. As far as the twentieth century is concerned, the Germans will be universally remembered for their savagery, whatever else they may have done.

This violent past does not and will not go away.[2] To be sure, recollections of war and genocide generally go through cycles of disavowal, intense concern, and disinterest, and there is no reason to assume that war and genocide in twentieth-century Europe will follow a different pattern. The very depth of public and scholarly engagement with the history of the two world wars and the belated but determined concentration on the deliberate slaughter of the Jews cannot be expected to last. But the cyclical nature of historical consciousness is not a good indicator for the continuing presence of this particular past. Why? Not because the events were unique, the war grander, the violence more villainous than those of other wars, or the murder of the Jews, the Holocaust, distinct from all other genocide.[3] Nor can we account for the persistence of recollection with the argument that genocide and war are the essence and destiny of being German or, for that matter, the founding memory of postwar national identity—and thus hardwired into national history.[4] Instead, the recollection of war and genocide will stay alive, first, because it is tied neither to any single source nor to any one national history. It has become part of a global historical record that is not controlled by a single master. Second, the effects of war and genocide are so tangible in the after-histories of Europe, and indeed the world, that even if its causes were to be forgotten the consequences would remain traceable.

[2] The phrase "the past does not go away" was famously coined by Ernst Nolte (*Das Vergehen der Vergangenheit. Antwort an meine Kritiker im sogenannten Historikerstreit* [Berlin, 1989]). Apparently, he wanted to suggest that although war and holocaust will not go away, they can be made to disappear by making them a response to internal and external provocation by Communists and Jews, respectively.

[3] This argument is made most impressively by Steven T. Katz, *The Holocaust in Historical Context* (New York, 1993).

[4] This argument sounds strange if put into a single sentence, but it reflects two widely argued convictions. As far as Germans are concerned, it states that ever since a certain moment in the making of the German nation (Luther, Kant and Fichte, Wagner), they were set on a course of aggressive war and mass murder. As far as Jewish victims are concerned, it expresses the belief, prominent in Judaic orthodoxies, that genocide was another instance in a history of kurban that began with the destruction of the Temple. There are similar Christian accounts, both Orthodox and Catholic, that again precede the Holocaust. See, for example, Brian Porter, *When Nations Began to Hate: Imagining Modern Politics in Nineteenth-Century Poland* (New York, 2000).

These are tall claims, but they are not without reason. Take the deep fear that the memory of genocidal war may be forgotten or disappear in postwar recovery and well-being, or, alternatively, that it may be submerged in (German and Allied) war talk.[5] Or consider the waves of concern that with war and genocide out of sight, they may be out of mind as well, or that with memory and historical recollection being commercialized and trivialized, they would become building blocks for all manner of fantastic fabrications. These concerns were and are real enough. German war talk about the honor and integrity of Wehrmacht soldiers did not yield without contestation.[6] Western memory still finds it difficult, despite captivating documentaries, to think of the eastern war as the crucial battle front. The fictitious and occasionally fake personal recollections of war and Holocaust will require much more serious debate because, for better or worse, they have become part and parcel of historical memory.[7] But the postwar fear of forgetting that haunted survivors proved to be unfounded. It is obviated not just by a huge and sprawling historiography, but also by the emergence of a memorial art, notwithstanding doubts about the representability of war and genocide.[8] The most striking thing about a half-century of recollection is the depth and breadth of the historical record and the very multiplicity of representations and histories.[9] This very diversity of memory and history is the single most important guarantee against forgetting.

In a world of proliferating national histories, the recollections of war and genocide have escaped national confines. The history of German war and genocide is written and told everywhere. It exists as a record of German thoughts and actions as well as in the memory and history of the victims of German violence. Both are worked over by an international scholarship and addressed to a multi-national audience. And this record has come to be used as a reference point against which other manmade mass death is held. Nobody can foretell, and historians have not really begun to think about, how this proliferation of per-

[5] Robert G. Moeller, *War Stories: The Search for a Usable Past in the Federal Republic of Germany* (Berkeley, 2001).

[6] Hamburger Institut für Sozialforschung, ed., *Besucher einer Ausstellung. Die Ausstellung "Vernichtungskrieg. Verbrechen der Wehrmacht 1941–1944" in Interview und Gespräch* (Hamburg, 1998).

[7] The cause celèbre is Binjamin Wilkomirski, *Fragments: Memories of a Wartime Childhood*, trans. Carol Brown Janeway (New York, 1996).

[8] James E. Young, *At Memory's Edge: After-Images of the Holocaust in Contemporary Art and Architecture* (New Haven, 2000).

[9] On the Holocaust as global memory, see Yehuda Bauer, *Rethinking the Holocaust* (New Haven, 2001).

spectives will be sorted out. What we tend to emphasize are the negative effects. German apologists of genocide, as opposed to the outright
holocaust deniers, have tended to drown out German deeds in a universality of violence.[10] By the same token, the multiplication of the record of victimizations has led to an ugly "competition of victims," and
some scholarship seems to like it that way.[11] Various scholars, pundits,
and audiences have protested against what they perceive as the Americanization of the Holocaust.[12] Before we enter such debates, however,
we should note the truly remarkable outcome of a half-century's historical recollection. German history has become part of a web of global
memory articulated worldwide. It echoes in the histories of Germans,
of those who fought them, of those who were the victims of their violence, and of all those who use these accounts as a reference in their
own histories.

The grandest achievement of German historiography is its consider-
ation of this egregious loss of autonomy over the national past as a
chance for a new cosmopolitanism of scholarship and national memory. A German history of extreme violence has come to exist that, in
the same breath, tells of German agency and reclaims the memory and
history of its victims. Induced only in part by total defeat, Germans
have turned against their past in a most remarkable process of conversion that has opened a space in German history for its victims. This is
cosmopolitanism in the wake of genocidal war because the postwar
German recollection, in acknowledging the worldwide echoes of these
German deeds, created a testimonial to the life of all those whom war
and genocide meant to vanquish.[13]

The second argument about the consequences of war and genocide
and the imprint they leave is more difficult, not the least because historians have not found a good way of dealing with loss. Victimization,
yes, but irretrievable loss, no. History as a discipline is life-affirming
and tends to contemplate (mass) death only inasmuch as it is overcome
in the continuity of individual survivors, the family, the nation, the
human species, life itself. Historians dwell on war and genocide as survivors on a far shore looking back. In this assertion of, and insistence
on, a new beginning, historical scholarship reflects a broader public

[10] This, in any case, was Habermas' claim, which started the Historikerstreit. Jürgen
Habermas, *Eine Art Schadensabwicklung* (Frankfurt am Main, 1987).

[11] Jean-Michel Chaumont, *La concurrence des victimes: génocide, identité, reconnaissance*
(Paris, 1997).

[12] Peter Novick, *The Holocaust in American Life* (Boston, 1999).

[13] Harold Marcuse, *Legacies of Dachau: The Uses and Abuses of a Concentration Camp,
1933–2001*(Cambridge, 2001).

sentiment. Would it not seem to be high time to leave this entire catastrophe behind? It is not a matter of forgetting but of putting it aside and storing it—for which the German language has the tantalizing word *"aufheben,"* with its triple meaning of undoing, laying aside, and preserving—or, suitable for more commercial tastes, writing if off, entering it in the debit column of history. Why stay marooned in so sinister a nightmare?

Because extreme acts of violence must be recalled in ever-renewed catharsis, counsels civilizational wisdom. Because loss has irreversibly altered the course of German and European history, is perhaps the more palatable answer for historians. This is to argue that what twentieth-century German and European histories have become cannot be extrapolated, without caesura, from what they have been. Life continued and survivors picked up the pieces, but none of them picked them up quite where they left off and what they picked up was not what they had left behind. The gap that opens is made from irretrievable loss. The experience and the memory gained are irreversibly tainted with genocidal violence.

We have yet to fathom what the death of tens of millions of people in Central and Eastern Europe and Russia, the un- and re-settlement of countless numbers of people (quite apart from more familiar border and regime changes), and the destruction of an old urban landscape did to European civilization. Of all the desiderata in the historical record, these weigh most heavily. They are the dark matter of twentieth-century history—the history of an absence, a deafening silence, yet to be recovered. We can say with more insight and knowledge that the destruction of the great variety of Jewish communities throughout Europe, culminating in the deliberate murder of all Jews, was, and is, an irreversible loss for both Jews and gentiles. While true for all of Europe, the effect of this loss pertains most particularly to Jewish-German culture because so much of what is quintessentially modern in German culture emerged out of German-Jewish struggles for emancipation, equality, and recognition. And inasmuch as these struggles have disastrously failed, the entire project of an enlightened multi-nation of citizens has become suspect.[14] Not that the loss of trust cannot be repaired, or that the trauma of violence and uprooting cannot be overcome. But the disenchantment over the German betrayal of civilization, as an effect of the actual loss, will remain—and thus this genocide casts its

---

[14] Anson Rabinbach, *In the Shadow of Catastrophe: German Intellectuals between Apocalypse and Enlightenment* (Berkeley, 1997); and Steven E. Aschheim, *Culture and Catastrophe: German and Jewish Confrontations with National Socialism and Other Crises* (New York, 1996).

spell over the living, is passed on to future generations, and moves from place to place.

In these losses and their effects we encounter a history that broke apart in extirpation and genocide. They mark the tear that separates one state of the past from another. This tear is the reason why German and European histories are tied to their twentieth-century nightmares, much as postwar Jewish history will remain bound to the European *galut* and its destruction. This is also the reason why history, although life-affirming in principle, will always be concerned with the history of manmade mass death—the event, its prehistory and afterhistory of loss, and the remaking of a civilization.

Inasmuch as historiography has dealt with these challenges of a globalization of the historical record on the one hand and of the irreversibility of loss for Europe on the other, it has done so in an unselfconscious manner. Its primary and overwhelming concern has been succinctly and truthfully to show and tell what happened. The best postwar history on war and genocide was investigative in nature. The difficulties were extraordinary and it took a long time until historians began doing what they reputably do best: to reconstruct from sources and their traces a historical record of the res gestae of violent times. There was a paucity of what traditionally would have been considered crucial records of decisions and actions that turned out to be an intrinsic feature of the genocidal regime. Also, this was a history in which the main actors could not be trusted to tell the truth, permitting deception—such as the double-talk surrounding war crimes and murder—to creep into the very process of recording actions and events. Moreover, it was a history in which the sheer scale of events threatened to overwhelm historians. Yet a rich and diverse chronology of events, a careful, if controversial, assessment of agency and agents, and a caring recollection of the life, suffering, and death of victims, has emerged as the result of evermore painstaking, detailed, and encompassing research and of the innovative preservation of many facets of the record.

The very best accounts of the Holocaust, like Browning's *Ordinary Men*, Friedländer's *Nazi Germany and the Jews*, Kaplan's *Between Dignity and Despair*, or Bartov's *Murder in Our Midst*, as well as the recent wave of German scholarship represented in Herbert's *National Socialist Extermination Policies*, stay close to the ground.[15] The worst narratives single-

---

[15] Chistopher R. Browning. *Ordinary Men: Reserve Police Batallion 101 and the Final Solution in Poland* (New York, 1993); Saul Friedländer, *Nazi Germany and the Jews. Vol I: The Years of Persecution,1933–1939* (New York, 1997); Marion Kaplan, *Between Dignity and Despair: Jewish Life in Nazi Germany* (New York, 1998); and Ulrich Herbert, ed., *National Socialist Extermination Policies: Contemporary German Perspectives and Controversies* (New York, 2000).

mindedly drive home an argument that, even though it is half right, as was the case with Goldhagen's *Willing Executioners*, does injustice to the event and its subjects.[16] The study of war, and of genocidal war, in particular, still suffers from the narrow-mindedness of most military history, especially in the English-speaking world. It is also held back by the relative inaccessibility and, perhaps even more, the unfamiliarity with Soviet and Eastern European records. Still, works in the more traditional manner of military history—such as Beevor's work on *Stalingrad*, studies on genocidal war commissioned by the Militärgeschichtliche Forschungsamt, or new works on German occupation such as Mazower's *Inside Hitler's Greece* or Gerlach's *Kalkulierte Morde*—have set new standards.[17] If initially it seemed that American historians were in the lead, it is now British, Israeli, and German scholars who are doing some of the most important work. "We Now Know," as John Lewis Gaddis put it in the context of the Cold War, and can begin to understand what happened, when, and where—not always with sufficient clarity and detail, and only rarely with a multiple perspective on all people implicated in or drawn into war and genocide, but with enough evidence to reject out-of-hand any and all efforts to deny the facts of genocidal war and the Holocaust.[18] In this sense, historiography has lived up to its first and most important charge.

Historiography has done less well with "the insertion of the 'Final Solution' into a global historical interpretation"[19] and putting World War II, as well as the age of wars, into the context of a general history. There are several interrelated problems. The first of these problems concerns the tendency among historians to slice up an era of extreme violence into its component parts. There is good reason, both empirical and conceptual, why one must distinguish between war, genocide, and the Holocaust, but it makes no sense to keep them apart once their distinguishing features are recognized. Second, because the violence that makes up this era is not seen in its composite gestalt, the effort to make sense of any one aspect (war, genocide, or holocaust), irrespec-

---

[16] Daniel Jonah Goldhagen, *Hitler's Willing Executioners: Ordinary Germans and the Holocaust* (New York, 1996).

[17] See the ten-volume series, *Das Deutsche Reich und der Zweite Weltkrieg*, [English] ed. Militärgeschichtliches Forschungsamt (New York, 1990–), of which six volumes have been completed; Mark Mazower, *Inside Hitler's Greece: The Experience of Occupation 1941–1944* (New Haven, 1993); and Christian Gerlach, *Kalkulierte Morde. Die deutsche Wirtschafts- und Vernichtungspolitik in Weissrussland 1941 bis 1944* (Hamburg, 1999).

[18] Richard J. Evans, *Lying about Hitler: History, Holocaust, and the David Irving Trial* (New York, 2001).

[19] Saul Friedländer, "The 'Final Solution': On the Unease in Historical Interpretation," in Saul Friedländer, ed., *Memory, History, and the Extermination of the Jews of Europe* (Bloomington, 1993), 102–16, here 104.

tive of the others, must fall short. As a result of such parsing, historians are not even capable of handling straightforward issues such as the nature of Allied bombing in comparison with German genocide. Third, before we can begin putting the Holocaust into a global perspective, we would do well to put it into the context of a genocidal war with global effects. In turn, before trying to make sense of the origins and causes of genocide, we need to reflect on the nature of war and of German war in particular—without folding one into the other indiscriminately. This puts a great deal of weight on the weakest link in historiography. Despite formidable studies such as Gerhard Weinberg's *A World at Arms*, we understand neither the conduct of war in this particular age nor its place in history.[20] Hence, genocide and the Holocaust remain erratic blocks in the historiography of war, even while they epitomize the age of war in public memory.

Caught in investigating one or the other element of extreme violence, historians hesitate to explore the time and place, the history, of this era of wars. In the end, it comes down to great men or crazy ideas. Both had their place, but any interpretation could clearly profit from putting them into the context of the violent remaking of European social and political order in a cauldron of resettlement, expulsion, ethnic cleansing, and exterminism.[21] Whether or not the cataclysmic remaking of social order is the *raison* of this violent era (replacing an older *raison d'état*), how we might possibly explain the peculiar grammar of twentieth-century European violence, and how exterminist ideologies find their place in this context is all largely unresolved.

The need for a "general" history has gained urgency with the change in generations, dramatized by the end of the Cold War. The moment is approaching when historians will write about this era of violence in the absence of the living testimony of eyewitnesses and survivors. Throughout the second half of the twentieth century, this memory gave the historical record an unsurpassed acuity and authority. That victims of genocide and mass murder—not in equal measure, but with great breadth—have spoken was one of the most stunning features of the postwar memory culture. Conversely, that the perpetrators could not hide and use their testimony to swing history in their favor set in motion a most remarkable reversal in which the history of war and genocide, even and especially among Germans, followed the lead of the victims. In the new post–Cold War world, however, histori-

---

[20] Gerhard L. Weinberg, *A World at Arms: A Global History of World War II* (Cambridge, UK, 1994).

[21] The most convincing starting point is Mark Mazower, *Dark Continent: Europe's Twentieth Century* (New York, 1999).

ans will have to shoulder the burden of recollecting a violent past in the absence of living testimony from survivors. They will be able to rely on memory cultures' and new media's recording and storing testimonies that have taken shape over the past half century, but these memories and testimonies themselves will need renewal for future generations—hence the concern for what a general history of German war and genocide might entail. What was the violent German "signature of the age?"[22]

Anti-Semitism, Civil War Ideology, and the Holocaust

"Holocaust" is the commonly used American name for the premeditated, deliberate, and systematic murder of any and all Jews in Germany and Nazi-occupied Europe between 1939–41 and 1945. The deliberation and foresight of this act of collective murder, the totality of its ambition, and the persistence and pervasiveness of its implications distinguish it from other genocides. It was the endpoint in a process of deepening and expanding exclusion and segregation that accelerated rapidly. German initiative merged with local actions across occupied Europe. It met opposition and resistance only intermittently—enough, though, to suggest that one could find everywhere people who made it their business to know about and counter the murderous design. Jews fought back, although Jewish communities were divided about the proper course of action. Their struggle was hampered by a lack of cooperation and countered by the systematicity of German action. Murder was initiated, organized, and committed by a very large, but nonetheless circumscribed group of perpetrators, acting on their own free will and mostly out of conviction, although people of all ranks, soldiers and civilians, were caught up and participated. These actions were condoned or, in any case, tolerated, by the vast majority of gentile Germans and Europeans. Approximately six million Jewish men, women, and children, out of a dispersed population of approximately nine million, were killed. Slightly more than half of them were exterminated in death camps such as Chelmno, Belzec, Sobibor, Treblinka, Majdanek, and Auschwitz. A few less than half of the victims were worked or marched to death, or starved, tortured, mutilated, strangled, stabbed, bludgeoned, or shot. Survivors suffered lasting physical and mental injury in addition to the loss of family and kin as well as property and

---

[22] Jan Philipp Remtsma. "Die 'Signatur des Jahrhunderts'—ein kataleptischer Irrtum?" *Mittelweg* 36, (1995), no. 5: 7–23.

citizenship. Escape did not provide shelter from trauma. The Holocaust destroyed thriving Jewish community cultures throughout continental Europe, especially in eastern Europe, and dramatically diminished the communities that survived. It undid more than a century of
struggle for equality, emancipation, and integration that had become
the signature of the modern nation-state in Europe, and cast doubt on
the very foundation of European civility.

The historiography of the Holocaust has been a fifty-year struggle
between what we deem right (that monstrous events have unequivocal
causes) and what historians encounter as a murky and multi-layered
process. Furthermore, it has become a struggle with the profound implications of systematic murder (what does it tell us about civility in
Europe?) and the contingent and transient nature of the event, with its
altogether sudden manifestation and its abrupt termination with German defeat. Historians are pulled between the poles of diffuse gesta-
tion of murder and the unequivocal nature of the deed, just as they
are caught between recognition of the universality of genocide and the
singularity of this particular act.

Their response has been to turn these opposites into rival interpretations. Initially, the debate focused on the German state and its transformation subsequent to Nazi seizure of power, with one side arguing for
a conspiracy of Nazi leadership to initiate their ideological program of
conquest and genocide, and the other side holding out for a process
of radicalization in a regime that relied on mass-mobilization for its
support.[23] Lately, these older debates have been overlaid by another
polarity. As the Holocaust has moved into the center of historiographic
attention, one group interprets the murderous act as an extreme variant of more general trends in Western society, be it the politics of imperial aggrandizement or schemes of social engineering and population
management (in short, biopolitics), whereas another group highlights
the power of beliefs, of a compelling world picture that captured significant elements of the population in the manner of mass seduction.[24]
One might call the former group "rationalists" because they argue,
with varying degrees of conviction, that the motivation for genocide
resulted from (putative) rational calculation, whereas the latter group

[23] See the now dated controversies in Lothar Kettenacker and Gerhard Hirschfeld,
eds., Der "Führerstaat", Mythos und Realität. Studien zur Struktur und Politik des Dritten
Reiches. The "Führer State," Myth and Reality: Studies on the Structure and Politics of the
Third Reich (Stuttgart, 1981).

[24] Compare Götz Aly, "Final Solution": Nazi Population Policy and the Murder of the European Jews, trans. Belinda Cooper and Allison Brown (London, 1999), to Michael Burleigh,
The Third Reich: A New History (New York, 2000).

can be labeled "idealists" in that they insist on the power of world-views and of sentiment. In a curious twist, the former identify calculation with the enlightenment, while the latter consider deeply held beliefs to be religious, with the confusing effect that we are confronted with a romantic enlightenment and an evil religion.

The genuine contribution of these recent debates to an understanding of the Holocaust is that both sides have come to think of Nazi genocide as the articulation of a world picture (whether rational or irrational) that aimed at appropriating and remaking the world, and, in this context, was capable and willing to make and unmake entire societies. The argument that the Holocaust is the outcome of deliberate action by identifiable groups of people to remake society and the world is compelling. Before we accept this understanding, however, it is worth spelling out the stakes. Why, one may ask, resort to a general argument about the making and unmaking of society when radical anti-Semitism serves as a sufficient explanation for the Holocaust? Is radical anti-Semitism or, perhaps, a uniquely German anti-Semitism not the better answer?[25] We do not think so. There is sound reason to distinguish the Holocaust within the context of a more encompassing genocidal politics of the Third Reich and, for that matter, among the universality of modern genocides. But the time and place of the Holocaust were set in a politics of war that aimed at (re)generating the body politic and remaking the world through violence. One without the other makes as little sense as a history of the Holocaust without both Germans and Jews.

It still remains embarrassing to recall how marginal anti-Semitism had been for much of the historiographic debate on the Third Reich. Not that anyone would have denied the fact of it, but anti-Semitic beliefs were carried along as "Nazi ideology" to be strategically placed rather than opened to scrutiny.[26] This has changed dramatically and for the better, although the change has also raised a whole series of new questions. Can we say that the Holocaust grew out of a long history of European-Christian anti-Semitism? Was German anti-Semitism somehow more virulent than other European anti-Semitism? Is it appropriate to speak of a concatenation of circumstances that catalyzed anti-Semitism into a deadly furor and, if so, what were they? Was it furor or cold-blooded calculation? Unequivocal answers are difficult to find, but they exist, even if they are fragmented.

---

[25] The signal contributions to this debate come from Dan Diner, *Beyond the Conceivable: Studies on Germany, Nazism, and the Holocaust* (Berkley, 2000).

[26] Typically Andreas Hillgruber, *Die Zerstörung Europas. Beiträge zur Weltkriegsepoche 1914 bis 1945* (Frankfurt, 1988).

Modern anti-Semitism (like its opposite, the movement for equal rights of Jews and, much more tentatively, recognition of Jewish community life and religious practice) was a product of the modern nation-state and grew out of an older (Christian) anti-Judaism. Both as sentiment and as grassroots movement, modern anti-Semitism waxed and waned throughout the long nineteenth century, and by the end, thrived on biological or racial thought.[27] This cast of thought was radicalized in the wake of World War I, in defeat, revolution, and postwar chaos.[28] The Judaeophobia of the postwar German Right developed a few peculiar features, none of them new, but extraordinary in their combination. The attribution of postwar chaos, and, more importantly, defeat and revolution to a Jewish conspiracy, and the obsession with Jewish sexuality and miscegenation as expressions of a debilitating subversion of the body social (and with it the call for the extirpation of the Jews, especially those who had immigrated from eastern Europe), have been noted repeatedly.[29] This shrill anti-Semitism gained added force and danger when linked to a nationalism rooted in the catastrophic memory of the "war of liberation" against Napoleon and the Thirty Years' War. This resuscitated, catastrophic nationalism gave anti-Semitism an apocalyptic dimension that projected a cataclysmic remaking of German society with Jews as its sacrificial victims.[30] This postwar fusion of nationalism and anti-Semitism no longer contemplated the German self in relation to an abject Jewish other (to be excised) but took defeat as grounds for cathartic killing. The figure of the (German) sacrificer as both killer and victim took shape in the radical Right's image of the frontline soldier as representative of the German nation.[31] One might argue, therefore, with some justification, that exterminism arose from a spirit of eschatology, but in fact it was, notwithstanding its transcendental leanings that could be endlessly spun out,

---

[27] Shulamit Volkov, *Jüdisches Leben und Antisemitismus im 19. und 20. Jahrhundert* (Munich, 1990); and Peter Pulzer, *The Rise of Political Anti-Semitism in Germany and Austria* (London, 1988).

[28] Martin H. Geyer, *Verkehrte Welt. Revolution, Inflation und Moderne, München 1914–1924* (Göttingen, 1998).

[29] Werner Jochmann, "Die Ausbreitung des Anti-Semitismus," in Werner E. Mosse and Arnold Paucker, eds., *Deutsches Judentum in Krieg und Revolution* (Tübingen, 1971), 409–510.

[30] Uwe Lohalm, *Völkischer Radikalismus. Die Geschichte des Deutschvölkischen Schutz- und Trutz-Bundes, 1919–1923* (Hamburg, 1970); and Michael Geyer, "Insurrectionary Warfare: The German Debate about a levée en masse in October 1918," *Journal of Modern History* 73 (September, 2001): 459–527.

[31] Bernd Hüppauf, "Schlachtenmythen und die Konstruktion des 'Neuen Menschen'," in Gerhard Hirschfeld and Gerd Krumeich, eds., *Keiner fühlt sich hier mehr als Mensch . . . Erlebnis und Wirkung des Ersten Weltkrieges* (Essen, 1993), 43–79.

fueled by a popular sense of pride and revenge that found in the Jews a very predictable enemy. The postwar fusion of nationalism and anti-Semitism was so ominous because it reached beyond older nationalist milieus and mobilized more traditional (religious, liberal, and populist) German sensibilities. It made hatred of Jews the core of a war ideology that predicated overcoming defeat on the excision of Jews from Germany. Perhaps most importantly, this hybrid ideology infused what had been a muddle of anti-Semitic outbursts with a striking sense of mission and activism, which was carried forward by an elite that looked for results rather than rhetoric. Thus, anti-Semitism was turning both deadly and efficient.

Anti-Semitism undulated with the political fortunes of the Weimar Republic but remained the defining element for the hard core of the radical Right and a nascent Nazi party.[32] It was a key issue on the Nazi political agenda once they had come to power and surfaced at every threshold of the consolidation—and the demolition—of the Nazi regime: 1933, 1935–36, 1938–39, 1941–42, 1944–45.[33] The quick succession of these moments reflects a general acceleration of politics in the Third Reich. What matters in terms of anti-Semitism as ideology is, first, that the vibrant anti-anti-Semitism of the Weimar Republic was terrorized into submission. Jews faced the full force of anti-Semitic outbursts. Their exclusion from public life destroyed footholds for opposition and resistance. The remnants of liberal-democratic, gentile society were either pushed into privacy or co-opted.[34] Second, otherwise heterogeneous anti-Semitic traditions—the divisions within German society and culture had produced varieties of anti-Semitism—were dragged out of their respective milieus and made over into a single and, indeed, singular issue, "the Jewish Question." Only now a genuinely national anti-Semitism took shape that spoke to Protestants, Catholics, Nationalists, and Socialists alike.[35] It emerged as a mass-based (as opposed to milieu- or class-bound) ideology—and in this respect differed significantly from the virulent French or the exterminist Rumanian anti-Semitism. Third, anti-Semitism entered public consciousness through a range of micro-politics that systematically tied Nazi propaganda to ev-

[32] Uwe Dietrich Adam, *Judenpolitik im Dritten Reich* (Düsseldorf, 1972); and Erich Goldhagen, "Weltanschauung und Endlösung. Zum Antisemitismus der nationalsozialistischen Führungsschicht," *Vierteljahrshefte für Zeitgeschichte* 24 (1976): 73–89.

[33] The most compelling account is Raul Hilberg, *The Destruction of the European Jews*, 3 vols., rev. and definitive ed. (New York, 1985).

[34] Marion Kaplan, *Between Dignity and Despair: Jewish Life in Nazi Germany* (New York, 1998).

[35] David Bankier, *Probing the Depths of German Anti-Semitism: German Society and the Persecution of the Jews, 1933–1941* (New York, 2000).

eryday life. To be sure, Germans proved susceptible both to hate propaganda and to more general arguments about racial hygiene.[36] But anti-Semitism was habitualized in the busy work of lawyers and bureaucrats who separated and segregated Jews and a Jewish spirit (in music, art philosophy, taste) in an avalanche of minute directives. Jews and Germans became strangers in the course of cumulating acts of segregation. Fourth, public and popular anti-Semitism downplayed the apocalyptic edge of the radical fringe and surfaced as a ticket for the good life. This could take the crude form of buying cheap at secondhand markets for Jewish valuables and goods. It could also be articulated in an aesthetic of healthy "Aryan" bodies or in the promise of happiness for all (Germans).[37] Saul Friedländer has pointed out how much anti-Semitism was linked to the promise of salvation and redemption, but these grand ideological themes only make sense if translated into daily existence where they signaled a beautiful, prosperous life.[38] Very little of this beauty was in sight, and prosperity was limited to Nazi high society, but the idea of the good life was carried over as a deferred dream into the postwar years, where it survived long after the Nazis were defeated and discredited.

As pervasive as anti-Semitism became in the Third Reich, however, neither habits of the heart nor ideological commitment was enough to turn it from idea into genocidal practice. Susceptible as the Germans were to anti-Semitism, most of them hesitated to endorse state terror and recoiled from street violence.[39] Furthermore, if it had been a matter of ideological commitment, Alfred Rosenberg, the chief ideologue of the Nazi regime, or Julius Streicher, the notorious and powerful anti-Semitic *Gauleiter*, would have been in charge. But they were bypassed in the formation of anti-Semitic politics. The mark of distinction in the Third Reich was not beliefs, but action—and it is in this realm of action that anti-Semitic politics took shape. Here, however, we enter a crowded field and we discover that actions against Jews evolved in a much larger arena of National Socialist racial activism.

One of the main sites of this kind emerged in the medical intervention into the body social (*Volkskörper*), which encompassed a variety of

---

[36] David Bankier, *The Germans and the Final Solution: Public Opinion under Nazism* (Oxford, 1992).

[37] Frank Bajohr and Joachim Szodrzynski, *Hamburg in der NS-Zeit. Ergebnisse neuerer Forschungen* (Hamburg, 1995); and Sander L. Gilman, *The Jew's Body* (New York, 1991).

[38] Friedländer, *Nazi Germany and the Jews*, who made this argument most clearly, tends to think of redemption as too spiritual a process. Redemption through consumption was far more prominent.

[39] Ian Kershaw, *Popular Opinion and Political Dissent in the Third Reich, Bavaria 1933–45* (Oxford, 1983).

initiatives. The Nazi desire to forge a strong and heroic people teamed up with the interest of the medical world that had long lobbied for public hygiene and in the 1910s and 1920s had come under the sway of racial hygiene.[40] With the Nazi seizure of power, these interests gathered under the banner of protecting and fortifying the nation against internal and external enemies. The result was initiatives to sterilize men and women deemed unfit to procreate and to put to death the mentally handicapped, measures that were introduced in 1934 and 1938, respectively.[41] Medical doctors and health officials effectively claimed power over life and death. Historians disagree on the question of what was ideological and what was medical about National Socialist biopolitics.[42] But what matters in the first place is the dramatic expansion of the right to kill (traditionally limited to the military and the penal systems) and the claims to biopolitical surveillance over the entire population as a means to both punitive (sterilization) and ameliorative (prenatal) intervention—and how generally these rights and claims were deemed appropriate by the medical profession and public health officials. The technical expertise that was acquired in the context of euthanasia formed a link to genocide of the Jews, although the two arenas remained substantially separate.[43]

The most prominent arena of Nazi activism concerned the suppression of its political enemies. To this end, a concentration camp system sprang up in the wake of the seizure of power, initially as a "wild" regime of terror by National Socialist fanatics against their many critics and opponents. Jews got caught up in the first wave of terror together with many others, especially communists, who were the main target. This terror of the street was quickly regularized, but the emergent system of camps remained outside the rule of law and within the purview of the Nazi Party, which made them into a self-financing and, indeed, profit-making scheme. The rapidly growing regime of detention and incarceration was advertised for its capacity to remove internal ene-

---

[40] Paul Weindling, *Health, Race and German Politics between National Unification and Nazism 1870–1945* (Cambridge, UK, 1989); and Michael Burleigh and Wolfgang Wippermann, *The Racial State: Germany 1933–1945* (Cambridge, UK, 1991).

[41] Gisela Bock, "Sterilization and 'Medical' Massacres in National Socialist Germany," in Manfred Berg and Geoffrey Cocks, eds., *Medicine and Modernity: Public Health and Medical Care in Nineteenth- and Twentieth-Century Germany* (Washington, D.C., 1997), 149–72; and Michael Burleigh, *Death and Deliverance: "Euthanasia" in Germany ca. 1900–1945* (New York, 1994).

[42] Richard F. Wetzell, *Inventing the Criminal: A History of German Criminology, 1880–1945* (Chapel Hill, 2000), is a good example of this discussion.

[43] Henry Friedlander, *The Origins of Nazi Genocide: From Euthanasia to the Final Solution.* (Chapel Hill, 1996).

mies and, thus, as essential to national revival.[44] By 1938, this regime of extralegal violence was used not only to detain those the regime deemed hardened criminals and political opponents, but also to incarcerate social outcasts such as vagrants, "work-shy" and "a-socials" (as they were called), unruly youths, homosexuals, and members of such religious groups as the Jehovah's Witnesses. These latter groups increasingly filled the camps under the otherwise quite popular cover of keeping dangerous elements from the population and having them converted to socially responsible behavior through hard labor and violence.[45] Again, what matters is the readiness to incarcerate entire groups of people, the commitment of officials and Nazi activists to protect society (and Nazi rule) by means of deadly terror, and the general popularity of these measures with their promise to clean up German society. In sum, within a very short time, a sphere of population management emerged at the edge of the penal system, with incarceration and physical terror as its main characteristics. It served the political ends of the regime by articulating a popular desire to clean up German society and make it new and better.

Piece by piece, this regime of camps was amalgamated with the nationalized police forces to form the security apparatus under Heinrich Himmler. The latter is best known for the SS and the Gestapo but was part of "a burgeoning security empire" that was run by a young and action-driven elite encompassing murderous thugs as much as academic think tanks.[46] The dramatic growth of this machine—its emergence as extralegal domain based on the will, embodied in the *Führer*, to rid Germany of its internal enemies, its claims to total surveillance of all aspects of life, its emergence as a comprehensive "thought" police and racial guardian, its unlimited right to prosecute and detain, and, above all, its accrued powers over life and death, exemplified in the institution of the concentration camp and symbolized in the death's head insignia of the guards—has come under evermore detailed scrutiny.[47] Historians have pointed to the homogenization and attempted professionalization of its members in a state security corps.[48] The pur-

---

[44] Robert Gellately, *Backing Hitler: Consent and Coercion in Nazi Germany* (Oxford, 2001); and Eric A. Johnson, *Nazi Terror: The Gestapo, Jews and Ordinary Germans* (New York, 1999).

[45] Ulrich Herbert, Karin Orth, and Christoph Dieckmann, eds., *Die nationalsozialistischen Konzentrationslager—Entwicklung und Struktur*, 2 vols. (Göttingen, 1998).

[46] Burleigh and Wippermann, *Racial State*, 120

[47] Gerhard Paul and Klaus-Michael Mallmann, eds. *Die Gestapo. Mythos und Realität* (Darmstadt, 1995).

[48] Karin Orth, *Die Konzentrationslager-SS. Sozialstrukturelle Analysen und biographische Studien* (Göttingen, 2000).

pose of this apparatus, however, was to wage "a permanent war against the interior enemy."[49]

If the expansion of the security machine and the evermore inclusive definition of its tasks were breathtaking before the war, it truly came into its own when charged with "security" behind the advancing armies in the occupied territories during the war. The Security Police not only considered the occupied territories outside of the law and subject solely to German security needs, but from the start, in pursuit of control in occupied areas, they waged war against noncollaborationist groups and parties, partisans, bandits, racial groups, and anyone suspected of being or becoming an enemy of the Germans.[50] They covered the occupied areas with an elaborate system of surveillance and control, supported by networks of informers and collaborators. Typically, the Security Police also launched, with the goal of securing German rule, a broad politics of population transfers and ethnic cleansing that were meant to create an ethnically stratified, but at its core homogeneous, consolidated, and racially pure Germanic homeland, with the boundaries of the Reich significantly moved both east and west. The full brunt of this politics of ethnic cleansing and resettlement could first be seen in Poland, where immediate concerns for security—Poland was the staging ground for the war against the Soviet Union—merged with grandiose plans for "reclaiming" German lands and repopulating them with ethnic Germans.[51] In the dual capacity of waging war against the interior enemies of the regime and securing German rule in occupied territories, Himmler's security machine became one of the most powerful forces in the Third Reich.

This obsession with making society safe by protecting it against its purported enemies has not received the attention it deserves in recent historiography. Of course, we cannot trust the security claims by Nazi officials, but the very fixation on security and the centrality of this concern for Third Reich politics matter greatly as the key feature of this right-wing regime. The Nazis concentrated with singular determination on combating society's enemies in all spheres of life. In this very concrete sense, rolling back the evil that had afflicted German society,

[49] Karl-Dietrich Bracher, *Die deutsche Diktatur. Entstehung, Struktur, Folgen des Nationalsozialismus* (Cologne, 1976), 391.

[50] Ahlrich Meyer, *Die deutsche Besatzung in Frankreich 1940–1944. Widerstandsbekämpfung und Judenverfolgung* (Darmstadt, 2000).

[51] Bogdan Musial, *Deutsche Zivilverwaltung und Judenverfolgung im Generalgouvernement. Eine Fallstudie zum Distrikt Lublin, 1939–1944* (Wiesbaden, 1999); and Götz Aly and Susanne Heim, "Deutsche Herrschaft 'im Osten'. Bevölkerungspolitik und Völkermord," in Peter Jahn und Reinhard Rürup, ed., *Erobern und Vernichten. Der Krieg gegen die Sowjetunion 1941–1945. Essays* (Berlin, 1991), 84–105.

captured in the reference to "the criminals of November [1918]," the Nazis formed a civil war regime. We discover here a popular presumption that the nation was incomplete—wanting—and needed its task-masters, who gave it shape and form. If some historians describe this determination as "revolutionary," it is not merely for the sheer radicality and totality of the measures taken. Rather, in rolling back a revolution and in uprooting its supporters, the Nazis looked forward to remaking Germany in their own image. While right-wing politics was nostalgically hankering for the past, the Nazis were not. Historians are debating what this Nazi future might have entailed. It may suffice to say that there was no agreement beyond terror, although certain elements—such as grandiose designs for cities and suburbs, a fascination with speed (a fast rail system, autobahns, cars), and a culture of the spectacle (films, revues)—stand out.[52] In all these deliberations and fantasies, though, two things were more certain than others. First, the remaking of Germany could only be accomplished through war and, second, the transformation of the German body politic would lead to a Germany without Jews.

Nazi politics directed against the Jews conformed to the overall project of securing and expanding Germany, yet also exceeded it. The difference is most readily apparent in the separation of anti-Jewish measures from others within the expansive realm of state terror—a division of labor first encountered within Germany and subsequently repeated in Nazi-occupied Europe. But while telling, this differentiation does not quite capture the peculiar nature of the "excess" of anti-Semitic politics. Rather, we might think of anti-Jewish measures as distinct acts of war—as acts of war against what the Nazis perceived as their most intransigent, internal, and external enemy. In the terror against the Jews, the Nazi civil war ideology came into its own. We have already seen how war and anti-Semitism intertwined in the sacrificial fantasies of postwar catastrophic nationalism. But in the early 1920s these were the ideological gyrations of a political movement in defeat. By 1938 the question was how, when, and with what means a victorious and self-assured Nazi Party and its leadership would wage this war. After five years of stepping up its terrorism against the Jews (and remarkably synchronous with the overall decision to launch interstate wars of conquest), the Third Reich crossed a decisive threshold in November 1938 when it began to seek a "final solution" for "the 'Jewish problem.'"

[52] See, for example, Edward Dimendberg, "The Will to Motorization: Cinema, Highways, and Modernity," *October* 73 (1995): 91–137.

In the wake of the *Reichskristallnacht* (November 9, 1938), Hitler charged Hermann Göring with resolving the Jewish question "one way or the other."[53] With this, at first sight, strange choice he signaled the concentration of concerns critical to the regime in the hands of an inner circle of loyalists who straddled Party and state positions. Within the first few months of 1938, Hitler had taken charge of the Wehrmacht, Himmler had consolidated his security apparatus (and had begun to put it on a war footing), and Göring had begun to deal with the threat that Nazis considered the most implacable enemy. Hitler also completed the process of disempowering the activist grassroots anti-Semitism (the preserve of *Gauleiter* and the Propaganda Ministry, headed by the *Gauleiter* of Berlin, Goebbels), much as he had disempowered the SA in 1934 in preparation for general conscription, instead handing over the solution of the Jewish question to the man in control of war preparations. Therefore, it makes sense to put Hitler's curious choice into the context of the controversial and crisis-ridden decision, in 1938, to begin waging war within a year.[54] Even if we consider decision-making in the Third Reich to be a helter-skelter affair, in terms of waging war, things were falling into place. The Jewish question came to figure prominently in this context—and remained there until 1945.

Placing the Jewish question within the context of war did not, by itself, determine how to proceed. Notwithstanding repeated threats to annihilate the Jews, a "solution" was still sought through forced emigration and resettlement schemes.[55] From a Nazi vantage point, such schemes offered a most expeditious way of removing a threat (and of profiting from the act). Raul Hilberg has persuasively argued that the step from a rhetoric of annihilation to putting extermination into practice was huge.[56] One might add that limiting all-out war fit Hitler's— one might say, intuitive—pattern of breaking down war into individual campaigns. Much as a final solution of making the German domain *judenfrei* was sought, there was flexibility as to when, where, and how. As it happened, the 1938 option of expulsion and forced emigration

[53] Richard Breitman, *The Architect of Genocide: Himmler and the Final Solution* (Hanover, 1991).

[54] Klaus-Jürgen Müller, *General Ludwig Beck. Studien und Dokumente zur politisch-militärischen Vorstellungswelt und Tätigkeit des Generalstabschefs des deutschen Heeres 1933–1938* (Boppard am Rhein, 1980); and Michael Geyer, "Crisis of Military Leadership in the 1930s," *Journal of Strategic Studies* 14 (1991): 448–62.

[55] Götz Aly, " 'Jewish Resettlement': Reflections on the Political Prehistory of the Holocaust," in Ulrich Herbert, ed., *National Socialist Extermination Policies: Contemporary German Perspectives and Controversies* (New York, 2000), 53–82.

[56] Raul Hilberg, *The Destruction of the European Jews* (New York, 1979), 1 vol., 646–62

opened a final, narrow window of survival for German, Austrian, and Czech Jews. This window, however, was shut rapidly.

With the invasion of Poland on September 1, 1939, the ground began to move. Initiative had already shifted to Himmler's apparatus and within the apparatus, to Reinhard Heydrich, the former naval officer and head of the Security Police under whom Eichmann had developed his emigration scheme in Vienna.[57] With the onset of war, the Security Police began to take charge on a number of levels. First, Jews were instantly targeted as the main security threat everywhere.[58] Jewish men were taken hostage and killed en masse, especially with the invasion of Poland, the occupation of Serbia (April 6, 1941), and, on a grand scale following detailed preparation, with the advance into Soviet-occupied territories and the Soviet Union (June 22, 1941). While rationalized as a preventive measure against partisan threats and as a deterrent to ascertain control over territories and people, these mass killings had all the makings of deliberate genocide.[59] Second, the evolving politics of ethnic cleansing and population transfers also had Jews as its first and main target. Escalating and accelerating older tactics of expulsion (as, for example, in the deportation of "eastern" Jews across the Polish border in 1938), Jews were collectively expelled and eventually concentrated in so-called ghettos. These ghettos served, among other things, as labor preserves.[60] Third, the horrendous situation was compounded by *Gauleiter* efforts to remove all Jews from German territory, with the effect that eastern European Jews were killed to make space for Western Jews, and soon the recently deported were killed to make space for new arrivals. The result was a relentless ratcheting up of anti-Jewish pogroms into acts of mass extermination that, by September-October 1941, extended to the killing of women and children.[61] The murder of entire Jewish communities, as well as of concentrations of Jews in transit camps in sweeping police raids, had become a systematic aspect of German occupation.

This was genocide of unprecedented dimensions. Most historians follow the sensible lead of Christopher Browning, who has argued for

---

[57] Hans Safrian, *Eichmann und seine Gehilfen* (Frankfurt, 1995).

[58] Walter Manoschek, *"Serbien ist judenfrei"—Militärische Besatzungspolitik und Judenvernichtung in Serbien 1941/1942* (Munich, 1993).

[59] Christoph Dieckmann, "The War and the Killing of the Lithuanian Jews," in Ulrich Herbert, ed., *National Socialist Extermination Policies: Contemporary German Perspectives and Controversies* (New York, 2000), 240–75.

[60] Christopher R. Browning, *Nazi Policy, Jewish Workers, German Killers* (Cambridge, UK 2000).

[61] Christopher R. Browning, *The Path to Genocide: Essays on Launching the Final Solution* (Cambridge, UK, 1992).

summer (and surely September-October) 1941 as the beginning of the all-out murder of the Jews.[62] Nevertheless, exceedingly involved debates continue about the exact timing because each adjustment of the date shifts the cast of responsible actors. Was all-out murder due to local initiative emanating from the occupied East or issued from Berlin, ultimately on Hitler's authority? Was it the effect of cold-blooded calculation of Nazi officials (such as the population managers just mentioned) or did a murderous anti-Semitism break the dam? Did the fatal turn come in the flush of expected victory or the foreboding of possible defeat? In shifting responsibilities, the grand historical narratives change as well. The more that historians emphasize the local conditions, the more they make the genocide of the Jews an aspect of a cruel occupation regime. The more they put the weight on Berlin, the more they see the determining feature in the virulence of anti-Semitic ideology. In the face of such debates, one does well to remind oneself of the hitherto unthinkable: Never before had Germans, with a record of all manner of atrocities in their history, engaged in this kind of all-out murder. Never before had Jews, who had suffered through many extirpations and pogroms in their history, experienced the threat they felt beginning in September-October 1941. The systematic killing and the totality of enmity signal the advent of a new form of genocide.

And yet the sweeps of the Security Police in 1941 were but the beginning. New, industrial forms of killing through mass asphyxiation with gas and the disposal of corpses through incineration had yet to be developed. These extermination camps, above all Auschwitz, began operating between 1942 and 1944.[63] Further, the totality of killing had yet to be established as a programmatic initiative and as a hard fact. This meant that it had to be agreed upon (and subsequently negotiated with local authorities) that all Jews in Nazi-occupied Europe were to be swept up into the killing machinery.[64] Guidelines had to be developed for schemes to use Jewish labor (which mushroomed into an elaborate system of camps and sub-camps while the killings proceeded) were strictly transitional. This required a heretofore absent operational intelligence that was provided by Reinhard Heydrich and his staff who, in the summer of 1941, were charged by Göring to prepare for the "final solution" of the "Jewish problem."[65] This former naval

[62] In addition to Browning, *Path to Genocide*, see his "The Euphoria of Victory and the Final Solution: Summer-Fall 1941," *German Studies Review* 17 (1994): 473–81.

[63] Deborah Dwork and Robert Jan van Pelt, *Auschwitz 1270 to the Present* (New York, 1996).

[64] Martin Gilbert, ed., *The Macmillan Atlas of the Holocaust* (New York, 1982), is a most graphic account.

[65] See Browning, *Path to Genocide*; and Breitman, *The Architect of Genocide*.

officer and his staff turned mass genocide into a systematic undertaking, calibrating means to ends and coordinating the complex machinery that made this operation feasible. What emerged is a politics of annihilation, famously observable at the Wannsee Conference in January 1942, which managed coordination and cooperation and a military-style operational knowledge that turned genocide into a systematic campaign of extermination. Through the portal of thorough planning for an internal war against the Jews, we enter a world of total annihilation. Three elements—the systematicity of murder, the encompassing nature of the scheme to capture any and all Jews, and the foresight and deliberation of making violent death their inescapable destiny—turned an unprecedented genocide into what we have come to call the Holocaust.

This was Heydrich's campaign, conducted in the spirit of civil war that commenced in the fall of 1941. The calibration of Heydrich's annihilation campaign, however, shifted, if only slightly, in the course of late 1941 and early 1942. In a startling essay, a young historian, Christian Gerlach, has attributed this shift to the intervention of Hitler in December 1941.[66] We take Gerlach's findings to suggest that what we find in December 1941 is a return to the ideological origins of a Nazi catastrophic nationalism with its strong sense of sacrificial killing

The circumstances in late 1941 were dramatic. With Operation Barbarossa in jeopardy and Operation Typhoon (the seizure of Moscow before winter) just under way, Hitler talked himself into a rage both privately, at the dinner table, and in public, through speeches that were transmitted on radio to a national audience.[67] In his bursts of unmitigated anger, he rehearsed ideas and images that he had originally formulated between the end of World War I and the aftermath of the failed coup in 1923. His fulminations culminated (in the wake of the Soviet counteroffensive and the American entry into the war) in a secret address to Nazi dignitaries (*Reichsleiter* and *Gauleiter*) on December 13, 1941. Goebbels reports the key passage.

> In regard to the Jewish question, the Führer is determined to clear the table. He warned the Jews that if they were to cause another world war, it would lead to their own destruction. Those were not empty words. Now the world war has come. The destruction of the Jews must be its necessary

[66] Christian Gerlach, "The Wannsee Conference, the Fate of German Jews, and Hitler's Decision in Principle to Exterminate all European Jews," *Journal of Modern History* 70, no. 4 (1998): 759–812.

[67] Klaus Reinhardt, *Moscow—The Turning Point: The Failure of Hitler's Strategy in the Winter of 1941–42* (Oxford, 1992).

consequence. We cannot be sentimental about it. It is not for us to feel sympathy for the Jews. We should have sympathy rather with our own German people. If the German people have to sacrifice 160,000 victims in yet another campaign in the east, those responsible for this bloody conflict will have to pay for it with their lives.[68]

Hitler had made similar statements. He called for "the destruction of the Jews" at a moment when a regime of mass shooting was in place and killing with gas was being introduced.[69] In the face of the already rolling annihilation campaign, it would be farfetched to argue that the Holocaust resulted from Hitler's determination. The crux of the matter is that Hitler's intervention put Heydrich's campaign at the center of the Nazi war effort. The annihilation of the Jews became a strategic imperative. From that point the Third Reich fought a war of extermination with such determination that at times it appeared that the outer war was but a shrinking shell to facilitate the interior one. A year later when Goebbels and Göring talked about the effects of the Holocaust, they noted, in particular, one of its more indirect consequences. They thought that with the bridges burnt behind them, the Germans could not but fight to the point of self-destruction.[70] This is where the ideological circle closes: The Jews, as the imaginary culprits of German defeat, would now ascertain, through the fact of having been murdered, that a fickle and weak German nation could only fight to its own death—and that generations to come would draw a spirit of vengeance from such heroic disaster. Catastrophic nationalism had its very own politics of memory.

The notion that war was to be fought simultaneously inside and outside, as annihilation of the enemy and as destruction of inimical forces within, is a recurrent theme in the history of war, discussed under the rubric of "civil war" since Thucydides. Yet, in 1941–42 the unthinkable happened: In waging a war to salvage the nation from defeat, an entire nation and, indeed, an entire continent were thrown into a war of annihilation against any and all Jews. That there could be such implacable enmity makes the Holocaust a singular and "incompliant" event.[71]

[68] Goebbels diaries (December 13, 1941), quoted in Gerlach, "Hitler's Decision," 785.

[69] Peter Longerich, *Politik der Vernichtung. Eine Gesamtdarstellung der nationalsozialistischen Judenverfolgung* (Munich, 1998), 419–71.

[70] Joseph Goebbels, *Die Tagebücher von Joseph Goebbels. Sämtliche Fragmente*, 15 vols., Elke Fröhlich, ed. (Munich, 1987), II/7, 454.

[71] Dan Diner, "Uncompliance of an Event: Integrating the Holocaust into the Saeculum's Narration" (Manuscript, Tel Aviv, 2000).

The Era of World Wars and the
German Quest for Dominance

The sequence of wars that stretches from World War I in 1914 to 1918, through World War II in 1938–39 to 1945, to the Cold War in 1945 to 1961–63, suggests deep rifts in the makeup of Europe. The state of deadly turmoil only subsided because the two grand imperial forces of the age, the Soviet Union and the United States, withdrew from the brink of nuclear war when they faced each other over Berlin and Cuba.[72] That peace came as the result of a détente among the two intercontinental powers rather than an intra-European arrangement, is an indication of how Europe's place in the world had changed as a result of these wars. It also points to the inability of the Europeans to give themselves an order that would reconcile the aspirations of their people. Throughout the twentieth century, Europe was an unsettled continent.

Germany and its ambitions were at the center of Europe's twentieth-century wars. For even the Cold War had, as far as Europe was concerned, Germany as its main object. Fritz Fischer defined the nature of these ambitions for post–World War II historiography, picking up on controversies over German war aims that reached back to World War I.[73] He stressed the expansive nature of German war aims and the aggressiveness of a Prussian-German elite in pursuing them. Europe's troubles were thus seen as originating in the imperial designs of atavistic and militaristic German elites.[74] While most every aspect of Fischer's "thesis" has been challenged, his basic argument has stuck, mostly for the lack of a better one.[75] For instance, it proved difficult to square the conventionalism of Wilhelmine elites with the radicalism of National Socialist war. The Third Reich appeared to fight an entirely different war for which, eventually, the term *Weltanschauungskrieg*, or ideological war, was coined. This notion proved extremely useful, but exactly what an ideological war is (beyond the Nazis' own definition), how it might relate to Wilhelmine politics, and how both can be situated in a European context remains unresolved. We suggest that an answer, elucidating both the nature of ideological war and the role of

[72] Marc Trachtenberg, *A Constructed Peace: The Making of the European Settlement 1945–1963* (Princeton, 1999).

[73] Fritz Fischer, *Germany's Aims in the First World War* (New York, 1967), and *From Kaiserreich to Third Reich: Elements of Continuity in German History, 1871–1945* (London, 1986).

[74] The structuralist approach then became the new orthodoxy. See Volker Berghahn, *Germany and the Approach of War in 1914*, 2nd ed. (New York, 1993).

[75] There is no lack of alternatives, such as Klaus Hildebrand, *German Foreign Policy from Bismarck to Adenauer: The Limits of Statecraft* (London, 1989).

Germany in Europe, can be found by looking more closely at the politics of war between 1938 and 1942.

Historians follow the lead of contemporaries when they make World War I into the pivotal moment at which the world irrevocably changed.[76] They have in mind the machine-like slaughter of trench warfare, the "total" mobilization of entire nations and their recourse to worldwide resources, and the transformation of the international order, captured in the 1917 Bolshevik revolution in Russia, the entry of the United States into the war, and, one might add, in nationalizing revolutions the likes of which Europe had not seen since 1848.[77] These were, indeed, signs of things to come. But looking back at the twentieth century, we find that Europe was turned upside down between 1938 and 1942. Within barely four years, Nazi Germany radicalized war, not only to encompass "total" or "industrial" warfare on an unprecedented scale (soon to be outdone by the Allies), but also to engage in an utterly savage war of destruction, primarily in Eastern Europe and Russia, which left millions upon millions of soldiers and civilians dead or bereft and entire countries devastated. In 1941 Nazi Germany fought interstate wars as genocidal war. Simultaneously, German political and military leadership escalated with breathtaking speed from local wars over positioning Germany in central Europe to the level of intercontinental wars encompassing the entire world by the end of 1941. These were wars not simply across immense spaces, but over global geopolitics—acts of war that pushed aside the remnants of a European world order in favor of global competition. What European society of a gilded, imperial age had darkly anticipated in 1914, the end of their world, had become reality by 1941–42. War leapt beyond the constraints that a restorative nineteenth century had imposed on it. International affairs had become global. Violence had become genocidal.

Thinking of this as an "ideological war" helps us make sense of the explosive aggressiveness that brought about such a momentous rupture. But caution is necessary in putting ideology into the history of war, lest it appear as some extraneous principle or dogma that is handed down to a hapless officer corps, a conscript army, and the German nation. The image of ideology as imposed dogma misses the reasons that ideology got into the armed forces in the first place and was able to become such an important and deleterious force in the conflict.

[76] Jay Winter and Blaine Baggett, *The Great War: The Shaping of the Twentieth Century* (New York, 1996); and Wolfgang Michalka, ed., *Der Erste Weltkrieg. Wirkung, Wahrnehmung, Analyse* (Munich, 1994).

[77] Niall Ferguson, *The Pity of War* (New York, 1999).

The latter had a great deal to do not with the Nazis but with the German way of fighting war.

While all combatants in World War I had appealed to the spirit of their nation, none was more insistent in putting "mind over matter" and stressing the need for individual and social self-motivation in mobilizing and fighting war than the German military. The entire nation would have to wage war for Germany to succeed; soldiers would have to become self-motivated if they wanted to prevail in battle; both army and nation would have to be transformed by stimulating their fighting spirit. Germans understood war, by its very conduct, as a profoundly spiritual affair, in sharp contrast, for example, to the British.[78] In this sense ideology became the essential power in mobilizing the nation at large and in making the soldiers fight. It was all the more devastating when the army and the nation stopped fighting in 1918—or, as the common right-wing view claimed, were kept from fighting by revolutionaries, Jews, and other conspirators. The experience of 1918—the fear of mutiny in the armed forces and of civilian defeatism—was so deep-seated because the German military was committed to the idea of war as, first and foremost, a spiritual act.

It would be misleading, however, to look for any particular doctrine or mission that generated this fighting spirit. All efforts to inculcate some kind of national message failed in both world wars, but success came with the call for individual and collective achievement. The "spirit" was that everybody must do their job to the best of their ability. It was the "achieving," the very subjective involvement in one's own war, that mattered. Against considerable internal resistance, performance became the key criterion for judging (and punishing) soldiers and officers.[79] Performance was doubled-edged. Using World War I tactics as precedent, the Wehrmacht and the Nazi regime were set on instilling in each soldier (and non-combatant) both a sense of the utter importance of individual effort and the absolute dependence on the group, a combination marking the ideological core of the Wehrmacht.[80]

[78] Omer Bartov, *Mirrors of Destruction: War, Genocide, and Modern Identity* (Oxford, 2000); and Allan R. Millett and Williamson Murray, *German Military Effectiveness*, 3 vols. (Boston, 1988).

[79] MacGregor Knox, "1 October 1942: Adolf Hitler, Wehrmacht Officer Policy, and Social Revolution," *The Historical Journal* 43, No. 3 (2000): 801–25; and Bernd Kröner, "Auf dem Weg zu einer 'nationalsozialistischen Volksarmee'," in Martin Broszat, ed., *Von Stalingrad zur Währungsreform. Zur Sozialgeschichte des Umbruchs in Deutschland* (Munich, 1988), 651–82.

[80] Martin van Creveld, *Fighting Power: German and U.S. Army Performance, 1939–1945* (Westport, 1982), uses the American notion of "primary group behavior," which misses the point quite badly. Omer Bartov, *Hitler's Army: Soldiers, Nazis, and War in the Third Reich* (New York, 1991), in critiquing van Creveld, does not explore the notion of "die

German experts spoke of the individual and collective "will" to fight as the key to fighting war. The supreme ideological act of the Nazi regime consisted of reinforcing these tendencies within the armed forces and society.[81] They apparently did something "right" because, in contrast to World War I, the military at large, although increasingly weary, fought in a blinding spirit of solidarity to the very last days of the war. The Wehrmacht fought its most lethal battles in the war's waning months, with more soldiers and exponentially more non-combatants killed during 1944–45 than in the entire war.[82]

With the power of self-motivation and a strong attachment to one's unit or group came a sense of exclusion and exclusiveness, a rejection of all those who were deemed unfit or did not belong, and, in the course of the war, an ever deeper resentment against those who did not fight. It was the source for a sense of superiority that marked German soldiers even when defeated. This sense of superiority could be reinforced by racial doctrine and other such beliefs, but it did not have to be. It was the main source for the profound disregard for the life and integrity of enemy nations and people that became so central an aspect of the German conduct of war. To be sure, overt ideological commitment to Nazi causes and a more covert embrace of racial stereotypes played a distinct role in developing this disrespect, especially when and where it reinforced the generational experience of all those who grew up, as children or adolescents, in the Third Reich and, born around 1920, made up the bulk of the fighting forces. The Hitler Youth cohorts, whether in the SS or in army divisions, were among the most ferocious warriors Germany had ever seen.[83] Still, even when war ideology took on an overtly dogmatic form—as the case of war against the Soviet Union—it remained embedded in, and could fall back on, a peculiarly effectiveness-oriented rationale and a concomitant sense of superiority that made German warfare so lethal and destructive.

This is to say that *Weltanschauungskrieg*, or ideological war, developed first and foremost from this spirit of fighting war. The notion of unconstrained efficiency, derived from World War I, shaped the Wehrmacht conduct of war in two ways. The first lesson consisted in using bold initiative and concentrating overwhelming force (both strategi-

---

Gruppe" either. There is no study to date that draws out the prewar (youth movement) and postwar (group dynamics) linkages.

[81] Klaus Jürgen Müller, *Armee, Politik und Gesellschaft in Deutschland 1933–1945. Studien zum Verhältnis von Armee und NS-System* (Paderborn, 1979).

[82] Rüdiger Overmans, *Deutsche militärische Verluste im Zweiten Weltkrieg* (Munich, 1999).

[83] See, among others, the quite stunning recollections of Gerhard Zwerenz, *"Soldaten sind Mörder". Die Deutschen und der Krieg* (Munich, 1988).

cally and tactically) to gain, not simply breakthrough capability, but a devastating sense of superiority before which enemy armies and entire enemy nations would buckle. Given the overall lack of numerical and technological superiority, the skillful creation of this sense was the essence and pride of German warfare. Manfred Messerschmidt, the foremost German military historian, has pointed to the deep roots of this "technocratic" impulse, as he called it, in the Prussian- German military. But it is the actual use of this impulse as operating principle—the overwhelming and, in fact, excessive use of force against military and civilian targets—that matters.[84] This principle—in whatever form of violence it used—was glamorized by German propaganda (as, for example, in the image of daring tank commanders and dashing dive-bomber pilots) and was picked up as "*Blitzkrieg* strategy" in the postwar literature and cinema.[85] There is no such thing as "Blitzkrieg strategy" except in propaganda. But what we find is conduct of war that encouraged the uninhibited, strictly achievement-oriented use of force, unconstrained by rules of war. The normativity of excess, captured in the holy grail of performance-driven command tactics, holds the key to the German conduct of war.

The second and equally important lesson consisted of putting a premium on securing and exploiting occupied territories so that their surrender fed the war machine, with the effect of marshaling an ever-expanding resource base while diminishing the cost of war on the home front. Military operations were thus always and in principle combined operations. As the main forces advanced along narrow fronts much like spearheads, security forces, both military and police units, moved in the opposite direction, extending control to the rear and initiating a war, as it were, on an interior front. In contrast to the exterior war, this interior war never ended. While there were vast differences from country to country, military and police forces everywhere engaged in a permanent war of occupation, even when and where resistance was minimal.[86] Terror was the primary means of achieving and maintaining control over occupied territories. The German conduct of war built on achieving both total submission and absolute superiority. Terror, of course, was the job of the Security Police. But its intended effect, a sense of absolute superiority, reverberated in common aspirations,

---

[84] Manfred Messerschmidt, *Militär und Politik in der Bismarckzeit und im Wilhelminischen Deutschland* (Darmstadt, 1975).

[85] Omer Bartov, "From Blitzkrieg to Total War: Controversial Links between Image and Reality," in Ian Kershaw and Moshe Lewin, eds., *Stalinism and Nazism: Dictatorships in Comparison* (Cambridge, UK, 1997), 158–84.

[86] The best study on this subject is Mark Mazower, *Inside Hitler's Greece: The Experience of Occupation 1941–1944* (New Haven, 1993).

such as a sense of exclusivity, and was clearly meant to combat fears, such as a sense of vulnerability in the midst of alien populations.[87] This attitude of pride and fearlessness, the body armor of the German soldier, was glorified in propaganda that celebrated the natural and biological advantage of the German master race, which some believed although many others did not.[88]

Against this background, the radicalization of war in eastern Europe gains sharper contours. Although all sorts of arrangements were struck with local leaders (in Slovakia, Croatia, Rumania, and Hungary), wars in the east, against Poland, and in the southeast (against Serbia, in particular) were fought, not to disarm, but to destroy states, their civic institutions, and civil constitutions. Invasion and occupation were geared toward producing peoples without rights. There was no reason for restraint in the first place and none was applied, because there was no institution and no social body in its own right with whom the Germans wanted to cooperate or with whom they considered concluding a peace. German rule was unconditional.[89] The effect was the systematic subjection of the Polish population and, as its perquisite, an annihilation campaign against its elites as well as a ruthless war against any form of resistance—and unfolding in this context was first the concentration and then the total extermination of the Jewish population.[90] The situation differed somewhat in Serbia because control over the country was so much more difficult to achieve and armed resistance was greater from the start. But the effect was remarkably similar.[91] The initial war of conquest turned into a war-in-permanence, which in turn was driven by a world picture portraying Poles and Serbs as a subaltern mass of people rather than a defeated nation. Jews, of course, not only lacked civil rights but lost their right to life long before the systematic Holocaust set in.

This worldview established the ground rules for the German conduct of war in the East. Its key was an ideology of unadulterated, unrestrained violence, limited only by expediency, in a world of conquered

---

[87] Klaus Latzel, *Deutsche Soldaten—nationalsozialistischer Krieg? Kriegserlebnis—Kriegserfahrung 1938–1945* (Paderborn, 1998).

[88] René Schilling, "Die 'Helden der Wehrmacht'—Konstruktion und Rezeption," in Rolf-Dieter Müller and Hans-Erich Volkmann, eds., *Die Wehrmacht. Mythos und Realität* (Munich, 1999), 550–72.

[89] Bernhard R. Kroener, Rolf-Dieter Müller, and Hans Umbreit, *Organisation und Mobilisierung des deutschen Machtbereiches*, Vol. 5/1: *Kriegsverwaltung, Wirtschaft und personelle Ressourcen, 1939–1941* (Stuttgart, 1988).

[90] Martin Broszat, *Nationalsozialistische Polenpolitik, 1939–1945* (Stuttgart, 1961).

[91] Jonathan Steinberg, *All or Nothing: The Axis and the Holocaust 1941–1943* (London, 1991).

people without rights. Older traditions of seeing eastern Europeans as "people without history" and, hence, without nationality, as well as a distinctly anti-Polish and anti-Serbian animus or, more generally, an anti-Slavic racism, articulated and legitimated this regime of terror. This prejudice undoubtedly had a deep history, but as far as the Nazis were concerned, it was actualized in the self-assertion of eastern European nations in the present. Inasmuch as there was an agenda or mission, it was to roll back and destroy the nationalizing revolutions of 1918, to make nations into subject populations through the inherent political and ideological message of unrestrained National Socialist violence.

The most egregious case of war driven by ideology was "Operation Barbarossa," the initial campaign against the Soviet Union.[92] This campaign calculated the destruction, in whole or in part, not only of (imagined and real) armed resistance, but of entire populations. Operation Barbarossa explicitly risked the death of millions of noncombatants for lack of food and shelter, and expressly approved the death of a majority of POWs and slave laborers. It was a genocidal war with the objective of destroying the enemy society as a coherent and self-sustaining body.[93]

The key elements of the war against the Soviet Union require a brief review.[94] First, orders handed down to unit level called for extreme violence as standard and normal in the conduct of war. Excessive violence against the enemy population was now expressly excluded from prosecution. Second, certain enemy groups—Soviet commissars, Jews, Asian minorities, and, apparently, female soldiers in the Red Army[95]— were slated for outright liquidation, mostly to be done by the Security Police but not infrequently performed by military detachments. Third, the entire population of the occupied territories was treated, in principle, as hostile and suspect of supporting partisans (even if differences were made along racial lines, so that Ukrainians were considered least unfriendly and Jews innately hostile) and, hence, the targets of preventative measures such as hostage taking, demonstrative massacres, de-

---

[92] Horst Boog et al., *Der Angriff auf die Sowjetunion* (Munich, 1983); and Bernd Wegner, ed., *From Peace to War: Germany, Soviet Russia, and the World, 1939–1941* (Providence, 1997).

[93] Hannes Heer, "Killing Fields: The Wehrmacht and the Holocaust in Belorussia, 1841–1945," *Holocaust and Genocide Studies* 11 (1997): pp. 79–101.

[94] Jürgen Foerster did pioneering work in "Das Unternehmen 'Barbarossa' als Eroberungs- und Vernichtungskrieg," in Horst Boog et al., eds., *Der Angriff auf die Sowjetunion* (Stuttgart, 1983), 413–47.

[95] Hans-Adolf Jacobsen, "Kommissarbefehl und Massenexekutionen sowjetischer Kriegsgefangener," in Hans Buchheim et al., eds., *Anatomie des SS–Staates*, vol. 2 (Olten, 1965), 161–278.

struction of buildings and towns, and the creation of dead zones. Deur-banization, the forced removal of the urban population, and the depopulation of security zones along transportation routes were the basic means of control. Fourth, the material and physical resources of the land were preferentially used for the fighting forces, the occupation regime, and the homeland with the effect that concentrations of subject populations—especially POWs and urban populations—died en masse through the deliberate strategy of starvation.[96] Fifth, the remaining "human resources" were used as auxiliaries in the army and as local labor or deported en masse to Germany.[97] Each one of these measures violated existing conventions of war. Put together as military strategy, however, they made the war against the Soviet Union singular in its savagery.

"Operation Barbarossa" did not accomplish its goal, the defeat of the Red Army, which clawed its way back into the conflict and aggravated the process of brutalization by forcing the issue and using harsh tactics of its own, apparently meant to stiffen the backs of its soldiers.[98] With no way out, they surmised, Soviet soldiers had no choice but to fight, and the further collapse of entire army fronts (as in July–August 1941) could be averted. Meanwhile, the German side followed its own ex-plicit doctrine of genocidal warfare, which common soldiers saw vin-dicated by rumored and actual Soviet atrocities. With the Wehrmacht unable to defeat the Red Army, and both sides locked in mortal combat that extended deep behind German-occupied territories, an internal debate began by 1942–43 within the German political and military leadership to cut back the more overtly "ideological" elements of their annihilation doctrine, resulting in the return to expediency or *Kriegs-brauch* (in fact: an eye for an eye), which worsened the situation. The "ideological" conduct of war in 1941, with its rhetoric of exterminating the Jewish-Bolshevik world conspiracy did not yield to more restraint before the Red Army's fierce fighting but encouraged an escalation to more relentless tactics that gave no quarter and left behind only scorched earth, a wasteland bereft of people and barely suitable to sus-tain life. War behind the lines caught everyone not protected by one side or the other, with people becoming trapped by either the German

[96] Christian Streit, *Keine Kameraden. Die Wehrmacht und die sowjetischen Kriegsgefangenen 1941–1945* (Bonn, 1991); and Gerlach, *Kalkulierte Morde*.

[97] Ulrich Herbert, *Hitler's Foreign Workers: Enforced Foreign Labor in Germany under the Third Reich* (Cambridge, UK, 1997). There is still little work on Wehrmacht auxiliaries and the Organisation Todt.

[98] Alexander Werth, *Russia at War: 1941–1945* (New York, 1964); and David Glantz and Jonathan M. House, *When Titans Clashed: How the Red Army Stopped Hitler* (Lawrence, 1995).

or the Soviet maelstrom. The German advance was cruel and ideological, but their retreat was barbarous,[99] and, in turn, the Soviet advance into eastern Europe and Germany responded in kind.[100] In the long history of wars fought by Germans and Russians, both at their colonial frontiers and in Europe, the war on the Eastern Front was unprecedented in its savagery. The point is not that any particular element of warfare was new or even absent for long but that the deliberate combination of elements surpassed any former or concurrent event. The extraordinary death toll among combatants and non-combatants, the destruction of cities, and the devastation of the countryside were the outward signs of this savagery, which is still barely recognized.

The essence of *Weltanschauungskrieg*, though, was not found primarily in overwhelming physical destruction but consisted of acts of vast displacement and the destruction of self-sustaining community networks.[101] This war orchestrated social death on a grand scale—and in this tenet we find both the similarity to and the difference from the Holocaust. While the intrinsic difference of the war against the Soviet Union and against the Jews is obvious, we should note their coincidence. The extermination of all Jews, the Holocaust, commenced just when the ideological war against the Soviet Union culminated, and it reached its zenith during the two-year period when German and Soviet forces fought their war on a retreating Eastern Front. While these campaigns were separate and distinct, even where they overlapped, they were part and parcel of the same complex of ambitions and goals of Nazi Germany, and the deliberation and ferocity with which each was fought put them at the very heart of German warfare.

This coincidence of genocidal war and holocaust raises the question of what *Weltanschauungskrieg* is and to what end it was fought. The problem is that the one sustained historiographic effort to conjoin the war against the Soviet Union and the war against the Jews is not convincing.[102] Arno Mayer has used the stereotypical Nazi reference to a Jewish-Bolshevik conspiracy to align genocidal war and the Holocaust in a hierarchy of goals that emphasized the centrality of anti-

---

[99] Omer Bartov, *Hitler's Army: Soldiers, Nazis, and War in the Third Reich* (New York, 1991).

[100] Norman Naimark, *The Russians in Germany: A History of the Soviet Zone of Occupation, 1945–1949* (Cambridge, Mass., 1995).

[101] Gerlach, *Kalkulierte Morde*. For a more cautionary view, see Theo J. Schulte, *The German Army and Nazi Policies in Occupied Russia* (Oxford, 1989). The latter is an important corrective because we discover the tendency of ordinary soldiers to stay out of trouble as long as possible.

[102] Arno J. Mayer, *Why Did the Heavens not Darken? The "Final Solution" in History* (New York, 1988).

communism. Given the overt ideological link and the practice to liqui-
date both commissars and Jews, sanctioned in the so-called Commis-
sar Order, this would seem a promising interpretation, but neither the
abundant ideological synchronization nor the practical overlap of
genocidal war and holocaust are sufficient grounds for merging them.
Indeed, by December 1941, they had developed into distinctly separate theaters of war—the genocidal campaign against the Soviet
Union characterized by a withdrawal from overt ideology, and the
Holocaust unfolding from what, in spring and summer 1941, still
could be interpreted as racialized security sweeps behind the front
into overtly anti-Semitic exterminism.

The Intent of Nazi
War Aims

The problem remains that while we understand the conduct of Nazi
war and the Holocaust, we have great difficulties grasping the nature
and purpose of the Nazi pursuit of war. The latter poses a particular
problem because the Nazi leadership, while deliberate in its conduct
of war, was quite opaque about its goals or aims. This has led some
historians to speculate, not entirely without reason, that the Nazis' appetite grew with action, but they only knew what they wanted when
they got it.[103] In view of the deliberate nature of both genocidal war
against the Soviet Union and the Holocaust of the Jews, however, this
argument also misses the mark.

The kernel of truth in this latter argument is a highly developed
Machiavellian sense in the Nazi leadership that Hitler applied with
singular cunning to waging war.[104] Military-diplomatic historians have
long marveled about the flexibility of Hitler's politics of war, his deceptions and feints, as well as his pursuit of seemingly contrary options for which the German-Soviet pact of 1939 is the classic case.[105]
Holocaust historians, in turn, have emphasized the "twisted road" to
Auschwitz.[106] But the same historians also agree that the play of diplomacy and the variegations of bringing the "Jewish problem" to a solu-

---

[103] Hans Mommsen, "The Realization of the Unthinkable," in *From Weimar to Auschwitz* (Princeton, 1991).

[104] Andreas Hillgruber, *Hitlers Strategie. Politik und Kriegführung, 1940–1941* (Frankfurt
am Main, 1965).

[105] Donald C. Watt, *How War Came: The Immediate Origins of the Second World War, 1938–
1939* (London, 1989).

[106] Karl A. Schleunes, *The Twisted Road to Auschwitz: Nazi Policy toward German Jews,
1933–1939* (Urbana, 1970).

tion had their limits. The National Socialist leadership never left any doubt that they wanted war and terror—and while they admired violence as such, they also knew well that only combined violence and war could produce what they wanted. The problem is identifying precisely what they wanted within the maze of diplomatic indirections and impulsive pronouncements about their ideological intent. Nonetheless, four main thrusts of the Third Reich's politics of war emerge very clearly and, in turn, lead us back to the zenith of the German war, genocidal war against the Soviet Union, and the Holocaust.

The first war aim of National Socialist Germany was the subordination of eastern Europe under German hegemony and the subjection of all those countries and people, foremost Poland and Serbia, who were seen as the main champions of national liberation in eastern Europe. Since subjection of the East also entailed a profound challenge to France, the achievement of this goal ultimately depended on victory over the French, but possibly this conquest was only an indirect, though inevitable target of Nazi aggression. Nazi Germany tolerated subordinate client states, but not independent nations—and in this sense developed a distinctly post- and antirevolutionary agenda, if we see the nationalizing revolution as the grand revolution of the twentieth century. The essence was to roll back the process of nationalization that followed the collapse of the old monarchies. Nazi war politics differed from a more conservative program of "revision" that pursued a course of border adjustments, often in conjunction with the goal of achieving more "ethnic" borders for German speakers. The latter could be heard within the Nazi movement as well, but the goal for Nazi politics was not border adjustment, as with the Sudentenland, but conquest, subjection, and eradication of eastern European identities, which they pursued by erasing national cultures and eliminating national elites.

Second, there is broad agreement that, radical as this pursuit of dominance in Eastern Europe was, it counted only as a transitory and preliminary move, a prerequisite for the grander ambitions of imperial conquest. Here the discrepancy between older, Wilhelmine imperial fantasies and Nazi ideas, inchoate as they were, are most clearly evident. For although many voices within the Nazi party and surely among Nazified traditional elites (as, for example, the naval officer corps) clamored for a British-style colonial empire and, hence, considered Britain their main enemy, this was not what the Nazi leadership and Hitler wanted. In fact, Hitler steadfastly believed for a long time that there would be no conflict of interest between Britain and Nazi Germany, which is why he did not want to fight a war with Britain and regularly deplored it.[107] The war that he considered absolutely essential, the one without which Nazi Germany categorically could not do without, was against the Soviet Union. He clearly felt Germany had to fight this war in his lifetime or the Nazi cause would be in vain. The reason for this determination was first and foremost strategic: Any European nation, even a dominant and dominating one, was too small and too vulnerable to be a truly autonomous actor on a global scale. Autonomy could only be achieved with control over the vast resources of Russia. Whoever held this advantage could consolidate its hold over Europe (given Europe's dependence on external resources). The conquest of the Soviet Union, in other words, was the key both for becoming a superpower (which European nations were incapable of achieving on their own) and for consolidating the hold over a notoriously uncontrollable Europe of squabbling tribes and vainglorious states. Without the Soviet Union, there was no global power and no Europe—and hence a permanent state of dependence and insecurity. German elites didn't recognize until 1942–43, however, that the Soviet Union could actually become a superpower in its own right, and resuscitated some of the anti-Bolshevik animus of 1918.[108] That the United States was seen as the other superpower can be assumed, but America entered the Nazi world picture by her own design.[109] Still, Nazi thinking was quite clear: Global power was needed to ascertain autonomy in the twentieth-century world, but European nations were too small to sustain this power on their own.

The global, geopolitical imperative was intimately and insolubly tied to a third, more distinct National Socialist war aim. At the heart of the National Socialist notion of conquest in eastern Europe and the Soviet Union lay the idea of reconstructing German territory and populations in a technocratic regime of settlement. The regime of biopolitics and population management within Germany was magnified in the conquest of the East. Assessing this grander biopolitical agenda is difficult, however, because the first steps toward implementation, in occupied Poland and the Baltic states in particular, caused pandemonium. When greed took over, wanton pillage was sometimes impossible to distinguish from long-term initiatives. These initiatives for creating a grander Germany, based on massive schemes of population management, were adopted and found considerable popular support with legions of officials, settlers, and hangers-on descending on the occupied

[107] Bernd Martin, *Friedensinitiativen und Machtpolitik im Zweiten Weltkrieg 1939–1942* (Düsseldorf, 1974).

[108] Hans-Erich Volkmann, ed., *Das Russlandbild im Dritten Reich* (Cologne, 1994).

[109] Andreas Hillgruber, *Der Zenit des Zweiten Weltkrieges, Juli 1941* (Wiesbaden, 1977).

East, but they should give us pause. The very abundance of agencies established for exploiting the land and its people caused bewilderment. Also, a closer look at key initiatives suggests, that remaking the land and its populations into the German image and a German ruling class was not just some nebulous scheme of agro-romanticism but a vast infrastructural endeavor to claim land, shuffle people, and establish transportation systems.[110] The contrast between reality and blueprints was stark and deadly, but the visions articulated, as, for example, in the *Generalplan Ost*, suggest the imposition of vast projects of social engineering on what the German experts considered a wild and irrational East, with the goal of putting the land and subject populations to productive use.[111] One should add that the plans for the indigenous people were even more lethal and destructive than the reality.

The fourth and final war aim consisted of remaking German populations into a racialized *Volk*, a German body politic with a core excised of both Jewish influence and Jewish persons. The genealogy of this project, which can be traced back to the nineteenth century, does not concern us as much as the intimate and violent link between the excision of Jews and the constitution of Germans as a superior, biologically improved *Volk*. To this tradition of right-radical thought we should add a second strand, which brings us back to the notion of catastrophic nationalism and Fischer's war aims. Fischer, and an entire generation of historians, curiously underestimated the very deep sense of vulnerability and past grievance that undergirded so much of the most extreme war aims debate in Germany.[112] The sense of abjection simply did not register, although this sense of utter panic over German weakness (often captured as progressive degeneration) distinguished the radical Right from Gilded Age nationalists. The intimate and emotional ties to a radical anti-Semitism are unexplored, for the most part, because the very idea of the nation as an emotional state had not yet entered the debate.[113] Defeat and revolution in 1918 and the Versailles Treaty only confirmed the radical Right's long-held belief that they were the butt of global abuse and internal conspiracy, with Bolshevism being added to racial anti-Semitism, and that Germans would only become a superior race or people by shaking off this global and intimate conspiracy embodied in the Jewish image. The biopolitical schemes fit

[110] Dwork and van Pelt, *Auschwitz*.

[111] Mechthild Rössler and Sabine Schleiermacher, eds., *Der "Generalplan Ost". Hauptlinien der nationalsozialistischen Planungs- und Vernichtungspolitik* (Berlin, 1993).

[112] Roger Chickering, *We Men Who Feel Most German: A Cultural Study of the Pan-German League, 1886–1914* (Boston, 1984).

[113] Etienne François, Hannes Siegrist, and Jakob Vogel, eds., *Nation und Emotion. Deutschland und Frankreich im Vergleich, 19. und 20. Jahrhundert* (Göttingen, 1995).

this end, but the most telling formulation of this war aim came with the ambition, which can be traced back into World War I, to undo the modern history of German migration and diaspora by repatriating and reconsolidating all Germans into a single racial territory that would expand deep into the East and be serviced by ethnic underclasses.[114] We rediscover in these efforts to re-embody Germans as a people an unconditional craving for superiority, premised on a sense of past abjection that could send Nazi leaders, as well as ordinary soldiers and officials, into paroxysms of rage. Hitler's call for all-out extermination, the Holocaust, in December 1941 can, therefore, be seen both as a momentary exasperation in a critical moment of the war and as the deliberate pursuit of a final solution that remade Germans into a race of masters as the ultimate act of war, the assertion of superiority through the elimination of the Jews.

In terms of Nazi ideology, all this was the fulfillment of age-old dreams and the realization of German destiny. For the population managers and settlement experts, it was their chance to create *Lebensraum* for better German living and a superior European order. For the security forces and their henchmen, it was the testing ground to demonstrate ruthless efficiency. For ordinary Germans, it was a bit of everything—and a lot of second-guessing if anything but grief would come from these Nazi schemes. If we look more closely into the society of conquerors we discover greed, jealousies, hatreds, backstabbing, and breathtaking inefficiencies and slovenliness, together with all manner of abuse and brutality—as one might expect from a class of conquerors who wielded absolute power. But the pettiness of the enterprise should not obscure the fact that its effect was the destruction of eastern Europe—the annihilation of the Jewish population, the death and uprooting of millions upon millions of people, the unmaking of a venerable urban tradition, the erasure of national cultures, and the unraveling of grown solidarities and bonds of belonging. It was an unprecedented deadly regime of conquest, which says much for a region that had been devastated many times in the bloody terror of nationalist upheavals and civil wars.

But what was the historical place of this horrendous enterprise? And why was it so difficult to prevent? In a manner, Fischer was on the right track, for what we saw unfold was the radical-Right and ultra-nationalist answer to the "German question."[115] This German

---

[114] Michael Geyer will explore this issue in some detail in his forthcoming study on catastrophic nationalism.

[115] Wolf D. Gruner, *Die deutsche Frage. Ein Problem der europäischen Geschichte seit 1800* (Munich, 1985).

question had always been how to unify the ethnically fragmented and religiously and socially divisive German people, how to hold together the global German diaspora, and how to make the German nation safe in a world of empire. It was exacerbated when the initial solution, the Second Empire, fell apart in World War I and older memories of deleterious defeat (Napoleon) and disastrous civic disunity (Thirty Years' War, Peasant Wars) resurfaced. The radical nationalist answer was that Germany would either have an empire, ruled by a racially homogeneous, repatriated nation, or it would be nothing at all; that Europe would either have to band together under German leadership or disappear in the competition of global regimes; and that the imperial people would have to be purified from their internal sources of discord, exemplified by the Jews, so that they could rule or they would fall apart. What the Nazis offered is a whole series of final solutions, which all amounted to one choice—either constitute a German people by force or cease to exist at all.[116] Germans have had to learn to live with the disastrous consequences of this genocidal strategy for becoming a nation ever since.

[116] Isabel Hull is preparing a study on "final solution" as a German way of problem-solving.

5

The Totalitarian Temptation[1]: Ordinary Germans, Dictatorship, and Democracy

Appalled by the Nazi seizure of power, the Jewish scholar Victor Klemperer recorded the establishment of a "party dictatorship" in his diary in the spring of 1933: "It is depressing [to see] how day by day naked violence, breaches of law, most terrible sanctimoniousness and barbaric spirit openly appear as governmental orders." Though realizing that he had now become a hostage to anti-Semitism, he actually felt "more shame [for Germany] than fear . . . because the left gave up without a fight and the rest went along opportunistically under the pressure of the nazified street."[2] Twelve years later, an exhausted Klemperer experienced "a great feeling of relief and gratitude (towards whom?) for having really survived all this incredible, hardly romantic danger." As the Third Reich crumbled, he noted ironically, "now everybody has *always* been an enemy of the party," making it "all the more puzzling, how Hitlerism could ever have won out." But on his

[1] Jean-François Revel, *The Totalitarian Temptation* (Garden City, N.Y., 1997).
[2] Victor Klemperer, *Ich will Zeugnis ablegen bis zum letzten. Tagebücher 1933–1945*, vol. I (Berlin, 1995), 6 ff.

difficult trek home to Dresden, this astute observer began to suspect that liberation from one dictatorship might mean the beginning of another: "What I have experienced under the Russians so far does not look like personal freedom and security."[3]

How can one explain Germany's shocking "departure from the community of 'civilized peoples' " that allowed the dictators of the Right and the Left to seize and maintain power? Hitler's success has been attributed to diverse reasons, such as a deep-seated "eliminationist anti-Semitism" or a particular power constellation in January 1933,[4] but the question of origin is not posed with the same urgency for the communist dictatorship because it is seen as a "Soviet homunculus."[5] Able to attract only a minority of committed followers, each extremist movement was forced to rely on the support of ordinary people to put its dictatorship into power and keep it there. Since the apparatuses of repression symbolized by the Gestapo and the Stasi were not large enough to control either population by force alone, the Nazi and communist systems needed a surprising amount of voluntary cooperation from below for their smooth functioning.[6] If Alexander Solzhenitzyn is correct in asserting that the victims could have halted their oppression by refusing to comply, the analytical challenge consists of explaining the reasons for the "reluctant loyalty" of those masses that provided support for the NS and SED regimes.[7]

Though diametrically opposed, both terrorist states might perhaps be understood as rival versions of a basic transformation of European politics during the early twentieth century. Hannah Arendt pointed out the importance of the rise of masses of "atomized and isolated individuals" as a result of advancing industrialization to explain the passive following of totalitarian movements.[8] In Germany the problem was particularly severe because the demand for wider participation rights from many workers, artisans or peasants, and some intellectuals in leftist parties and trade unions clashed with the semiconstitutional structure of the Empire. Afraid of losing their power, some members

---

[3] Victor Klemperer, *Tagebücher 1942–1945*, vol. II (Berlin, 1995), 760 ff.

[4] Daniel J. Goldhagen, *Hitler's Willing Executioners: Ordinary Germans and the Holocaust* (New York, 1996), 4 ff.; and Henry Ashby Turner, *Hitler's Thirty Days to Power: January 1933* (Reading, Mass., 1996).

[5] Norman Naimark, *The Russians in Germany: A History of the Soviet Zone of Occupation, 1945–1949* (Cambridge, Mass., 1995).

[6] Ian Kershaw, *The Nazi Dictatorship: Problems and Perspectives of Interpretation* (London, 1993); Jürgen Kocka, ed., *Historische DDR-Forschung. Aufsätze und Studien* (Berlin, 1993).

[7] The term is from Klaus-Michael Mallmann and Gerhard Paul, *Herrschaft und Alltag: Ein Industrierevier im Dritten Reich* (Bonn, 1991), 327 ff.

[8] Hannah Arendt, *The Origins of Totalitarianism*, 3rd ed. (New York, 1973), 305 ff.

of the nobility and the *Großbürgertum* resorted to populist countermo-
bilization strategies of acclamation, Bonapartism, and manipulation
from above.[9] At the same time, the desire of the poor and exploited for
greater prosperity and security necessitated an expansion of the role of
government by reducing economic risks and regulating social changes.
This clamor for increased public assistance, when amplified by academic reformers, led to the establishment of a social service bureaucracy that produced an "authoritarian welfare state," trading paternalist aid for political acquiescence.[10]

Competing attempts at conceptualization, inspired by the subsequent contest between dictatorship and democracy, might offer a theoretical starting point for solving this puzzle. Already during 1933
Klemperer "equated National Socialism and Communism: both are
materialist and tyrannical, both disregard and negate intellectual and
personal freedom."[11] After World War I, political theorists who were
fascinated by these similarities of both dictatorships developed the
concept of "totalitarianism" to account for the novelty in the extent
and methods of repression.[12] During the 1970s liberal analysts, seeking
to soften the German division, proposed a less judgmental comparison
between various policies of the Communist and the western democratic systems so as to analyze their actual functioning.[13] After 1990
the collapse of communism revived the totalitarian approach by looking back from the second dictatorship to the first to probe the interrelationship of both repressive regimes in a systematic *Diktaturvergleich*.
But this dual perspective must be expanded through the incorporation
of the preceding and succeeding democracies to account for the full
complexity of the struggles between political regimes in the twentieth
century.[14]

[9] Geoff Eley, ed., *Society, Culture and the State in Germany, 1870–1930* (Ann Arbor, 1996);
and Hans-Ulrich Wehler, "A Guide to Future Research on the Kaiserreich?" *Central European History* 29 (1996): 541–72.

[10] Young-Sun Hong, *The Contradictions of Modernity and the Politics of Welfare Reform:
Welfare, Citizenship, and the Formation of the Weimar State, 1919–1933* (Princeton, 1997).

[11] Klemperer, *Tagebücher*, vol. I, 75.

[12] Eckhard Jesse, ed., *Totalitarismus im 20. Jahrhundert. Eine Bilanz der Internationalen
Forschung* (Baden Baden, 1996); and Alfons Söllner, ed., *Totalitarismus. Eine Ideengeschichte
des 20. Jahrhunderts* (Berlin, 1997).

[13] Peter Christian Ludz, *Parteielite im Wandel. Funktionsaufbau, Sozialstruktur und Ideologie der SED-Führung* (Cologne, 1968). See also the diatribe by Jens Hacker, *Deutsche
Irrtümer. Schönfärber und Helfershelfer der SED-Diktatur im Westen*, 3rd ed. (Frankfurt,
1994).

[14] Francois Furet, *Le passé d'une illusion. Essai sur l'ideé communiste au XXe siècle* (Paris,
1995), suggests such a broader framing. Cf. the more limited papers of Eckhard Jesse
and H. Pohl in Bundeszentrale für politische Bildung, ed., "Demokratie und Diktatur in
Deutschland" (conference documentation, Berlin, 1998).

Any rethinking of this three-cornered contest between the rival ideologies would benefit from focusing on the issue of popular support
with the help of some of the methodologies of everyday and cultural
history. To transcend the preoccupation of totalitarianism with coercion from above, a more subtle analysis of grassroots participation
might conceive of "*Herrschaft* as social practice," thereby leaving room
for the attempts of ordinary people to determine their own lives
through a stubborn *Eigen-Sinn*.[15] To escape emphasis on *Durch-
herrschung*, prevalent in studies of dictatorship, comparisons of dictatorships and democracy could be broadened to open up other dimensions such as economic measures and social policies that generated
loyalty through improving people's lives.[16] To go beyond sociostruc-
tural determinism, complex cultural questions might also be asked
about the power of language and discourse in producing a self-disci-
plining *Herrschaftsdiskurs* of voluntary internal compliance.[17] Such a
methodological perspective could allow historians to compare support
for dictatorship and democracy, and to see a traditional subject in a
new way.

The Transformation of Politics

Around the turn of the century the newly established German national
state faced an unexpected challenge in the rise of mass politics. As portrayed in Fontane novels, *Honoratiorenpolitik* had traditionally been a
matter of local notables meeting at an inn to propose candidates and
rally the wealthy as well as educated for programs that would be supported by their inferiors out of a sense of deference. But around 1900,
Catholic processions, as well as Socialist demonstrations, began to disturb that order by bringing thousands of people into the streets to lis-
ten to incendiary speeches filled with calls for increased participation

---

[15] Alf Lüdtke, ed., *Herrschaft als soziale Praxis. Historische und sozialanthropologische Studien* (Göttingen, 1991); and Thomas Lindenberger, "Projektvorstellung: Herrschaft und
Eigen-Sinn in der Diktatur," *Potsdamer Bulletin für Zeithistorische Studien* 5 (December
1995): 37–52.

[16] Ian Kershaw and Moshe Lewin, eds., *Stalinism and Nazism: Dictatorships in Comparison* (Cambridge, 1997); Günther Heydemann and Christopher Beckmann, "Zwei Diktaturen in Deutschland. Möglichkeiten und Grenzen des historischen Diktaturvergleichs,"
Deutschland-Archiv 30 (1997): 12 ff.

[17] Martin Sabrow, "Projektvorstellung: Geschichte als Herrschaftsdiskurs in der DDR,"
Potsdamer Bulletin für Zeithistorische Studien 5 (December 1995): 53–63; and Georg G. Iggers,
Konrad H. Jarausch, Matthias Middell and Martin Sabrow, eds., "Die DDR-Geschichtswis-
senschaft als Forschungsproblem," *Historische Zeitschrift* special issue no. 27 (1998).

and remedying of social abuses.[18] The dismayed, largely Protestant noble or grand bourgeois leaders of the community responded by formalizing their networks into tight interest groups (*Verbände*) and rousing their own peasant or artisan following through nationalist, imperialist, and militarist rhetoric. The result of this unprecedented popular mobilization was an intensifying contest between leftist and rightist parties, pressure groups, or unions for the allegiance of the masses, necessary for winning parliamentary elections and obtaining political power.[19]

The imperative of appealing to a larger following meant that political elites had to become more responsive to the demands of the less fortunate for prosperity and security. From a mixture of cynicism and compassion, Prince Bismarck in the 1880s responded to academic debates about the "social question" by initiating a social policy of accident, health, and retirement insurance so as to insulate the poorer classes against subversive agitation by giving them "a stake in society." Intent on papering over the class struggle, bourgeois reformers collaborated with moderate socialists, especially on the municipal level, in extending this limited system to broader constituencies even before World War I. To the horror of Manchester liberals, this turn to social policy superseded older versions of private and religious charity and made the state responsible for taking care of its most unfortunate citizens. Since support measures tended to be popular with their putative recipients, they became linked with demands for inclusion in the conception of the modern welfare state.[20] German politics in the twentieth century revolved largely around the question of which version of participation and security would prevail.

By shattering the uneasy balance of the Second Reich, World War One intensified the ideological competition for popular loyalty. At first, the proclamation of a "truce in the castle" seemed to have restored a unity of national purpose, but soon the suspension of politics proved unworkable because military control favored the Right.[21] Although the Social Democrats were partially co-opted into the imperial system,

---

[18] Thomas Nipperdey, *Deutsche Geschichte, 1866–1918*, vol. I: *Arbeitswelt und Bürgergeist* (Munich, 1990); and Jonathan Sperber, *The Kaiser's Voters: Electors and Elections in Imperial Germany* (Cambridge, UK, 1997).

[19] Roger Chickering, *We Men Who Feel Most German: A Cultural Study of the Pan-German League, 1886–1914* (Boston, 1984); and Margaret L. Anderson, *Practicing Democracy: Elections and Political Culture in Germany* (Princeton, 2000).

[20] George Steinmetz, *Regulating the Social: The Welfare State and Local Politics in Imperial Germany* (Princeton, 1993).

[21] Konrad H. Jarausch, *The Enigmatic Chancellor: Theodor von Bethman Hollweg and the Hubris of Imperial Germany, 1856–1921* (New Haven, 1973).

they began to agitate for a compromise peace, improved working conditions in the munitions factories, and political reforms that would lead to a true parliamentary government. At the same time, various right wing groups and conservative partisans gathered into a nationalistic mass movement, called *Vaterlandspartei*, to agitate in favor of annexationism, the unrestricted use of submarines, and outright victory, supporting the quasi-dictatorship of Hindenburg and Ludendorff. Impatient with the half-heartedness of the SPD majority and emboldened by Lenin's coup in Russia, a more radical minority, named after the Roman slave revolutionary Spartacus, called for an immediate end of the fighting as well as a social revolution.[22] World War I, therefore, initiated the ideological struggle between what would become competing visions of democracy, fascism, and communism.

Because of revulsion against Wilhelmine authoritarianism and hopes for Wilsonian self-determination, the initial victor in this three-cornered contest turned out to be, somewhat surprisingly, the Weimar Republic. In response to liberal middle-class calls for parliamentary government and socialist working-class aspirations for a better life, the first German democracy sought to enlarge rights of political participation, for instance for women, and to offer a greater amount of social security. While the communist schism with Social Democracy destroyed its parliamentary majority, various right-wing coups demonstrated the discontent of dispossessed elites, such hostile institutions as the army, and alienated social groups such as the peasantry.[23] Nonetheless, the Weimar Republic survived the crippling problems of a peace treaty that many considered punitive and of hyperinflation that wiped out part of the middle classes by broadening access to decision-making and enlarging the sphere of social responsibility of the state. Ultimately, the first attempt at democracy failed for a combination of reasons, such as adverse circumstances like the Great Depression, technical faults in its constitution, eroding support among segments of society, and cultural distance from conceptions of liberty.[24]

Coming to power as result of popular support and elite complicity, the Nazi movement promised a modern right-wing version of participation and security without political divisiveness and economic risks. To stem the disintegrative effects of individualism, the "national revo-

---

[22] See also Bernd Sösemann's edition of the Theodor Wolff diaries, *Tagebücher 1914–1919. Der erste Weltkrieg und die Entstehung der Weimarer Republik*, 2 vols. (Boppard, 1984).

[23] Hagen Schulze, *Weimar. Deutschland 1917–1933* (Berlin, 1982); and Heinrich August Winkler, *Weimar 1918–1933. Die Geschichte der ersten deutschen Demokratie* (Munich, 1993).

[24] Jürgen Falter, *Hitlers Wähler* (Munich, 1991). For a sectoral study, cf. Konrad H. Jarausch, *The Unfree Professions: German Lawyers, Teachers and Engineers, 1900–1950* (New York, 1990).

lution" suggested subordinating the self to the dictates of a dynamic leader in the name of regaining national unity and international influence. To give citizens a sense of involvement while absolving them of any responsibility, Hitler's helpers sought to mobilize the masses through endless rallies, various NS auxiliary organizations, and such massive campaigns as the *Winterhilfswerk*.[25] At the same time they propagated the ideal of a people's community, called *Volksgemeinschaft*, as a form of domesticated socialism that stressed symbolic equality between different strata and offered various benefits in exchange for abandoning the class struggle.[26] While full employment and initial victories made the Third Reich popular among those not suffering from persecution, its ultimate price turned out to be mass death, physical destruction, expulsion, and division not just for the victims but also for the perpetrators.

As left-wing negation of the nationalist dictatorship, the Communist experiment promoted yet another combination of mass involvement and social provision. To avoid democratic chaos or racist repression, Marxist-Leninist workers and intellectuals sought to realize the traditional aims of the German labor movement in a more radical antifascist fashion: On the one hand, the SED hardened the welfare agenda into a far-reaching social revolution by dispossessing the *Junkers* of their estates, depriving the capitalists of their ownership of industry, subsidizing food as well as transportation, offering free education to all, and granting women greater equality.[27] On the other hand, the GDR as a minority project that rested on Red Army bayonets, transformed its democratic trappings into a "dictatorship of the proletariat," ruling in a Rousseauian sense *for the people*. Honecker's "unity of social and economic policy" essentially represented a bargain of modest prosperity and security in return for political acquiescence in the rule of the SED.[28] But when the planned economy stalled and the Soviets withdrew their support, the very masses that the GDR claimed to serve chose to return to bourgeois democracy.

The totalitarian temptation was, therefore, a result of the double failure of the authoritarian paternalism of the Second Empire and of the

---

[25] Martin Broszat, *The Hitler State: The Foundation and Development of the Internal Structure of the Third Reich* (London, 1981); and Jost Dülffer, *Nazi Germany, 1933–1945: Faith and Annihilation* (London, 1996).

[26] Ronald Smelser, *Robert Ley: Hitler's Labor Front Leader* (Oxford, 1988); and Mallmann and Paul, *Herrschaft und Alltag*, 114 ff.

[27] Eric Weitz, *Constructing German Communism, 1890–1990: From Popular Protest to Socialist System* (Princeton, 1997).

[28] Hermann Weber, *DDR. Grundriß der Geschichte, 1945–1990*, 2nd ed. (Hanover, 1991); and Mary Fulbrook, *Anatomy of a Dictatorship: Inside the GDR, 1949–1989* (Oxford, 1995).

social democracy of the Weimar Republic.[29] While the former was associated with death and the defeat, the latter became synonymous with political chaos and socioeconomic suffering, thereby discrediting efforts of the liberal, Catholic, and socialist parties to combine participation with social reform. By joining forces in obstruction, the Nazis and Communists were strong enough to topple the unloved Republic, but, as minorities from opposite ends of the political spectrum, both required the acquiescence of a considerable part of the public to establish their own rule. Aided by an illiberal tradition of scapegoating presumed racial or class enemies, their ensuing dictatorships of the Right and the Left sought support by offering a greater degree of social security in exchange for political acclamation.[30] In Germany more than in any other country, creative intellectuals and ordinary people were caught in a contest between the fading promises of democracy and the futuristic claims of rival dictatorships. Which were the chief pillars that propped up both totalitarian regimes?

Coercion and Compliance

By definition, dictatorships rely more on compulsion than on persuasion to make their people comply with the wishes of the rulers. Informed by the resentment of defeated democrats, moving tales of suffering by victims, and occasional confessions of perpetrators, totalitarianism theory privileges the apparatus of repression and manipulation in its analysis. The famous catalogue of traits, developed by Carl J. Friedrich, stresses structural dimensions of rule such as control by a single, all powerful leader exercised through a governing party that holds a political monopoly; it also emphasizes aspects of intimidation of the populace by the military and the police that violate individual rights; and finally it highlights elements of ideological direction through propaganda and censorship that provide a broader rationale for the system.[31] By relying on bureaucratic evidence such as programs, orders, and guidelines from above, this ideal type has created a rather stylized understanding of dictatorship that focuses on the formal struc-

[29] Detlev J. K. Peukert, *The Weimar Republic: The Crisis of Classical Modernity* (New York, 1989), 241 ff.

[30] Fritz Stern, *The Failure of Illiberalism: Essays on the Political Culture of Modern Germany,* 2nd ed. (New York, 1992); and Konrad H. Jarausch, "Illiberalism and Beyond: German History in Search of a Paradigm," *Journal of Modern History* 55 (1983): 268 ff.

[31] Carl J. Friedrich and Zbingiew Brzezinski, *Totalitarian Dictatorship and Autocracy* (Cambridge, 1965). For Arendt's more dynamic emphasis on ideology and terror, see her *Origins of Totalitarianism*, 460 ff.

ture of power, the processes of repression, and the instruments of manipulation.

The strongest evidence for the importance of coercion is the prominence of the military, the police, and the secret service in a dictatorial regime. Pictures of the Third Reich abound with the field gray uniforms of the regular *Wehrmacht*, the brown shirts of the SA thugs, and the intimidating black of the SS elite, while the GDR evokes images of the neotraditional gray uniforms of the NVA, border guards, and factory militia or the olive green of the Red Army. Even the importance of the regular police, such as the Schutzpolizei or the Volkspolizei, increased since the maintenance of public order expanded into previously undreamed of areas. Moreover, the very names of the secret services—the Gestapo and SD or the Stasi, which virtually operated without legal restraint—have become synonymous with treachery and cruelty. If one adds the countless existing prisons and the rapidly proliferating institutions of the concentration camp system with their political, racial, and economic purposes, the apparatus of repression seems as ubiquitous as all-powerful. Because of their ever-expanding size and influence, both the SS and the Stasi have been called a "parallel society," a kind of cancer on the body politic that was ready to metastasize and devour the entire dictatorial state.[32]

The key to the successful functioning of state terror was its unpredictability and selectivity, which left most of those not victimized grateful to have escaped unscathed. Whereas Nazi fanaticism fastened on biological and racial targets, Communist doctrine focused on class adversaries, such as estate owners and industrial capitalists. Both dictatorships persecuted their political opponents but also constructed new ideological enemies in an arbitrary process with changing criteria. Though the Nazis condoned occasional "spontaneous" violence by zealots, both ruling parties preferred to control intimidation by the careful targeting of proscribed minorities. While terror established clear boundaries of what was permitted and reinforced the prohibitions with threats of sanctions, its selective imposition demonstrated to those who were not singled out that they could live in relative peace as long as they conformed. Moreover, the ruling party could claim credit for reestablishing law and order, reducing criminality, and spreading a general sense of security.[33] Klemperer noted the debilitat-

---

[32] George C. Browder, *Hitlers Informers: The Gestapo and the SS Security Service in the Nazi Revolution* (Oxford, 1996); and Karl Wilhelm Fricke, *Die DDR-Staatssicherheit: Entwicklung, Strukturen, Arbeitsfelder* (Cologne, 1982) .

[33] Eric A. Johnson, *The Nazi Terror: Gestapo, Jews and Ordinary Germans* (New York, 1999); Fulbrook, *Anatomy*, 21 ff.

ing effects of such terror: "Everything, literally everything, is overwhelmed by fear. No letter, no phone call, no word on the street is
secure. Everyone suspects the other as a traitor or spy."[34]

Some historians are beginning to complicate this picture of compulsion from above by uncovering evidence of large-scale and partially
voluntary compliance from below. They point out that from ideological
conviction, or from calculating opportunism, millions of ordinary Germans supported both dictatorships, apparently without any qualms. A
case in point is the importance of denunciations for the functioning of
the secret police. Since the Gestapo used only about twelve thousand
operatives to control eighty million people, it had to rely to a considerable degree on information volunteered by ordinary citizens who com-
plained about neighbors who engaged in illicit practices. Whatever
their personal motives, such as envy, revenge, or just nosiness, thousands of normal Germans informed on their *Volksgenossen*, thereby
providing endless leads and spreading a climate of suspicion.[35] Similarly, the much larger Stasi, though counting about 85,000 regulars toward the end of the GDR, thought it necessary to organize another
approximately 180,000 informal informants who reported on every
facet of East German society, from the most trivial to the highly trea-
sonous.[36] To function efficiently, the control of society by the organs of
repression apparently required a considerable amount of cooperation
from regular citizens.

Another indicator of compliance is the prevalence of "volunteering"
in the public campaigns for various causes, mounted by both dictatorial regimes. The Third Reich sought to whip especially the young into
a veritable frenzy of helping to bring in the harvest, collecting alms
for the coming winter, or marching in holiday parades. According to
Klemperer, students "*must* organize demonstrations and agitate with
every method" in Nazi campaigns, turning such volunteer work into
"the hardest compulsion."[37] Similarly, the GDR tried to mobilize workers to exceed their production targets, housewives to collect scarce raw
materials, writers to bring culture into the factories, young people to
march for peace, and the like. No doubt, some individuals found the
continual requests for acclamation irksome, but many others saw the
social pressure as an opportunity to break with the routine of school

[34] Klemperer, *Tagebücher*, vol. I, 14, 39, 50 f.

[35] Robert Gellately, *The Gestapo and German Society: Enforcing Racial Policy, 1933–1945*
(Oxford, 1990).

[36] David Childs and Richard Popplewell, *The Stasi: The East German Intelligence and
Security Service* (New York, 1996).

[37] Klemperer, *Tagebücher*, I: 66.

and work or to affirm their loyalty.[38] The craving for enthusiastic displays of popular feeling and the extensive reporting system on the public mood indicate in a perverse way the special dependence of dictatorships on visible manifestations of popular support.

Recent research on "the limits of dictatorship," therefore, suggests that viewing a dictatorial system as a controlled society, a *durchherrschte Gesellschaft*, may be correct but somewhat incomplete.[39] Microstudies of everyday life draw a far more complex picture of domination as a social interaction between rulers and the ruled in which both sides depended upon each other.[40] When facing postal clerks, traffic cops, or housing officials, ordinary people tried to obtain solutions for mundane problems such as late mail, rude drivers, or leaky apartments. But system representatives also wanted to have the public obey their regulations, participate in their campaigns, and not make any trouble. Countless daily encounters between both sides created mini-bargaining situations in which some criticism was allowed, and compliance presupposed responsiveness to one's concerns. The massive files of popular petitions to an inscrutable authority are an impressive record of attempts of the powerless to sway those in charge; similarly, the record of wildcat strikes illustrates that even humble workers had some possibility for refusal as long as they did not threaten the regime. Though the notion of a "negotiation society" may be overstated, the need for popular support limited coercion and made both Nazis and Communists look for more subtle methods of encouraging cooperation.[41]

Privilege and Performance

Although such scholars as Charles Maier recognize the role of positive incentives in maintaining oppressive regimes, their importance is rarely analyzed in detail. Most discussions of dictatorship center on

[38] Harald Focke, *Alltag unterm Hakenkreuz: Wie die Nazis das Leben der Deutschen änderten* (Hamburg, 1979); and Dietrich Mühlberg, "Die DDR als Gegenstand kulturhistorischer Forschung," *Mitteilungen aus der kulturwissenschaftlichen Forschung* 16 (1993): 7–85.

[39] Jürgen Kocka, "Ein deutscher Sonderweg: Überlegungen zur Sozialgeschichte der DDR," *Aus Politik und Zeitgeschichte* (1994) no. 40: 34–45; and Richard Bessel and Ralph Jessen, eds., *Die Grenzen der Diktatur: Staat und Gesellschaft in der DDR* (Göttingen,. 1996).

[40] See Konrad H. Jarausch, ed., *Dictatorship as Experience: Towards a Socio-Cultural History of the GDR* (New York, 1999); and Thomas Lindenberger, ed., *Herrschaft und Eigen-Sinn in der Diktatur. Studien zur Gesellschaftsgeschichte der DDR* (Berlin, 1999).

[41] Robert Gellately, *Backing Hitler: Consent and Coercion in Nazi Germany* (New York, 2001); and Wolfgang Engler, *Die zivilisatorische Lücke. Versuch über den Staatssozialismus* (Frankfurt, 1992).

the negative aspects of terror since historians seem reluctant to say anything that might be construed as positive about such systems. This omission is deplorable because mounds of fan mail, as well as ubiquitous references in SD-reports, provide ample evidence of Hitler's personal popularity and of his symbolic power as *Führer* of the Third Reich. Although they sometimes ridicule the "cult of personality," jokes about the GDR leaders suggest a reluctant respect for the feisty Ulbricht and a genuine admiration for his successor, affectionately called "Honi."[42] These indications of popular support are too widespread merely to be the result of coercion or propaganda from above, although conscious image building no doubt played a role. Since it often overshadowed private skepticism, the pervasiveness of such public popularity ought to raise questions about non-compulsive sources of regime support.

At least for beneficiaries of the regime in the ruling party and the state apparatus, potential privilege seems to have exerted a powerful attraction. While the NSDAP and SED cultivated a rhetoric of "service to the people,"membership in the movement appears to have afforded an intoxicating sense of power for previously unremarkable functionaries who could now make important decisions. With such influence came a considerable amount of corruption, such as the "shameless self-enrichment in cars, houses, food" among the "Old Fighters," SA thugs, the more stylish SS counter-elite, or collaborators in government and industry, especially during World War II, that sometimes even offended the party faithful. In the GDR with its "nomenclature" system of identifying, cultivating, and promoting cadres, the "Wandlitz syndrome" suggests a growing separation from the common folk in terms of shopping and living standards, albeit at a level of petit bourgeois taste.[43] By cooperating with the system, one could hope to share some modest privileges, such as access to foreign currency or travel abroad.

Secret *Stimmungsberichte* and fragmentary survey evidence show that the loyalty of the general population also rested to a considerable degree on the modest prosperity provided by a regime.[44] Since the Great Depression had cost one-quarter of the work force its jobs and

[42] Ian Kershaw, *The Hitler Myth: Image and Reality in the Third Reich* (London, 1987); and Monika Kaiser, *Machtwechsel von Ulbricht zu Honecker* (Berlin, 1997).

[43] Victor Klemperer, *So sitze ich denn zwischen allen Stühlen. Tagebücher 1945–1949*, ed. Walter Nowojski (Berlin, 1999), 127 f.; and Charles S. Maier, *Dissolution: The Crisis of Communism and the End of East Germany* (Princeton, 1997), 41 ff.

[44] Heinz Boberach, ed., *Meldungen aus dem Reich: Die geheimen Lageberichte des Sicherheitsdiensts der SS*, 17 vols. (Herrsching, 1984); and Heinz Niemann, *Meinungsforschung in der DDR. Die geheimen Berichte des Instituts für Meinungsforschung an das Politbüro der SED* (Cologne, 1983).

reduced another quarter to underemployment, job security seems to have been more important than actual wage increases. Breaking with the deflationary budget-cutting of the presidential cabinets, the Nazis engaged in massive deficit spending on public works and on clandestine rearmament to return to full employment. Even if this countercyclical policy was unsustainable in the long run, its short-term effect, inflated by Goebbels' propaganda, helped restore public hope. Motivated by the Depression trauma, the SED similarly struggled to overcome postwar destruction, hunger, and cold to restore a semblance of normalcy. It also engaged in labor-intensive smokestack industrialization and never tired of touting its full employment policies in contrast to capitalist insecurity.[45] The modest wage increases allowed a broadening of consumption by providing radios (*Volksempfänger*) or cars (*Trabis*) to the masses.[46]

Beyond job security, working people depended on the social policies offered by the respective regime to alleviate their lot. While both Nazis and Communists suppressed independent unions in the spirit of paternalism, their ideological attitudes and actual measures differed considerably. Much to the chagrin of radicals, the "German socialism" proclaimed by the NSDAP remained largely cosmetic since Hitler needed the support of big business for rearmament and foreign expansion. Some campaigns, such as the promotion of "beauty of labor," improved working conditions, but the bureaucracy of the party-supervised "German labor front" mainly promoted leisure as a means to improve industrial productivity.[47] In contrast, the Communist leaders sincerely tried to help the downtrodden by subsidizing basic foodstuffs, offering cheap transportation, and providing low-cost housing. Moreover, numerous policies, from the construction of free kindergartens to the establishment of daylong schooling, sought to facilitate the employment of women. Carrying some Nazi trends further, GDR industrial companies became centers of sport, entertainment, and other services.[48]

---

[45] Dietmar Petzina, *Autarkiepolitik im Dritten Reich* (Stuttgart, 1968); and Charles Maier, "Vom Plan zur Pleite," in Jürgen Kocka and Matrin Sabrow, eds., *Die DDR als Geschichte. Fragen—Hypothesen—Perspektiven* (Berlin, 1994), 109 ff.

[46] Lutz Niethammer, ed., *Lebensgeschichte und Sozialstruktur im Ruhrgebiet 1930–1960*, 2 vols. (Berlin, 1983); Lutz Niethammer, Alexander von Plato, and Dorothee Wierling, eds., *Die volkseigene Erfahrung: Eine Archäologie des Lebens in der Industrieprovinz der DDR* (Hamburg, 1991). See also Hannes Siegrist, Hartmut Kaelble and Jürgen Kocka, eds., *Europäische Konsumgeschichte. Zur Gesellschafts- und Kulturgeschichte des Konsums* (Frankfurt, 1997).

[47] Timothy W. Mason, *Sozialpolitik im Dritten Reich. Arbeiterklasse und Volksgemeinschaft*, 2nd ed. (Opladen, 1977).

[48] Peter Hübner, *Konsens, Konflikt und Kompromiß. Soziale Arbeiterinteressen und Sozialpolitik in der SBZ/DDR 1945–1970* (Berlin, 1995), 130 ff.

The Nazis and SED took special credit for improving the lives of ordinary people through offering affordable forms of leisure and entertainment. The German Labor Front was especially proud of its "strength through joy" program (KdF) which initiated mass tourism by providing cheap vacations within the country as well as organizing well-advertised cruises in the Mediterranean. Similarly, the East German yellow union FDGB constructed holiday facilities from the Baltic Sea to the Bohemian mountains to offer recreation within the GDR, supplemented by an increasing amount of travel to such Southern European neighbors as Hungary, Bulgaria, and Romania.[49] After heavy-handed efforts at indoctrination films foundered, Goebbels's propaganda ministry switched to producing lighter escapist fare by UFA to distract the population from the horrors of the war. The DEFA productions of the GDR show a parallel evolution from overt ideological messages to less political entertainment, albeit from a decidedly class perspective.[50] By exploiting mass entertainment for their own propaganda purposes, the German dictatorships sought to bolster their regimes with indirect means.

Beyond the effects of terror on crushing visible alternatives, the dictatorships' actual performance in providing tolerable lives, therefore, helped keep them in power. No matter their personal attitude toward the governing ideology, people would put up with political restrictions as long as the rulers offered them decent living conditions with some prospect of future improvement. According to Klemperer's informants, even intelligent Germans eventually came to believe that "the Nazis had undoubtedly done some good things."[51] Their more resolute style of decision-making, the outward unity of the governing party, and the rhetorical posturing for the common good seemed to offer "the really or apparently 'dispossessed' " an attractive vision of a national community. Similarly, the SED's real effort to topple "the pillars of reaction," such as Junkers and capitalists, offered workers and peasants unprecedented chances for mobility as well as a new sense of social equality.[52] Ironically, the GDR's extensive welfare system depended on economic performance and therefore remained vulnerable to a loss of support should it fail to deliver adequately.

[49] Paper by Shelly Baranowski on KDF tourism at GSA meeting, September 1997; and Gunhild Fuhrmann, "Ferienscheck und Balaton: Urlaub und Tourismus in den 1960ern," *Mitteilungen aus der kulturwissenschaftlichen Forschung* 16 (1993): 273 ff.

[50] Wolfgang Jacobsen, Anton Kaes, and Hans-Helmut Hinzler, eds., *Geschichte des deutschen Films* (Stuttgart, 1993).

[51] Klemperer, *Tagebücher*, vol. I, 171

[52] Klemperer, *So sitze ich*, 178. Cf. David Schoenbaum, *Hitler's Social Revolution: Class and Status in Nazi Germany* (New York, 1967); and Hartmut Kaelble, Jürgen Kocka, and Hartmut Zwahr, eds., *Sozialgeschichte der DDR* (Stuttgart, 1994).

Idealism and Ideology

In totalitarian theory, ideology plays a central role in explaining the conformity of the populace to the aims of the respective regime. Karl Dietrich Bracher defines the concept as an attempt to create "a comprehensive system of ideas, especially regarding the relationship of man to society and politics . . . which can reduce reality to a formula and distort it as well as obscure it in the interest of power politics." Scathingly, this historian of political ideas calls ideology a "conglomerate of deceptions and self-deceptions" that combines pseudoreligious needs, idealism, and perfectionism with a justification of violence. In a dictatorial context, he defines its most dangerous feature as "the tendency to an extreme reduction of complex realities" through the claim of presenting one truth and at the same time splitting the world dichotomously into friends and foes.[53] Although realizing that not only the masses but also intellectuals are vulnerable to this sort of thinking, the totalitarian understanding of ideology stresses the importance of propaganda in spreading a worldview to legitimize a dictatorial regime. Unfortunately, this instrumental perspective reduces ideology itself to a mere tool to be manipulated at will.

The attraction of ideological blueprints for ordinary Germans becomes more intelligible when one understands them as rival answers to the perennial crises of the Weimar Republic.[54] The curious amalgam of national-socialist ideas promised a return to law and order as well as to a healthy agricultural lifestyle to worried members of the middle class not put off by a populist style. Neoconservative intellectuals could hope that the *Führerstaat* would provide a solution to the problem of leadership, while volkish agitators might look forward to a racial cleansing of the body politic that would remove Jewish influences that threatened to lead to cultural and social decadence.[55] In contrast, Communism sought to capitalize on resentment against capitalist exploitation and Fascist suppression. Marxism appealed to the educated because of its origin in enlightenment aspirations, its uncompromising exposure of bourgeois selfishness, and its claim to scientific certainty. For workers, the revolutionary message promised an immediate im-

[53] Karl-Dietrich Bracher, *Zeit der Ideologien. Eine Geschichte des politischen Denkens im 20. Jahrhundert* (Stuttgart, 1982), 11–18.

[54] Anton Kaes, Edward Dimendberg, and Martin Jay, eds, *The Weimar Republic Sourcebook* (Berkeley, 1994).

[55] Erberhard Jäckel, *Hitlers Weltanschauung: Entwurf einer Herrschaft*, 2nd ed. (Stuttgart, 1981). See also Wolfgang Bialas and Manfred Gangl, eds., *Intellektuelle im Nationalsozialismus* (Frankfurt, 2000).

provement of their living conditions through the expropriation of the hated noblemen or capitalists as well as an eschatological hope of liberation from physical toil, and sharing of the fruits of their efforts.[56] Curiously enough, both oppositional visions involved a large element of faith.

Part of the power of ideology stems from the transformation of language that trickled down from political controversy into everyday usage. As a philologist, Klemperer noticed that the Nazis were misusing traditional words out of ignorance, employing euphemisms when they wanted to hide a distasteful action (like the anti-Semitic boycott), or coining entirely new phrases such as "battle for work." Borrowing from advertising, Goebbels's propagandists favored abbreviations like *Blubo* for "blood and soil" as well as mechanistic expressions like "putting on" or "coordinating" to describe planning a demonstration or taking control of an organization. Prominent in the primitive Nazi vocabulary were words that identified sinister enemies, such as "world Jewish conspiracy" or adjectives such as "Marxist" or "liberalist," which denoted proscribed ideas. The Third Reich also introduced biological metaphors to portray racial inferiority, such as *artfremd*, that struck contemporaries as misplaced when applied to people instead of animals. In a brilliant reflection on the *lingua tertii imperii*, Klemperer systematized his critique of Nazi linguistic dehumanization—and privately extended it to similar tendencies among the Communists, which he ironically called *lingua quatri imperii*. "Except for the ideology, I see no difference between the LTI and the LQI."[57]

The dictatorships also proved more adept at propaganda than the austere republic, since they appealed to emotions through symbols and mass rallies. Klemperer noticed that the Nazis repeated key phrases in the newspapers until such patently false claims as "there was no world war" were believed. The creative combination of a misappropriated Nordic imagery, such as the swastika, with modern technological means, such as the loudspeaker, the radio, and the movies, enthralled the population. Borrowed from military parades as well as demonstrations of the labor movement, the carefully staged "roaring jubilation" of the party rallies created a sense of overwhelming dynamism and community.[58] Although the SED could draw on working-class traditions, such as the red flag, and invoke Soviet models as well, it contin-

---

[56] Klemperer, *Tagebücher*, vol. I, 217. Cf. Furet, *Le passé d'une illusion*, passim.

[57] Klemperer, *Tagebücher*, vol. I, 21, 36 f. , 114, 128 ff, and *LTI: Die unbewältigte Sprache* (Munich, 1969), as well as *So sitze ich*, 76. Cf. Thomas Pegelow, "Towards a Stricter Separation: Constructions and Contestations of 'Jews' and 'Germans' in the Press of Nazi Germany, 1933–1938" (M.A. thesis, Chapel Hill, 1998).

[58] Klemperer, *Tagebücher*, vol. I, 172.

ued to employ the practice of marching thousands of workers before its leaders as visible proof of support. While the Nazis often favored a Germanic primitivism of style in their representations, the Communists preferred a more internationalized form of socialist realism, though both rejected avant-garde modernism as decadent. In contrast to democratic calls for reason, Klemperer noted that dictators heavily relied on irrational appeals. "With such phrases we are time and again force-fed, bludgeoned, and anesthetized."[59]

The transformation of language and the use of symbols combined to create a dictatorial discourse separate, self-referential, and hostile to open debate. As Klemperer quickly discovered, among Nazi zealots, ideology had primacy over reality in determining public consciousness, whereas among Communists, reasoning proceeded deductively by an exegesis of the Marxist-Leninist classics. In both regimes the Party reserved for itself the ultimate authority to provide interpretations of the belief system that would be binding for public speech, thereby determining the manner in which certain problems could be talked about as well as the kinds of solutions that could be proposed. A vital part of the respective ruling discourse was the definition of enemies, such as Jews or capitalists, against which the faithful had to be constantly on guard lest these foes deviously undermine the system. Since discussion could only take place within the basic premises of the ideology, any violation of the code had to lead to elaborate rituals of recanting or to dramatic expulsions from the circle of adherents. This *Herrschaftsdiskurs* was so effective because it functioned as a closed rhetorical system that determined content as well as limits of political consciousness.[60]

The instrumentalized view of ideology, therefore, ought to be expanded to take the visionary and discursive dimensions of its popular appeal into account. No doubt, both dictatorships made ingenious use of propaganda to indoctrinate their populace and employed harsh censorship to suppress any dissenting views.[61] But the emphasis on manipulation fails to appreciate the subtle but cumulative transformation of reality resulting from the alteration of language, the invocation of symbols, and the construction of a new ruling discourse. Klemperer noticed, with disgust, that a fanatical minority had abandoned all "healthy common sense" and instead preferred, in a profound self-

---

[59] Klemperer, *So sitze ich*, 49 f; and Weitz, *Constructing German Communism*, passim.

[60] Martin Sabrow, ed., *Verwaltete Vergangenheit: Geschichtskultur und Herrschaftslegitimation in der DDR* (Leipzig, 1997).

[61] Simone Bark and Siegfried Lokatis, *"Jedes Buch ein Abenteuer." Zensur-System und literarische Öffentlichkeiten in der DDR bis Ende der sechziger Jahre* (Berlin, 1997).

abdication, "only to believe in Hitler and victory." Ironically, the constant griping, joking about the system (such as a new Catholic holiday for "*Maria Denunziata*"), and speaking differently in public and in private only seemed to reinforce the hold of the ruling party upon its reluctant following.[62] A new cultural history perspective, therefore, suggests that one of the most amazing aspects of the dictatorships was the degree to which they depended upon the "self-control" of their repressed subjects. Essential for the stability of "consensus within a dictatorship" on a day-to-day level were the partly enthusiastic, partly reluctant, decisions of millions of individuals to keep themselves in line.[63]

Legitimacy of Democracy

The succession of five different systems within the span of a century suggests that German regimes have faced a profound problem of political legitimacy.[64] According to Max Weber's sociology of rule, governments gain acceptance either from tradition, bureaucracy, or charisma.[65] Because the overthrow of the Hohenzollerns destroyed the inherited bases of legitimacy, the ensuing systems had to rely upon some combination of bureaucratic control and charismatic leadership: The Weimar Republic faced a monarchist civil service and military, never finding a truly popular leader; the Third Reich rode on Hitler's personal mystique, but failed at creating an orderly administration; the GDR bureaucratized socialism, since its leaders lacked charisma; only the FRG succeeded in modernizing the civil service and finding such popular statesmen as Adenauer or Brandt. To refine the Weberian perspective, Sigrid Meuschel distinguishes between the fundamental legitimacy of a regime, based on adherence to its values, and a more superficial loyalty to a system, deriving from its actual performance: "If a society is not dominated by a belief in legitimacy but by loyalty, i.e., a primarily strategic and interest-dependent acceptance of a form of rule, then its permanence can be assumed to be precarious."[66]

---

[62] Klemperer, *Tagebücher*, vol. II, 749 ff. Cf. Fulbrook, *Anatomy of a Dictatorship*, 129 ff.

[63] Konrad H. Jarausch, "Historische Texte der DDR aus der Perspektive des *linguistic turn,*" *Historische Zeitschrift*, 261 ff. Gellately, *Gestapo*, 258, discusses "auto-policing." See also Lindenberger's introduction, *Herrschaft und Eigen-Sinn*, 13 ff; and Martin Sabrow, "Der Wille zur Ohnmacht und die Macht des Willens," *Deutschland Archiv* 33 (2000): 539–58.

[64] Eberhard Jäckel, *Das deutsche Jahrhundert: Eine historische Bilanz* (Stuttgart, 1996).

[65] Max Weber, *Wirtschaft und Gesellschaft* (Berlin, 1964), 157 f. Cf. Frank Wilhelmy, *Der Zerfall der SED-Herrschaft. Zur Erosion des marxistisch-leninistischen Legitimitätsanspruches in der DDR* (Münster, 1995).

[66] Sigrid Meuschel, *Legitimation und Parteiherrschaft in der DDR. Zum Paradox von Stabilität und Revolution in der DDR, 1945–1989* (Frankfurt, 1992), 23.

Ultimately both dictatorial systems in twentieth-century Germany X failed in their attempts to progress from loyalty to legitimacy by offering substitute versions of political participation and social security. The Nazi *Volksdiktatur*, which promised to reconcile nationalism with socialism by replacing public participation with acclamation, and emancipation with social paternalism, lost its popularity when the suffering of World War Two demonstrated that it could not fulfill the bargain of regaining international power for observing domestic docility.[67] Similarly, the Communist *Fürsorgediktatur*, which offered an antifascist alternative and a social revolution, foundered when increased contacts with Western consumerism revealed as unnecessary the exchange of maintaining reluctant acquiescence for obtaining equality and security.[68] In the long run both dictatorships could not maintain the compliance of their subjects since the mechanisms of terror and complicity, privilege and performance, and ideology and idealism on which they relied for support, gradually began to fail.[69] The test of adversity, such as the loss of World War Two and the fall of the Wall, revealed that in a fundamental sense, neither the Third Reich nor the SED regime achieved political legitimacy.

Because of the failure of dictatorial alternatives, democracy returned to Germany more by default than by design. On the one hand, the Federal Republic, prompted by Western occupation authorities, made a conscious effort to reject the noxious patterns of militarism and authoritarianism and to break with the racist nationalism of the Third Reich. Especially on the Left, revelations of Nazi atrocities combined with experiences of personal suffering to engender a strong sense of antifascism that sought to distance itself from the murderous past. On the other hand, the West German state was also a resolute attempt to counter the repressive and leveling policies of the Communist regime sponsored by the Soviet Union. Especially on the Right, the ideological confrontation of the Cold War inspired a sense of Russian danger and a fear of cultural Bolshevism that blended older prejudices into a new

---

[67] See Ian Kershaw, *Hitler 1889–1936* (Stuttgart, 1998). Cf. also Martin Sabrow, "Dictatorship as Discourse: Cultural Perspectives on SED-Legitimacy," in *Dictatorship as Experience*, 195 ff.

[68] Konrad H. Jarausch, "Realer Sozialismus als Fürsorgediktatur. Zur begrifflichen Einordnung der DDR," *Aus Politik und Zeitgeschichte* (1998) no. 20: 33–46.

[69] Heinz Boberach, ed., *Meldungen aus dem Reich 1938–1945. Die Geheimberichte des SD der SS* (Herrsching, 1984); and Ian Kershaw, *Der Hitler Mythos. Volksmeinung und Propaganda im Dritten Reich* (Stuttgart, 1980). Walter Süss, "Selbstblockierung der Macht. Wachstum und Lähmung der Staatssicherheit in den siebziger und achtziger Jahren," and Andre Steiner, "Zwischen Konsumversprechen und Innovationszwang. Zum wirtschaftlichen Niedergang der DDR," in *Weg in den Untergang. Der innere Zerfall der DDR*, 153 ff., 239 ff.

anticommunism. Both of these rejections of dictatorship joined in the conception of totalitarianism as a threat to Western civilization and human rights that provided the founding ideology of the FRG.[70]

It took a series of complex steps to transform an authoritarian, divided nation into a stable democracy, making observers agree that "Bonn is not Weimar."[71] The famous Basic Law was the product of a committed minority of politicians and jurists, seeking to blend German traditions of self-government with Western models, as advocated by the occupation authorities. The restored (SPD) and new (CDU, FDP) political parties sought to become *Volksparteien*, appealing to broader segments of the populace to overcome prior fragmentation. The revived parliament, called *Bundestag*, strove to produce a more stable government by requiring a constructive vote of "no confidence" when trying to topple a cabinet. The electoral system combined Continental traditions of proportional representation with Anglo-American single-member-district practices to eliminate splinter parties while remaining responsive to popular wishes. These constitutional innovations gradually convinced a skeptical majority to accept democracy as a superior solution for the problem of mass politics because it provided for more participation through representative institutions and for greater social security. Moreover, compared to the repression and social turmoil in the Soviet zone, the Western occupation and later alliance came to look benign.[72]

A generation later, impulses often associated with the youth revolt of 1968 triggered a further transformation toward grassroots participation that filled the institutional structures with a participatory spirit.[73] This process of internal democratization was important in supplanting formal compliance with democratic rules by an actual acceptance of their intention as a way of regulating interpersonal conduct, shaping institutional governance, and regulating public space. New Social Movements of pacifism, ecology, and feminism sponsored a rash of grassroots civic protest movements, based on hot button issues and carried on by informal networks that could mobilize masses of supporters. These loose coalitions of concerned citizens brought national questions down to a local level and suggested that individuals could

---

[70] M. Rainer Lepsius, *Demokratie in Deutschland. Konstellationsanalysen* (Göttingen, 1993).

[71] Fritz Rene Allemann, *Bonn ist nicht Weimar* (Cologne, 1956).

[72] Christoph Kleßmann, *Die doppelte Staatgründung. Deutsche Geschichte 1945–1955* (Göttingen, 1991); and Hans-Peter Schwarz, *Adenauer. Der Staatsmann* (Stuttgart, 1991).

[73] Carole Fink, Philipp Gassert, and Detlef Junker, eds., *1968: The World Transformed* (Cambridge, 1998); and Ingrid Gilcher-Holtey, ed., *1968. Vom Ereignis zum Gegenstand der Geschichtswissenschaft* (Göttingen, 1998).

make a difference in furthering peace, bettering the environment, or increasing equality between the sexes. Though some activists tried to force minority views upon the majority by civil disobedience and terrorism (RAF), they added a participatory layer to parliamentary politics and shook up the entrenched party system by founding a less bureaucratic alternative, the Green Party.[74]

After another two decades, the repudiation of Communism by the mass exodus, the peaceful protests, and reluctant SED reform confirmed the process of democratization by bringing Western institutions and practices to East Germany. Forced upon the small network of pacifist and environmental groups by police repression, the rediscovery of human rights repudiated the Communist model of democratic centralism, which had reduced elections to a sham.[75] The unexpected upwelling of democratic feeling in the fall 1989 demonstrations reestablished free debate, compelled the acceptance of a political opposition, triggered the overthrow of the gerontocratic Honecker regime, and forced the pragmatic SED leader, Hans Modrow, into a desperate effort to reform the GDR to stave off its collapse. The first free election in four decades, engineered by the Round Table, produced an overwhelming plebiscite for unification, which led to the accession of five Eastern states, and the diplomatic settlement accelerated the integration of the European Union, resolving the national issue so that Germany might be called "a postnational democracy."[76] Since none of these developments were automatic, explaining the post-totalitarian democratization remains a major challenge for contemporary history.

Perhaps the criteria used in analyzing support for dictatorial regimes might also shed some light on the surprising success of democracy within the same population. No doubt, a degree of coercion was necessary to reestablish self-government in Germany, since democracy had to be re-implanted from the outside through the mandate of the victors in 1945. To avoid a repetition of Weimar failures, the constitution of the Federal Republic proposed the conception of a militant democracy (*wehrhafte Demokratie*), capable of defending itself from political ex-

---

[74] Karl Werner Brand, Detlef Büsser, and Dieter Rucht, *Aufbruch in eine andere Gesellschaft. Neue soziale Bewegungen in der Bundesrepublik* (Frankfurt, 1986); and Gene E. Frankland and Donald Schoonmaker, *Between Protest and Power: The Green Party in Germany* (Boulder, 1992).

[75] Ehrhart Neubert, *Geschichte der Opposition in der DDR 1949–1989* (Berlin, 1997); and Detlef Pollack and Dieter Rink, eds., *Zwischen Verweigerung und Opposition. Politischer Protest in der DDR 1970–1989* (Frankfurt, 1997).

[76] Karl-Dietrich Bracher, *Turning Points in Modern Times: Essays on German and European History* (Cambridge, 1995), 232 ff. Cf. Konrad H. Jarausch, "Die Postnationale Nation: Zum Identitätswandel der Deutschen 1945–1995," *Historicum* (Summer 1995): 30–35.

tremism through forbidding the SRP and KPD.[77] Greater possibilities for personal participation, however, created stronger bonds of voluntary compliance than under the dictatorships. After some initial skepticism, the electorate turned out in record numbers to vote, people joined the newly established parties, and many also were willing to serve in public office. At the same time, citizens revived an amazing variety of voluntary associations, creating a dense network of interest organizations that established a functioning civil society. And from the 1970s on, a great number of grassroots groups coalesced around such topics as peace, the environment, and equal rights, forming a citizens' movement, an unprecedented *Bürgerbewegung*.[78]

Bouts of self-doubt notwithstanding, many West Germans ultimately came to see the Western way of life as more attractive than Nazism or Communism. Overcoming much reluctance, Konrad Adenauer managed to incorporate remnants of the old elites into a democratic system by reestablishing some of their earlier privileges, such as restoring a professional civil service and reintegrating former Nazi collaborators into society.[79] In contrast to the perennial crises of the Weimar Republic, the chancellor democracy that evolved under his leadership also succeeded in radiating authority, maintaining public order, and protecting private lives. Ludwig Ehrhard's gamble on returning to a modified form of neoliberal competition restarted the economy, led to an export boom, created a firm currency in the Deutsche Mark, and eventually brought even the working class a measure of prosperity. At the same time, the social legislation of the Equalization of Burdens Law and other subsequent acts took care of the war victims, such as widows, orphans, veterans, and refugees, while gradually extending welfare provisions to larger segments of the population.[80] By the 1960s, the public considered the FRG's performance clearly superior to prior regimes, as well as to the rival in the East.

Even if committed democrats were in a minority in 1945, ideals of self-government established firm roots in the West and eventually also spread to the East. No doubt, the hesitant conversion was aided by American propaganda during the Cold War, which painted horrifying pictures of the Bolshevik danger and appealed to conservatives to defend a mythical Western civilization (*Abendland*). Although the discipline of political science was imported from the United States to

---

[77] These aspects are sometimes underestimated in the literature.

[78] Dennis L. Bark and David R. Gress, *A History of West Germany,* 2 vols. (Oxford, 1989).

[79] Michael Hayse, "Recasting West German Elites: Higher Civil Servants, Business Leaders and Physicians in Hesse, 1945–1955" (Ph.D. dissertation, Chapel Hill, 1994).

[80] Nicholls, *The Bonn Republic*, passim.

provide theoretical justification for the fledgling democracy, it did eventually manage to obtain academic respectability.[81] Even skeptical Germans learned by doing—criticizing occupation policies, pursuing their own interests, negotiating with opponents, and gradually grasping the virtues of compromise. Intellectually as well, the preoccupation of postwar writers with exposing the horrors of the Third Reich slowly established a critical public in the media, theaters, and schools that understood freedom as precondition for its own voice. By a remarkable process of cultural osmosis, most Germans not only formally accepted democracy but also ultimately internalized its values, developing an emotional attachment to their state that became evident at its fiftieth anniversary.[82]

In contrast to the static and normative theories of democracy, a historical analysis of the complex transformation of German political culture during the second half of the twentieth century will need to focus on several successive processes. First, it was necessary to overthrow the NS dictatorship by military intervention to make space for Western alternatives and to give the liberal minority a chance to remake their ruined polity. Then a lengthy learning process was required to wean the illiberal elites from ingrained authoritarian traditions, pragmatically accept a parliamentary framework, and understand the beneficial results of self-government. Moreover, popular values and behaviors also had to be gradually transformed through habituation and generational succession to internalize patterns of responsible participation in public affairs and acquire greater tolerance for differences of opinion. Finally, an emotional bonding was needed to attach citizens to democracy beyond the vagaries of regime performance, making the rule of law a value worthy of sacrifice beyond any presumed concrete benefits. Such a comprehensive explanation that would conceptualize the democratic transformation as a prolonged and contested process of cultural reorientation has yet to be written.[83]

Has democratic government at last found political legitimacy in Germany at the end of the twentieth century? If durability is any indication, the FRG can claim to have met the challenge of providing participation through parliamentary institutions and welfare through a social market economy. Data on attitudes toward the Basic Law, therefore,

[81] Rupieper, *Die Wurzeln der westdeutschen Nachkriegsdemokratie*, passim.

[82] Axel Schildt, *Ankunft im Westen. Ein Essay zur Erfolgsgeschichte der Bundesrepublik* (Frankfurt, 1999).

[83] Arndt Bauerkämper, "Aneignung als Verfremdung: Die Aufnahme und Vermittlung anglo-amerikanischer Demokratiemodelle in Westdeutschand von 1945 bis zur Mitte der sechziger Jahre" (MS, Potsdam, 2000). For a first step, see Peter Graf Kielmansegg, *Nach der Katastrophe. Eine Geschichte des geteilten Deutschland* (Berlin, 2000).

indicate a shift from a variable performance orientation to a gradual acceptance of democracy as a value on its own, denoted in the term "constitutional patriotism." Many of the lessons of the past have been heeded since leftist antifascism and rightist anticommunism are giving way to a broader anti-totalitarianism as underlying political consensus.[84] But a lingering link between public opinion and regime performance offers some reasons for continuing concern: The emotional attachment to democracy seems to be less deep-rooted in the Eastern states; a tide of repatriation, immigration, and asylum has sparked ugly outbreaks of xenophobia; and pressures of global competitiveness coupled with costs of unification have strained the state's capacity to maintain welfare levels.[85] Nonetheless, the 1998 election of a social-democratic and green government as well as early policies, such as the reform of citizenship, give grounds for guarded optimism that democracy in Germany will continue to meet such challenges.

[84] Dolf Sternberger, *Verfassungspatriotismus*, in *Schriften*, vol. 10 (Frankfurt, 1990), 11–38. See also Jürgen Habermas, *Eine Art Schadensabwicklung* (Frankfurt, 1987), 161 ff.

[85] Konrad H. Jarausch, ed., *After Unity: Reconfiguring German Identities* (Providence, 1997).

6

From Empire to Europe:
The Taming of
German Power

At the turn of the twentieth century Germany belatedly joined the race for overseas empire that already held other European nations in thrall. Instead of being content with its renown as "land of the poets and thinkers," the newly created Second Reich wanted to catch up in acquiring colonies, seeking, in Chancellor Bülow's inimitable phrase, "a place in the sun." The building of William II's favorite toy, the imperial navy, and ill-considered gestures such as sending a gunboat to Agadir, projected an abrasive political style that frightened neighbors and provoked competitors.[1] In contrast, one hundred years later Chancellor Helmut Kohl clearly distanced himself from the legacy of imperialism during his effort to reunify the remainder of the former Reich. Pledging to respect wishes for peace and to continue the process of European integration, he promised, "The FRG stands without ifs, ands or buts to its European responsibility—because especially for us Germans this is true: Europe is our destiny."[2] This commitment to integra-

[1] Bernhard von Bülow, *Denkwürdigkeiten*, 4 vols. (Berlin 1930–31); and Wolfgang J. Mommsen, *Großmachtstellung und Weltpolitik. Die Außenpolitik des Deutschen Reiches 1870 bis 1914* (Frankfurt, 1993).

[2] Helmut Kohl, *Deutschlands Zukunft in Europa. Reden und Beiträge des Bundeskanzlers* (Herford, 1990), 163–180. See also Volker Berghahn, Gregory Flynn, and Paul-Michael

tion betrayed a more modest, multilateral approach based on a chastened understanding of power.

Explaining this drastic transformation of attitudes requires a historical approach to the meaning of power as the ability to project cultural, economic, and political influence beyond a country's borders.[3] Because of its flagrant abuse during the past century, the concept of power has become unfashionable in the German context, but it is, nonetheless, necessary to address its implications since they have governed interactions with neighboring states. Recent discussions in the field of international relations have broadened the narrow neorealist definition, based primarily on military potential, and developed a structural approach that looks at three additional dimensions—culture, economy, and politics.[4] Already during the peace movement of the 1980s, the political scientist Hans-Peter Schwarz called FRG leaders the "tamed Germans," criticizing that in repudiating the expansionist pretensions of their predecessors they had forgotten how to deal with power at all. The return of a unified national state in 1990 raises questions about the accuracy of this chastening thesis: How did the "taming" of German power come about in the postwar period and will it continue to hold for the larger "Berlin Republic?"[5]

From a European perspective, the issue can be restated as inserting a German national state into the established order by negotiation or confrontation.[6] In the past, the informal pentarchy had proven flexible enough to drop some old members such as Portugal, Spain, Holland, or Sweden and to include such newcomers as Russia or Prussia. But in testing new aspirants, the balance of power system ultimately had to resort to war since it lacked any alternative for verifying the relative strength of prospective players. If a state such as Napoleonic France sought to establish its hegemony, the others formed coalitions to put the pretender down, sometimes by diplomatic threats but more often

---

Lützeler, "Germany and Europe: Finding an International Role," in Konrad H. Jarausch, ed., *After Unity: Reconfiguring German Identities* (Providence, 1997), 173–99.

[3] For the multiple meanings of the concept, see *Webster's Third International Dictionary of the English Language Unabridged* (Springfield, 1968), 1778–79; and Peter J. Katzenstein, ed., *Tamed Power: Germany in Europe* (Ithaca, 1997), 1–48.

[4] Andrei S. Markovits and Simon Reich, *The German Predicament: Memory and Power in the New Europe* (Ithaca, 1997), 1–20. Max Otte, *A Rising Middle Power: German Foreign Policy in Transformation, 1899–1999* (New York, 2000), 4–7, distinguishes between realist, institutionalist, and constructivist conceptions of power.

[5] Hans-Peter Schwarz, *Die gezähmten Deutschen. Von der Machtbesessenheit zur Machtvergessenheit* (Stuttgart, 1985). The purpose of the book was to call for a "responsible power policy."

[6] Concept in Dwight E. Lee, *The Outbreak of the First World War: Causes and Responsibilities*, 4th ed. (Lexington, Mass., 1975).

by military force.[7] Integrating the German national state, created in 1871, was complicated by a double legacy—the memory of the Holy Roman Empire, which suggested a hegemonic role as leader of Christendom, and the recollection of territorial division after the Thirty Years War, which implied restraint. The Second Reich, therefore, had to choose whether to be content with mere membership in the concert of great powers, solidified by cooperation, or to aspire to become its conductor, at the risk of provoking hostility.[8]

Unfortunately, the scholarly literatures on German power are so segmented that they have failed to relate the various dimensions of this problem to one another. Since the Fischer controversy, debates on foreign policy have come to revolve around the question of its aggressive versus defensive intent, largely ignoring its structural underpinnings.[9] Studies on the international implications of German culture are rare and controversial, focusing almost exclusively on foreign cultural policy measures.[10] Similarly, the complex econometric research concerns itself more with theoretical questions of uneven development than with the political implications of various business cycles, growth patterns, and the like.[11] Most of the work on European integration is, moreover, limited to the postwar era and preoccupied with institutional development of the Common Market or European Union but not systematically related to a broader historical context.[12] To deal with the complicated reversal of the German role in Europe, it is necessary to draw these various strands together into one analytical approach.

Perhaps a cultural perspective on conceptions, structures, and contexts of power might help shed some new light on such a traditional subject as the "German problem." Recent discussions of "international

[7] Paul Schroeder, *The Transformation of European Politics, 1763 to 1848* (New York, 1994).

[8] Ludwig Dehio, *Germany and World Politics in the Twentieth Century* (New York, 1967). For the persistence of Reich mythology, see also Heinrich-August Winkler, *Der lange Weg nach Westen. Deutsche Geschichte*, 2 vols. (Munich, 2000).

[9] Fritz Fischer, *Griff nach der Weltmacht. Die Kriegszielpolitik des kaiserlichen Deutschland 1914/18* (Düsseldorf, 1961); Andreas Hillgruber, *Die gescheiterte Großmacht. Eine Skizze des deutschen Reiches, 1971–1945* (Düsseldorf, 1980); and Klaus Hildebrand, *Das vergessene Reich. Deutsche Außenpolitik von Bismarck bis Hitler, 1871–1945* (Stuttgart, 1995).

[10] Kurt Düwell and Werner Link, eds., *Deutsche auswärtige Kulturpolitik seit 1871. Beiträge zur Geschichte der Kulturpolitik* (Cologne, 1981); and Hans Arnold, *Foreign Cultural Policy: A Survey from the German Point of View* (London, 1979).

[11] Hans-Joachim Braun, *The German Economy in the Twentieth Century* (London, 1990). See also Knut Borchardt, *Perspectives on Modern German Economic History and Policy* (Cambridge, 1991).

[12] The historiography of European integration is generally disappointing. For a useful introduction, see Derek Urwin, *The Community of Europe: A History of European Integration since 1945*, 2nd ed. (London, 1995); and Wilfried Loth, *Der Weg nach Europa. Geschichte der europäischen Integration 1939–1957* (Göttingen, 1996), 2nd rev. ed.

history" have begun to address the "unspoken assumptions" of the decision makers of the July crisis in 1914 and uncover cultural dimensions of national policies, such as the American reconstruction of Germany.[13] But it is also necessary to develop cultural approaches to economic questions since topics such as the symbolic power of the deutsche Mark as currency seem to cry out for such a reading.[14] Finally, it will be important to go beyond chronicles of the European idea and shift from the social dimension to the cultural aspects of European integration.[15] Because of the paucity of preparatory studies, this chapter can only take a first stab at dealing with some of the learning processes of the elites that ultimately produced a different foreign policy agenda and style. Since this shift was motivated by responses to experiences, the discussion has to begin with the disastrous attempts at outright hegemony in order to reconstruct the successive shocks that led to the taming of German power during twentieth century.

Failed Attempts at Domination

The creation of a German national state in 1871 was bound to upset the established European system because it was at once too large to fit in and too small to dominate outright. Otto von Bismarck therefore counseled his countrymen to assuage "the ill feelings which our establishment as a real great power has created by using our might in an honest and peace-loving manner" so as to make German ascendancy in Europe more tolerable than French, Russian, or English dominance. Though he himself had unleashed three wars during the Prussian conquest of Germany, the Iron Chancellor thereafter pursued a defensive *Realpolitik*, designed to reassure "that we are pacified and peace-loving," claiming to be intent only on "equality with the other great powers of Europe" rather than on further aggrandizement.[16] The new Reich, therefore, posed a dual challenge to the existing order: On the

[13] James Joll, *The Origins of the First World War* (London, 1992); and Michaela Hönicke, "Know Your Enemy: American Interpretations of National Socialism, 1933–1945" (Ph.D. dissertation, Chapel Hill, 1998).

[14] Hansjörg Siegenthaler, "Geschichte und Ökonomie nach der kulturalistischen Wende," *Geschichte und Gesellschaft* 25 (1999): 276–301, takes too narrow an approach.

[15] In the cultural area, nothing compares to Hartmut Kaelble, *A Social History of Western Europe, 1880–1980* (London, 1989); and Wolfgang Schmale, *Geschichte Europas* (Vienna, 2000).

[16] Otto von Bismarck, *Gedanken und Erinnerungen* (Stuttgart, 1928), 543 ff. See also Lothar Gall, *Bismarck. Der weiße Revolutionär* (Frankfurt, 1980); and Ernst Engelberg, *Bismarck*, 2 vols. (Berlin, 1985 and 1990).

one hand, its inexperienced elites needed to learn to live within the informal European system; on the other hand, the neighboring countries had to figure out how to deal with the power rising in their midst.[17]

One foundation of German influence was the renown of *Kultur*, a high culture that extended well beyond its own frontiers. At the beginning of the twentieth century, German was not only spoken by ethnic descendants in eastern Europe, and North and Latin America, but also by neighbors in Scandinavia and central and eastern Europe. Such poets as Wolfgang von Goethe, playwrights as Friedrich Schiller, philosophers as Immanuel Kant, and social critics as Karl Marx were famous the world over. By promoting self-cultivation and the research ethic, German universities set the international standard for science, and were widely imitated, sparking the development of graduate schools in the United States.[18] As the case of Elias Canetti shows, this conception of *Kultur* proved attractive to the Jewish middle class in east central Europe because it drew upon liberal values of rationality and individuality that seemed to formulate human universals. Unfortunately, its inclusive optimism was increasingly challenged by an intolerant Pan-German, volkish, and anti-Semitic strain.[19]

Another source of the Reich's increasing power was the belated but rapid growth of the economy in the last decades of the nineteenth century, which turned the trademark "made in Germany" from a stigma into a sign of excellence. For instance, the basic measure of industrial production expanded tenfold between 1871 and 1913. The lateness of industrialization made for greater speed, larger unit size, more state involvement, and reliance on new technology, such as in electronics and chemicals. Marked as it was by the growing pains of the Great Depression, the process of expansion also produced new forms of industrial organization, which have been dubbed "organized capitalism," to highlight the interdependence between government and industry as well as tendencies toward monopolization and carteliz-

[17] Gerhard Ritter, *Das deutsche Problem. Grundfragen deutschen Staatslebens gestern und heute* (Munich, 1962); David Calleo, *The German Problem Reconsidered: Germany and World Politics, 1870 to the Present* (Cambridge, 1979).

[18] Konrad H. Jarausch, "The Universities: An American View," in Jack R. Dukes and Joachim Remak, eds., *Another Germany: A Reconsideration of the Imperial Era* (Boulder, 1988), 207 ff.; and Henry Geitz, Jürgen Heideking, and Jurgen Herbst, eds., *German Influences on Education in the United States to 1917* (Cambridge, 1995).

[19] Fritz Stern, *The Politics of Cultural Despair: A Study in the Rise of the Germanic Ideology* (Berkeley, 1961); George Lachmann Mosse, *The Crisis of the Volkish Ideology: Intellectual Origins of the Third Reich* (New York, 1964); and Konrad H. Jarausch, "Illiberalism and Beyond: German History in Search of a Paradigm," *Journal of Modern History* 55 (1983), 268–84.

ation.[20] Even if population growth and urbanization created social problems, the increasing wealth, celebrated as *Volkswohlstand* by the banker Karl Helfferich, gave contemporaries a heady sense of pride, dynamic movement, and unlimited possibilities for change. This psychological effect of economic advance made the Empire turn into a "restless Reich."[21]

Cultural tensions and economic success contributed both a strident rhetoric as well as an aggressive style of imperialism that made Germany look threatening to the outside world. Ironically, most colonial possessions had already been acquired by Bismarck during the 1880s, not quite in "a fit of absent-mindedness," but at least in a cautious manner that did not upset continental security.[22] But around 1900 historians, economists, and publicists began to present social-Darwinist analyses of a transition of the international system from Continental to world politics, supported by neo-mercantilist arguments of the need to protect markets and raw materials. Max Weber forcefully argued in his inaugural lecture: "We must understand that German unification would be a youthful folly, committed by an aged nation, that should better have been left undone because of its costs, if it were the conclusion and not the beginning of a German world power policy."[23] Ironically, it was, therefore, the second round of imperialism, coupled with the building of a battle fleet and brusque but unsuccessful efforts to acquire more territory, that provoked alarms over "the German danger," transforming Berlin into a threatening enemy.[24]

The first bid for German hegemony in the Great War was, therefore, a curious amalgam of offensive measures and defensive intentions.[25] The failure of the Kaiser's fleet to protect the colonies and the inability of the new submarines to break the British blockade quickly ended all

---

[20] Hans Rosenberg, *Große Depression und Bismarckzeit. Wirtschaftsverhalten, Gesellschaft und Politik in Mitteleuropa* (Berlin, 1967); and Gerald D. Feldman, ed., *Organisierter Kapitalismus. Voraussetzungen und Anfänge* (Göttingen, 1971).

[21] Michael Stürmer, *Das ruhelose Reich. Deutschland 1866–1918* (Berlin, 1983).

[22] For a somewhat overstated case, see Hans-Ulrich Wehler, *Bismarck und der Imperialismus* (Cologne, 1969). See also Wolfgang J. Mommsen and Jürgen Osterhammel, eds., *Imperialism and After: Continuities and Discontinuities* (London, 1986).

[23] Max Weber as quoted in Fritz Fischer, *Krieg der Illusionen. Die deutsche Politik von 1911 bis 1914* (Düsseldorf, 1969), 69 f.

[24] Paul Kennedy, *The Rise of the Anglo–German Antagonism, 1860 to 1914* (London, 1980). The cultural construction of foreign enemies is a subject that still needs to be investigated.

[25] For the endless debate on the outbreak of the war, see Konrad H. Jarausch, "World Power or Tragic Fate? The *Kriegsschuldfrage* as Historical Neurosis," *Central European History* 5 (1972), 72–92; Samuel R. Williamson, *Austria-Hungary and the Origins of the First World War* (New York, 1991); and Hildebrand, *Das vergangene Reich*, 303 ff.

dreams of an overseas empire. But during the initial victories on land, industrial spokesmen, generals, politicians, and Prussian bureaucrats formulated demands for annexationist war aims that Chancellor Bethmann Hollweg combined into his September Program.[26] Defining as the purpose of the war "the safeguarding of the German Empire for the foreseeable future" through weakening France and pushing back Russia, he proposed, aside from a series of limited territorial gains, "the formation of an economic organization of central Europe through mutual customs agreements" among neighboring countries. In the ensuing stalemate the liberal politician Friedrich Naumann also suggested an indirect form of hegemony in his bestseller *Mitteleuropa*, but with the defeat of Russia, the military and industrialists insisted on outright domination in the Treaty of Brest-Litovsk.[27]

The conduct of World War I, instead, revealed the limitations of a German power that was strong enough to hold a superior coalition at bay for five years but insufficient to achieve ultimate victory. Exploiting regional conflicts, Berlin did manage to acquire some allies, such as the Turks and Bulgarians, but its vision of central Europe reeked too much of hegemony to attract popular enthusiasm elsewhere. Moreover, the failure of the war of movement, anticipated in the Schlieffen Plan, forced the Supreme Command to switch to a strategy of attrition on the western front, which the inferior manpower of the Central Powers would find difficult to sustain. Finally, the economic blockade by the Royal Navy exposed the inadequacy of the raw material base, which no amount of ingenuity in creating substitutes (nitrogen), tighter organization (Rathenau), or labor mobilization (the Hindenburg Program) could overcome.[28] The first bid for hegemony foundered not just on a series of political gaffes, military mistakes, and economic blunders, but on structural reasons, such as authoritarianism, militarism, and limited resources, that nationalist purveyors of the "stab-in-the-back " legend refused to understand.[29]

The development of a more cooperative approach was hampered by the Versailles Treaty, which sought to curb German economic and military power without destroying the national state. The territorial reduction of one-seventh, population loss of one-tenth, massive disarmament, and so on, may have been less severe than contemporaries

---

[26] Konrad H. Jarausch, *The Enigmatic Chancellor: Bethmann Hollweg and the Hybris of Imperial Germany* (New Haven, 1973), 185 ff.

[27] Friedrich Naumann, *Mitteleuropa* (Berlin, 1916). See also the survey by Jörg Brechtenfeld, *Mitteleuropa and German Politics: 1848 to the Present* (New York, 1996), 39 ff.

[28] Roger Chickering, *Imperial Germany and the Great War, 1914–1918* (Cambridge, UK, 1998); and Niall Ferguson, *The Pity of War* (London, 1998).

[29] Peter Fritzsche, *Germans into Nazis* (Cambridge, 1998).

supposed, but lack of negotiations, attribution of war guilt, and the size of the reparations' bill signaled a spirit of revenge that boded ill for the future. These punitive aspects overshadowed the constructive features of the Wilsonian program that were directed toward democratization, self-determination, and cooperation in the League of Nations. The terms shocked not just rabid nationalists but also bourgeois democrats and working-class socialists, indicating that most Germans, unprepared for defeat, viewed the treaty not as a hand of peace but as a form of punishment. The paradoxical nature of a settlement that was too harsh to be accepted by the losers and too lenient to permanently hold them down suggests that the victors also failed to figure out how to incorporate the Germans into a European order.[30]

Only in the mid-1920s did Foreign Minister Gustav Stresemann succeed in breaking the postwar cycle of confrontation in Europe with his "fulfillment policy." The end of the Franco-Belgian Ruhr occupation and the scaling down of reparations with the Dawes Plan induced Berlin to promise in the Locarno Treaty that it would accept the peace treaty and respect its western frontiers. Similarly, the introduction of the *Rentenmark*, backed by a sounder fiscal policy, burst the bubble of the hyperinflation, which had devalued the currency by one trillion, and restored confidence in the economy.[31] If the 1920s were golden at all, it was only between 1924 and 1929 when the brief, but intense, flowering of modernism, called "Weimar Culture," reached its feverish climax.[32] Even in these good years, Stresemann pursued a "revisionist" policy that sought to change the eastern frontiers with Poland by peaceful means.[33] But the Great Depression ended all hopes for peaceful cooperation in Europe by toppling the Weimar Republic and returning German policy to a naked pursuit of dominance.[34]

Despite its professions of peace, the Nazi dictatorship put a premium on the restoration of military might as a precondition for an ex-

---

[30] Klaus Schwabe, *Deutsche Revolution und Wilson-Frieden. Die deutsche und amerikanische Friedensstrategie zwischen Ideologie und Machtpolitik 1918/19* (Düsseldorf, 1971); and Peter Krüger, *Die Außenpolitik der Republik von Weimar* (Darmstadt, 1985).

[31] Carl-Ludwig Holtfrerich, *The German Inflation 1914–1923* (New York, 1986); and Gerald D. Feldman, *The Great Disorder: Politics, Economics, and Society in the German Inflation, 1914–1924* (New York, 1993).

[32] Anton Kaes, Martin Jay, and Edward Dimdenberg, eds., *The Weimar Republic Sourcebook* (Berkeley, 1994).

[33] Henry Turner, *Stresemann and the Politics of the Weimar Republic* (Princeton, 1963); Heinrich-August Winkler, *Weimar 1918–1933. Geschichte der ersten deutschen Demokratie* (Munich, 1993).

[34] Harold James, *The German Slump: Politics and Economics, 1924–1936* (New York, 1986); and Detlev J. K. Peukert, *The Weimar Republic: The Crisis of Classical Modernity* (New York, 1989).

pansionist policy. As a former volunteer for the imperial army, the Austrian-born chancellor dedicated himself to throwing off the shackles of the Versailles treaty, reversing the defeat of World War I, and creating a greater German Reich. He succeeded so quickly in establishing his dictatorial rule because he could count on a revanchist consensus of the diverse monarchist, neoconservative, volkish, and racist groupings that comprised the nationalist right.[35] Financed by massive borrowing and shielded by international barter, the return to full employment via public works even silenced many skeptics in the working class. The concurrent rearmament program that first proceeded clandestinely but came out into the open by the mid-1930s, was designed to provide the necessary weapons for another attempt to establish German hegemony. Based upon a seemingly flourishing economy and rising military strength, Hitler brazenly pursued the goal of treaty revision, cleverly mixing offers of cooperation with threats, cajoling and intimidating at the same time.[36]

The second German effort to seize hegemony by force was, therefore, more thorough in preparation, radical in goals, and merciless in execution than the first. Directed at reversing an earlier defeat, the Nazi attack sought to learn from earlier failures by avoiding through Russian neutrality a two-front war, keeping up domestic morale by isolating the civilian population from the fighting, and marshalling limited resources to achieve local superiority. The novel strategy of the *Blitzkrieg* was not just designed to combine armor and tactical air power to break through enemy lines, trap large numbers of opposing forces, and compel them to surrender by destroying their communication lines. It also husbanded Germany's still limited military resources such as tanks, planes, and artillery by fighting one opponent at a time, then resupplying the *Wehrmacht* and shifting the costs of the continued war onto the already defeated enemy. At the same time, this lightening-strike warfare also attempted to isolate opposing countries politically, promising a share of the spoils to potential allies, and holding out the hand of peace to those countries willing not to get involved. By turning German liabilities into assets, this *Blitzkrieg* strategy proved spectacularly successful in Poland, Scandinavia, and France.[37]

The conception of German power that animated the Nazi crusade was quite primitive, colliding time and again with the exigencies of

<hr/>

[35] Eberhard Jäckel, *Hitler's Weltanschauung* (Middletown, 1972); and Ian Kershaw, *Hitler, 1889–1936*, 2 vols. (New York, 1999–2000).

[36] Gerhard A. Weinberg, *The Diplomacy of Nazi Germany*, 2 vols. (Chicago, 1970, 1980).

[37] Richard J. Overy, *War and Economy in the Third Reich* (Oxford, 1994); and Gerhard A. Weinberg, *A World at Arms: A Global History of World War Two* (Cambridge, UK, 1994).

modern warfare. Hitler, NS ideologues and the SS brain trust thought of might as spatial, believing that the possession of territory rather than a mobile use of military force provided security, a view that would ultimately hasten defeat in the East. At the same time, the party leaders supported an agrarian vision of a healthy body politic, renourished through direct work on the soil, a conception that stood in crass contradiction to the technological innovations required by industrial warfare. Moreover, the NS movement carried from its origins as a free corps a gendered view of male bonding that reduced women to birthing machines, to be kept at home rather than mobilized for war production. Finally, the Nazi elite argued in racial terms, touting the superiority of Aryans, and considering all other races, especially Slavs, Jews, and Roma, as genetically inferior. As a result it spent scarce resources to resettle ethnic Germans, and at the same time engaged in an extermination program through work or industrial killing of entire populations, desperately needed as slave-laborers to produce the weapons for its sputtering war machine.[38]

Because of the boundlessness of its Reich mythology and ruthlessness toward others, the second bid for German hegemony failed to an even greater degree than the first. The frantic effort by Goebbels' propaganda machine to enlist volunteers from NS client states under the banner of "Fortress Europe" could only postpone the inevitable defeat. In cultural terms, the Nazi message of anti-Bolshevism did not resonate since Aryan purity and superiority hardly proved inspiring to non-Germans—instead, its involvement justifying SS crimes tarnished the heritage of *Kultur*. In economic terms, Berlin's dreams of controlling the continent foundered on the inadequacy of material resources and on the military's slowness to recognize the significance of inventions, such as the jet fighter or the atomic bomb. In political terms, the project of creating a new European order collapsed since its instrumental attitude toward potential allies, for instance, Vichy France or a white Russian army, showed that Nazi hegemony left no space for sincere collaboration.[39] Ultimately, the quest for racial exploitation and extermination ruined the entire continent that it set out to conquer and ended the European system that it had wanted to dominate.

---

[38] As entry into the vast Holocaust literature, see Saul Friedländer, *Nazi Germany and the Jews*, vol. I (New York, 1997). Only a few members of the old elites in the resistance opposed the Nazis on the basis of a more limited understanding of German power. Cf. Theodore S. Hamerow, *On the Road to the Wolf's Lair: German Resistance to Hitler* (London, 1997), 267 ff.

[39] Robert O. Paxton, *Vichy France: Old Guard, New Order* (New York, 1972); and Omer Bartov, *Hitler's Army: Soldiers, Nazis and War in the Third Reich* (New York, 1992). Cf. Hildebrand, *Das vergessene Reich*, 886 ff.

Learning Cooperation
through Recovery

After the disastrous end of the Third Reich, evident impotence and reluctant insight combined to impose a fresh approach to the German problem within Europe. Unlike 1919, 1945 saw little revanchism since the fighting on German soil, the conquest of Berlin, and the foreign occupation made defeat incontestable. Moreover, the loss of sovereignty created a hiatus for national politics since it broke the continuity of such institutions as the central government and the Reichstag. Also, the gradual division of the country into lost territories in the East and rival occupation zones with different ideologies destroyed political unity, reducing the remnants to objects of international politics. At the same time, the bombing of plants, the destruction of railroads, the dismantling of factories, and the imprisonment of male workers suggested that the economy was ruined and would be unable to provide a basis for restoring power. Finally, the Nazi defeat also shattered a nationalist and racist belief system, leaving the population spiritually adrift, searching for answers to their incomprehensible misery.[40]

As a result of Nazi abuse of its traditions, German *Kultur* lost its attraction and turned into an object for pathological investigation after 1945. Critical intellectuals wrote volumes to uncover the ideological sources of the NS dictatorship, with explanations ranging all the way from Luther's half-hearted religious Reformation to the poetic otherworldliness of Romanticism, the material interests of big business, or the paternalist authoritarianism of child rearing. As a result, German language use in other countries collapsed, and such neighbors as Sweden and Holland, which had previously oriented themselves toward Berlin, now refashioned themselves as outposts of Anglo-American civilization. Spurred by some returning exiles, German intellectuals hungrily sought to recover the displaced legacy of Weimar culture, and with the help of international exchange programs strove to import the styles and contents of that high modernism, which had been proscribed in the Third Reich. In the West youth culture Americanized rapidly through rock music and consumer products, while in the East the Communist party made strenuous efforts to Sovietize its population.[41]

[40] Alexander von Plato and Almut Leh, eds., *"Ein unglaublicher Frühling." Erfahrene Geschichte im Nachkriegsdeutschland, 1945–1948* (Bonn, 1997). Cf. Klaus-Dietmar Henke, *Die amerikanische Besatzung Deutschlands* (Munich, 1995).

[41] Konrad H. Jarausch and Hannes Siegrist, eds., *Amerikanisierung und Sowjetisierung in Deutschland 1945–1970* (Frankfurt, 1997); Reinhold Wagnleitner, *Coca-Colonization and*

Somewhat paradoxically, Konrad Adenauer attempted to regain sovereignty for the Federal Republic through close cooperation with the West. The neighboring countries welcomed this reconciliation since they realized that their security required dealing with the Germans, and the American Marshall Plan stipulated a transnational approach to recovery. The joint French, Italian, and German initiative to establish a European Coal and Steel Community in an economic lead sector represented an attractive compromise between continued control of the Ruhr Basin and a lifting of various kinds of economic restrictions.[42] Also, Adenauer's unpopular offer of limited rearmament during the Korean War seemed helpful to British and French governments, who were embroiled in severe decolonization conflicts elsewhere on the globe. Although the failure of the European Defense Community forced the restoration of a national army in the *Bundeswehr*, this force became tightly integrated into the North Atlantic Treaty Organization in 1955.[43] As a result of considerable domestic opposition, mobilized by the SPD leader Kurt Schumacher, West Germany thereafter followed a policy of civilian control, international restraint, defensive orientation, and military integration.[44]

The founding of the German Democratic Republic in the Soviet zone represented a similar attempt to regain a degree of independence, albeit with a less autonomous Communist state. Even if there was some curiosity in the Russian victors, Sovietization proceeded largely by pressure from above through the German-Soviet Friendship Society. In the East, the economy became a tool for social revolution because the 1946 Saxon plebiscite against Fascists and their collaborators initiated a process of expropriation of landowners and entrepreneurs that led to the collectivization of agriculture and to state ownership of business. Initially, the Soviet leadership seems to have vacillated between hopes for a united socialist Germany and the more pragmatic establishment of a satellite state, until the FRG's entry into the Western alliance settled the issue in favor of the second alternative.[45] The consequence was

---

the Cold War (Chapel Hill, 1994); and Uta Poiger, *Jazz, Rock and Rebels: Cold War Politics and American Culture in a Divided Germany* (Berkeley, 2000).

[42] Walter Lipgens, *A History of European Integration, 1945–1950* (Oxford, 1982); and Alan S. Milward, *The European Rescue of the Nation State* (Oxford, 1992).

[43] Konrad Adenauer, *Erinnerungen*, 2 vols. (Stuttgart, 1965–66). See also Wolfgang Hanrieder, *Deutschland, Europa, Amerika. Die Außenpolitik der Bundesrepublik Deutschland, 1949–1994*, 2nd ed. (Paderborn, 1995).

[44] David Clay Large, *Germans to the Front: West German Rearmament and the Adenauer Era* (Chapel Hill, 1996); and Otte, *Rising Middle Power*, 30–33.

[45] Wilfried Loth, *Stalin's Unloved Child: The Soviet Union's German Policy and the Founding of the GDR* (New York, 1998). See also Konrad H. Jarausch, ed., *Dictatorship as Experience: Towards a Socio-Cultural History of the GDR* (New York, 1999).

the integration of the GDR into the Warsaw Pact that sealed the division. Each successor state was small enough to be easily incorporated into its respective bloc, with partition serving as insurance against a resurgence of aggressive German power.

The discrediting of their culture and limitations on sovereignty left the Germans only the economic card to play. In the West, as a necessary response to the Reichsmark's erosion, it was the currency reform, which restarted business activity so spectacularly that it has become a founding myth of the FRG. Ludwig Erhard's decision to dismantle economic controls gradually restored competition and freed the forces of the market, transforming black-market barter into regular business activity. But it is often forgotten that at the same time, some of the social measures, such as the controversial Equalization of Burdens Law, restored buying power to disabled veterans, widows, orphans, and refugees, which helped fuel demand. This dual approach was enshrined in the composite concept of the "Social Market Economy," which served as basis for the proverbial economic miracle that exceeded prewar standards by the mid-1950s.[46] Because of heavier reparations, burdens, and planning constraints, the Eastern recovery came later and remained more modest, but both German states soon became economic leaders in their respective camps.[47]

For many West German businessmen the process of European integration provided a welcome escape from the confines of the national market and the burden of guilt. Even if the French merchant Jean Monnet spearheaded its relaunching in the Messina conference, the Germans participated constructively in the deliberations that led to the Rome Treaties, which founded the Common Market in 1957. The project of a customs union, designed to eliminate all internal tariffs, was to profit not just French farmers but also German industrialists, a bargain that offered the latter access to wider markets and the chance to grow by circumventing social regulations. They were confident that the quality and design of their medium-high technology in areas such as automobiles, chemicals, and electronics would hold its own against competitors from other member nations. The rapid success of the Common Market allowed a generation that had been caught up in Hitler's continental schemes to resume their activities beyond the FRG—this time not as conquerors but as participants in multilateral cooperation.[48]

---

[46] Werner Abelshauser, *Wirtschaftsgeschichte der Bundesrepublik Deutschland 1945–1980* (Frankfurt, 1983); and Antony J. Nicholls, *Freedom with Responsibility: The Social Market Economy in Germany, 1918–1963* (Oxford, 1994).

[47] Jörg Rösler, *Das Wirtschaftswachstum in der Geschichte der DDR, 1945–1970* (Berlin, 1986).

[48] This psychological effect has been underestimated by conventional histories of European integration. Cf. Paul Kleinewefers, *Jahrgang 1905. Ein Bericht* (Stuttgart, 1977).

In contrast, the integration of the GDR into the COMECON yielded fewer benefits since the Eastern market remained dominated by the bilateral needs of the Soviet Union.

An equally important learning process involved the abandonment of Cold War confrontation and the move toward reconciliation in what became known as the new *Ostpolitik*. By the mid-1960s it was becoming clear that the legal insistence on the borders of 1937, in response to refugee demands for a return to the homes from which they had been expelled, would remain a fiction. Moreover, the Hallstein Doctrine of not recognizing the Communist rival in the East grew increasingly un- workable as more and more Third World states established relations with the GDR for economic or ideological reasons. But it took the cou- rageous decision of the Brandt-Scheel Cabinet in 1969 to jettison these positions and embrace a conciliatory course toward Germany's neigh- bors in the East, most importantly the Soviet Union, by symbolically admitting Nazi guilt and pledging peaceful relations in the future. While the Four Powers worked out an access guarantee for Berlin, the two German states concluded a Basic Treaty to regulate their special relationship. These steps gradually softened the barrier of the Wall through small concessions in regard to travel, communication, and so on.[49] Though initially quite contested, this reversal reinforced the les- son of cooperation through its growing success.

The commitment to multilateralism, styled as *Verantwortungspolitik*, paid ample dividends in increasing German influence in various are- nas. Entry into the United Nations gave Bonn a larger platform from which to operate and increased its legitimacy as a democratic state. Participation in the Helsinki negotiations made it possible to include a clause on "peaceful change" in the border guarantee of the CSCE final act, which allowed a future unification of the two German states. Economic cooperation with the six other leading industrial countries cushioned the Oil Shocks of OPEC's price increases and permitted col- lective action to create a European currency "snake" that helped stabi- lize exchange rates. The close friendship between French President Giscard d'Estaing and German Chancellor Helmut Schmidt facilitated the compromises of the Single European Act, which marked important progress in integration. Finally, improving relations with Moscow dampened the arms race of the Second Cold War, while growing ties to East Berlin created a German-German "community of responsibil- ity." The FRG elite gradually learned that it could better weather the

---

[49] Willy Brandt, *Erinnerungen* (Berlin, 1989). See also Timothy Garton Ash, *In Europe's Name: Germany and the Divided Continent* (New York, 1993).

inevitable tensions of international affairs through peaceful cooperation than through blustering.[50]

Growing economic success also created pride in the "German model"
and began to exert a new form of indirect influence upon neighboring
countries. The notion of "Rhenish capitalism" came to mean a peculiar
combination of traits: First, it connoted an unusual amount of labor discipline, because of large-scale union organization and a ritualized form
of collective bargaining that tended to produce moderate wage increases. Second, it implied a corporate form of nonadversarial decision-
making by bringing together different interest groups, for instance, on
the board of public TV networks. Third, it meant fiscal restraint as well
as a strong currency, with the deutsche Mark becoming a symbolic identifier of economic influence rather than military power. Fourth, it also
suggested a generous welfare system, which made it possible for socially less fortunate groups, such as pensioners or single mothers, to
share some degree of prosperity. Finally, it came to stand for a high standard of living that produced a mass consumer society with an unprecedented amount of material goods, vacations in far away places, and the
like.[51] Though critics denounced multilateralism as "oblivion of power,"
it was this economic and social success that made the German example
once again attractive elsewhere.[52]

In contrast, the stalling of the GDR economy hastened the domestic
erosion of the SED regime. No doubt, during the 1980s East Germany
reached the zenith of its international prestige with the Bonn visit of
Secretary General Erich Honecker and the athletic triumphs that were
not just the result of superior training methods but also of massive
doping. But the often repeated claim that the GDR was the tenth
largest industrial state rang increasingly hollow as the foreign currency
debt piled up, productivity stagnated, and plant equipment as well as
the infrastructure in housing or transportation wore out. Ultimately,
the failure of the planned economy to finance social provisions and
consumption broke the bargain between the Party and the population
of receiving increasing prosperity in exchange for political abstinence
and produced the mass flight in the summer of 1989. The surprising
fall of the Wall suggests that constant comparisons with the more suc-

---

[50] Helmut Schmidt, *Menschen und Mächte* (Berlin, 1987). See also Wolfram Hanrieder,
ed., *West German Foreign Policy, 1949–1979* (Boulder, 1980).

[51] For an alarmist version, see Edwin Hartrich, *The Fourth and Richest Reich* (New York,
1980). See also Hartmut Kaelble, *Der Boom 1948–1973. Gesellschaftliche und wirtschaftliche
Folgen in der BRD und Europa* (Opladen, 1992).

[52] Schwarz, *Gezähmte Deutsche*, 23–59. See also Christian Hacke, *Weltmacht wider Willen. Die Außenpolitik der Bundesrepublik Deutschland*, 2nd ed. (Frankfurt, 1993).

cessful West were a prime reason for the erosion of the SED's dictatorial power.[53]

The subsequent process of unification might also be understood as a reward for the successful taming of German power in the difficult decades after the war. The strength of American support, and French as well as British restraint in opposition, were in part a result of Germany's cultural westernization and the reliability of the FRG as ally in NATO. The willingness of Hungarian reformers, Polish dissidents, and liberal elements in the Soviet leadership to gamble on the restoration of a united German state had much to do with making amends for Nazi crimes, placating fears of revanchism, and offering material help. The groundswell of popular feeling for a rapid accession of the East German states to the Federal Republic was largely a product of the population's recognition of the economic superiority of the West German model of social democracy over their own "welfare dictatorship." Finally, the rapid achievement of a diplomatic settlement in the two-plus-four negotiations was a product of a restrained use of resurgent German power that did not provoke its partners by an aggressive style.[54] Only with a chastened FRG were foreign skeptics willing to take the risk of restoring a reduced national state.

Reluctant Regional Dominance

Ironically, the accession of the five new states to the FRG in a way recreated the original problem of fitting a German national state into an emerging European polity. Although territorially reduced by the loss of its former eastern provinces, united Germany had a population that was one-third larger than its neighbors and an economy that surpassed its direct competitors by the same amount or more. No wonder that fearful foreign observers and domestic critics immediately warned of a "fourth Reich" that would come to dominate Europe by economic power, just as its predecessors had through military force. As proof, Cassandras could point to the reputable political scientist Hans-Peter Schwarz, who called united Germany "the central power of Europe," and conservative commentators who demanded greater assertiveness

---

[53] Konrad H. Jarausch, *Die Unverhoffte Einheit* (Frankfurt, 1995); and Charles S. Maier, *Dissolution: The Crisis of Communism and the End of East Germany* (Cambridge, 1997).

[54] Philip Zelikov and Condoleezza Rice, *Germany Unified and Europe Transformed: A Study in Statecraft* (Cambridge, 1995); and Werner Weidenfeld, *Aussenpolitik für die deutsche Einheit. Die Entscheidungsjahre 1989/90* (Stuttgart, 1998).

in the pursuit of national interests.[55] But more sanguine observers countered that their earlier catastrophes had chastened the Germans and that they were now tightly embedded in a web of international organizations such as NATO, the EU, and the UN. How would the Germans use their regained power and how would a larger Germany fit into an emerging Europe?

The initial steps of the enlarged FRG showed such fears to be exaggerated, since the adjustment to the new, postunification role proved quite difficult. For example, the addition of the moribund planned economy turned out to be a rather mixed blessing for West German business since filling East German consumer needs did produce a short-lived boom, but in the long run the market transition exacted enormous costs. The 1.5:1 exchange rate of eastern for western money in the currency union helped Kohl win the election of 1990 but proved a severe handicap since it gave the East Germans more buying power than their productivity warranted. The subsequent run on western products and the concurrent collapse of East European markets resulted in severe deindustrialization, managed by the Treuhandanstalt, a government receivership charged with transforming state enterprises into competitive market businesses. The rebuilding of the decrepit infrastructure was so expensive as to demand the imposition of a 7.5 percent income tax surcharge, specifically to finance Eastern improvements.[56] The immediate effect of unification was, therefore, increased German self-absorption with the problems of integrating the East.

In international affairs, united Germany also continued to move rather cautiously, disappointing President Bush's expectations for a "partnership in leadership." This diffidence was partly the result of concern for not disturbing the Soviet troop withdrawal, which took until 1994, and of the need to integrate Eastern soldiers into the Western *Bundeswehr*. But it also showed the strength of the West German culture of multilateralism that dominated Genscher's *Auswärtiges Amt*, which refused to accept any GDR diplomats after unification. When Washington demanded German military involvement in the Gulf War, Bonn fell back on its practiced reflex of offering logistic support and paying seventeen billion deutsche Mark, a considerable share of the fighting costs. Public opinion responded with instinctive pacifism, and only after prominent critics like Wolfgang Biermann pointed out that

[55] Harold James and Marla Stone, eds., *When the Wall Came Down: Reactions to German Unification* (London, 1992), 221 ff.; Hans-Peter Schwarz, *Die Zentralmacht Europas. Deutschlands Rückkehr auf die Weltbühne* (Berlin, 1994).

[56] Gerlinde and Hans-Werner Sinn, *Kaltstart. Volkswirtschaftliche Aspekte der deutschen Vereinigung*, 2nd ed. (Tübingen, 1992). Cf. W. R. Smyser, *The Economy of a United Germany* (New York, 1992).

Saddam Hussein endangered Israel did support for the war effort grow. The one exception to this reticence was the early recognition of Croatian independence, which could be justified on the basis of self-determination, but which caused much resentment in the West.[57]

Belying alarms about resurgent skinhead nationalism, the enlarged FRG also maintained its commitment to European integration. The re-election of Chancellor Kohl returned a leader for whom the European anchoring of Germany was a personal conviction, while business expected material advantages and intellectuals saw Europeanization as a way to protect the Germans from themselves. Nonetheless, the Maastricht Treaty also demanded considerable sacrifices from Bonn, such as the attenuation of the just-recovered nation-state and the forsaking of the identity symbol, a strong deutsche Mark. But the united elites managed to convince a skeptical electorate to take this risk by arguing for the advantages that a common currency would present to travelers as well as to businessmen. It helped that after much wrangling the new European Central Bank was located in the banking capital, Frankfurt, and that the other partners made visible efforts to adopt the German standard of low inflation, low budget deficits, and low borrowing for convergence. Though foreign critics attacked the Euro experiment as German monetary hegemony, it also required the Germans to jump over some of their own shadows.[58]

In the classic areas that define power, united Germany continues to face considerable impediments that have limited its potential hegemony. For instance, German culture has been so much marred by its association with the Holocaust that it remains an intellectual provocation rather than a model for neighboring countries to emulate. Even after partial recovery, the German language, once a leading conduit to learning, has slipped to distant third place behind Spanish and French in North America, and its dramatic revival in Eastern Europe seems to have economic rather than empathetic reasons. The FRG possesses impressive instruments of foreign cultural policy in the some 150 Goethe institutes, the German Academic Exchange Service, or the Alexander von Humboldt Foundation, but because of their mediocre reputation German universities are attracting proportionally fewer foreign students than a century earlier. Finally, foreign intellectuals are often more

---

[57] Hans Dietrich Genscher, *Erinnerungen* (Berlin, 1995), 899 ff. Cf. Daniele Conversi, *German-Bashing and the Breakup of Yugoslavia* (Seattle, 1998), Donald W. Treadgold Papers in Russian, East European, and Central Asian Studies number 76.

[58] Rolf H. Hasse et al., *The European Central Bank: Perspectives for a Further Development of the European Monetary System* (Gütersloh, 1990); Carl F. Lankowski, *Germany and the European Community: Beyond Hegemony and Containment?* (New York, 1993).

interested in exploring the dark shadows of the Third Reich than prob-ing the vibrant pluralized culture of the democratic Germany of today.[59]

In contrast to the cliches of militarism, the Federal Republic also re-mains reluctant to use military power for foreign political ends. The *Bundeswehr* is a regional force of 340,000 soldiers without nuclear, bio-logical, or chemical (ABC) weapons that has great difficulty even main-taining troop strength because of budget cuts. Moreover, the German draft has a liberal provision for conscientious objection, allowing about half of an age cohort to choose alternative service helping the elderly, working in hospitals, and the like. It took a bitter political struggle, therefore, to abandon the reticence of the elites and to permit German participation in such humanitarian UN missions as in Somalia. When the Balkan wars posed the question of active peace-keeping, the Ger-man Supreme Court was required to endorse the constitutionality of such action in July 1994, if authorized by a defensive alliance such as NATO, before two German brigades could participate in the mop-up in Bosnia in 1995. Finally, horrifying television pictures of Serbian atrocities in Kosovo were required to produce a broad majority in the Bundestag (except for the postcommunists) that endorsed German sol-diers' actually fighting in the air war and deploying for pacification on the ground. This is hardly the behavior of a country that seeks to im-pose its will by force.[60]

The best case for regional dominance can be made in the economic arena—but even here some limitations are becoming apparent. With 30 percent of its gross national product produced through exports, the FRG is the most export-dependent country in the EU, and it accumu-lates the largest trade surplus, mostly returned abroad in the form of investment or tourist expenditures. After the collapse of Communism, Germans have resumed their traditional trading ties with their Central and Eastern European neighbors, far outstripping any competitors in terms of bilateral trade and direct investments. But this impressive per-formance is marred by an increasing structural rigidity that has pro-duced a high level of irreducible unemployment of around 10 percent and is exacting a considerable welfare cost. Moreover, a combination of corporate conservatism, labor restrictions, and green resentment against technology has slowed down the development of the new lead sectors in microelectronics and biotechnology. Only if the Schroeder-Fischer government further reduces public deficits, pares social bene-

---

[59] Carolyn Höfig, "Foreign Cultural Policy," in *The German Predicament*, 183 ff. Cf. also Frank Trommler, ed., *The Cultural Legitimacy of the Federal Republic: Assessing the German Kulturstaat* (Washington, 1999).

[60] Markovits and Reich, *The German Predicament*, 137 ff.

fits, and creates greater flexibility in the service sector, will the economy remain competitive in the long run.[61]

Despite its global business interests, the FRG's policies remain clearly focused on the European continent. According to M. Rainer Lepsius, the EU is an unprecedented hybrid that combines supranational features (the quasi-cabinet of the Commission) with international aspects (such as using the Council of Ministers as final arbiter). This ambiguous shape is the result of compromises between French desires for ascendancy through a wider base, British free trade suspicions of central power, and German professions of supranationalism coupled with practical reluctance. The German public is increasingly frustrated that the EU continues to be mired in problems such as a democracy deficit, centripetal regionalism, lack of a common culture, inability to tax, military weakness (except for the Eurocorps), and failure to agree on a common foreign policy. No doubt some of these can be remedied by piecemeal solutions, such as variable speeds and geometries or subsidiarity, but clashing visions and interests make integration a long-range project with an uncertain outcome.[62] In this indistinctly emerging European polity the Germans, much like Gulliver, are fettered in multiple ways, ways that reflect their economic influence but do not allow them to bully the other members.

In contrast to the crowded West, there is more room for German leadership in Central and Eastern Europe, but this is also the region with the bitterest memories of earlier domination. In the complicated NATO discussions about eastward expansion, the FRG was noticeably quiet since it wanted to improve its security position by pushing the defense perimeter eastward without provoking Russian enmity. In the debates about the acceptance of new members into the EU, the Germans have pushed for greater speed, at least verbally, since they feel bound to bring in such neighbors as the Hungarians, who helped during the process of unification. At the same time, Berlin is insisting on first solving some current EU problems and getting the candidates ready to meet European requirements since the public fears an unrestricted influx of cheap labor and goods from the East. As the takeover of the Czech car maker Skoda by VW shows, the East Europeans themselves are also quite ambivalent in their attitudes, welcoming German investment on the one hand, and fearing economic domina-

---

[61] Frank Westermann, "Germany's Economic Power in Europe," *The German Predicament*, 150 ff.; and Otte, *Rising Middle Power*, 61–75.

[62] M. Rainer Lepsius lecture in Berlin, July 1999. Much of the European Studies literature on integration is a strange blend of analysis and policy advising. Cf. Gary Marks et al., eds., *Governance in the European Union* (Beverly Hills, 1996).

tion on the other. Almost by default, Germany has taken the lead in helping east Central Europe and Russia with symbolic gestures and exchange programs that are likely to increase their regional role.[63]

Does the greater assertiveness of the Schröder-Fischer Cabinet since 1998 show that the old, insensitive Germans of a century earlier are back? As members of the first truly postwar generation, the Social-Democratic and Green leaders no longer feel quite as burdened by the Nazi past as did their predecessors. True enough, they have been ready to settle the slave labor claims through negotiations and have accepted the construction of a central Holocaust memorial in Berlin. But at the same time Chancellor Schröder has begun to pursue German interests more vigorously, for instance in the question of contributions to the EU that he finds excessive, thereby upsetting other countries that had gotten used to a more circumspect language and compromising stance. Yet in the difficult negotiations to end the bombardment of Yugoslavia, German mediation efforts proved quite useful in brokering a compromise between Russian support for the Serbs and western desires to help the Kosovars. Although it is only an incremental change from earlier reticence, the more self-assured style, suggested by the claim that Germany is "a great power in Europe," represents a gradual normalization in foreign policy that is becoming increasingly willing to pursue its own interests.[64]

Projecting Structural Power Softly

Over the tumultuous course of the twentieth century, German leaders painfully learned to revise their conception of power from military bluster to civil self-restraint. This reversal was partly facilitated by profound changes in the social composition of the elite. Gone are the arrogant East Elbian Junkers, paternalistic industrial tycoons, and the militarist generals or chauvinist professors that dominated the Empire. Also removed are the racist agitators, merciless SS henchmen, greedy war profiteers, and adventurous *condottieri* who characterized the Nazi leadership. They have been replaced by cosmopolitan managers who have studied abroad, speak English with ease, frequently meet with

---

[63] The articles in *Daedalus*, special issue, "A New Europe for the Old?" (Summer 1997), are mostly focused on Eastern Europe. See also Tony Judt, *A Grand Illusion: An Essay on Europe* (New York, 1996), 45 ff.

[64] Volker Herres and Klaus Waller, *Der Weg nach oben. Gerhard Schröder—eine politische Biographie* (Munich, 1998), 243 ff. Cf. also Otte, *Rising Middle Power*, 196–219.

European partners, and own vacation houses at the Costa Brava in Spain. In spite of occasional scandals, the political class of the FRG affects a more modest demeanor, conscious of its dependence upon a mass electorate and the fickle favor of the media. Similarly the prominent scientists and researchers are part of a transnational enterprise oriented toward Anglo-American models. As a result of the double defeat, the traditional elites have disintegrated and new social groups, who have a more international cast of mind, have taken their place.[65]

The chastening of German power was also the result of a cultural learning process regarding conceptions of national interest, which has been insufficiently explained so far. Why was the revanchist resolve to make another, better-prepared play for outright hegemony after the defeat in 1918 not repeated after 1945? No doubt, the decimated successor states of the Third Reich had little choice but to comply with their respective occupiers' wishes, but the objective weakening of the German position does not quite explain the transformation of subjective outlooks on how and for what ends to use the remaining influence. In contrast to the somewhat cynical fulfillment of Stresemann, the policies of Adenauer and Brandt created a different civil and multilateral approach that redefined German interests as reconciliation with the West and subsequently also the East to overcome division. In part, the rethinking reflected a wider European reassessment of the consequences of unbridled power politics after World War II. In part, the evident success of efforts at cooperation promoted a shift away from outright reliance on military or political force to indirect economic incentive, cultural example, or friendly persuasion.[66]

This reorientation was the prerequisite for unification and the return of a considerable amount of "structural power," making the Germans implicitly dominant in Europe. In spite of the low birth rate, the accession of the five new states has made the FRG the most populous country west of Russia, since economic migrants, ethnic resettlers, and asylum seekers make up the deficit. Notwithstanding the shrunken borders, united Germany has over a dozen neighbors and occupies a central place in the continental geography, as the multitude of foreign license plates of trucks crisscrossing the *Autobahnen* demonstrates. Regardless of the costs of incorporating the former GDR, the German

---

[65] Michael R. Hayse, "Recasting the West German Elites: Higher Civil Servants, Businessmen and Physicians in Hessen, 1945–1955" (Ph.D. dissertation Chapel Hill, 1995). The East German rupture was even deeper. Cf. Peter Hübner, ed., *Eliten im Sozialismus. Beiträge zur Sozialgeschichte der DDR* (Cologne, 1999).

[66] Explaining this chastening process would require a more cultural approach to international affairs than the standard histories of German post-war diplomacy offer. Cf. Otte, *Rising Middle Power*, 13 ff.

economy continues to lead the EU in GNP as well as trade, and the deutsche Mark has become the standard by which the success of the Euro will be measured. Although the FRG is so tightly integrated into international organizations as to prevent unilateralism, it has thereby gained a crucial position in the counsels of NATO, the EU, and the like.[67] Since the Germans, however insecure they may be, cannot run away from their structural power, the question becomes how they will use it and to what ends.

As a result of a painful process of learning from history, the FRG has developed a soft approach that understands the limits of its mid-sized power and tries to employ its influence constructively. Unlike their Wilhelmian or Nazi predecessors, the postwar political class has internalized a "culture of restraint" that generally eschews prestige policies and looks for negotiated solutions to problems. One reason is an acute consciousness of the burden of the German past, which conjures up associations with a domineering behavior that ought not to be repeated because it produced so much suffering. Another cause of self-limitation is the realization of German security dependence on the United States, its vital interest in European cooperation, and its need for stability in the east, which disposes Berlin to play a mediating role. A final motive of reticence is the evident success of the strategy of multilateralism, patiently seeking to convince partners in NATO, the EU, or the UN instead of bullying them, and in maintaining a peaceful environment, essential for a country so dependent upon international trade.[68] This restraint has also been reinforced by a more cooperative stance of neighboring countries that have gradually recognized the need to overcome their historical aversions and to welcome a measure of German leadership in the pursuit of common aims such as prosperity and security.

To paraphrase Thomas Mann, the change of attitudes of the past century can, therefore, be understood as a trajectory from a Germanized Europe to an Europeanized Germany.[69] The former recalls the catastrophic efforts at conquest in the first half, whereas the latter suggests a gradual westernization and muting of aspirations in the second half. Why else would the Federal Republic actively work on surrendering

---

[67] Markovits and Reich, *The German Predicament*, 150 ff. See also Wolfgang-Uwe Friedrich, "In Search of Stability: German Foreign Policy and the Public in the 1990s," in David P. Conradt et al., eds., *Germany's New Politics* (Tempe, 1995), 253 ff.

[68] Simon J. Bulmer, "Shaping the Rules? The Constitutive Politics of the European Union and German Power," and Jeffery J. Anderson, "Hard Interests, Soft Power, and Germany's Changing Role in Europe," in *Tamed Power*, 49 ff., 80 ff.

[69] Thomas Mann, *Deutschland und die Deutschen 1945*, intro. by Hans Mayer (Hamburg, 1992).

some of its hard-won sovereignty to a higher cause, namely the construction of an integrated Europe? The actual formulation of a chastened European vision may, no doubt, still project some aspects of "the German model" to the outside, insisting on the adoption of successful solutions, such as a hard currency or a federalist structure. The new self-assurance of the Berlin Republic "which recognizes and formulates national interests" is bound to revive some old fears. But in contrast to earlier designs for outright hegemony, current efforts at building Europe proceed from democratic and capitalist values that recognize the aspirations of neighbors as legitimate and allow for compromise. Perhaps this basic internationalization of attitudes will make the regional leadership role into which united Germany is reluctantly growing more acceptable to others and constructive in its results.[70]

[70] Schröder interview statements appeared in *Der Weg nach oben*, 264 f. See also Fritz Stern, *Verspielte Größe. Essays zur deutschen Geschichte* (Munich, 1996).

7

Unsettling German Society: Mobility and Migration

Few issues are as contested in Germany as the questions of asylum and immigration. Led by the Catholic regional party CSU, conservative circles tenaciously maintain that "Germany is not an immigration country." In the 1999 Hessian state elections, CDU candidate Roland Koch mobilized xenophobic fears with a postcard campaign against "dual citizenship," warning that it would "privilege foreigners," create conflicting loyalties, and establish ghettos of unintegratable Moslems.[1] Outraged, the liberal association Pro Asyl denounced this exclusionist mindset as "shameful and blind to history," arguing for a "special obligation" of Germans to prevent the recurrence of such humanitarian disasters as the failure to accept the expelled Jews in the 1930s. Going even further, the leftist Green Party demanded "a transparent and human-rights-oriented immigration policy" that would reconcile the wishes of foreigners for protection and the needs of an aging society

[1] CSU press release, "Dr. Gauweiler antwortet Cumali Naz zum Thema 'Einwanderungsland," 5 March 1998; Detlef Kleinert, "Klarstellung in Hessen: Deutschland ist kein Einwanderungsland" (n.p., n.d.)

for youthful labor.[2] Since these arguments appeal to deep-seated feelings, there is no agreement in sight over which course to pursue.

The prevalent German self-image of stability is a result of an extraordinary act of amnesia that has repressed memories of the varied outward and inward migrations in Central Europe. Klaus Bade, a leading scholar in this field, notes with considerable frustration: "Contemporary public debate has largely chosen to ignore the fact that throughout German history the movement of peoples across borders and the consequent clash of cultures has not been the exception but the norm." Since spatial mobility has not been sufficiently incorporated into the competing national narratives, internal and external migration appear only episodically as subsidiary themes, not as central characteristics of the German past. "It has also been forgotten that many native inhabitants are descendants of foreigners who immigrated to Germany and that millions of German emigrants were strangers in foreign countries, just as many foreigners today are strangers in united Germany."[3] The failure to incorporate experiences of migration into the national story has created a misleading historical consciousness that treats "German" as a fixed ethnic category, although it is rather fluid.

In contrast to American discourse, German opinion does not represent mobility as liberating and enriching, because it is usually associated with negative experiences. Stories of emigration are told in terms of failure, bemoaning ethnic losses to America, Canada, or Australia, rather than in terms of success for assimilating such strangers as Poles or Jews. References to foreign labor tend to emphasize its economic utility rather than its human quality, and often reveal a bad conscience because of past or present exploitation. Compulsory efforts to "Germanize" Danes, Alsatians, or Poles through the movement of national frontiers across people can hardly be recalled with pride since they largely foundered on the resistance of those concerned. Finally, the shocking memory of ethnic cleansing or violent elimination of racial undesirables in the Holocaust has left a deep trauma. The German vocabulary of mobility uses such terms of resettlement as *Umsiedler* and *Aussiedler* in referring to ethnic kin but reserves the migration concepts of asylum or immigration for foreigners. Surprisingly enough for a

---

[2] PRO ASYL press release, "PRO ASYL erinnert an die gescheiterte Flüchtlingskonferenz von Evian. Deutschland heute Hardliner der europäischen Abschottungspolitik," 6 July 1998; "Interview von Hartmut Kriege mit Heiko Kaufmann," *Deutschlandfunk*, 8 July 1998; Green Party press release, "Neuorientierung in der Migrationspolitik—für eine weltoffene Republik!" 5 May 2000.

[3] Klaus J. Bade, "From Emigration to Immigration. The German Experience in the Nineteenth and Twentieth Centuries," in Klaus J. Bade and Myron Wiener, eds., *Migration Past, Migration Future* (New York, 1997), 1–37.

people prizing world-wide tourism, mobility seems to have unpleasant connotations that prove troubling rather than uplifting.[4]

The growing body of migration scholarship has been unable to shake these cultural preconceptions since its sophisticated but technical discussions remain marginalized and divided into distinctive subfields. Fortunately, the division between an "emigration literature," which studies the motives of departure, and an "immigration literature," which works on the new arrivals, is being overcome by migration studies, which follow subjects from their origin to their destination to grasp the complexities of transferring people and customs.[5] But much work remains statistical rather than cultural, counting heads rather than exploring experiences of strangeness or belonging. Moreover, much of the scholarship is highly fragmented, treating each particular spatial movement as a discrete set of events rather than asking questions about the broader pattern of migration. The prevalent focus on voluntary individual movement pays too little attention to the compulsory and violent character of collective population shifts. Finally, for all the attention to exile and diasporas, the lengthy processes of cultural transformation involved in becoming or unbecoming "German" still remain largely in the dark.[6]

A comprehensive approach to German migration within European patterns therefore needs to draw together a set of literatures not often combined. A starting point must be the demographic scholarship that deals with population growth, gender balance, or age structure, since presumed excess or lack of population fuels outward or inward movement.[7] Another dimension has to involve economic perceptions of labor needs, because claims for additional or cheaper manpower lie at the basis of recruitment of foreigners, be it by incentives or by force.[8] A more unusual facet that also should be considered is the work on

---

[4] Ibid. The question of representation of migration and mobility needs to be explored more systematically. Cf. Klaus J. Bade's *Europa in Bewegung. Migration vom späten 18. Jahrhundert bist zur Gegenwart* (Munich, 2000); and Rudy Koshar, *German Travel Cultures* (Oxford, 2000).

[5] Exemplary in this regard is the work of Walter Kamphoefner, *The Westfalians: From Germany to Missouri* (Princeton, 1987).

[6] Compare Dirk Hoerder and Leslie Page Moch, eds., *European Migrants: Global and Local Perspectives* (Boston, 1996), to Mitchell Ash, Jeffrey Peck, and Christiane Lemke, "Germans, Strangers and Foreigners," in Konrad H. Jarausch, ed., *After Unity: Reconfiguring German Identities* (New York, 1997).

[7] Steve Hochstadt, *Mobility and Modernity: Migration in Germany, 1820–1989* (Ann Arbor, 1999); and the forthcoming study by Annette F. Timm on "The Politics of Fertility: Population Politics and Health Care in Berlin, 1919–1972."

[8] Klaus Bade, ed., *Population, Labor and Migration in 19th and 20th Century Germany* (Leamington Spa, 1987).

national conflict, biopolitics and ethnic cleansing, which deals with discrimination and violent transplantation.[9] Yet another aspect is the legal provisions that regulate economic activity as well as the citizenship rules governing membership in the political community.[10] Finally, there is also the recent discussion of the patterns of conflict and coexistence among multiethnic communities and the investigations of cultural processes of assimilation or acculturation.[11] If combined, these approaches reveal an astounding pattern of mobility and metamorphosis among German speakers that is full of unexpected twists and ironies.

The Emigration Axiom

Although millions of newcomers have thronged to the FRG during the last half-century, German self-conceptions remain focused on the experience of emigration. Many nineteenth-century folksongs celebrate the journeyman's custom of "wandering," required for learning a trade, but the lyrics of such well-known tunes as *Nun ade du mein lieb Heimatland* and *Muss i denn* focus on the pain of departure rather than the joy of new discovery.[12] This sense of sadness also informs thousands of "emigrant letters" from abroad, which are replete with nostalgia for a home that has been irretrievably lost, even if these reports also take great pains to emphasize the material benefits that have been gained in return.[13] Though major writers ignored the subject, such popular authors as Johannes Gillhoff and Friedrich Gerstäcker fictionalized the collective emigration experience in such well-known titles as *Jürnjacob Swehn, der Amerikafahrer*, a story of a Mecklenburg farmhand in the United States, and *Die Regulatoren in Arkansas*, a tale of the American

[9] See the contributions of Hans Lemberg and Götz Aly in Dittmar Dahlmann and Gerhard Hirschfeld, eds., *Lager, Zwangsarbeit, Vertreibung und Deportation. Dimensionen der Massenverbrechen in der Sowjetunion und Deutschland 1933 bis 1945* (Essen, 1999), 485–99. Cf. also Norman Naimark, *Fires of Hatred: Ethnic Cleansing in Twentieth Century Europe* (Cambridge, Mass., 2001).

[10] Rogers Brubaker, *Citizenship and Nationhood in France and Germany* (Cambridge, Mass., 1992), 165 ff.

[11] Klaus J. Bade, *Europa in Bewegung*, passim; and Christhard Hoffmann, "Einwanderung, Ethnizität, 'Rassismus'. Konzepte der Migration und Minderheitsgeschichte am Beispiel Grossbritanniens," *Historische Zeitschrift* 266 (1998): 671–85.

[12] Hans Breuer, *Der Zupfgeigenhansel. Das Liederbuch der Wandervögel* (Leipzig, 1913), starts with a section called *Abschied*. These songs were still played on transatlantic steamers in the 1950s to mark the departure of emigrants.

[13] Wolfgang Helbich, Walter Kamphoefner, and Ulrike Summers, eds., *News From the Land of Freedom: German Immigrant Letters Home* (Ithaca, 1991), is the most comprehensive selection.

West seen through German eyes.[14] These various sources constructed a pervasive cultural cliche of emigration conceived as loss, a traumatic uprooting from a sentimentalized *Heimat* with uncertain personal outcomes that diminished the ethnic community. The historical source of this perception were several massive movements of German-speakers beyond their original settlement areas. Mislabeled as the *Drang nach Osten*, the first was the Germanic "re-colonization" of central Europe under the banner of Christianization in the early Middle Ages that spilled over into Silesia, East Prussia, and the Baltic states. The second was the early modern surge of colonists, invited by local princes, that formed German-speaking population islands in Transylvania (Siebenbürgener Sachsen), Hungary (for instance in the Banat), and also in czarist Russia (along the banks of the Volga and on the shores of the Black Sea).[15] Third was the nineteenth-century transatlantic migration of a mixture of religious sectarians, land-seeking farmers, and finally, socialist factory workers. In three waves from 1846 to 1852, from 1860 to 1873, and once again from 1880 to 1893, over five million German speakers emigrated to the United States, accounting through their partial descendants for about one-quarter of the country's Caucasian population.[16] This partly violent and partly peaceful movement created a deep cultural memory of emigration as well as an awareness of a far-flung German diaspora scattered in foreign parts.

The public debate, fueled by the transatlantic exodus, came to associate emigration with negative consequences for the strength of the emerging nation. Supporters of mobility argued in terms of the individual's right to leave for a better life elsewhere or in terms of a collective "safety valve" that would relieve the body politic of population pressure. Opponents of migration pointed, instead, to the continued loss of manpower, personal initiative, and cultural capital that weakened the Second Reich in international competition. Hence, the Colonial and Pan German leagues argued strenuously for a policy of channeling emigrants to settlement colonies, but unfortunately, the late German acquisitions were singularly unsuited to European habitation.

[14] Johannes Gillhoff, *Jürnjacob Swehn, der Amerikafahrer* (Berlin, 1917), had well over half a million copies printed, and Friedrich Gerstäcker, *Die Regulatoren in Arkansas. Ein Roman aus dem amerikanischen Pflanzerleben* (Frankfurt, reissued 1988), had a similar success.

[15] Volker Press, "Von der mittelalterlichen zur frühneuzeitlichen Ostsiedlungsbewegung—ein Rückblick," in Klaus J. Bade, ed., *Deutsche im Ausland—Fremde in Deutschland. Migration in Geschichte und Gegenwart* (Munich, 1992), 29 ff.

[16] Günter Moltmann, *Germans to America: Three Hundred Years of Immigration, 1683–1983* (Stuttgart, 1982); and Kathleen Conzen, *Immigrant Milwaukee, 1838–1860: Accommodation and Community in a Frontier City* (Cambridge, Mass., 1976). See also Hartmut Keil, ed., *German Workers Culture in the US, 1850–1910* (Washington, D.C., 1988).

Because of Bismarck's resistance, Germany had to wait until 1897 for the passage of a national emigration law that sought to regulate the outflow "to maintain the German nature of the emigrants and to make use of emigration for the interests of the mother country" by directing the flow "to suitable destinations."[17] Since this effort remained ineffective, the Association for Germans Abroad (VDA) launched a vigorous campaign to preserve the language and culture for those ethnic Germans living in eastern Europe and overseas.

At the same time, imperial Germany, ironically, started to attract immigrants, even if earlier migrants such as French Huguenots had largely faded from view. Because of fears of disease and prejudice, the authorities insisted that the nearly five million Jewish, Polish, and other Slavic emigrants from eastern Europe cross the Reich as quickly as possible to embark from Bremen or Hamburg to America.[18] But the demand for backbreaking labor in the coal mines and steel factories drew about half a million Catholic Poles and Protestant Masurians from Upper Silesia, West Prussia, and other eastern provinces into the Ruhr Basin. Though political agitation was prohibited, the "Ruhr Poles" were allowed to speak their language, worship in Catholic churches, and create a vibrant associational life, "clear signs of a true immigration process."[19] Even more tightly regulated were the almost 1.2 million seasonal laborers from the east and south who worked partly in industrial jobs and partly as farmhands on Prussian estates. Desperately needed to fuel the prewar boom, these "cheap and willing" workers were forced to carry permits and return home during the winter to prevent their permanent settlement. Such Polish laborers formed an exploited subproletariat, and their seasonal migration kept the fiction of nonimmigration alive.[20]

The imperial citizenship law of 1913, which superseded older territorial provisions, addressed both concerns about ethnic emigration and fears of immigrating foreigners. To "preserve Germandom abroad," an intense agitation sought to help German language islands in eastern Europe survive in the face of Slavic nationalism and to delay the accul-

---

[17] Bade, *Vom Auswanderungsland zum Einwanderungsland*, 25 ff. See Roger Chickering, *We Men Who Feel Most German: A Cultural History of the Pan-German League, 1880–1914* (Boston, 1984); and Gerhard Weidenfeller, *VDA. Verein für Deutschtum im Ausland, deutscher Schulverein 1881–1918* (Bern, 1976).

[18] Michael Just, *Ost- und Südosteuropäische Amerikawanderung 1881–1914. Transitprobleme in Deutschland und Aufnahme in den Vereinigten Staaten* (Stuttgart, 1988).

[19] Christoph Kleßmann, *Polnische Bergarbeiter im Ruhrgebiet 1870–1945. Soziale Integration und nationale Subkultur einer ethnischen Minderheit in der deutschen Industriegesellschaft* (Göttingen, 1978); and Richard Murphy, *Gastarbeiter im Deutschen Reich. Polen in Bottrop 1891–1933* (Wuppertal, 1982).

[20] Klaus J. Bade, " 'Billig und Willig'—die 'ausländischen Wanderarbeiter' im kaiserlichen Deutschland," in *Deutsche im Ausland*, 311 ff.

turation of overseas emigrants in English-speaking countries. At the same time, volkish nationalists mounted an assimilation and settlement campaign against Polish speakers in West Prussia, or Posnan, whose increase threatened to undo the German character of these provinces. As a solution to this double problem, the imperial government and the conservative Reichstag majority insisted upon adopting the principle of jus sanguinis, which considered ethnic descent rather than birthplace as the source of citizenship. This patrilinear framework would allow Germans living abroad to retain their right of return, while the law's administration by the states made it exceedingly difficult for children of foreigners born in Germany to be naturalized.[21] Because of its intent of cultural and racial homogenization, this ethno-nationalist philosophy of inclusion simultaneously excluded strangers, ignoring the paradox of Polish, French, and Danish minorities within the Reich.

Despite legal restrictions against foreigners, the Second Reich gradually turned into a de facto immigration country. During the prewar boom outward migration slowed to a trickle while immigration increased dramatically, rendering positive the migration balance between 1890 and 1910. The number of legal foreigners increased about six times between 1871 and 1910, from about 207,000 to 1,260,000. Not all eastern Jews who were supposed to emigrate actually left, since some were too ill to travel, and about 78,000 found loopholes to stay.[22] As Max Weber pointed out, the settlement policy of the Hatakist League foundered on both the reluctance of German farmers to move to the East and the estate owners' desire for cheap Polish labor, which made them circumvent official prohibitions.[23] Such cities as Berlin and Breslau grew into multiethnic communities, with entire quarters inhabited by legal or illegal migrants, such as eastern Jews or Russian Poles. In spite of discriminatory regulations against foreigners, many Germans actually managed to coexist with newcomers, allowing the latter to keep their languages and customs as long as they did not challenge political authority.[24] The Empire, therefore, left an ambivalent legacy of ethnic sentimentalism and fearful xenophobia.

[21] Dieter Gosewinkel, "Die Staatsangehörigkeit als Institution des Nationalstaats," in Rolf Grawert et al., eds., Offene Staatlichkeit (Berlin, 1995), 359–78. See also Dieter Gosewinkel, " 'Unerwünschte Elemente'—Einwanderung und Einbürgerung der Juden in Deutschland 1848–1933," Tel Aviver Jahrbuch für deutsche Geschichte 27 (1998): 71–106.

[22] Marschalck, Bevölkerungsgeschichte Deutschlands, 178 ff. See also Jack Wertheimer, Unwelcome Strangers: East European Jews in Imperial Germany (New York, 1987).

[23] Max Weber, Die Verhältnisse der Landarbeiter im ostelbischen Deutschland, Schriften des Vereins für Socialpolitik, vol. 55 (Berlin, 1892).

[24] Charles Robert Garris, "Becoming German: Immigrants, Conformity and Identity Politics in Wilhelmian Berlin, 1880–1914" (Ph.D. dissertation, Chapel Hill, 1998). See also Till van Rahden, "Juden und andere Deutsche in Breslau" (Ph.D. dissertation, Bielefeld, 1999).

The Trauma of Forced Mobility

The outbreak of World War I inaugurated a half-century of unprecedented hatred and violence that replaced individual migration by the forced mobility of entire populations. With vicious propaganda the belligerents inflamed nationalist passions against external enemies, whipping young men into a fighting frenzy, pressuring the national community to close ranks, and making all aliens suspect as subversives.[25] Millions of young men were drafted, assembled at collection points, moved in railroad cars to the front, and marched into enemy territory. Hundreds of thousands of captured soldiers were held in POW camps under unspeakable sanitary conditions, suffering from hunger and disease. Tens of thousands of refugees clogged the roads behind advancing enemies, seeking to save their very lives or salvage some possessions by retreating into the interior. Thousands of suspect foreign civilians were rounded up and interned, lest they engage in acts of sabotage.[26] At the same time, the war produced extremes of motion and immobility, removing people involuntarily from their peaceful pursuits at home or forcibly detaining them without any chance to leave.

interesting observation

When mobile warfare turned into a struggle of attrition, the demand for labor rose dramatically, prompting efforts to attract foreign workers by incentive or force. Since idle prisoners were difficult to guard, the Germans put about two-thirds of the 2.5 million captured soldiers to work in the fields (45 percent) and factories and mines (20 percent) to replace civilians in uniform. The authorities also insisted on retaining the 1.2 million foreign, largely seasonal laborers by prohibiting their return home and making them sign longer contracts, which tied them to one employer. When the Hindenburg program of mobilizing overaged men and women for factory work proved inadequate, the government shifted from incentives to roundups as a method of impressing about half a million Polish laborers from conquered Russian territories. Since a similar tactic of deporting the unemployed from Belgium created an international outcry, the authorities returned to offering positive incentives to entice about 130,000 workers to sign up.[27] The war,

---

[25] Roger Chickering, *Imperial Germany and the Great War, 1914–1918* (Cambridge, 1998).

[26] Novels like Erich Maria Remarque's *All Quiet on the Western Front* (Berlin, 1928), as well as snapshots from the war, show this forced mobility—but migration studies have largely ignored this dimension.

[27] Ulrich Herbert, *Geschichte der Ausländerbeschäftigung in Deutschland 1880 bis 1980. Saisonarbeiter, Zwangsarbeiter, Gastarbeiter* (Bonn, 1986), 82 ff., updated as *Geschichte der Ausländerpolitik in Deutschland* (Munich, 2001). See also Jürgen Rund, *Ernährungswirtschaft und Zwangsarbeit im Raum Hannover 1914 bis 1918* (Hannover, 1992).

therefore, transformed voluntary foreign workers into forced laborers toiling under brutal conditions.

The return of peace unleashed another wave of migration that tried to reverse the wartime displacement but also added new dislocations of its own. Demobilization meant the return of millions of defeated, sick, and hungry soldiers, as well as the repatriation of millions of POWs and forced laborers to their home countries. By moving borders across people, the various Paris peace treaties precipitated additional migrations because the breakup of the multiethnic empires uprooted masses of people, for instance, necessitating a bloody population transfer between Greeks and Turks.[28] Hence thousands of Germans returned from the Alsace while tens of thousands of officials, business people, or professionals moved back to the Reich from lost provinces such as West Prussia or parts of Upper Silesia.[29] The establishment of national states in east central Europe turned former rulers into endangered minorities, left to the tender mercy of the new governments that tried to create an ethnically homogenous citizenry. Since the protection of the League of Nations proved inadequate, the mixture of self-determination and revenge, embodied by the Versailles Treaty, created fierce nationality struggles over the postwar borders that bore the seeds of future conflicts.

With increasing stability, the Weimar Republic restored earlier patterns of voluntary migration, albeit on a noticeably lower level. Postwar dislocation and hyperinflation triggered a fourth wave of transatlantic migration to America, but its highest number reached only 115,000 per annum, and the destinations became more diverse, extending to Argentina, Brazil, and Chile.[30] Because the remaining agricultural territories in the east still required Polish farm laborers, a more humane system of *Arbeitsnachweis* allowed entry merely to those who were really required and provided better protection for the migrant workers. Since the labor unions largely succeeded in keeping competitors out of the factories, only 236,000 non-German workers were employed during the peak year.[31] Despite a sizable influx of Russian émigrés and east European artists or intellectuals, drawn by modernist culture, the number of resident foreigners also declined to three-quarters of a million. But Weimar's welfare measures attracted a growing share of remigrants, turning the migration balance once

---

[28] Dan Diner, *Das Jahrhundert verstehen. Eine universalhistorische Deutung* (Munich, 1999), is one of the few historians who is aware of this irony.

[29] Konrad H. Jarausch, *Unfree Professions: German Lawyers, Teachers and Engineers, 1900–1950* (New York, 1990), 40 ff. Since most of the returnees belonged to prior elites, they intensified the postwar competition for better jobs.

[30] Bade, *Vom Auswanderungsland*, 18 ff.

[31] Herbert, *Geschichte der Ausländerbeschäftigung*, 114 ff.

again positive during the early 1930s.[32] The world economic crisis, however, stopped all mobility by erecting new protective barriers.

The Nazi seizure of power ended the brief interlude of individual movement and revived the World War I pattern of forced migration in an even more extreme form. Coming from the radical fringe, the NSDAP propagated an exclusionary, racist vision of the ethnic community and possessed the will as well as the means to put its numerous resentments into practice. To consolidate control, Hitler used the Reichstag fire as pretext to persecute the political opposition, rounding up Communists, Socialists or other Democrats, forcing the rest underground and propelling about twenty-five to thirty thousand people into political exile. With the symbolic book burning, the Nazi Student League signaled a deep-seated cultural antimodernism that silenced the critical avant-garde and triggered what has been called "the flight of the muses," involving another six to ten thousand intellectuals. A wave of anti-Semitic boycotts and professional purges, followed by the Nuremberg Laws and culminating in the pogrom of the *Kristallnacht*, harassed, discriminated, and intimidated the Jewish community. As a result, about four hundred fifty to six hundred thousand German-speaking Jews had to flee central Europe by 1939, desperate to gain entry to any country that would admit them.[33] These expulsions amounted to an internal form of ethnic cleansing, removing political opponents and racial inferiors from the *Volksgemeinschaft*.

As a positive counterpart, the Nazis also made strenuous efforts to return desirable Aryans individually or collectively *Heim ins Reich*. Through such organizations as the VDA they campaigned in support of Germandom abroad and sought to induce disappointed emigrants to return, actually persuading a few thousand to follow the call. More successful was the attempt to incorporate neighboring communities of German speakers by claims to ethnic self-determination, thereby reversing the losses of the Great War. The first priority was the *Anschluss* of eight million Austrians from Hitler's own birthplace through a mixture of subversion, intimidation, and plebiscite in the spring of 1938. The second step was the use of the Henlein movement to force the "liberation" of two-and-a-half million Sudenten Germans, followed by the annexation of the rest of Czechoslovakia. Though the Nazis could make a better case for reclaiming ethnically German Danzig, their third effort to bludgeon Poland into concessions regarding transportation

---

[32] Karl Schlögel, *Berlin, Ostbahnhof Europas. Russen und Deutsche in ihrem Jahrhundert* (Berlin, 1998); Marschalck, *Bevölkerungsgeschichte*, 175 ff.

[33] Werner Röder, "Die Emigration aus dem nationalsozialistischen Deutschland," in *Deutsche im Ausland*, 345–53.

routes across the Corridor led directly into World War II.[34] While they triggered new waves of flight, these revisions of the Versailles Treaty went a long way toward realizing old Pan-German goals of gathering the *Volk* in one state.

To shield Aryan women and civilians, Hitler's war machine once again relied on the slave labor of about 7.8 million foreigners. Ignoring their xenophobia, the Nazis used a mixture of POWs and civilians, especially after the start of the Russian campaign, to provide about one-fifth of the workforce by 1944. The number of Polish, then French, and finally Russian prisoners grew to 1.831 million, while civilians accounted for another staggering 5.295 million foreign laborers, about one-third of whom worked in agriculture and two-thirds of whom toiled in war-related industries. By the middle of the war, the entire country was covered with slave labor camps, containing a complicated ethnic hierarchy based on prejudice: western workers from France, Belgium, or Holland, some of whom had hired on voluntarily, stood at the top; Poles and Czechs, who had a long history of seasonal work, were in the middle; and Russian or Ukrainian *Ostarbeiter*, largely obtained by force, remained at the bottom. While farm workers were often better fed, industrial laborers were brutally exploited, starved, and beaten—with cruelty limited only by the need to retain some productivity. During the final phase of the war, almost half a million concentration camp inmates were also forced to work in rocket and ammunition factories, often with the express purpose of their murder.[35]

Even more ambitious was the gigantic project to conquer living space in the east to relieve what Hitler considered an excess population pressure. Captured in the title of a ponderous Hans Grimm novel, *Volk ohne Raum*, this ideology proposed the acquisition of contiguous agricultural colonies to restore ethnic health, increase military might, and augment economic prosperity. Coordinated by Heinrich Himmler and the SS, this effort aimed at nothing less than an ethnic *Umvolkung* that would transform the balance of nationalities in central Europe and extend the boundaries of the Third Reich far to the east. Starting with the Polish victory, a Volksdeutsche Mittelstelle organized the resettlement of a million diasporic Germans from Wolhynia to the Baltics into a coherent area in Posen or West Prussia. To make room, millions of native Poles and Jews had to be forcefully removed to the Polish government general while their farms and possessions were reassigned. After the

---

[34] Gerhard Weinberg, *Hitler's Foreign Policy: Diplomatic Revolution in Europe, 1933–1936* (Chicago, 1970), and *Hitler's Foreign Policy: Starting World War Two, 1937–1939* (Chicago, 1980).

[35] For a concise summary, see Ulrich Herbert, " 'Ausländer-Einsatz' in der deutschen Kriegswirtschaft, 1939–1945," in *Deutsche im Ausland*, 354–67.

attack on Russia, Nazi visions became even grander, extending to the Ukraine, and the lack of suitable territories for further expulsion logically suggested annihilation.[36] The roundups, cattle-cars, and concentration camps of the "Generalplan Ost" that have come to represent the Holocaust are symbols of an unprecedented and violent mass migration that inevitably led into death.[37]

The experience of compulsory mobilization eventually rebounded to include the German population as well. For the privileged Aryans, the mass rallies, labor service, harvest duty, building of superhighways, or border defenses might have been an exciting break with provincial routine and a chance to widen horizons. The initial victories of the war promised soldiers adventurous travel to far-flung places from the Arctic Circle to North Africa, from the coast of Brittany to the Caucasus Mountains.[38] But with defeat approaching, the consequences of forced dislocation began to dawn on even the most fanatic Nazi supporters: Civilians were evacuated from the cities to escape the bombing raids, children were separated from their families to be shipped to the countryside, women were forced to gather their families and possessions for a long trek to safety, and dispirited men in uniform struggled in endless retreats to avoid capture by the Red Army.[39] Eventually, the forced population movement initiated by the Nazis would engulf the Germans themselves, obliterating all racial distinctions and universalizing its trauma.

An Unacknowledged Immigration Country

The end of World War Two set off massive collective and individual movements that sought to restore some semblance of demographic order in Europe. Millions of Allied occupation soldiers established a

[36] As an entry point into a vast literature, see Götz Aly, "*Endlösung.*" *Völkerverschiebung und der Mord an den europäischen Juden* (Frankfurt, 1995); and Ulrich Herbert, ed., *Nationalsozialistische Vernichtungspolitik 1939–1945. Neue Forschungen und Kontroversen* (Frankfurt, 1998). Part of the process was also an ethnic selection in the East, which created a *deutsche Volksliste* with four categories of Germanness entitling to citizenship, whereas the rest of the native population would have to be disposed of.

[37] Emigré descriptions and survivors' accounts are replete with portrayals of such forced migration. See Elie Wiesel, *La nuit, l'aube, le jour* (Paris, 1969). See also Arno Herzig and Ina Lorenz, eds., *Verdrängung und Vernichtung der Juden unter dem Nationalsozialismus* (Hamburg, 1992).

[38] The positive connotations of mobilization are often forgotten in discussing dictatorship.

[39] For a graphic description of chaotic mobility during the breakdown of the Third Reich, see Victor Klemperer, *Ich will Zeugnis ablegen bis zum letzten* (Berlin 1995), especially volume 2, which concerns 1942 to 1945.

new, privileged population of foreigners that lived in separate quarters but fraternized for the sake of companionship, fathering a generation of children and taking some of their mothers along as war brides.[40] The defeated German soldiers were gathered in POW camps, thoroughly screened, and only gradually released. Major offenders were kept for years to repair war damage in Russia, with the last ten thousand returning from the Soviet Union only in 1955.[41] Moreover, the denazification process and the various war crime trials also spurred many perpetrators in the NSDAP and the SS to go underground and escape via illegal routes to friendly countries, mostly in Latin America. Finally, the mutilated and divided country held out little hope for a better future, setting off a final wave of transatlantic migration that propelled another million emigrants to friendlier shores.[42] No wonder that the guilt-ridden and dispersed Germans, above all, wanted strangers to leave and relatives to come home.

Shocked by the magnitude of human suffering left by the Third Reich, the occupation forces tried to help repatriate the foreign victims. The liberated POWs were quickly returned by their own militaries to their home countries, although they were received with suspicion in the Soviet Union and sometimes incarcerated again. More complicated was the fate of the 10.5 to 11.7 million civilians who were concentration camp survivors or former slave laborers, but who also included some Nazi collaborators fleeing Stalin's grasp. Deliriously happy to be rescued, these half-starved "displaced persons" often resented their exploiters and engaged in acts of retribution (for instance, the burning of Frankfurt/Oder), so that they had to be collected in special DP camps to be controlled. The UN Relief and Rescue Agency organized their repatriation, shipping as many as thirty thousand per day back home during 1945. But because of the movement of borders, many could not or would not return, forcing the IRO to attempt to "resettle" about three-quarters of a million in the United States, Australia, and Canada.[43] Since they were greeted with mutual relief, these departures left little trace in collective recollections.

[40] Klaus-Dietmar Henke, *Die amerikanische Besatzung Deutschlands* (Munich, 1995); and Elfriede B. Shukert, *The War Brides of World War Two* (Novato, Calif., 1988).

[41] Arnold Krammer, *Nazi Prisoners of War in America* (New York, 1979); and Albrecht Lehmann, *Gefangenschaft und Heimkehr. Deutsche Kriegsgefangene in der Sowjetunion* (München, 1986).

[42] Johannes-Dieter Steinert, "Drehscheibe Westdeutschland. Wanderungspolitik im Nachkriegsjahrzehnt," in *Deutsche im Ausland*, 386–92.

[43] Wolfgang Jacobmeyer, *Vom Zwangsarbeiter zum Heimatlosen Ausländer. Die Displaced Persons in Westdeutschland 1945–1951* (Göttingen, 1985). See also Fritz Bauer Institut, ed., *Überlebt und unterwegs. Jüdische Displaced Persons im Nachkriegsdeutschland* (Frankfurt, 1997).

A huge movement in the opposite direction was the flight of about 12.5 million Germans who were expelled from former Reich provinces in the east. Propelled by propaganda claims and real experiences of Russian brutalities, hundreds of thousands of old men, women, and children embarked upon the long trek westward in the winter of 1944–45 to escape the Red Army. Eager to get rid of their former oppressors, the local populace resorted to lynching, beatings, plunder, and rape—a spontaneous retribution that the Polish, Czech, Romanian, Hungarian, and Yugoslav governments ratified through a formal policy of expulsion. Because of the discovery of the concentration camps, the Allied leaders had little sympathy for German suffering, approving systematic eviction to stabilize the new borders, only feebly insisting that the evacuation be carried out in an "orderly and humane" manner. Somewhere between one hundred and two hundred fifty thousand were killed by partisans or militias, while another two million refugees died of starvation, exhaustion, cold, or other "natural" causes. From Finland to Greece, postwar ethnic cleansing emptied east Central Europe of virtually all Germans, creating another immense tragedy.[44] Ignored by most western historians, this *Vertreibung* has through personal retellings and collective advocacy become one of the mainstays of postwar memories.[45]

Another sizable group moving westward were about 3.8 million East Germans who fled the Communist state before 1961—about seven times the number of Westerners who went in the opposite direction. This migration occurred in several waves: about 408,000 left in 1953 in connection with the workers' uprising; around 396,000 fled in 1956 in response to the Hungarian crackdown; and yet another 233, 000 got out in 1961 before the border was sealed.[46] These East German refugees consisted of people with different motivations and skills. Most vocal were the anticommunists in the bourgeois parties—among former Social Democrats and even Communist dissidents, who left to avoid persecution. Quite prominent, also, were the "bourgeois class enemies,"

---

[44] Wolfgang Benz, ed., *Die Vertreibung der Deutschen aus dem Osten. Ursachen, Ereignisse, Folgen* (Frankfurt, 1985). See Philipp Ther, *Deutsche und polnische Vertriebene. Gesellschaft und Vertriebenenpolitik in der SBZ/DDR und in Polen 1945–1956* (Göttingen, 1998).

[45] Rainer Ohliger, "Vertreibungsforschung. Ost(europa)forschung, 'Deutschtumsforschung'? Zwei Debatten—ein Konflikt," H-Soz-u-Kult, 9 June 2000. See also the problematic account by Alfred de Zayas, *A Terrible Revenge: The Ethnic Cleansing of the East European Germans, 1944–1950* (New York, 1994).

[46] Helge Heydemeyer, *Flucht und Zuwanderung aus der SBZ-DDR 1945/1949–1961. Die Flüchtlingspolitik der Bundesrepublik Deutschland bis zum Bau der Mauer* (Düsseldorf, 1994), 43. The exact numbers are somewhat in dispute since not all refugees registered with the authorities and there was also some movement eastward.

landowners, or industrialists who were expropriated under antifascist pretenses so as to make way for the collectivization of agriculture and the nationalization of factories. Less visible were thousands of professors, students, and professionals who resented intellectual censorship and the imposition of Marxist-Leninist orthodoxy. Most numerous were the workers who tired of being exploited by the Soviets and who dreamed of a better life in a consumer economy.[47] This continual population hemorrhage was so debilitating that the SED was finally forced to build the Wall to stop the flow.

A last group of ethnic immigrants were about two million *Aussiedler* who resettled in West Germany from Eastern Europe between 1950 and 1989. Increasingly, those who had not fled, who felt discriminated against by the nationalist majorities, or who had been deported to other regions in the Soviet Union during the war, wanted to return to Germany. Initially, only a few thousand managed to circumvent Communist restrictions, but in the second half of the 1950s a first wave of over 100,000 succeeded in leaving Poland; because of the material concessions made by the Brandt government, about 50,000 could emigrate annually from the mid-1970s onward; and in the improving climate of détente, a veritable torrent of over 200,000 in 1988 and 375,000 in 1989 poured into West Germany. About three-fifths of the migrants came from Poland, another one-sixth hailed from Romania (Transylvania), and only about one-tenth came from Russia. In many families only the older generation still spoke some German, making a determination of a family's Germanness a difficult bureaucratic challenge. A sense of ethnic estrangement from their surroundings and the prospects of a better life in a Western country proved attractive enough to motivate tens of thousands to try living as "Germans among Germans."[48]

These groups of immigrants were rarely recognized as such since they came from the same ethnic stock, were considered citizens, and were assumed to be quickly integrated. Even if newcomers were resented in the difficult postwar years, the shared language and culture made appeals for help politically difficult to resist. In response to the human tidal wave, the Basic Law reaffirmed the ethnic conception of citizenship in Article 116 that provided a right of return and supported the freedom of movement across the zonal borders in Article 117. A

[47] Klaus Bade, "Fremde Deutsche: 'Republikflüchtlinge'—Übersiedler—Aussiedler" in *Deutsche im Ausland*, 401–10; Rainer Münz and Ralf Ulrich, "Changing Patterns of Immigration to Germany, 1945–1995: Ethnic Origins, Demographic Structures, Future Prospects," in *Migration Past, Migration Future*, 74. See also Inge Bennewitz and Rainer Potratz, *Zwangsaussiedlungen an der innerdeutschen Grenze* (Berlin, 1997).

[48] Münz and Ulbrich, "Changing Patterns of Immigration," 70f; and Bade, "Fremde Deutsche," 403 ff.

special refugee ministry set up a screening process, the *Notaufnahme-verfahren*, to discourage frivolous movement, but it gradually turned into a form of refugee registration. New arrivals were gathered in camps such as Friedland near the border, debriefed on their flight, provided with immediate necessities, and held until they could be assigned to one of the states. By 1953 a special law, the *Bundesvertriebe-nengesetz*, provided an increasing amount of help with housing, hiring, and the like, while refugees were even included in the social insurance system and the Equalization of Burdens Law. Although various interest groups clamored for revenge and additional help, these policies eventually succeeded in sufficiently integrating the newcomers to render superfluous such separate refugee parties as the BHE.[49]

The inconceivability of immigration also governed the renewed recruitment of temporary foreign workers to compensate for the drying up of the ethnic influx in the 1960s. Although some Italian farm laborers were already welcomed in 1955, the achievement of full employment only prompted the signing of additional rotating labor agreements with Spain and Greece in 1960 as well as Turkey in 1961. By 1980 one-third of the so-called *Gastarbeiter* hailed from Turkey with another one-seventh from Yugoslavia and Italy each. Drawn by material incentives, these foreign workers nonetheless proved a cheap reserve army for industry since they could be paid lower wages, housed in substandard compounds, and were willing to take on the dirty and dangerous jobs that local union members increasingly refused. Their number grew to 2.6 million until the oil crisis of 1973 triggered a halt in further recruitment; attempts to send now-superfluous laborers home reduced their number to 1.7 million by the late 1980s. Surprisingly, the majority refused to leave and, instead, insisted on having their families join them, more than doubling their number during the same time.[50] In spite of exploitation, many of the supposedly temporary "guests" ultimately decided to stay permanently.

This presence of "native foreigners" created a set of unanticipated problems with practical as well as psychological implications. Since the *Gastarbeiter* families spoke their own languages, possessed distinctive cultures, and worshipped other religions, they could not easily be integrated into the existing community. While nationals of Italy or Yugoslavia were generally accepted as soon as they learned some German,

---

[49] Heydemeyer, *Flucht und Zuwanderung*, 331 ff. Cf. Also Ian Connor, "The Integration of Refugees and Foreign Workers in the FRG since the Second World War," *Bulletin of the German Historical Institute London* 22 (2000): 18–31.

[50] Klaus Bade, "Einheimische Ausländer, Gastarbeiter, Dauergäste, Einwanderer," in *Fremde in Deutschland*, 393 ff.

peasants from Anatolia, with their different physical appearance, particular dress, and Islamic customs, did not just blend in. Turks gathered in parts of cities where the rents were low, and created their own colonies with newspapers, radio broadcasts, mosques, and shops offering special foodstuffs. Because of high reproductive rates, foreign children began to outnumber German pupils in some urban schools, making assimilation all the more difficult. When xenophobia grew as a result of structural unemployment, the CDU government tried various incentives to get foreign laborers to leave and vigorously resisted all liberal efforts at integration.[51] By the 1980s the Federal Republic of Germany, therefore, showed all the hallmarks of an unacknowledged immigration country.

East Germany similarly tried the foreign worker route when the country's labor-intensive smoke-stack economy ran out of reserves because of its continual population loss. When the SED could mobilize no more women, it tried to recruit temporary workers from the neighboring Warsaw Pact countries. Except for some Polish commuters who worked in the silicone factory at Frankfurt/Oder, this effort foundered on the negative memories of World War II. By the mid-1970s the GDR recruited in pro-Socialist countries in North Africa or Cuba, but once again these attempts, labeled occupational training, bore little fruit since their instrumental purpose was all too apparent. Finally, a special agreement with Vietnam yielded about eighty thousand contract workers who were willing to work for a fixed term in textile and other factories under hard restrictions. These *Fremdarbeiter* were tightly controlled by the police, rigidly segregated from the natives, and not allowed to integrate at all. Predicated on the same instrumental attitude, Communist contract labor turned out to be even harsher than capitalist practice.[52]

Toward Contested Multiethnicity

In the early 1990s unexpected population movements, triggered by the collapse of Communism and by increasing globalization, created another crisis that forced a painful rethinking of attitudes toward migra-

[51] Karl-Heinz Meier-Braun and Martin A. Kilgus, eds., *40 Jahre "Gastarbeiter" in Deutschland. 4. Radioforum Ausländer bei uns* (Baden-Baden, 1995), 17–35.

[52] Sandra Gruner-Domic, "Zur Geschichte der Arbeitskräftemigration in die DDR. Die bilateralen Verträge zur Beschäftigung ausländischer Arbeiter 1961–1989," *Internationale Wissenschaftliche Korrespondenz zur Geschichte der Arbeiterbewegung* 32 (1996), 204–230.

tion. On the one hand, the breakdown of the Soviet empire set in motion hundreds of thousands of people who could claim admission to the Federal Republic according to ethnic preference as Germans. On the other hand, the poverty of the Third World and civil wars in the former Yugoslavia uprooted similar numbers who invoked the asylum clause of the Basic Law because there was no provision for any other form of immigration. Since these new arrivals coincided with unification and structural unemployment, the massive in-migration met with a mixed political reaction. Exploiting xenophobic fears, the Right responded with such slogans as *Ausländer raus!*, while the Left bravely continued to celebrate multiculturalism as enrichment.[53] The very dimension of the new problems suggested that old attitudes toward migration had to be revised and that fresh political answers had to be found in order to cope with this issue in the future.

The first movement was the mass exodus of the East German population to the West in the summer of 1989 that helped to destabilize the SED dictatorship. Even after the Wall was built, a few thousand GDR citizens annually had managed to escape or had been been allowed to resettle in the FRG, a number that increased to several tens of thousands in the more permissive 1980s. With the lifting of the Iron Curtain in Hungary, 11,700 fled in July 1989, 133,400 escaped in November with the fall of the Wall, and the outflow continued well into the summer of 1990, bringing altogether about 582,000 East Germans to the West.[54] While the first refugees were welcomed with bands, balloons, and speeches, later migrants were considered a public problem since they could claim official help from the local communities in finding subsidized housing, being placed into new jobs, and the like. Among the poorer strata of the local population, such preferential treatment caused much "social envy," creating pressure on the Kohl government to find a political and economic solution that would keep the East Germans from leaving their homes—in effect, hastening the process of unification. Even after the currency union, the East-West migration continued at a lesser rate, insufficiently counterbalanced by a reverse flow.[55]

The second stream consisted of the remigrants from Eastern Europe who used the collapse of Communism to realize their dream of returning to Germany. During 1989 and 1990 about three-quarters of a

---

[53] For a documentation of press clippings from the early 1990s, see Klaus Bade, ed., *Ausländer, Aussiedler, Asyl in der Bundesrepublik Deutschland* (Bonn, 1992).

[54] Konrad H. Jarausch, *Die Unverhoffte Einheit 1989–1990* (Frankfurt, 1995), 100; and Axel Schützsack, *Exodus in die Einheit. Die Massenflucht aus der DDR 1989* (Melle, 1990), no. 12 of *Deutschland-Report*. The discrepancy stems from the question of registration.

[55] Münz und Ulrich, "Changing Patterns of Immigration," 74 ff. Between 1989 and 1993, 1.4 million migrated from East to West, while only 352,000 went the other way.

million ethnic Germans flowed into the Federal Republic, compounding the problems caused by the GDR refugees. After most of those wanting to leave Poland and Romania had gotten out, the break-up of the Soviet Union allowed greater numbers of ethnic Germans in Russia to leave for the West.[56] To stem the tide, the Bundestag passed a law restricting the acceptance of resettlers (Aussiedleraufnahmegesetz) in 1990 that required applicants to file in their home countries, and complete a fifty-page questionnaire to establish ethnic origin. As a result the number admitted in 1991 dropped to 221,000. A year later public pressure led to a further tightening of procedures, fixing the previous annual number as a quota for ethnic immigrants, and requiring a language test.[57] The integration of these remigrants was becoming increasingly difficult, since many no longer spoke German and structural unemployment made unskilled jobs difficult to find. Though they continued to be treated as ethnic kin, these remigrants were, in effect, rapidly becoming foreign immigrants.

Because of their cultural and physical distinctiveness, asylum seekers were the most controversial group knocking at the door of the FRG. Between 1953 and 1978 the guarantee of Article 16 of the Basic Law, that "persons persecuted for political reasons have the right to asylum," posed little problem since only 7,100 people applied annually. After surpassing 100,000 in 1980, requests dropped until the late 1980s, when the Balkan Wars pushed the number up to 438,200 in 1992.[58] This steep increase produced a conflict between conservatives, wanting to discourage immigration, and liberals, insisting on maintaining an open door for the persecuted. The bureaucracy responded by dropping the rate of recognition from 80 percent during the Cold War to less than 10 percent in the early 1990s. But administrative tightening would not suffice since petitioners could stay for months until their cases were decided. By 1994, 1.7 million registered for asylum in the FRG, with 650,000 refugees temporarily tolerated, 415,000 applicants under review, and 350,000 considered victims of civil war—but only 267,000 were officially recognized as eligible.[59] Less restricted were Jewish peti-

---

[56] Christa Hartmann, Aussiedler aus der Sowjetunion. Sozialisationsgeschichte der Rußlanddeutschen (Berlin 1992), working paper no. 13 of the Pädagogisches Zentrum Berlin.

[57] Münz and Ulrich, "Changing Patterns of Immigration," 71 ff.

[58] Die Ausländerbeauftragte der Senatsverwaltung Berlin, Flüchtlinge aus Bosnien in Berlin (Berlin 1992), and Vietnamesen in Berlin—Bootsflüchtlinge und 'Gastarbeiter' wider Willen, 2nd ed. (Berlin, 1990).

[59] Klaus Bade, "'Politisch Verfolgte geniessen...' Asyl bei den Deutschen—Idee und Wirklichkeit," in Deutsche im Ausland, 411–22. See also "Zeitschrift Grundgesetz im Profil. BAUSTEINE Grundgesetzänderung Asyl," as well as "Asylrecht. Fünf Jahre Art. 16 a GG—enttäuschte Hoffnungen" on the Web.

tioners from Russia, who were admitted to reverse the effects of the Holocaust by reestablishing a Jewish community in Germany.[60]

The rising demand for asylum provoked a heated public debate about legal remedies that might stop the influx. Welcoming ethnic remigrants, the CDU and conservatives sought to raise barriers against economic migrants, while the SPD and the left proposed legalizing immigration, maintaining asylum, and easing naturalization. After protracted negotiations, the government forced through a "compromise" in 1993 that eliminated "abuses" from the asylum process through an amendment to the Basic Law. First, asylum seekers coming in through the European Union or the Eastern European countries that were considered "safe" enough, would be sent back to that state on the assumption that they ought to have asked for acceptance there. Second, to deny applications from citizens of certain states, the application procedure was simplified by establishing a list of countries declared free from persecution. This policy shifted the enforcement of land borders to the German neighbors, leaving only the airports or harbors patrolled directly by the BSG. In the long run, the tightening of administrative practice, which decreased admission percentages to less than 5 percent, had the expected effect of discouraging applications, dropping their number to about one hundred thousand in subsequent years.[61]

The result of such massive migration was a wave of ugly xenophobia, especially in the new German states of the former East. Between 1984 and 1994, 1.6 million ethnic remigrants plus 2.5 million foreigners thronged into the FRG, increasing the number of non-German residents to 7.3 million. To a people that clung to the conception of ethnic homogeneity, this sudden influx seemed threatening, especially since it was exploited by negative media coverage that linked the newcomers with a rise in the crime rate and spectacular incidents of violence, for instance, between Kurds and Turks. Already in 1989, 75 percent of the respondents of a national survey claimed that there were "too many foreigners" in Germany, making various measures of reducing the flow popular.[62] The consequence of adult aversion was a proliferation of youthful anti-foreigner violence, such as beatings of visually different people, fire-bombing of asylum homes, and the like. Gangs of skinheads pursued not only leftists but anyone of different skin color, often with the tacit approval of the community and the police. Conservative

[60] Y. Michal Bodemann, ed., *Jews, Germans, Memory: Reconstructing Jewish Life in Germany* (Ann Arbor, 1996); and Michael Brenner, *After the Holocaust: Rebuilding Jewish Life in Post-War Germany* (Princeton, 1997).

[61] Münz and Ulrich, "Changing Patterns of Immigration," 84 ff.

[62] Claus Leggewie, " 'Stolz ein Deutscher zu sein. . .'—die neue Angst vor dem Fremden," in *Deutsche im Ausland*, 423–30.

politicians remained reluctant to condemn such outbursts until hundreds of thousands of liberal spokesmen, clergymen, and intellectuals demonstrated for tolerance with chains of candlelight.[63]

With the 1998 election of the Schröder-Fischer government, the political wind finally turned sufficiently to allow a revision of the 1913 citizenship law. For over a decade liberal academics, religious leaders supporting church asylum, Green politicians, and progressive intellectuals had clamored for an easing of naturalization procedures. But the CDU, desperate for an issue to reverse its national defeat, fastened upon popular resentment against dual citizenship in a nasty campaign that unseated the SPD state government in the 1999 Hessian election. The red-green coalition, therefore, contented itself with a more limited option model that allowed second-generation children under twenty-three years of age the choice of becoming German by simple declaration and shortened to eight years the lengthy residence requirement for naturalization by adults. Though this reform did not go as far as the pro-immigration lobby wanted, it did break with the jus sanguinis tradition and introduced the principle of jus soli into German law.[64] Initial indications are that the simplified procedure has allowed more foreigners to take out papers, but because of the high costs and a language test, the response has fallen somewhat short of its goal.[65]

The labor needs of a high-tech economy sparked another revival of immigration discussions in the spring of 2000. At the Hanover world exposition Chancellor Schröder proposed the temporary admission of twenty thousand computer specialists via a "green card" to attract trained programmers from abroad. While industrialists were delighted, the CDU countered with the populist slogan *"Kinder statt Inder;"* nonetheless, it lost the North-Rhine-Westphalian elections. Since unemployment numbers were gradually receding, the cabinet succeeded in turning this initiative into law.[66] At the same time, concern about keeping social security payments stable without raising contributions further, shifted attention to a drastic reproduction deficit,

[63] Rainer Erb, "Rechtsextremistische Jugendszene in Brandenburg," in the discussion forum of the "Aktionsbündnis gegen Gewalt, Rechtsextremismus und Fremdenfeindlichkeit," Potsdam, 1999.

[64] *Einbürgerung, das neue Staatsbürgerschaftsrecht. Ein Informationsangebot der Beauftragten der Bundesregierung für Ausländer* (Bonn, 2000). Brubaker, *Citizenship and Nationhood,* 179 ff.

[65] Center for Turkish Studies in Essen, press release, "Einbürgerungen werden trotz Sprachtest und hohen Gebühren weiter zunehmen," 9 February 2000, and "Dauernde Verbleibabsicht der türkischen Zuwanderer im Freistaat Bayern," 27 March 2000.

[66] Resolution of the Greens, "Auch Inder haben Kinder. Für eine zeitgemässe, offene und faire Green-Card-Regelung," 21 March 2000, sowie Hans-Jürgen Leersch and Peter Schmalz, "CSU und Gewerkschaften kritisieren Green Card," *Die Welt,* 15 March 2000.

caused by an insufficient birth-rate. Demographers pointed out that Germany was turning into a "republic of the childless" and would either have to reduce its fat pensions or at last become an immigration country. In a courageous speech, Federal President Rau called for an end to xenophobia since "we will in the future need immigration out of self-interest."[67] When even the CDU-CSU dropped its opposition, the subsequent debate about introducing an immigration law no longer revolved around whether any immigrants ought to be admitted, but how many and in what form.[68]

Rethinking German (In)Stability

Neither the Germans themselves nor outside commentators have quite appreciated the extent of the reversal from emigration to immigration country during the last century. The ethnic definition of identity that stemmed from romantic conceptions of the *Volk* and grew into racial prejudice, has blocked a recognition of the pattern of massive population movements in central Europe.[69] Official memory culture recalls only some German aspects of population movement, such as the transatlantic emigration or the postwar expulsion, but forgets such foreign dimensions as the rotation of seasonal workers or the exploitation of slave laborers. The negative connotations associated with such "A-words" as *Ausländer*, *Aussiedler*, and *Asyl* indicate a defensive mentality that considers difference a threat rather than an opportunity for enrichment.[70] Ironically, it has taken the emergence of "native foreigners" in the children of the *Gastarbeiter* to undermine the distinction between natives and foreigners, while it required the arrival of "foreign natives" such as the Russian resettlers to question ethnic preferences. The cognitive lag, based on an image of stability, can only be overcome by a more comprehensive history of migration that transcends the distinction between ethnic (r)emigration and foreign (im)migration.

[67] Rainer Münz, "Republik der Kinderlosen. Ohne Zuwanderung vergreist die deutsche Gesellschaft—Plädoyer für ein Einwanderungsgesetz," *Die Zeit*, 31 May 2000. See also Johannes Rau, "Ohne Angst und ohne Träumereien. Gemeinsam in Deutschland leben," Berlin speech of 12 May 2000.

[68] "Kirchen fordern Einwanderungsgesetz für die Bundesrepublik," *Frankfurter Rundschau*, 29 November 1999; "DGB-Chef Schulte für Einwanderungsgesetz," *ticker.de*, 28 April 2000; and "Das Einwanderungsgesetz kommt," *Die Welt*, 7 July 2000.

[69] Joseph B. Schechtman, *Postwar Population Transfers in Europe, 1945–1955* (Philadelphia, 1962).

[70] Bade, *Ausländer, Aussiedler, Asyl in der Bundesrepublik Deutschland*, 9ff.

From such a perspective, twentieth-century Germany, therefore, ought not to be conceptualized as a bedrock of stability but rather considered as an "unsettled society." The repeated population shifts in central Europe suggest an extraordinary record of individual or collective, voluntary or forced, pacific or violent, transitory or permanent movement. For many more Germans than is usually assumed, migration was a crucial part of their individual or collective experiences. About one-quarter of the population of the Federal Republic consists of newcomers since World War II—and these twenty million do not include a nearly equal number of slave laborers, DPs, rotating workers, and occupation soldiers who have moved in the other direction.[71] The passages of all these different peoples have left traces of different depth in German society and culture that have yet to be more systematically recovered. Moreover, recollections of these massive population movements are also intimately involved in the attitudes of the Federal Republic's neighboring countries. Perhaps the German craving for a self-image of stability should itself be thought a response to a profound feeling of unsettlement. Is it not time to incorporate the story of this mobility into larger historical narratives and to acknowledge the role that migrants played in the German past?

The cultural implications of this demographic mobility can hardly be exaggerated because they challenge the fixity of ethnic stereotypes. As a result of the migrations of the last century, participation in German culture has been extraordinarily fluid: Millions of German speakers have assimilated into other cultures, fading from members of a vibrant immigrant community to bearers of a vague sense of cultural background in the United States, while preserving their language and customs somewhat better in Latin America. At the same time, millions of Polish and Jewish foreigners have also acculturated themselves in Germany, blending into the dominant fabric with hardly a trace of difference, while other newcomers, such as Turkish guest workers, have clung to a more contested dual identity. Membership in the ethnic community has, therefore, been subject to constant transformations in both directions, creating hybrids such as German-Americans and gradually also changing strained references to "Turkish fellow citizens" into more tolerant allusions to "Germans of Turkish background." Fixated upon a stable sense of ethnicity, the political system has unfortunately failed to come to recognize these multiple transformations. Instead of being

---

[71] Münz and Ulrich, "Changing Patterns of Immigration to Germany," 66 ff. See also Jan Motte, Rainer Ohlinger, and Anne von Oswald, eds., *Fünfzig Jahre Bundesrepublik—Fünfzig Jahre Einwanderung* (Frankfurt, 1999).

ignored as marginal exceptions, processes of becoming and "unbecoming" German need to be considered an essential part of the story.[72]

The overdue recognition of the importance of multiple migrations for German development may help suggest more humane and pragmatic solutions for the problems of *Zuwanderung*. According to its chair, Rita Süssmuth, the non-partisan commission on remigration, asylum, and immigration departed from the premise that German national interest required "the creation of a labor-market-oriented immigration" policy. Despite its insistence on a German *Leitkultur*, the Right is beginning to concede that demographic deficits and labor requirements demand an immigration law that will abolish ethnic distinctions and find a compromise between the capacity of German society to absorb and the need of outsiders to come in. At the same time, the Left is starting to understand the need for a concerted effort at integration to help newcomers leave their separate colonies by including them in the mainstream.[73] Children of guest workers have to be brought out of their limbo between their background and their German context; rural East European remigrants need to acquire language skills to compete; and asylum seekers must make a more rapid transition into their new world. Even if fears of international terrorism have made the task of framing appropriate legislation more difficult, the passage of an immigration bill in the spring of 2002 that combines a labor-market dependent liberalization of entry with an insistence on cultural integration is a more hopeful sign.[74]

---

[72] Klaus Bade, ed., *Migration, Ethnizität, Konflikt. Systemfragen und Fallstudien* (Osnabrück, 1996). See also Fredrick C. Luebke, *Germans in the New World: Essays in the History of Immigration* (Champaign, 1990).

[73] "Mit Rita Süssmuth an der Spitze. Schily stellt Einwanderungskommission vor," *Der Tagesspiegel*, 13 July 2000. For the commission report, see Rita Süssmuth, ed., *Zuwanderung gestalten, Integration fördern. Bericht der Unabhängigen Kommission "Zuwanderung"* (Berlin, 2001). Cf. also "Ein neues Recht für die Ausländer in Deutschland," *Süddeutsche Zeitung*, 4 August 2001.

[74] Klaus Bade, "Politik in der Einwanderungssituation. Migration—Integration—Minderheiten," in *Deutsche im Ausland*, 442 ff. See also Klaus J. Bade and Rainer Münz, eds., *Migrationsreport 2000. Fakten—Analysen—Perspektiven* (Frankfurt, 2000), 7–22.

8

A Struggle for Unity: Redefining National Identities

"What is a German's fatherland?" This question, posed by the poet Ernst Moritz Arndt during the Wars of Liberation against Napoleon, has received many different answers during the last two centuries.[1] A simple enumeration of states from the Holy Roman Empire to the German Confederation, the Second Empire, the Weimar Republic, the Third Reich, the German Democratic Republic, and the Federal Republic of Germany, indicates a dizzying variety of constitutional arrangements, external borders, and internal structures. Similarly, a glance at Austria and Switzerland, the language islands of Eastern Europe, or transatlantic emigration communities suggests that not all German speakers were included in these German states, but that numerous Danes, Poles, French, and voluntary immigrants and forced laborers, especially from the east and south, did belong to them. No wonder that during the modern era legal and cultural definitions of who was supposed to be German have varied more drastically than for any other European nationality.

[1] Peter Longerich, *"Was ist des Deutschen Vaterland?" Dokumente zur Frage der deutschen Einheit, 1800–1990* (Munich, 1990).

Ever since Friedrich Meinecke reflected on "cosmopolitanism and the national state," scholars have conceptualized this issue as the rise of nationalist ideology.[2] Horrified by the war, such intellectual historians as Hans Kohn defined the essence of the "German mind" as a romantic, ethnic deviation from Western Enlightenment and citizenship.[3] Social scientists, such as Helmut Plessner and Ralf Dahrendorf, attributed German incapacity for democracy to structural reasons rooted in a belated and defective form of modernization of economy and society.[4] In contrast, such recent critics as Benedict Anderson and Homi Bhabha suggest that nationalism be understood as "an imagined community," and stress the "production of nation as narration" or the significance of "othering."[5] By focusing on cultural processes of inclusion and exclusion, such interpretations point to the need to explain the construction of national sentiment and to probe the shift of allegiances from the local or the national level. While a vague sense of community may already date from the Renaissance, the transformation into modern nationalism in the nineteenth century made German self-definitions profoundly problematic.[6]

The creation of a German state must be analytically separated from discussions of nationalism since both were combined only for three-quarters of a century. The lateness of German unification in 1871, the troubled record of a unified Germany in Europe, the division of 1945, and the surprising reunification of the successor states in 1990, suggest that the combination of "nationness" and statehood in Central Europe cannot be taken for granted.[7] Recent analysts stress that early modern

---

[2] Friedrich Meinecke, *Weltbürgertum und Nationalstaat. Studien zur Genesis des deutschen Nationalstaats* (Munich, 1911). Cf. Dieter Langewiesche, "Nation, Nationalismus, Nationalstaat. Forschungsstand und Forschungsperspektiven," *Neue Politische Literatur* 40 (1995): 190–236.

[3] Carlton J. Hayes, *Nationalism: A Religion* (New York, 1960); and Hans Kohn, *Nationalism: Its Meaning and History* (Princeton, 1955).

[4] Helmut Plessner, *Die verspätete Nation. Über die politische Verführbarkeit des bürgerlichen Geistes* (Frankfurt, 1982); Ernest Gellner, *Nations and Nationalism* (Ithaca, 1983); and Anthony D. Smith, *Theories of Nationalism* (London, 1971).

[5] Benedict Anderson, *Imagined Communities: Reflections on the Origin and Spread of Nationalism*, 3rd ed. (London, 1986); Homi Bhabha, ed., *Nation and Narration* (New York, 1990); Eric J. Hobsbawm, *Nations and Nationalism since 1780: Program, Myth, Reality* (Cambridge, 1990); and Lloyd Kramer, *Nationalism: Political Cultures in Europe and America, 1775–1865* (New York, 1998).

[6] Wolfgang Hardtwig, *Nationalismus und Bürgerkultur in Deutschland, 1500–1914* (Göttingen, 1994). Cf. Dieter Langewiesche, "War da was vor 1871?" *Frankfurter Allgemeine Zeitung*, 12 December 2000.

[7] Reinhart Koselleck "Volk, Nation, Nationalismus, Masse," in Werner Conze and Reinhart Koselleck, eds., *Geschichtliche Grundbegriffe. Historisches Lexikon der politisch-sozialen Sprache in Deutschland* vol. 7 (Stuttgart, 1992), 141–431. See James J. Sheehan, "What is

state-building largely proceeded on the level of individual territories, complemented by looser confederations, until the Prussian conquest of Germany combined both tendencies in an entity that resembled a nation-state.[8] The imperial hybrid of middle-class agitation and dynastic interests proved constitutionally unstable, changing to republic, dictatorship, and back; moreover, its borders were extraordinarily undefined, surging forward during wartime to include nonethnic territory and shrinking back after defeat to leave behind many German speakers. Hence the explanatory challenge is not just the particular nature of central European nationalism, but its disastrous effect on the internal and external politics of German statehood.

Misled by claims of uniformity, much of the literature fails to mention that the national project was in fact promoted by competing minorities, each seeking to shape the nascent polity in its own image.[9] In the particularistic world of the Holy Roman Empire, such educated advocates of a cultural renaissance as Johann Gottfried Herder struggled hard to formulate arguments that would persuade the majority of the burghers to shift their local loyalties away from their princes to the future nation. For two-thirds of the nineteenth century Catholic and Austrian partisans of a larger Germany clashed with the Protestant and Prussian supporters of a lesser Germany over the geographical extent, dynastic allegiance, and confessional composition of future statehood. It took even longer for radical democrats or socialists to gain attention for their socially more inclusive visions of the nation-state, while proponents of other religious or ethnic minorities continued to be silenced. The very fragmentation of region, religion, and class that nationalism hoped to overcome was reflected in these contending, largely male blueprints for unity, in the force used to convert the reluctant, and in the exclusion of unassimilatable others.[10]

The notion of a "German identity" might provide a more useful perspective on shifting definitions of Germanness than the presumption of a "national character."[11] Compared to an essentialist understanding

---

German History? Reflections on the Role of the Nation in German History and Historiography," *Journal of Modern History* 53 (1981): 1–23.

[8] John Breuilly, *Nationalism and the State*, 2nd ed. (Manchester, 1993); and Hagen Schulze, ed., *Nation Building in Central Europe* (Leamington Spa, 1987).

[9] Otto Dann, *Nation und Nationalismus in Deutschland 1770–1990*, 2nd ed. (Munich, 1994); and Hagen Schulze, *Staat und Nation in der europäischen Geschichte* (Munich, 1994).

[10] Thomas Nipperdey, *Deutsche Geschichte 1806–1866. Bürgerwelt und starker Staat* (Munich, 1983); and Jonathan Sperber, *The Kaiser's Voters: Electors and Elections in Imperial Germany* (Cambridge, 1997).

[11] Harold James, *A German Identity, 1770–1990* (New York, 1990). See also Ansgar and Vera Nünning, *Der Deutsche an sich. Einem Phantom auf der Spur* (Munich, 1994).

of fixed traits, this flexible approach points to the constructed character, the contested nature, and the changing configurations of such a
sense of self over time. While the transposition of a psychological concept from individual development to collective consciousness runs
some risk of reification, this shift of focus from the "I" to the "we" also
highlights the emotional and gendered dimensions of self-definitions
that do not exhaust themselves in rational considerations of interest
alone. In spite of its inflation, a cultural understanding of identity as
"a great diversity of constantly changing meaning structures embodied
in and mediated by discourse practices and codified in a variety of
texts"[12] can help suggest new questions about the conflicted notions of
Germanness.[13] Such a congeries of contested and changing claims
imply a socially grounded, discursive approach, looking in turn at the
creation of self-definitions, the hypertrophy of nationalism, and attempts at distancing from the nation.[14]

Contending Visions
of Germanness

In many ways the inception of nationalism can be understood as an
attempt to break out of the confines of the local patriotism that dominated the patchwork map of central Europe in 1800. The small worlds
of over three hundred ecclesiastical principalities, free cities, and imperial knights might have offered a sense of belonging, but the territorial
states appeared stifling to an educated middle class dedicated to the
removal of the myriad of princely privileges, corporate restrictions, or
trade barriers that hampered the free development of individuals, public life, and trade. The rediscovery of a common language and culture
in the writings of the literary revival aimed at creating a translocal public that would advance the cause of popular *Aufklärung*. The pamphlets

---

[12] Konrad H. Jarausch, "Reshaping German Identities: Reflections on the Post-Unifi-
cation Debate," and Andreas Pickel, "Creative Chaos: A Methodological Postscript on
Interdisciplinary Cooperation," in Konrad H. Jarausch, ed., *After Unity: Reconfiguring
German Identities* (Providence, 1997), 1–23, 201–10.

[13] Aleida Assmann and Heidrun Friese, eds., *Identitäten* (Frankfurt, 1998); Lutz Niethammer, *Kollektive Identität. Heimliche Quellen einer unheimlichen Konjunktur* (Reinbeck,
2000); and Uffa Jensen, "Keine 'Identität' ohne Identitäter? Sammelrezension," in H-soz-
kult, 19 November 2000.

[14] Geoff Eley and Ronald Suny, eds., *Becoming National* (New York, 1997). Cf. Heinz-
Gerhard Haupt and Charlotte Tacke, "Die Kultur des Nationalen. Sozial- und kulturgeschichtliche Ansätze bei der Erforschung des europäischen Nationalismus im 19. und
20. Jahrhundert," in Wolfgang Hardtwig and Hans-Ulrich Wehler, eds., *Kulturgeschichte
heute* (Göttingen, 1996), 255–83.

of Karl von Moser were also animated by a palpable resentment against the political impotence of the Germans, the result of their manifold divisions.[15] While united in rejecting Napoleonic domination and in creating a national state, advocates of nationalism remained deeply at odds over what this new Germany ought to look like.

Critics of German nationalism often forget that many initial leaders of nation-state building were south German and Catholic.[16] After all, centuries of tradition in carrying the imperial crown pointed to the Hapsburg dynasty as the logical champion of a closer union of German states that would incrementally build on existing structures. In 1814 the Catholic publicist Joseph Görres argued for "a strong unity in free diversity," appealing to the princes for leading the way to the creation of a common state and for mobilizing the citizenry by greater participation through a constitution. In June 1815 the Austrian foreign minister, Clemens von Metternich, created the German *Bund* "for the purpose of maintaining the external and internal security of Germany as well as the independence and inviolability of the individual German states."[17] While using some of the new language of nationalism, this loose confederation fell far short of the hopes of bourgeois patriots because its protection of territorial sovereignty offered neither constitutional government at home nor effective military power abroad.

Although the Catholic vision could rely on Austrian support, it was weakened by a number of internal limitations that ultimately account for its failure. Since the attempt to re-Catholicize the land of the Reformation had stalled during the Thirty Year's War, the religious message appealed to less than one-half of the population, putting off many Protestants, Jews, and free-thinkers. The restoration emphasis on the monarchy attracted merely its defenders at the courts, such as the nobility, the bureaucracy, the clergy, and the peasantry, but antagonized the liberal educated and propertied middle class as well as the restive artisans and farmers seeking to cope with the disruptions of the market. Reliance on existing authorities of state and church hampered enthusiasm, stirring up popular support only when Catholicism became a rallying point against outside domination. Finally, various schemes

---

[15] Dann, *Nation und Nationalismus*, 38 ff. See also Dieter Langewiesche, "War da was vor 1871?" *Frankfurter Allgemeine Zeitung*, 12 December 2000.

[16] Jim Sheehan, *German History 1770–1866* (New York, 1989), and David Blackbourn, *The Long Nineteenth Century: A History of Germany, 1870–1918* (Oxford, 1998), have been instrumental in drawing attention to the importance of the Catholics in German nationalism.

[17] Joseph Görres, "Die künftige teutsche Verfassung," *Rheinischer Merkur*, 18 and 20 August 1815; and Act of German Confederation in Rolf Huber, *Dokumente der deutschen Verfassungsgeschichte*, vol. 1, 84 ff.

to turn the confederation into a "national union of the Germans" foundered on the unwillingness of the princes to cede sovereignty.[18] Only the failure of this larger conception of Germanness paved the way for the foundation of the more limited Bismarckian Empire.

Scholars of nationalism, therefore, have focused their attention on the more successful Protestant north German national movement.[19] Were not most of the prominent spokesmen, such as Ernst Moritz Arndt, Johann Gottlieb Fichte, or Friedrich Ludwig Jahn, members of the Protestant *Bildungsbürgertum*? Moreover, some of the crucial organizations, such as the student movement of the *Burschenschaft*, were also largely Protestant groups that cited Martin Luther as a national hero and celebrated the three hundredth anniversary of his provocative theses in 1817 at the Wartburg castle. But emphasis on the religious basis of nationalism fails to explain why the Protestant movement succeeded in elaborating a more inclusive conception of the nation than the Catholic alternative. A closer look at the rhetoric of "enlightened nationalism" reveals that its secularized vision, which equated Protestantism with progress, reform, and liberation, proved more accessible because any Catholic or Jew who was willing to jettison traditional religion could participate in this national community.[20] Only the ultramontane or orthodox, the French, Polish, or anybody else who refused to join this cultural version of Protestant Germanness would remain excluded as an enemy.

The state to which these nationalists looked was Prussia—the Protestant champion in the German lands. The relationship between the national movement and the Hohenzollern dynasty, however, remained contradictory because the monarchy continued, as the refusal of the crown during the 1848 revolution indicates, to waver between protecting Prussian interests and risking German leadership. Only decades of agitation by gymnastic clubs, singing societies, literary festivals, or campaigns for monuments made the bourgeois aspiration of unification popular enough among artisans and peasants to supplant older regional loyalties.[21] It also required successive reforms for the state to

[18] Program of the German Reform association, 28 October 1862; Austrian memorandum on the reform of the constitution of the German Confederation, 13 July 1863 in Longerich, *Vaterland*, 83 ff.

[19] From Hans Kohn, *The Idea of Nationalism: A History of its Origins* (New York, 1944) to Liah Greenfeld, *Nationalism: Five Roads to Modernity* (Cambridge, Mass., 1992).

[20] Matthew Levinger, *Enlightened Nationalism: The Transformation of Prussian Political Culture, 1806–1848* (New York, 2000). Cf. also Helmut Walser Smith, *German Nationalism and Religious Conflict: Culture, Identity and Politics, 1870–1914* (Princeton, 1994).

[21] Dieter Düding, *Organisation des gesellschaftlichen Nationalismus in Deutschland (1808–1847). Bedeutung und Funktion der Turner- und Sängervereine für die deutsche Nationalbewegung* (Munich, 1984).

shed its authoritarian and militarist image after the Napoleonic defeat and then again during the 1848 revolution to make Prussia attractive to some constitutionalists and liberals in western and southern Germany. Because the Protestant version also fell short of a majority, it only succeeded when Bismarck cut the Gordian knot by military force, offering the princes a federation led by the Prussian monarchy and the national movement a parliament elected by universal manhood suffrage.[22]

More neglected by historians is a third democratic and, eventually, also socialist strand that articulated its national aspirations in opposition to chauvinism. During the *Vormärz* and the 1848 revolution, radicals, inspired by American and French ideals of freedom and equality, developed a grassroots conception of the nation based upon a free union of the *Volk* governing itself in a Republic. Its advocates, such advanced intellectuals as Friedrich Hecker and Karl Marx, were supported mostly by small producers, artisans, and farmers who chafed at the arbitrary repression of their local state or church authorities. These lower-middle-class members as well as the laboring people in the crafts and factories sought in the nation a greater solidarity against the unpredictable swings of the emerging markets of early industrial economies.[23] Their vision was more inclusive than that of the Catholic federalists or Protestant nationalists since it comprised the entire productive population and expressed sympathy for the concurrent liberation movements in Italy, Poland, and the like. Merely the priest, the bureaucrat, the officer, the landed noble, and the factory owner were considered the people's enemies.

The state orientation of this democratic nationalism was virulently anti-Prussian, especially after Berlin's troops put down the uprisings of the spring and summer of 1849 in the south and west. The radicals were also divided about the work of the Frankfurt parliament, agreeing with its declaration of rights and attempts at national unification, but rejecting the "hereditary emperor" compromise as well as the laissez-faire orientation of its economic policies. In contrast to the liberals' appeals to local notables, the democrats tried to reach a mass audience through radical newspapers (such as the *Neue Rheinische Zeitung*), broadsheets read in taverns, fiery speeches at rallies, and rebellious *Katzenmusik*. The impressive membership numbers of democratic clubs, the growing size of later labor unions, and the eventual electoral

---

[22] For the partly instrumental, partly genuine relationship of Bismarck to the national movement, see Otto Pflanze, *Bismarck and the Development of Germany: The Period of German Unification, 1815–1871* (Princeton, 1963); and Ernst Engelberg, *Bismarck, Urpreuße und Reichsgründer* (Berlin, 1985).

[23] Jonathan Sperber, *Rhineland Radicals: The Democratic Movement and the Revolution of 1848–1849* (Princeton, 1991), 257 ff., 470 ff.

success of socialist parties indicated the potential resonance of a democratic nationalism in Germany.[24] But the defeat of the second revolution pushed this radical nationalism underground and made the Marxist labor movement overtly internationalist, rejecting nationality as "the principle of barbarism."[25]

The establishment of the Second Empire fundamentally altered the terms of the identity struggle since it posed the challenge of internally unifying the disparate subjects of over thirty separate states. Since the creation of the Reich could not overnight turn reluctant Badensians or Pomeranians into Germans, only a lengthy process of redirecting allegiances and interests eventually produced citizens who could feel at home in the new national state.[26] As regional loyalties in such conquered territories as Hanover did not disappear immediately and resentment against Prussia ran high among the partisans of the losing Austrian or south-western alternatives, it required a complicated federal structure, couched in medieval terminology and dynastic iconography, to make national allegiance appear superior as well as complementary to existing provincial loyalties.[27] The vigorous movements to assert *Heimat* in places as disparate as the Palatinate or Württemberg indicate a prolonged renegotiation of emotional ties that sought to reconcile a pride in local origins with a widening perspective of a national community.[28]

The cultural process that turned the inhabitants of the Second Empire into German citizens remains somewhat mysterious. Bismarck's counterproductive effort to compel loyalty by ostracizing the Catholics in the *Kulturkampf*, breaking with the Liberals to escape parliamentarization, and persecuting the labor movement with the anti-Socialist laws is well known. But the impact of positive efforts at inclusion— such as the linking of regions with railroads, the creation of a national public through the postal service, the legitimizing effect of *Reichstag* elections as well as of the measures to produce fiscal, economic, and legal uniformity, and the emergence of tourism—has received less at-

---

[24] John Snell, *The Democratic Movement in Germany, 1789–1914* (Chapel Hill, 1976); and Dieter Groh, *Vaterlandslose Gesellen. Sozialdemokratie und Nation 1860–1990* (Munich, 1992).

[25] Wilhelm Liebknecht, Reichstag speech, in *Verhandlungen des Deutschen Reichstages*, 25th session, 15 January 1866, 536 ff.

[26] Gordon A. Craig, *Germany, 1866–1945* (New York, 1978); and Thomas Nipperdey, *Deutsche Geschichte 1866–1918* 2 vols. (Munich, 1990).

[27] The literature on German federalism is disappointing. Cf. Johann Huhn and Peter Christian Witt, eds., *Föderalismus in Deutschland. Tradition und gegenwärtige Probleme* (Baden Baden, 1992).

[28] Celia Applegate, *A Nation of Provincials: The German Idea of Heimat* (Berkeley, 1990); and Alon Confino, *The Nation as Local Metaphor: Württemberg, Imperial Germany and National Memory, 1871–1918* (Chapel Hill, 1997).

tention.[29] Such cultural efforts of bonding as the use of imperial symbols by the Hohenzollern dynasty, the celebration of such new national holidays as Sedan's day, the service in the separate but joined armies, the rewriting of textbooks in line with a Prusso-centric interpretation of history, suggest the need for a concerted strategy to overcome local, religious, and class resistance to the imposition of a Prussian version of Protestant Germanness. Ultimately, nationalization succeeded because federalism promoted at the same time a culturalized form of regional loyalty.[30]

During the nineteenth century, Germans radically reconfigured their identities, adding to a sense of linguistic, cultural, and historical affinity a new dimension of common citizenship in a national state. There seemed to be ample reason for pride: The Second Reich included more German speakers than its predecessors, provided a federal structure that allowed some degree of regional diversity, offered a larger market for economic development, created a wider public for intellectual debates, and provided a more powerful platform for international affairs. But such self-satisfaction tended to overlook the losses in the normalization process, such as the exclusion of the German-speaking Austrians, discrimination against Catholics, persecution of Socialists, and the rise of a racial anti-Semitism, not to mention other repugnant traits, such as militarism and authoritarianism, caricatured by Heinrich Mann.[31] Through unification, the prior conflicts over identity were transferred from external rivalries to internal contests in a common state, albeit under a changed power relationship which privileged that particular dynastic and educated middle-class hybrid found in Prusso-German nationalism.

The Rise of Hypernationalism

Instead of satisfying national aspirations, the incompleteness of the Second Reich as national state ironically triggered a more integral form of nationalism. Since some of the founding compromises left an unfinished agenda at home and abroad, nationalists felt challenged to com-

[29] Margaret L. Anderson, *Practicing Democracy: Elections and Political Culture in Imperial Germany* (Princeton, 2000).

[30] Siegfried Weichlein, "Nationalbildung und Regionsbildung nach der Reichsgründung 1866–1890" (Habilitationsschrift, Berlin, 2002).

[31] For changing evaluations, see Hans-Ulrich Wehler, *Das deutsche Kaiserreich 1871–1918* (Göttingen, 1973), and the more differentiated treatment in volume III of his German social history, *Von der deutschen Doppelrevolution bis zum Beginn des Ersten Weltkrieges 1849–1914* (Munich, 1995), 934 ff.

plete the state building. Domestically, the Empire contained numerous non-German minorities, some, like the Danes and the French speakers in Alsace-Lorraine, who looked to existing national states, and others, like the Poles, who hoped for the resurrection of their state. Their refusal to assimilate to the Prusso-German mold triggered systematic Germanization policies that provoked much resistance and created fierce nationalities struggles within the Reich. Internationally, the exclusion of numerous German speakers in defeated Austria and the existence of language islands throughout east central Europe encouraged demands for bringing these "Germans" home and for elaborating an ethnic conception of citizenship.[32]

Once again, it was a handful of odd critics of imperial culture who spearheaded the transformation of the liberal national movement into an aggressive nationalism. In the 1870s, such marginal writers as Julius Langbehn and Paul de Lagarde created a stir with their critique of the shallowness of official *Kultur*, xenophobic warnings against decadence, and neoromantic insistence on basing the new state more squarely on the German *Volk*.[33] The onset of the Great Depression turned attention to speculators, fostered calls for ending Jewish emancipation, and created an audience for cranks like Wilhelm Marr who advocated a new brand of racial anti-Semitism. When the popular historian Heinrich von Treitschke picked up these slogans, student activists responded by founding *Vereine Deutscher Studenten*, which propagated a novel version of nationalism based on social reform, ethnic purity, and imperial ambition.[34] Though it started merely as a cultural countercurrent, this volkish critique, supported by the neoromantic operas of Richard Wagner and the philosophy of Friedrich Nietzsche, gradually infected wider circles of the educated middle class, giving nationalism an intolerant sectarian edge.

During the Wilhelmian era, volkish nationalism widened its audience by organizing a network of powerful pressure groups. Most vocal among them was the Pan-German league, which sought to support ethnic Germans abroad and advocated a foreign policy of conquest and settlement. But other groups, the Army League, the Navy League, the anti-Polish Eastern Marches Society, and the Colonial League,

---

[32] The term comes from Peter Alter, *Nationalism*, 2nd ed. (London, 1994), 26 ff. Wehler prefers "radical nationalism."

[33] Fritz Stern, *The Politics of Cultural Despair: A Study in the Rise of the German Ideology* (Berkeley, 1961); and George L. Mosse, *The Crisis of the German Ideology: Intellectual Origins of the Third Reich* (New York, 1964).

[34] Konrad H. Jarausch, *The Rise of Academic Illiberalism: Students, Society and Politics in Imperial Germany* (Princeton, 1982); and Norbert Kampe, *Studenten und Judenfrage im Kaiserreich. Die Entstehung der akademischen Trägerschicht des Antisemitismus* (Göttingen, 1988).

joined in demanding military preparedness, settlement on eastern estates, and the acquisition of colonies. These patriotic associations were financed by such special interests as arms manufacturers, large landowners, and colonial merchants, who stood to gain materially from their propaganda, while parties of the Right welcomed their efforts as auxiliaries, able to provide a greater mass base. Educated Protestants provided much of their leadership, while the followers consisted of members of the lower middle class threatened by the changes of rapid industrialization and urbanization.[35] In pursuit of *Weltpolitik*, these pressure groups formed a "national opposition" against what they considered to be too circumspect an imperial government by loudly clamoring for more forceful policies.

The Empire, nonetheless, also provided political space for attempts to broaden definitions of Germanness to make them more inclusive and democratic. Around the turn of the century, a women's movement, more moderate than the English suffragettes, began to attack male prerogatives in education and the professions, proposing a de-gendering of notions of citizenship. Moreover, the unstoppable rise of the trade unions and of the Social Democratic Party gave the industrial proletariat an economic representation and a political voice, and promoted a de-bourgeoisification of conceptions of national community. Additionally, the emancipation of the Jews through increasing legal equality, business success, and access to such professions as law and medicine, de-Christianized ideals of Germanness by introducing religious diversity. Finally, the reluctant assimilation of Poles and other minorities de-ethnicized definitions of German identity since it added people of different backgrounds to the mix.[36] To volkish nationalists, these tendencies toward diversification were profoundly unsettling since they threatened their vision of patriarchal, middle-class, Christian, and Teutonic Germanness.

It took World War I to provide integral nationalism with a mass following since the experience of the fighting created a militant sense of a national community. The spontaneous enthusiasm of the August days, encapsulated in the "ideas of 1914," indicated that the Empire had succeeded, somewhat in spite of itself, in integrating the Catholics and even most Socialists into the nation-state. Countless official proclama-

---

[35] Geoff Eley, *Reshaping the German Right: Radical Nationalism and Political Change After Bismarck* (New Haven, 1980); and Roger Chickering, *We Men Who Feel Most German: A Cultural History of the Pan-German League* (Boston, 1984).

[36] Volker Berghahn, *Imperial Germany, 1871–1914* (Oxford, 1994), stresses this differentiation. See also Charles Robert Garris, "Becoming German: Immigration, Conformity and Identity Politics in Wilhelminian Berlin, 1880–1914" (Ph.D. dissertation, Chapel Hill, 1998).

tions, patriotic rallies and speeches, nationalist pamphlets and posters repeated the message that the danger of the war had forged a "national community," struggling for survival against tremendous odds. The suspension of formal politics through martial law and the creation of a military quasi-dictatorship reinforced chauvinist appeals while forbidding any kind of criticism as unpatriotic. Nationalist pressure groups had a field day in advocating annexationist war aims and unrestricted submarine warfare, and in collecting, when the war dragged on, all disparate groups into a *Vaterlandspartei*, dedicated to victory at all costs. The comradeship in the trenches and the solidarity of the home front seemed to validate a militant understanding of German superiority and separateness.[37]

The rising tide of chauvinism prompted Catholic and Socialist Germans to define more democratic conceptions of patriotism that did not insist on complete victory. Although the number of outright pacifists was small, there was more opposition against the outbreak of the war than conventional accounts allow.[38] While Catholics were ready to defend the Reich, many chafed under Prussian command and failed to harbor annexationist dreams. Moreover, a significant segment of the Socialist Left opposed the "imperialist war," eventually broke with the party, and formed the Spartakist League as precursor of German Communism.[39] By the spring of 1917 antiwar strikes in the factories grew so large that the majority SPD reconsidered its commitment to the national struggle and joined disgruntled Catholic as well as Progressive deputies in passing a resolution against annexations and indemnities.[40] Ultimately, the war polarized politics, not only feeding nationalist sentiment but also strengthening a democratic patriotism that demanded constitutional reform and a compromise peace.

Born in defeat and revolution, the Weimar Republic finally offered the Catholic, democratic, and socialist skeptics of Bismarckian unification a chance to reconstruct a shrunken Germany in a more progressive image. The discrediting of Wilhelmine authoritarianism allowed its critics to build a "strong German people's state," which sought to reconcile conflicting views on the shape of national community by stress-

[37] Jeffrey Verhey, *The Spirit of 1914: Militarism, Myth and Mobilization in Germany* (Cambridge, 2000). Cf. Dann, *Nation und Nationalismus*, 208 ff.

[38] Volker Ullrich, *Die nervöse Großmacht. Aufstieg und Niedergang des deutschen Kaiserreichs 1871–1918* (Frankfurt, 1997).

[39] Willibald Gutsche, *Der erste Weltkrieg. Ausbruch und Verlauf, Herrschende Politik und Antikriegsbewegung in Deutschland* (Cologne, 1984).

[40] Konrad H. Jarausch, *The Enigmatic Chancellor: Theobald von Bethmann Hollweg and the Hubris of Imperial Germany* (New Haven, 1983); and Jürgen Kocka, *Facing Total War: German Society, 1914–1918* (Leamington Spa, 1984).

ing "the political freedom and responsibility, the ethical dignity of democracy."[41] This republican vision of individual and collective self-
determination was more tolerant of conflicting ethnic, ideological, religious, class, and gender definitions of Germanness, and sparked that
extraordinary flowering of creativity known as "Weimar culture." But
its focus on procedural guarantees could be exploited by antidemocratic forces, its reticence in symbolic self-representation failed emotionally to bond the population to the Republic, and its adversarial politics was unable to cope with the material challenges of the Great
Depression. Hence, critics could misconstrue the constant political in-
fighting as a lack of community and denounce the Weimar system as
fundamentally "un-German."[42]

Tragically, this effort to establish a modern democratic Germanness
triggered a further radicalization and popularization of the Right. The
defeat produced throngs of deeply disgruntled people, such as displaced imperial bureaucrats, dismissed officers, refugees of lost provinces, and victims of the hyperinflation, who provided a fertile ground
for a politics of resentment. Although some monarchists clung to the
expatriate Kaiser, most elites embraced a newer kind of neoconserva-
tism, stressing the restoration of bureaucratic, industrial, and military
authority.[43] Younger members of the Free Corps idolizing the comradeship of the trenches, unemployed academics envious of their Jewish
competitors, or members of the lower middle class afraid of the factory
and the department store, responded to the more egalitarian volkish
message supporting various radical fringe groups. Although deeply
fractured, the competing right wing factions were bound together by
their hatred of the *Diktat* of Versailles, their fears of cultural decadence,
and their neo-Bismarckian longing for stronger leadership. The failure
of republican politics ultimately paved the way for its antithesis, the
irresponsible populism of the Nazis.[44]

The uneasy coalition of the Old and New Right, which seized power
on January 30, 1933, rested on complementary versions of extreme nationalism. Conservative DNVP rhetoric was directed toward tradi-

---

[41] Friedrich Ebert to the *Nationalversammlung*, 6 February 1919; and Hugo Preuss before the same body, 24 February 1919, in *Verhandlungen der Nationalversammlung, erste
Sitzung* (Berlin, 1919), 1 ff., 284 ff.

[42] Peter Gay, *Weimar Culture: The Outsider as Insider* (New York, 1968); Detlev J. K.
Peuckert, *The Weimar Republic: The Crisis of Classical Modernity* (New York, 1989).

[43] See Larry E. Jones and James Retallack, eds., *Between Reform, Reaction and Resistance:
Studies in the History of German Conservatism Between 1789 and 1945* (Oxford, 1993).

[44] Peter Fritzsche, *Rehearsal for Fascism: Populism and Political Mobilization in Weimar
Germany* (New York, 1990); Michael Kater, *The Nazi Party: A Social Profile of Members and
Leaders, 1919–1945* (Cambridge, 1983).

tional targets, such as restoring Germany's power abroad and returning to law and order at home.[45] The more radical Nazi vision aimed at creating a *Volksgemeinschaft*, a close-knit national community that would abolish all distinctions of politics, class, region, religion, and the like. Seeking to wipe out the historical differences that divided German speakers was a profoundly revolutionary project that attempted to force an unprecedented degree of unity by dissolving organizational distinctions and fusing all members of the nation in one overarching movement. Since this was once again a minority view, promoted largely by Protestant males from the middle and lower middle class, it required an ever more repressive dictatorship to enforce it upon reluctant Catholics and proletarians. Nonetheless, Goebbels's incessant propaganda succeeded to a considerable degree in identifying National Socialism with Germanness as such.[46]

The results of this hypernationalism were initially disastrous for Europe and, eventually, also for the Germans. Hitler's successive elimination of internal rivals in the party and of the old elites removed restraints, while his economic and foreign policy successes created popular support for a policy of internal exclusion and external conquest. Domestically, the integral version of nationalism meant an unprecedented purging of the *Volk* through discrimination, persecution, and ultimately annihilation of political opponents, biological inferiors, and racial enemies. Internationally, ethnic radicalism implied the reunification of all German speakers in eastern central Europe with the Reich, which began with the rhetoric of self-determination but soon transcended the boundaries of nationalism by instrumentalizing the *Volksdeutsche* for empire building over non-German neighbors. The ensuing Second World War brought both projects together in the unspeakable atrocities of the Holocaust, which tried to cleanse the body of the nation and clear land for settlements.[47] Intended to establish a racial version of German power for the ages through the conquest of *Lebensraum*, the implementation of Hitler's nationalist fantasies made the German name unwittingly synonymous with repression, war, and genocide.

During the three-quarters of a century following the creation of the national state, conceptions of Germanness, therefore, became more

---

[45] For this important distinction, see Larry E. Jones, "Edgar Julius Jung: The Conservative Revolution in Theory and Practice," *Central European History* 21 (1990): 142–74.

[46] Eberhard Jäckel, *Hitler's Weltanschauung: A Blueprint for Power* (Middletown, Conn., 1972); and Jay W. Baird, *The Mythical World of Nazi War Propaganda* (Minneapolis, 1974).

[47] Götz Aly, *"Endlösung". Völkerverschiebung und der Mord an den europäischen Juden* (Frankfurt, 1996); Omer Bartov, *Murder in our Midst: The Holocaust, Industrial Killing and Representation* (New York, 1996).

militant and narrowed disastrously. Not content with propaganda-induced compliance, the Nazis' movement was a frantic effort to obliterate the remaining regional, religious, and class differences, which aimed at total uniformity through legal discrimination and physical elimination. The second, more ruthless, attempt to erect German hegemony over Europe rested not merely on voluntary collaboration of diverse allies but demanded complete subjugation and exploitation. Leaving no room for otherness, this fanatical racial redefinition of Germanness provoked most neighboring countries to fight back in resistance movements and in the incongruous Grand Alliance. Only a small minority of voices in internal opposition or external emigration argued that "Hitler is not Germany" to salvage freer and more tolerant definitions of Germanness as a basis for a more peaceful postwar order.[48] By abusing nationalism for imperial ends and engaging in untold atrocities, the Nazis in effect destroyed the very national state that the Party claimed to serve.

Denationalizing the Germans

The reeducation of the Germans after 1945 required yet another redefinition of identities to break the spell of nationalism. At the Yalta Conference the soon-to-be-victorious Allies proclaimed their "unbending will to destroy German militarism and National Socialism and to take care that Germany will never again be able to disturb world peace." Such perceptive commentators as Thomas Mann called for "a liberation from the clutches of a disastrous delusion of grandeur" to ensure the survival of a reformed country by disassociating Germanness from nationalism. The dire experiences of the killing at the front, the bombing at home, the raping and pillaging during the expulsion, and the incarceration of the POWs, dramatized the consequences of hypernationalism, raising troubling questions about individual complicity and collective responsibility.[49] Loss of statehood, Allied occupation, and the Cold War confrontation threw the Germans back upon a prepolitical local identity, forcing them to reconstruct a more internally tolerant and externally acceptable sense of self.

[48] Erich Weinert, speech of 12 July 1943, cited in Longerich, *Was ist des deutschen Vaterland?*, 132 ff. Cf. Theodore S. Hamerow, *On the Road to the Wolf's Lair: German Resistance to Hitler* (Cambridge, 1997).

[49] Allied declaration at the Yalta Conference, February 1945, cited in Longerich, *Was ist des Deutschen Vaterland?*, 138 ff. Thomas Mann, *Deutsche Hörer! 55 Radiosendungen nach Deutschland*, 2nd ed. (Stockholm, 1945), 111f.

In the Soviet occupation zone the surviving or returned antifascists undertook drastic steps toward creating a better Germany. A minority of Communists, Socialists, and bourgeois spokesmen or religious leaders could count on the moral bonus of having resisted the Third Reich and on the active help of the Soviet occupation authorities. Representing the progressive and Marxist strain of German patriotism, these activists insisted on a thorough purge of active Nazis and prominent collaborators but were often more lenient toward fellow travelers and made exceptions in such strategic areas as industry or defense.[50] Following Dimitrov's class definition of fascism as the most advanced element of monopoly-capitalism, these critics of nationalism unleashed a fundamental social revolution, expropriating the large landowners and nationalizing the property of leading capitalists to eliminate the societal basis of militarism. A stream of antifascist proclamations and literary works blamed the Junkers, industrialists, and bourgeois politicians for the war, thereby discrediting Prussian traditions but also indirectly absolving the ordinary East Germans from much of their complicity.[51]

By promoting a substitute Marxist identity, the GDR failed to resolve the national issue. Because the Russians shifted Poland to the west and annexed part of East Prussia, their occupation zone was smaller and less populous than the territory of the Western powers. Although his intentions remain controversial, Stalin wavered between the options of trying to revolutionize all of defeated Germany, neutralizing a united Germany through a peace treaty, or making his own zone into a Communist satellite.[52] As leader of the ruling SED, Walter Ulbricht apparently wanted the Sovietization of East Germany at the same time as the "unity of an antifascist democratic Germany" that included the West, even if these two aims turned out to be contradictory in practice. When the Western people did not follow his blandishments, the Eastern successor state was forced to invent a tortuous class theory of nationalism based not on ethnic identity but on membership in the proletariat to justify its own separate existence. In the end, Erich Honecker sought to square the circle by distinguishing between citizenship as East German and nationality, which he still allowed to be German.[53]

---

[50] Timothy R. Vogt, "Denazification in the Soviet Occupation Zone of Germany: Brandenburg, 1945–1948" (Ph.D. dissertation, Davis, 1997).

[51] Norman Naimark, *The Russians in Germany: A History of the Soviet Zone of Occupation, 1945–1949* (Cambridge, 1995); and Jürgen Danyel, ed., *Die geteilte Vergangenheit. Zum Umgang mit dem Nationalsozialismus in den beiden deutschen Staaten* (Berlin, 1995).

[52] Wilfried Loth, *Stalin's ungeliebtes Kind. Warum Moskau die DDR nicht wollte* (Berlin, 1994); and Michael Lemke, *Die Berlinkrise 1958 bis 1963. Zwänge und Handlungsspielräume der SED im Ost-West Konflikt* (Berlin, 1995).

[53] Klaus Erdmann, *Der gescheiterte Nationalstaat. Die Interdependenz von Nations- und Geschichtsverständnis im politischen Bedingungsgefüge der DDR* (Frankfurt, 1996).

The Western zones initially had more difficulty in distancing themselves from the Third Reich since they were intent on maintaining
some sense of continuity. Shocking revelations presented at the Nuremberg Trials of the major war criminals helped to make the emerging
leaders Konrad Adenauer, Kurt Schumacher, and Theodor Heuss repudiate National Socialism as the incarnation of evil.[54] But the uneven
success of a denazification procedure that caught many smaller perpetrators but let some more important figures off the hook gave antifascism a bad name. Also, limiting the disassociation to the political realm
of democratizing institutions allowed the traditional elites to recover
some of their previous authority, diminished only by the multiple disruptions of the defeat. Moreover, the struggle for daily survival in destroyed cities without power and food soon created a sense of victimization among ordinary Germans that reduced their empathy for the
Nazi victims and silenced their consciences with the argument that
others were little better than they themselves.[55] The West also rejected
the Nazi legacy, but some nationalist strains were initially able to survive in a chastened form.

In the long run, the cultural rupture went, nonetheless, deeper in
the Federal Republic because the ascendancy of Catholicism and the
geographic shift to the Rhine helped Westernize the Germans to an
unprecedented degree. Though the newly founded Christian Democratic Party also included Protestants and verbally insisted on reunification, it concentrated on establishing ties to the West by achieving
reconciliation with the French and promoting European economic integration. At the same time, West German society experienced an unparalleled process of Americanization of popular culture in film, music,
dress fashion, leisure habits, and the like, that removed many of the
traditional hallmarks of "Germanness." The success of Ludwig Erhard's liberal approach to rebuilding in the economic miracle also established a new vision of a "social market economy," based on mass
consumerism, that created other sources for pride and helped popular-
ize democratic institutions. While, as successor to the prior German
national state, the FRG paid billions of deutsche Marks in restitution
payments to Israel, it was the gradual process of Westernization that
ultimately helped overcome the nationalist legacy.[56]

[54] Jeffrey Herf, *The Divided Memory: The Nazi Past in the Two Germanys* (Cambridge,
1997).

[55] Michael Hayse, "Recasting German Elites: Senior Civil Servants, Business Leaders
and Physicians in Hessen, 1945–1955" (Ph.D. dissertation, Chapel Hill, 1994); and Elisabeth Heineman, "The Hour of the Woman: Memories of Germany's 'Crisis Years' and
West German National Identity," *American Historical Review* 101 (1996): 345–95.

[56] Konrad H. Jarausch, "Die post-nationale Nation. Zum Identitätswandel der
Deutschen, 1945–1995," *Historicum* Summer (1995): 30–35. See also Anselm Doering-

A further step in the denationalization process was the postmaterial shift, propelled by the youth revolt of the late 1960s. Though part of an international movement in the wake of the Vietnam War, this generational rebellion assumed a particularly German twist in the divided country. In the FRG the rejection of adult authority added an element of secondhand antifascism that accused the parent generation of struggling for material prosperity and of being deafeningly silent regarding its complicity with Nazi crimes. The students justified their challenge with a curious melange of democratic radicalism, unorthodox Marxism, and individualized anarchism that clamored for increased participation, structural reform, and lifestyle experimentation. In turning against the materialism of their elders, the young repudiated the hallowed secondary virtues of hard work, order, and discipline, instead turning to a series of New Social Movements such as pacifism, feminism, and environmentalism. In spite of its terrorist excesses in the RAF, this cultural revolution democratized West German society internally, launched an external *Ostpolitik* to decrease the Cold War tensions, and created a curiously non-German Germanness.[57]

By the 1980s Germans in both successor states seemed well on their way to establishing separate identities in their public and everyday lives. In the East a growing Stasi apparatus sought to stem disaffection in the wake of the silencing of the Prague spring and Willy Brandt's *Ostpolitik* by stricter surveillance and public acclamation.[58] In the West, the Basic Law created a parliamentary democracy characterized by corporate interest group bargaining and increasing grassroots participation in various protest movements. Under Honecker, the Eastern way of life was based on party-controlled welfare provisions that regulated work as well as vacations, subsidized food, transportation, and housing, and, eventually, provided a modest prosperity.[59] The Western standard of living derived from an ever more prosperous consumer capitalism where money could fulfill every wish and the social safety net only sought to catch the less fortunate. As a result, Easterners re-

---

Manteuffel, *Wie westlich sind die Deutschen? Amerikanisierung und Westernisierung im 20. Jahrhundert* (Göttingen, 1999).

[57] There is no good account of 1968 in the German context. See Elisabeth Peifer, "1968 in German Political Culture, 1967–1993: From Experience to Myth" (Ph.D. dissertation, Chapel Hill, 1997), and essays in Philipp Gassert, Carole Fink, and Detlev Junker, eds., *1968: The World Transformed* (Cambridge, 1998).

[58] Armin Mitter and Stefan Wolle, *Untergang in Raten. Unbekannte Kapitel der DDR-Geschichte* (Munich, 1993), 367; Mary Fulbrook, *Anatomy of a Dictatorship: Inside the GDR 1949–1989* (Oxford, 1995), 193 ff.

[59] Konrad H. Jarausch, "Realer Sozialismus als Fürsorgediktatur. Zur begrifflichen Einordnung der DDR," *Aus Politik und Zeitgeschichte* (1998) no. 20: 33–46.

mained more provincially German, group dependent, and state oriented, whereas Westerners became cosmopolitan, individualistic, and
suspicious of too much government authority.[60]

Despite growing divergence, "a sense of belonging to one nation"
among Germans somehow survived the decades of division.[61] This
identification, which exceeded sympathy with the Austrians and Swiss
neighbors in surveys, was the product of a shared sense of history, of
common customs, and of persistent communication links that again
strengthened during the 1980s. For instance, inter-German trade, clas-
sified as domestic rather than international, flourished despite inter-
mittent confrontation and actually kept the GDR afloat during the last
years through Western hard currency credits. Popular culture, centered
on radio and especially television, rather than literary exchanges of
well-known writers, penetrated the Iron Curtain so that East Germans
used more FRG media on a daily basis than their own and developed
a virtual affinity to the West. The Brandt-Schmidt policy of human improvements succeeded in revitalizing East-West travel, initially for retirees and close family members but eventually for an ever-growing
number of artists, youth groups, athletic teams, delegations from sister
cities, and the like. This manifold network of ties helped maintain a
sense of closeness to weather the division.

The surprising collapse of Communism and reunification into a single state prompted another profound reconfiguring of German identities. An incessant stream of refugees during the summer of 1989 indicated to the unprepared politicians in the East and West that the Iron
Curtain was rusting through and the postwar division of Europe might
be overcome. In an amazing rejection of their prior complicity, ever-
larger numbers of East Germans began to turn out for demonstrations
during the fall, demanding human rights such as free speech, the abdication of the old guard, and the opening of the impenetrable Wall.
Once they had regained freedom of expression and formed such opposition groups as the New Forum, ordinary East Germans parted com-
pany with intellectual partisans of a "Third Way," calling instead for a
rapid unification with the more prosperous and freer West.[62] Internationalized citizens of the Federal Republic who knew little of the East

[60] Wolfgang Engler, *Die Ostdeutschen. Kunde aus einem verlorenen Land* (Berlin, 1999).

[61] Walter Scheel, "Das demokratische Geschichtsbild," in Bernhard Pollmann, ed., *Lese-buch zur deutschen Geschichte*, vol. 3 (Nördlingen, 1984), 333 ff. Cf. Konrad H. Jarausch, "Nation ohne Staat. Von der Zweistaatlichkeit zur Vereinigung," *Praxis Geschichte* 13 (2000): 6–11.

[62] Konrad H. Jarausch, *Die unverhoffte Einheit 1989–1990* (Frankfurt, 1995); and Charles S. Maier, *Dissolution: The Crisis of Communism and the End of East Germany* (Princeton, 1997).

found themselves confronted with long-lost "brothers and sisters" who demanded sacrifices from them in the name of a common national past. The process of unification itself overturned many Cold War certainties and made the unthinkable suddenly possible.

The unforeseen return of national unity in 1990 required further unsettling adjustments in German self-definitions. For leftist Western intellectuals who had accepted partition as atonement for Nazi atrocities, the thought of a united country was frightening, while many Easterners soon forgot their earlier repression and waxed nostalgic over the relative security of the GDR. Patriotic commentators welcomed the "normalization" that ended the postwar political division, overcoming the confrontation of ideologies or social systems and regaining full sovereignty by sending Soviet occupation troops home. A triumphalist Right felt vindicated in its belief in national unity and insisted on a "re-nationalization" that would keep out immigrants and asylum seekers while demanding a more assertive foreign policy of pursuing German interests. Though flare-ups of xenophobic violence revealed an ugly nationalist strain among disadvantaged youths, huge candlelight demonstrations for tolerance showed that the civility learned by West Germans in the postwar period would continue to dominate their political culture. In many ways the surprise after unity was the strength of Western attachments in spite of the influx of seventeen million Easterners who were more provincially German.[63]

The Germans' effort during the second half of the twentieth century to live down their hypernationalism produced a fundamentally different sense of postnational identity. The term "postnational democracy," proposed by the political scientist Karl-Dietrich Bracher, suggests, in analogy to other "post" concepts, that Germans have lived through, learned from, and gone beyond nationalism.[64] While traumatic memories of dying at the front, being bombed at home, or fleeing from the East, discredited nationalism and militarism, growing prosperity, imported consumer goods, and extensive foreign travel widened horizons, fostering a more cosmopolitan outlook. Some intellectuals, like Günter Grass or Christa Wolf, so strongly felt the burden of guilt that they developed a veritable "Holocaust identity" that fastened upon

[63] Konrad H. Jarausch, "Normalisierung oder Re-Nationalisierung? Zur Umdeutung der deutschen Vergangenheit," *Geschichte und Gesellschaft* 21 (1995): 571–84. See also essays in Konrad H. Jarausch, ed., *After Unity: Reconfiguring German Identities* (Providence, 1997).

[64] Karl-Dietrich Bracher, *Wendezeiten der Geschichte. Historisch-politische Essays 1987–1992* (Stuttgart, 1992). See also Dolf Sternberger's concept of "constitutional patriotism" in his *Verfassungspatriotismus* (Frankfurt, 1990), popularized by Jürgen Habermas.

German crimes as a negative exemplar of human evil in general.[65] These distancing processes inspired a strong support for European integration that not only was motivated by practical self-interest but also served a deeply-felt need of trying to prevent the recurrence of the past. It is this Western recovery of civility rather than the Eastern experience of collaboration and resistance that has come to inform the identity of the restored German national state.

A Fragmented Nation

From a historical perspective, the most striking aspect of the development of German identities over the last two centuries is their variability. The contradictions in the national stereotypes amply demonstrate that perceptions of Germans have ranged from unpolitical poets and thinkers to arrogant Junkers, from brilliant scientists to fanatical SS killers, from arrogant GDR border guards to high-minded dissidents, from enterprising FRG businessmen to protesting Greens. Moreover, the developmental trajectory from the provincial cosmopolitanism of the late Holy Roman Empire to the liberal nationalism of the 1848 revolution is impressive. The subsequent transformation from the Prusso-German nationalism of the Second Reich via the democratic patriotism of the Weimar Republic to the racial hypernationalism of the Third Reich is astounding. And finally the changes from the postwar antifascism of the GDR and the constitutional patriotism of the FRG to the postnationalism of the Berlin Republic are breathtaking.[66] The one constant in these descriptions seems to be their extraordinary malleability.

These frequent changes suggest that German self-definitions were uncommonly contested between various minorities that sought to project their particular views upon the entire nation. The three most important strands—political Catholicism, Protestant nationalism, and Socialist patriotism—not only competed with each other for the loyalty of the population and control of the national state but were often deeply divided among themselves. For instance, Catholics had to contend with secular lay and ultramontane clerical wings; Protestants were polarized between various shades of liberals and conservatives, not to

---

[65] Bernhard Giesen, *Die Intellektuellen und die Nation. Eine deutsche Achsenzeit* (Frankfurt, 1993), 236–55. See also Martin and Sylvia Greiffenhagen, *Ein schwieriges Vaterland. Zur politischen Kultur im vereinigten Deutschland* (Munich, 1993).

[66] Gordon A. Craig, *The Germans* (New York, 1982); Werner Weidenfeld, ed., *Die Identität der Deutschen* (Munich, 1983); and Konrad H. Jarausch, "Huns, Krauts or Good Germans? The German Image in America, 1800–1980," in James F. Harris, ed., *German-American Interrelations* (Tübingen, 1985), 145–59.

mention the volkish fringe; and radicals splintered into democratic, social-democratic, and communist factions. At the same time other, cross-
cutting identifications developed that put primacy on membership in
a social class, a specific gender, or a particular race, both reinforcing
and complicating the contending claims for allegiances. Because none
of these competing blueprints succeeded in capturing the national
space entirely, their main point of convergence was the incessant conflict over what it meant at any given time to be German.[67]

In trying to define themselves, German speakers also continually set
themselves off against others, giving meaning to familiarity by emphasizing difference. On the inside, Bismarck's cultural struggle against
the Catholics in the 1870s inaugurated a disastrous tradition of "negative integration," which tried to create unity by stigmatizing political
opponents, such as the Socialists, as enemies of the Empire. This intolerant conflation of Germanness with a particular linguistic, religious,
or state loyalty sparked contradictory policies of discrimination toward the Jews and assimilation toward the Poles that ultimately escalated into annihilation. Additionally, the Iron Chancellor's construction of foreign enemies such as the French in the War-in-Sight-Crisis
of 1875 eventually undercut his finely spun network of alliances in the
non-extension of the Reinsurance Treaty with Russia, which diplomati-
cally isolated the Reich. The odd mixture of admiration and envy toward western neighbors and prejudice as well as fear toward the Slavs
of the east fell back upon the Germans as ascriptions from others,
tinged with increasing hostility.[68]

The repetition of efforts to produce a stable identity indicates that
the attempts to force a uniform self-conception upon the Germans have
largely resulted in failure. After 1945, all but a small right-wing minority wanted to distance themselves from the horrible Nazi crimes and
strenuously tried to appear antifascist, democratic, European, or cosmopolitan. Since Hitler had conflated his own movement with the German nation and misappropriated many of its traditions, subjects as in-
nocent as folk songs became tarnished and were thereafter taboo for
progressive intellectuals. As a result many Germans developed a negative identification with national symbols, such as flags and anthems,
and professed a rather low degree of collective self-esteem. This self-

[67] James, *German Identity*, 210 ff. See also Lloyd Kramer, "Nations as Texts: Literary
Theory and the History of Nationalism," *The Maryland Historian* 24 (1993): 71–82.

[68] Mitchell Ash, Christiane Lemke, and Jeffrey Peck, "Natives, Strangers and Foreigners: Constituting Germans by Constructing Others," in *After Unity*, 61–102. Cf. Valeria
Heuberger, Arnold Suppan, and Elisabeth Vyslonzil, eds., *Das Bild vom Anderen. Identitäten, Mentalitäten, Mythen und Stereotypen in multiethnischen europäischen Regionen* (Frankfurt, 1998).

deprecation often led to an arrogant insistence on the high moral ground—claiming to be more peaceful, ecologically conscious, socially just, and so on, than their more self-assured neighbors. By blocking a positive identification, the Holocaust has created among succeeding generations a deep uncertainty about what qualities "German" could or should stand for.[69]

The sense of Germanness that suggests a shared "we" to contemporaries, therefore, remains difficult to pin down. Even if they might be embarrassed about their background, certain people in an international crowd would define themselves and be identified by others as Germans. No doubt, the possession of a passport issued by a "German" government, which does indicate citizenship, would have something to do with it. The ability to speak the language fluently and to appreciate a certain version of *Kultur* would be another identifier, although not all citizens might share it and some foreigners might master it as well. More important in creating a feeling of ethnic belonging would be a set of customs, for instance, celebrating holidays with certain songs, such as Silent Night, or eating specific foods, such as *Lebkuchen*. Finally, a store of common experiences intertwining individual life stories with a collective *Schicksalsgemeinschaft* in surviving the catastrophes of the century ought to be relevant. Too changeable and complex to be defined by a single label, this elusive quality can only be reconstructed historically.[70]

Such a cultural approach would understand Germany as a fragmented nation struggling to reconcile enormous diversity with desired unity. Because of the untold territorial divisions in the Holy Roman Empire, the national movement longed for a nation-state on the French or British model, seeing unification as a magic solution to political repression and impotence. The "eternal confederation" of princes that constituted the Bismarckian Empire sought to combine regional autonomy with central authority through a monarchical form of federalism dominated by Prussia. The shrunken Weimar state strengthened popular sovereignty but experienced even greater internal strife and external irredentism because of its economic troubles and territorial losses. In many ways the Nazi *Führerprinzip*, coordination of organizations, and abolition of the states was a desperate attempt at last to dictate a uniform version of Germanness. In contrast, the revived federalism of

---

[69] Joyce Marie Mushaben, *Postwar to Post-Wall Generations: Changing Attitudes Toward the National Question and NATO in the Federal Republic of Germany* (Boulder, 1998), 47 ff.

[70] Konrad H. Jarausch, "Reshaping German Identitites: Reflections on the Post-Unification Debate," in *After Unity*, 1–23. Cf. also Hermann Bausinger, *Wie deutsch sind die Deutschen?* (Munich, 2000).

the Bonn Republic permitted regional differences, pacified religious strife between Catholics and Protestants, and muted the class struggle through the mediation of the social market economy. Ironically, the East German people ultimately found this looser framework more attractive than their own Communist brand of uniformity and, therefore, returned to the federation and reconstituted unity.[71]

The challenge for united Germany will be to recognize that the restored nation-state can only remain internally stable and internationally acceptable if it develops a pluralized western conception of Germanness.[72] For this purpose the Basic Law is an auspicious starting point since it only demands respect for its bill of rights and procedural safeguards of parliamentary politics, leaving all other issues to individual choice. In theory, members of different regions, religions, classes, genders, and races are equal before the law, making these distinctions private concerns rather than matters of state. The practice, however, does not always live up to this ideal of diversity since a sizable traditionalist minority still clings to ethnic definitions of uniform Germanness that are coded in regional, Christian, middle-class, male, or white terms and feel threatened by new forms of cultural differences. In spite of continuing skinhead violence, the growing support for immigration signals a broadening of self-definitions that is becoming more ready to accept the hybridity of such groups as Turkish-Germans.[73] Even the Germans might acquire a more "relaxed sense of self" and learn to live with multiple identities if they see local, state, national, and European loyalties not as mutually exclusive but as complementary.[74]

---

[71] Heinrich August Winkler, "Rebuilding of a Nation: The Germans Before and After Unification," as well as Jürgen Kocka, "Crisis of Unification: How Germany Changes," *Daedalus* (Winter 1994): 107 ff., 173 ff.

[72] Richard Schröder, *Deutschland, schwierig Vaterland. Für eine neue politische Kultur* (Freiburg, 1993). Cf. also Heinrich-August Winkler, "Demokratie und Nation in der deutschen Geschichte," in Fraunhofer Gesellschaft, ed., *Reden und Ansprachen. Jahrestagung 1994* (Munich, 1994), 34–56.

[73] Larry E. Jones, ed., *Crossing Boundaries: German and American Experiences with the Exclusion and Inclusion of Minorities* (New York, 2001); and Mary Fulbrook, *German National Identity After the Holocaust* (Cambridge, UK, 1999).

[74] Richard Schröder, "Mysterium Germaniae," *Der Spiegel* (2001) no. 40: 138–47.

9

Defining Womanhood: The Politics of the Private

Few areas of the past are as dominated by ascriptive clichés as the history of German women. In the early twentieth century, American observers fastened upon the stereotype of the *Hausfrau*, a loving mother and wife, caring and competent but somehow asexual and limited to the horizon of *Kinder, Küche, und Kirche*, the narrow confines of children, kitchen, and church.[1] American GIs were, therefore, not a little surprised when they encountered a different kind of woman after the defeat of the Third Reich, vivacious and seductive, willing to violate social conventions for the sake of some food or companionship. In describing these leggy blondes, American magazines began to marvel about the *Fräuleinwunder*, a miracle no smaller than the rapid economic recovery.[2] Five decades later, German magazines, though sporting bare-breasted pinups on the cover, tend to be full of emancipated career women in well-tailored suits who forsake rearing a family for the

[1] Claudia Koonz and Renate Bridenthal, "Beyond *Kinder, Küche, Kirche*: Weimar Women in Politics and Work," in Renate Bridenthal, Atina Grossmann, and Marion Kaplan, eds., *When Biology Became Destiny: Women in Weimar and Nazi Germany* (New York, 1984), 33 ff.

[2] Annette Brauerhoch, " 'Foreign Affairs'—Fraeuleins as Agents," paper delivered at "Fifty Years of the FRG Through a Gendered Lens," Chapel Hill, September 1999.

sake of professional success.[3] These contradictory images raise the issue of what has changed in the past century—the visual representations or the actual lives of German women?

Answering this question requires breaking with the essentializing tendency that has bedeviled both political debate and academic scholarship on women's issues. Even a cursory look at a turn-of-the-century volume of the lavish art magazine *Moderne Kunst* reveals an enormous range of visual depictions and textual descriptions of women in the 1890s. The pages are full of neoclassical sculptures of nude goddesses, impressionist watercolors of timid maidens, realist engravings of arrogant society ladies, exotic pictures of dancing gypsies, naturalist drawings of poor fishmongers, fanciful images of bucolic shepherdesses, and studiously simple depictions of bourgeois domesticity. Most surprising of all is a continuing column dedicated to commenting on the emergence of "the modern woman," including such subjects as female doctors, bicycle-riding, and painting.[4] This discrepancy among representations suggests that "woman" may be a somewhat "deceptive term" because it conveys a rather static and "monolithic collective experience . . . in which differences based on gender, sexuality, national identity, etc., are overridden by the commonality of femaleness."[5]

Since the 1960s, research has begun to illuminate some of the changes in and differences among female experiences, but its impact is hampered by the ideological controversies swirling around women's studies. A straightforward social approach to investigating the living conditions as well as aspirations of women throughout the centuries often appears to its politically committed critics as too limited.[6] A more explicitly feminist effort to trace the development of the women's movement can in turn be criticized for measuring past lives by contemporary standards of emancipation and thereby misconstruing the intentions of earlier actors.[7] Even a gender perspective that addresses the

---

[3] For instance, "Karriere. Die neuen Waffen der Frau," *Der Spiegel* (1999) no. 49: 84–109.

[4] *Moderne Kunst in Meister-Holzschnitten. Nach Gemälden und Skulpturen berühmter Meister der Gegenwart*, vol. IX (Berlin, 1895), passim.

[5] Sabine Hark, "Disputed Territory: Feminist Studies in Germany and its Queer Discontents" (MS, Potsdam, 1999). See also Nira Yuval-Davis, *Gender and Nation* (London, 1997), 5–11.

[6] Compare Richard Evans, *The Feminist Movement in Germany, 1894–1933* (London, 1976), with John C. Fout, ed., *German Women in the Nineteenth Century* (New York, 1984). See the dispute between Louise Tilly, ed., *Women, Politics and Change* (New York, 1990), and Joan W. Scott, ed., *Feminism and History* (New York, 1996).

[7] Compare Isabel V. Hull, "Feminist and Gender History Through the Literary Looking Glass: German History in Postmodern Times," *Central European History* 22 (1989),

interaction between males and females to stress the social rather than biological construction of womanhood might also be faulted for its overemphasis on cultural determination and disregard for the constraints of childbearing.[8] In the debates on how to reconcile the imperative of equality with the assumption of difference among the sexes, demarcating one's positionality within contemporary identity politics often clashes with a contextualized historical reconstruction.[9]

Because of such cleavages, the growing literature on women's history has enriched our understanding of female lives in the past but has also left some important issues unresolved. The new stress on women's experience has broadened approaches to traditional subjects from war to social mobility to education, making it impossible to write about them only in male terms. Problematizing the distinction between the private and public spheres has opened to research entirely new areas, ranging from the politics of abortion or divorce to the patterns of consumption or popular culture.[10] Particularly controversial in the Third Reich, the issue of women's agency has been redefined from the view that all women were victimized to a sense of active participation, even in some of the atrocities.[11] But corresponding research on male roles or sexuality has been slow to develop beyond promising, but still tentative, beginnings.[12] Thus far, women's history has been more successful in producing a critical counternarrative of its own than in rewriting the stories of nation, class, or modernization, complementing rather than replacing older views.

279–300, to Gertrude Himmelfarb, *On Looking into the Abyss: Untimely Thoughts on Culture and Society* (New York, 1994), 131 ff.

[8] Kathleen Canning, "Gender History," in *International Encyclopedia of the Social and Behavioral Sciences* (Amsterdam, 2001); Ann Allen, "Feminism and Motherhood in Germany and in International Perspective, 1800–1914," in Patricia Herminghouse and Magda Mueller, eds., *Gender and Germanness: Cultural Productions of Nation* (Providence, 1997), 113–28.

[9] Andreas Pickel, "Creative Chaos: A Methodological Postscript on Interdisciplinary Cooperation," in Konrad H. Jarausch, ed., *After Unity: Reconfiguring German Identities* (Providence, 1997), 201 ff. Cf. Hans Medick and Anne-Charlott Trepp, eds., *Geschlechtergeschichte und Allgemeine Geschichte. Herausforderungen und Perspektiven* (Göttingen, 1998).

[10] Nancy Fraser, "Rethinking the Public Sphere," *Social Text* 25-26 (1990), 56–80; and Joan Landes, ed., *Feminism, the Public and the Private* (New York, 1998).

[11] Compare Gisela Bock, *Zwangssterilisation im Nationalsozialismus. Studien zur Rassenpolitik und Frauenpolitik* (Opladen, 1986), to Claudia Koonz, *Mothers in the Fatherland: Women, the Family and Nazi Politics* (New York, 1986). Cf. Adelheid von Saldern, "Victims or Perpetrators? Controversies about the Role of Women in the Nazi State," in David Crew, ed., *Nazism and German Society* (London, 1994).

[12] George Lachmann Mosse, *The Image of Man: The Creation of Modern Masculinity* (New York, 1996); and Thomas Kühne, *Männergeschichte, Geschlechtergeschichte. Männlichkeit im Wandel der Moderne* (Frankfurt, 1996).

From a cultural vantage point, one promising avenue to putting gender issues into a broader context is a comparison of successive constructions of German womanhood. Such an approach would treat the competing definitions as efforts to shape a heterogeneous group into a common mold, not just by prescriptive rhetoric but also by legislation and sanctions to enforce compliance. It would make possible the analysis of the agendas or interests of male doctors or social reformers, while still paying attention to female aspirations and agency. At the same time, this perspective would allow an assessment of the various degrees of success of contending normalizations and permit a discussion of changes in the experiences of women over time.[13] Although such themes as sexuality, legal status, and education are also important, the subsequent brief reflections are limited to the key issues of reproduction, work, and public involvement, which were particularly significant for making the private political. How did the contending definitions of womanhood reflect and transform the lives of German women in the twentieth century?

The Cult of Motherhood

In the patriarchal society of the early twentieth century, views of women were dominated by conceptions of maternalism that stressed the importance of physical or spiritual motherhood. To German speakers the term *Mutter* suggests not just lifegiver or caring parent but an almost mystical source of protection and nurturing. This cult of motherhood was based on an essentialist understanding of female difference that gradually evolved from philosophical considerations to biological arguments.[14] Especially for the middle class, such an understanding justified a gendered separation of public and domestic spheres in which women exercised considerable power over their family members, household concerns, and social relations. In the eighteenth century a genre of *Hausmütterliteratur* sought to prepare girls for their responsibilities in child rearing and housekeeping, while in the nineteenth century thinkers propounded an essentialist vision of femininity.[15] This ethic of social caring could also transcend the private

---

[13] For a largely successful example of a similar approach, see Kathleen Canning, *Languages of Labor and Gender: Female Factory Work in Germany, 1850–1914* (Ithaca, 1996).

[14] Ann Taylor Allen, *Feminism and Motherhood in Germany, 1800–1914* (New Brunswick, 1991). See also Marion A. Kaplan, *The Making of the Jewish Middle Class: Women, Family, and Identity in Imperial Germany* (New York, 1991).

[15] Marion Gray, *Productive Men and Reproductive Women: The Agrarian Household and the Emergence of Separate Spheres in the German Enlightenment* (New York, 1999); and Claudia

realm and extend to public issues, inspiring a raft of reform movements that sought to redress social ills from alcoholism to prostitution.[16]

As a result of increasingly conscious control over childbearing, political attention began to focus on the controversial area of reproduction. Statistical evidence of a declining birth rate around 1900 made pronatalist publicists sound alarms about "depopulation," which they feared would weaken military power, while eugenicists such as Adolf Hartnacke deplored the reluctance of the higher classes to produce children. Based on the ideal of a patriarchal family, the German Civil Code maintained a series of legal prohibitions of infanticide, abortion, and immorality that punished women who sought to limit their offspring by birth control or to abort unwanted pregnancies. Arguing in favor of motherhood as choice, the social reformer Helene Stöcker therefore founded the League for the Protection of Motherhood to help rear illegitimate children, while in 1908 the Federation of German Women's Associations called for the legalization of abortions on medical grounds. Although misogynists sought to use natalism to keep women in their traditional place, leading feminists employed the rhetoric of motherhood for the opposite purpose of establishing arguments for responsible choice.[17]

In anticipation of a later problem, the argument of a *Frauenüberschuß* similarly used appeals to maternalism to enlarge female educational or professional opportunities. Popularized by the organizer of religious women's groups, Elisabeth Gnauck-Kühne, the "demographic imaginary" of a surplus of women, especially among the bourgeoisie, could be used to open doors otherwise closed to them. If there was an increasing group of women who could not fulfill their "natural" destiny to marry because men were too few or too reluctant to begin families, other outlets for their mothering talents would have to be found lest they become irritable and superfluous spinsters.[18] One solution, proposed by the moderate reformer Helene Lange, was the improvement of female secondary schooling, transforming it from largely domestic preparation to an intellectually challenging course of general cultivation. As a consequence of allowing girls to take the prestigious *Abitur*,

---

Honegger, *Die Ordnung der Geschlechter. Die Wissenschaften vom Menschen und das Weib, 1750–1850* (Frankfurt, 1991).

[16] Elisabeth Meyer-Renschhausen, *Weibliche Kultur und soziale Arbeit. Eine Geschichte der Frauenbewegung am Beispiel Bremens, 1810–1927* (Cologne, 1989).

[17] James Woycke, *Birth Control in Germany, 1871–1933* (London, 1988). Cf. Amy Hackett, "Helene Stöcker: Left-Wing Intellectual and Sex-Reformer," in *When Biology Became Destiny*, 109 f.

[18] Catherine Dollard, "The Single Women: Unwed in Imperial Germany, 1871–1914" (Ph.D. dissertation, Chapel Hill, 1999).

female students had to be admitted to Prussian universities in 1907 on a footing equal to that of men. Another remedy was the expansion of access to such motherly occupations as teaching primary school and nursing the sick.[19]

As a result of such initiatives, the German women's movement developed a vibrant organizational subculture that was, however, split along ideological and class lines. In 1894 the *Bund Deutscher Frauenvereine* sought to create a common front for the growing number of local and topical groups. This moderate organization generally favored a liberal line of improving women's opportunities in education, and getting involved in various causes of social reform. A few years later Protestant (DEF) and Catholic counterparts were founded to provide alternatives for more conservative and religious women who were interested in charitable work.[20] Led by Clara Zetkin and instructed by her journal *Gleichheit*, working-class women instead subsumed their concerns largely under the general class struggle.[21] Local studies of Hanover and Frankfort show an enormous proliferation of self-help groups and reform circles, creating a dense network of women's groups.[22] Although in a semiconstitutional regime the suffragist movement, led by Minna Cauer, found only a limited resonance, these various associations gave German women an increasingly important public voice.[23]

Proving both a threat and an opportunity, World War I drew women farther into the public sphere. On the one hand, the conflict was a demographic disaster since the drastic drop in the birthrate could not be stopped by granting soldiers leaves and enforcing reproduction. Growing food shortages also drove up mortality, preoccupying women with a struggle for food, clothing, and heat to assure the bare survival of their families. On the other hand, the absence of men provided new opportunities for young and energetic women—for instance, raising

[19] James Q. Albisetti, *Schooling German Girls and Women: Secondary and Higher Education in the Ninetheenth Century* (Princeton, 1988). See also Joanne Schneider, "*Volksschullehrerinnen*: Bavarian Women Defining themselves through their Profession," in Konrad H. Jarausch and Geoffrey Cocks, eds., *German Professions, 1800–1950* (New York, 1990), 85 ff.

[20] Evans, *German Women's Movement*, 24 ff; and Ute Frevert, *Women in German History: From Bourgeois Emancipation to Sexual Liberation* (Oxford, 1988), 107 ff.

[21] Werner Thönnessen, *The Emancipation of Women: The Rise and Decline of the Women's Movement in German Social Democracy, 1863–1933* (London, 1976). See also Jean Quataert, *Reluctant Feminists in German Social Democracy, 1885–1917* (Princeton, 1979).

[22] Nancy Reagin, *A German Women's Movement: Class and Gender in Hanover, 1880–1933* (Chapel Hill, 1995); and Christina Klausmann, *Politik und Kultur der Frauenbewegung im Kaiserreich. Das Beispiel Frankfurt am Main* (Frankfurt, 1997).

[23] Irene Stoehr, *Emanzipation zum Staat? Der Allgemeine Frauenverein Deutscher Staatsbürgerinnen-Verband, 1893–1933* (Pfaffenweiler, 1990).

their number among university students. While maternalism forbade labor conscription, many women did volunteer to work in arms production or social services, accelerating the trend toward employment and temporarily shifting its location to industry. Swept away by the initial enthusiasm, the BFD founded a National Women's Service, coordinating volunteer social work to care for mothers and children as well as strengthen the morale of the home front with patriotic rhetoric. In the long run, however, the mounting deprivations created war-weariness among working women, amplifying the voices of pacifist and socialist critics of the fighting.[24]

The struggle to reconcile newer freedoms with older traditions during the Weimar Republic intensified the politicization of the private realm. As a creature of fashion and commerce, the "New Woman" projected a modern image, at once slim, sporty, and sexually liberated.[25] But the population crisis of two million dead soldiers and untold never-conceived babies reinforced the natalist pressure for motherhood just when many women were intent on escaping that burden. In contrast to imperial coercion, the democratic governments resorted both to welfare incentives, such as greater maternal benefits and child support, and to family propaganda to arrest the halving of the birth rate. At the same time, the liberalization of birth control, supported by medical efforts against sexually transmitted diseases, increased the possibility of choice. The social democrats and communists, however, only succeeded in reducing the penalties for abortion, outlawed under paragraph 218 of the penal code, since Catholic and Protestant parties, not to mention the racist right, were firmly opposed to its legalization. Although hotly contested, "the politics of the body" slowly revised older forms of compulsion and produced a voluntary conception of motherhood.[26]

Through the vagaries of hyperinflation and rationalization, women also made some important gains in the workplace. The 1925 census showed 11.48 million women gainfully employed, which at 35.6 percent amounted to a higher rate than other European countries. The killing of a large number of young men made the "surplus of women" an uncontestable reality, forcing many young widows or women without

---

[24] Ute Daniel, *The War Within: German Working-Class Women in the First World War* (Oxford, 1997). Cf. Belinda Davis, *Home Fires Burning: Food, Politics, and Everyday Life in World War One Berlin* (Chapel Hill, 2000).

[25] Examples are in Anton Kaes, Martin Jay and Edward Dimdenberg, eds., *The Weimar Republic Sourcebook* (Berkeley, 1994), 151 ff.

[26] Cornelie Usborne, *The Politics of the Body in Weimar Germany: Women's Reproductive Rights and Duties* (Ann Arbor, 1992), superseded the essays in *When Biology Became Destiny*, 66 ff.

partners to support themselves and their children. Although half of the females still worked in agriculture, the media fastened upon the feminization of white-collar occupations, the millions of well-dressed secretaries and sales girls who used work to bridge the time between school and marriage.[27] Under the banner of "social mothering," women also carved out other new careers by transforming charity into paid social work. But unemployed males resented their admission into such professions as medicine and law, claiming that they enlarged the ranks of an "academic proletariat."[28] Even if growing occupational possibilities failed to overcome maternalist stereotypes, the attractive image of the secretary helped promote the acceptance of female work as a transitional stage before marriage.

In the public sphere women achieved greatest advancement during the 1920s—and also experienced the deepest disappointment. Because of socialist, democratic, and suffragist pressure, women received the active and passive right to vote in 1918, making them full-fledged citizens capable of pursuing their own aims. Predictably, formal participation led to partisan polarization, closer ties of various organizations with corresponding political parties, and the emergence of female politicians. About 10 percent of the delegates of the constituent assembly were women, most of them prominent leaders of the *Frauenbewegung*, but their share subsequently declined. After initial support for left-wing parties, the female vote consistently favored the Center Party, the German Nationalists, and the People's Party, creating an unexpected gender gap. This conservative preference reflected the strength of religious ties (Catholic organizations supporting the Center, Protestant groups the DNVP or DVP), as well as of patriotic associations that favored traditional definitions of womanhood. Despite obtaining a guarantee of equal rights in the constitution, making impressive organizational gains, and influencing decisions on female issues, the silent majority clung to a modified version of "motherly politics."[29]

The Third Reich sought to reverse women's limited gains in the Weimar Republic by "emancipating women from emancipation," so to speak. To counter the drop of the birthrate from over 20 per 1,000 during the Second Reich to 15.1 per 1,000, Nazi "bio-politics" emphasized the need for Aryan reproduction since dreams of empire required a growing population. NS-policy created numerous incentives, ranging

---

[27] Usborne, *Politics of the Body*, 43ff; and Frevert, *Women in German History*, 176 ff.

[28] Young-Sun Hong, *Welfare, Modernity and the Weimar State, 1919–1933* (Princeton, 1998), 141 ff.; and "Femininity as Vocation: Gender and Class Conflict in the Professionalization of German Social Work," in Jarausch and Cocks, *German Professions*, 232 ff.

[29] Bridenthal and Koonz, "Beyond *Kinder, Küche, Kirche*," 35–44; Reagin, *German Women's Movement*, 203 ff; and Frevert, *German Women in History*, 168 ff.

from financial support for childbearing to symbols such as the "Cross of Honor for the German Mother" to the training for motherhood in the Reich Mothers' Service. Hence, the regime restricted access to birth control and reintroduced stiffer penalties for abortion and infanticide.[30] At the same time, the Nazis also sought eugenically to purify the *Volkskörper* by prohibiting "miscegenation" between Aryans and Jews, as well as by compulsory sterilization of the mentally ill and eventual euthanasia of those suffering from hereditary disabilities. Intent on maximizing desirable births, the Third Reich had little respect for families as such, easing divorce and supporting single mothers in the *Lebensborn*. Despite these pro- and antinatalist measures, the birth rate barely improved to 20.4 per 1,000 due to more frequent marriages, showing that many women remained impervious to public appeals.[31]

Nazi labor policy was even less consistent, vacillating between male chauvinism and grudging concessions to the manpower needs of the economy. In response to academic overcrowding, the Third Reich limited the access of girls to higher education, pushed married women out of public service by prohibiting "double earner" couples, and rescinded entry into some professions such as law and medicine.[32] But by 1937 the labor shortage, caused by rearmament, forced the Nazis to use premarriage female labor, requiring prospective students to participate in the Reich Labor Service, and future industrial or white collar workers to complete a Year of Duty, largely spent in working on farms. As a result, the Third Reich failed to reach its rhetorical goal of returning women to the hearth since the female labor force increased by 2.3 million in the wake of economic recovery. Half of the growth came from married women who wanted to supplement family incomes with low-wage jobs, which industrialists did not want to give up. In the pinch, economic needs, therefore, tended to win over ideological appeals.[33]

The Nazis' impact on women's public role was equally ambiguous since the Party offered opportunities in subordinate positions despite

---

[30] Atina Grossmann, *Reforming Sex: The German Movement for Birth Control and Abortion Rights, 1920–1950* (New York, 1995); Lisa Pine, *Nazi Family Policy, 1933–1945* (Oxford, 1997); and Irmgard Weyrather, *Muttertag und Mutterkreuz. Der Kult um die "deutsche Mutter" im Nationalsozialismus* (Frankfurt, 1993).

[31] Bock, *Zwangssterilisation im Nationalsozialismus*, 10 ff., as well as "Antinatalism, Maternity and Paternity in National Socialist Racism," *Maternity and Gender Policies*, 233 ff; and Gabriele Czarnowski, *Das kontrollierte Paar. Ehe- und Sexualpolitik im Nationalsozialismus* (Weinheim, 1991).

[32] Konrad H. Jarausch, *Deutsche Studenten 1800–1970* (Frankfurt, 1984), 176 ff; and Jacques. R. Pauwels, *Women and University Studies in the Third Reich, 1933–1945* (New York, 1984).

[33] Jill Stephenson, *Women in Nazi Society* (London, 1975); and Dörte Winkler, *Frauenarbeit im Dritten Reich* (Hamburg, 1977).

their crusade for domesticity. Although women were more reluctant than men to vote for or join NSDAP, the misogynist, though magnetic, Hitler could not have come to power without considerable female support.[34] To acquire such a following, he reluctantly authorized the creation of a girls' league, called BDM, and the consolidation of various women's auxiliaries into the *NS Frauenschaft*, led by Gertrud Scholtz-Klink. In the spring of 1933 the two groups absorbed the existing bourgeois competitors except for religious groups, eventually attracting 600,000 and 3.3 million members, respectively. Although always subservient to male control, Nazi women found much scope for activity in welfare policy (the NSV), the German Labor Front (especially the KdF branches), public campaigns (such as the *Winterhilfswerk*), and the removal of children to safe havens (KLV) during the war. Even if communist and Jewish women were victimized, many others responded to the rhetoric of motherhood and, in their domestic roles and working lives, acted as accomplices of the Third Reich.[35]

World War II revealed the instrumental nature of the Nazis' women's policy since it destroyed the very families it was claiming to protect. Despite all efforts to maintain the birth rate by providing soldiers with liberal leaves, the fighting created another demographic disaster, killing several million men at the front, as well as hundreds of thousands of women and children by air raids. Although Hitler tried to stabilize the Home Front by shifting the burden to slave laborers, camp inmates, and POWs, he eventually had to allow the recruitment of single women for arms production and the training of female students to replace drafted professionals.[36] In the various social organizations, the absence of men created opportunities for female advancement as temporary replacements that kept many programs going. In spite of private grumbling about euthanasia or bombing attacks, women rarely engaged in public resistance, individual exceptions like Sophie Scholl notwithstanding. A small group of especially fanatical followers even worked as concentration camp guards and became directly involved

[34] Michael H. Kater, *The Nazi Party: A Social Profile of Members and Leaders, 1919–1945* (Cambridge, Mass., 1983), 148–53; and Jürgen Falter, *Hitler's Wähler* (Munich, 1991), 136 ff. For the controversy, see Frauengruppe Faschismusforschung, ed., *Mutterkreuz und Arbeitsbuch. Zur Geschichte der Frau in der Weimarer Republik und im Nationalsozialismus* (Frankfurt, 1981).

[35] Koonz, *Mothers in the Fatherland*, 53 ff. See also Erich Kasberger, *Heldinnen waren wir keine. Alltag in der NS-Zeit* (Hamburg, 1995); and Marion A. Kaplan, *Between Dignity and Despair: Jewish Life in Nazi Germany* (New York, 1998).

[36] Leila Rupp, *Mobilizing Women for War: German and American War Propaganda, 1939–1945* (Princeton, 1978); and Elisabeth Heineman, *What Difference Does a Husband Make? Women and Marital Status in Nazi and Postwar Germany* (Berkeley, 1999), 44 ff.

in the Holocaust.[37] The Nazis therefore turned the cult of maternalism into its very opposite—making women into accomplices of a repressive regime and serving as a license for selective killing.[38]

The Shift to Egalitarianism and Individualism

During the total defeat, German women, struggling for survival, had little time to ponder what had gone wrong. With over three million men dead and about eleven million others in POW camps, it was the women who had to keep the families going—extending the tasks of motherhood in a previously unknown sense and becoming more independent by mastering adverse circumstances. Many women, though content in the 1950s to step back from this "involuntary matriarchy," eventually turned toward alternate definitions of womanhood that de-emphasized domesticity and instead stressed their personal freedom. In the East the legacy of the Socialist women's movement offered a degendered version of egalitarianism that proclaimed female equality in the workplace. In the West a growing resentment against the limitations of family restoration, reinforced by Anglo-American stress on individual rights, promoted a challenge to sexual restrictions and conventional roles.[39] What triggered these double redefinitions? Would egalitarianism or individualism provide better opportunities for women in the postwar era?

The death and imprisonment of German men created a severe gender imbalance after 1945 that disrupted reproductive relations. In the East, hundreds of thousands of hapless women were raped by vengeful soldiers of the Red Army—a trauma that created a lasting memory of collective shame.[40] In the West, there was more voluntary fraterniza-

---

[37] Ortrun Niethammer, ed., *Frauen und Nationalsozialismus. Historische und kulturgeschichtliche Positionen* (Osnabrück, 1996), 83 ff., 100 ff. Cf. Alison Owings, *Frauen: German Women in the Third Reich* (New Brunswick, 1983).

[38] Allen, *Feminism and Motherhood*, 229 ff; and Reagin, *German Women's Movement*, 249 ff. See also Victoria de Grazia, *How Fascism Ruled Women: Italy, 1922–1945* (Berkeley, 1992).

[39] The quotation is from Rosemarie Nave-Herz, *Geschichte der Frauenbewegung in Deutschland*, 4th ed. (Opladen, 1994), 58 ff. Cf. Hanna Schissler, "Women in West Germany from 1945 to the Present," in Michael G. Huelshoff, Andrei S. Markovits, and Simon Reich, eds., *From Bundesrepublik to Deutschland: German Politics after Unification* (Ann Arbor, 1993), 117–36.

[40] The best summary of this difficult topic is in Norman Naimark, *The Russians in Germany: A History of the Soviet Zone of Occupation, 1945–1949* (Cambrigde, Mass., 1995), 69

tion between the occupiers and *Fräuleins*, who sought material rewards or just a good time despite initial prohibitions.[41] The death or uncertain fate of husbands or lovers encouraged temporary liaisons with other German men, intent on forgetting the bloodshed. With 1.65 females to every male in the twenty to forty year age-bracket, the prospects of traditional marriage were dim, encouraging all sorts of other relationships and producing tens of thousands of children with uncertain parentage. This sense of sexual freedom taught women to make more conscious choices about their partners and to reject the efforts of their returned husbands to reestablish patriarchal control. As a result of these upheavals, divorce rates mushroomed and a new, truncated type of "mother family" emerged.[42]

In struggling for survival, women had to expand their definition of work to include many different forms of providing for the remnants of their families. During the hunger years, the most important task became scrounging for food, getting something on the table, no matter whether it was ersatz coffee, bread stretched with tree bark, or jam made from sugar beets. To supplement their meager rations, women used the smallest plots to grow something edible or traveled into the countryside to barter their silver for a sack of potatoes. Collecting wood for heating purposes from parks or searching railroad tracks for bits of coal also became a major preoccupation. Some of the more vigorous or NS-implicated women were employed by the city authorities to clear away the rubble, becoming the famous *Trümmerfrauen* that chipped mortar from fallen bricks to reuse them for building. Regular work was difficult to obtain since factories had been destroyed or dismantled; besides, gainful employment contributed less than scrounging or barter toward feeding families. The result of this wearying effort to get to the next day was an increasing sense of female self-reliance coupled with an idealization of the family.[43]

In the public effort to meet the postwar emergency, women, therefore, played a crucial role, albeit more in their homes, neighborhoods,

---

ff. See also Atina Grossmann, "A Question of Silence: The Rape of German Women by Occupation Soldiers," *October* 72 (April 1995): 43–63.

[41] Maria Höhn, "GIs, Veronikas and Lucky Strikes: German Reactions to the American Military Presence in the Rhineland-Palatinate During the 1950s" (Ph.D. dissertation, Philadelphia, 1995).

[42] Robert G. Moeller, *Protecting Motherhood: Women and the Family in the Politics of Postwar West Germany* (Berkeley, 1993), 8 ff. See also Dagmar Herzog, "The 'Sexual Misery' of the 1950s," paper at the German Studies Association meeting in Atlanta, 9 October 1999.

[43] Elisabeth Heineman, "The Hour of the Woman: Memories of Germany's 'Crisis Years' and West German National Identity," *American Historical Review* 101 (1996): 354–95.

and towns than in national affairs. They took the lead in organizing local welfare committees to take care of orphans, people homeless from bombing, refugees from the lost eastern territories, and returning POWs—in short, the human flotsam that the war had left stranded without help. In the Soviet Zone, various groups joined Socialist and Communist women in a women's league (DFD) that seized control of relief efforts and propounded a Marxist definition of womanhood.[44] In the West, the religious and liberal associations reconstituted the bourgeois women's movement, combining in 1949 into the *Deutsche Frauenring*, which considered itself the successor to the BDF. Breaking with Nazi maternalism, their lobbying succeeded in getting the principle of gender equality included into both the Eastern and Western constitutions. Reflecting a compromise between clashing views of the SPD and the CDU, the *Grundgesetz* guaranteed equal rights for women (article 3, paragraph 2), but also placed marriage, motherhood, and the family under the "particular protection" of the state (article 6).[45]

During the 1950s and 1960s German women slowly regained a sense of normalcy, though in a country divided by the Cold War. The restoration of order, the return of the POWs, and the resumption of work gradually reconstituted some regularity in their lives and recreated disrupted families. As a result, reproductive patterns returned to their previous shape, with illegitimacy rates, as well as divorces, falling precipitously. In rare unanimity, both Germanys responded to the wartime mortality and subsequent population deficit by reemphasizing natalist policies and legally protecting motherhood in 1950 and 1952, respectively. On the one hand, they ceased the practice of tolerating abortions by stiffening penalties and driving the termination of pregnancy underground. On the other hand, they used their meager resources to restore maternalist incentives by various kinds of motherhood benefits, child support payments, and so on. Supported by improving economic prospects, this effort to normalize sexual behavior by confining it to marriage and directing it to the production of children, returned the birth rate close to prewar levels, about 17–18 per 1,000 inhabitants.[46]

---

[44] Donna Harsh, "Approach/Avoidance: German Communists between Women's Anti-Communism and Proletarian Anti-Feminism in the Soviet Zone of Occupation," *Social History* 25 (2000), no 2.

[45] Irene Stoehr, "Staatsbürgerinnen in Pumps. Weibliche Staatsbürgerschaft und Frauenbewegung in der Gründungsphase der Bundesrepublik," paper delivered at the gender conference in Chapel Hill, September 1999. See also Moeller, *Protecting Motherhood*, 38 ff.

[46] Donna Harsch, "Society, the State and Abortion in East Germany," *American Historical Review* 102 (1997): 53–84; and Hanna Schissler, ed., *The "Miracle" Years: A Cultural History of West Germany, 1949–1968* (Princeton, 2000).

East and West Germany differed, however, on the appropriate place of women in the workforce or in the home. Because of egalitarian ideology and the post-war labor shortage the SED sought to move women into production by promising that work would "make them independent, allow them to develop all their capabilities, and give their life meaning and contentment." A combination of carrots, such as propaganda films picturing female tractor drivers, and sticks, such as the abolition of alimony, dramatically increased the proportion of working women to over two-thirds by the 1960s.[47] In contrast, the CDU, propelled by Catholic maternalism, sought to redomesticate women to resolve the postwar "crisis of the family." Pension laws reconstituted the male breadwinner, while welfare measures, such as "money-for-children," created natalist incentives. The paradoxical compromise of the Family Reform Law of 1957 reaffirmed female equality while reasserting ultimate male authority, and permitted outside work while tying women's roles to the household. But women continued to make inroads into the gendered workplace, with about one-half employed in the early 1960s, and acquired influence as crucial actors in an expanding consumer society.[48]

In the public realm, women made only limited gains since in both German states men dominated discussions, even those about female issues. In the GDR, the DFD, with over one million members, largely served as a transmitter of SED directives rather than as a representation of female interests. Within the hierarchy of the nomenclatura, women generally rose only to middling levels, remaining shut out of ultimate decisions. But the Women's Committees of industrial enterprises were more successful in increasing concrete benefits for working women.[49] In the FRG the *Frauenrat* served as a lobbying organization for women's issues in the *Bundestag*, coordinating the efforts of various religious, liberal, and topical groups. In confrontations with Family Minister Franz-Josef Würmeling, obtuse judges, and unbending bureaucrats, some women, such as Elisabeth Selbert and Marie-Elisabeth Lüders, played an important role, while others, such as Elly Knapp-Heuss and Annemarie Renger, were recognized as "founding moth-

---

[47] The quotation is from Donna Harsch, "The Revenge of the Domestic: East German Women and the Construction of State Socialism, 1945–1970" (MS, Pittsburgh, 1999). See also Heike Trappe, *Emanzipation oder Zwang? Frauen in der DDR zwischen Beruf, Familie und Sozialpolitik* (Berlin, 1995), 103 ff.

[48] Moeller, *Protecting Motherhood*, 76 ff.; Heineman, *What Difference does a Husband Make?*, 108 ff. See also Erica Carter, *How German Is She? Post-War West German Reconstruction and the Consuming Women* (Ann Arbor, 1997).

[49] Harsch, "Revenge of the Domestic," chap. 2; and Heineman, *What Difference Does a Husband Make?*, 176 ff.

ers" of the FRG. Although they agreed on the need to restore families, women's groups remained divided between a democratized maternalism and an individualist conception of rights.[50]

During the 1970s and 1980s women made greater strides due to the sexual revolution, growing career opportunities, and the rise of a new feminism. While the arrival of the Pill facilitated birth control, political conflict focused on the legalization of abortion. In the East, shifting sentiment among women and doctors persuaded the SED leadership to permit first trimester abortions without restrictions beginning in 1972. But this liberalization was accompanied by a host of pronatalist measures, such as marital housing preferences, the building of nurseries and kindergartens, extended maternity leaves, and a monthly day for housework for working mothers.[51] In the West, the social-liberal government responded to feminist pressure, signaled by the slogan "my belly belongs to me," by legalizing first-trimester abortions in April 1974. But prompted by strong church and CDU protests, the Supreme Court struck down this law, arguing that after the Nazi crimes, the protection of life had priority over individual choice. In 1976 the *Bundestag* worked out another solution to allow abortions, requiring doctor certification according to one of four criteria, based on medical, eugenic, criminal, or social hardship factors. With this cumbersome compromise, Western women in practice achieved something close to free choice.[52]

Public demands, structural changes, and political reforms also helped expand female careers, both for single women and working mothers. In the East, the SED launched a qualification offensive in the 1970s that promoted adult learning and increased girls' access to higher education. Because of financial need, incessant propaganda, and better training, over 90 percent of women were gainfully employed—the highest proportion in the industrial world. But male resistance to housework created a double burden of working and homemaking, while shopping and services remained notoriously difficult.[53] In the FRG, educational reforms also expanded female access to secondary and tertiary education dramatically, even if girls tended to choose pre-

---

[50] Moeller, *Protecting Motherhood*, 211 ff.; and Heineman, *What Difference Does a Husband Make?*, 239 ff.

[51] Harsh, "Society, the State, and Abortion in East Germany," 71 ff.

[52] Joyce Mushaben, Sarah Lennox, and Geoffrey Giles, "Women, Men and Unification: Gender Politics and the Abortion Struggle Since 1989," in *After Unity*, 137 ff.

[53] Trappe, *Emanzipation oder Zwang?*, 89 ff. See also Leo Ansorg and Renate Hürtgen, "The Myth of Female Emancipation: Contradictions in Women's Lives," in Konrad H. Jarausch, ed., *Dictatorship as Experience: Towards a Socio-Cultural History of the GDR* (New York, 1999), 163 ff.

sumably softer subjects like teaching instead of the hard sciences. The majority of the less well-schooled prepared for the expanding service sector, training to become hairdressers, salesgirls, secretaries, or receptionists. In response to a campaign for equal job opportunities, the courts gradually began to declare lesser pay and slower advancement illegal and to enforce such decisions. Even if they lagged behind their Eastern sisters, two-thirds of the Western women also entered the paid workforce as part-time, phased, or full-time employees.[54]

Frustrated with continuing discrimination, FRG feminists founded a new women's movement during the cultural revolution of the late 1960s. In dramatic confrontations disgruntled women demanded "an end to the bourgeois division between private and public spheres," and established "self-help groups" to create solidarity, share female experiences, and raise consciousness. Out of these initiatives developed numerous "women's projects," such as women's centers, shelters, bookshops and magazines (such as *Emma*), as well as cafes and crèches (*Kinderläden*). Heated discussions revolved around the priority of female autonomy expressed in lesbianism, a radical social revolution, or a more pragmatic transformation of gender relations in an egalitarian direction. Despite such divisions, the new women's movement succeeded in institutionalizing itself with public equality advocates, with women's studies programs at the universities, and in a quota system among political parties, initiated by the Greens.[55] In the East, women's issues could only be raised by such talented writers as Christa Wolf and in a few opposition groups.[56] The postwar redefinition of gender roles therefore created a mixed system that sought to reconcile new demands for equality with traditions of difference.

Clashing Concepts of Emancipation

With German unification in 1990, two distinctive sets of female experiences and aspirations encountered each other, becoming conscious of their respective differences. In the oversimplified diction of a recent book title, Eastern *Muttis* had achieved a good deal of practical independence from men because of easy divorce and abortion, and be-

---

[54] Frevert, *German Women in History*, 270 ff.

[55] Nave-Herz, *Geschichte der Frauenbewegung in Deutschland*, 65 ff.; and Angelika von Wahl, *Gleichstellungsregime. Berufliche Gleichstellung von Frauen in den USA und der Bundesrepublik Deutschland* (Opladen, 1999).

[56] Eva Maleck Lewy and Bernhard Maleck, "The Women's Movement in East and West Germany," in Carole Fink, Philipp Gassert, and Detlev Junker, eds., *1968: The World Transformed* (Cambridge, UK, 1998), 373–95.

lieved in reconciling work with family via free childcare and maternal benefits. Yet in public they were more group oriented, reluctant to make a fuss, and generally sorry to see the dismantling of socialist supports. In contrast, Western *Emanzen* prided themselves on their feminist consciousness and focused on individual independence, but often saw family life and professional careers as mutually exclusive alternatives. They were used to speaking out in public, organizing for common purposes, and being assertive in pursuit of their aims, sometimes implying that they would just as soon do without men altogether.[57] Unfortunately, these contrasting versions of partial emancipation could not meet halfway since the "unification crisis" forced the Easterners to adopt Western patterns in a hurry.

The result of the "unification shock" was the dramatic drop in the eastern birth rate, which amounted to a spontaneous, but effective, "birth strike." The transformation of a welfare dictatorship into a social market economy drastically increased insecurity for women since their ability to combine work and family depended upon universal childcare, which began to break down due to its high cost. To get a foot into a chaotic labor market, they now concentrated first on launching a career, hoping to enter into marriage after they had established themselves in an occupation. As a result, between 1988 and 1993, the number of births decreased by over two-thirds from about 220,000 to 70,000, a level that was only half of the already low West German rate! Many kindergartens and primary schools had to close since they no longer had the requisite number of pupils. Lacking sufficient funds and not wanting to fall back into traditional natalism, alarmed politicians could only hope that after completing the transition to Western reproductive patterns, the birth-rate would recover, which it did to some degree, although without attaining previous levels.[58]

The collapse of the Eastern labor market also affected women more fundamentally than it did men. The double transition from plan to market and from high-industrial to postindustrial production produced widespread deindustrialization in the new states. It hit women particularly hard since the breakup of the *Kombinate* privatized their social services and thereby destroyed many female jobs. Moreover, the reintroduction of a male breadwinner model also created preferences

[57] Kathrin Rohnstock, *Stiefschwestern. Was Ost-Frauen und West-Frauen voneinander denken* (Frankfurt, 1994); Ulrike Helwert and Gieselinde Schwarz, *Von Muttis und Emanzen. Feministinnen in Ost- und Westdeutschland* (Frankfurt, 1995); and Heike Ellermann and Katrin Klatt, *Bundesdeutsche Hausfrau?—Nie im Leben! Eine Studie zum Selbstverständnis von Frauen in Ost und West* (Berlin, 1995), 158 ff.

[58] Cover story on "Sterben die Deutschen aus?" *Spiegel-Online*, 6 January 2000; and Brigitte Young, *The Triumph of the Fatherland: German Unification and the Marginalization of Women* (Ann Arbor, 1999), 199 f.

for men in competitive hiring, eliminating women from occupations considered "gendered" by Western employers. Faced with such drastic changes, twice as many women as men lost their jobs, especially the older ones. It was cold comfort that East German widows received higher pensions than Western retirees because of their longer working lives. While some especially audacious individuals tried to establish small service businesses, many younger women flocked to retraining schemes (ABM) in the hope of bettering their skills. But women who had become accustomed to combining work and family resented as regressive the pressure to stay home.[59]

Faced with such elemental difficulties in their lives, East German women were slow to find a public voice that could articulate their grievances. On the one hand, the unification winners enjoyed the new consumer goods, possibilities for travel, and avenues for political participation, making the most of their opportunities. On the other hand, many losers contributed to a postcommunist nostalgia that remembered the positive aspects of community and social support, but elided the oppressive features of the SED regime. The small band of feminists that had founded an independent women's league (UFV) to democratize the GDR saw unification as "three steps backward in women's questions." But these radical activists proved unable to turn widespread resentment into public protest against female losses in the rush to unity since women concentrated on mastering the transition in their private lives.[60] East German women like Angela Merkel, Christine Bergmann, and Gunda Röstel assumed prominent positions in their national parties, but they did not combine forces to voice the concerns of their troubled constituency.

The first issue affecting both Eastern and Western women was the emotional abortion struggle, which forced them to close ranks. Since the unification treaty had been unable to resolve the differences between the GDR and FRG systems, the *Bundestag*, freed of party discipline, basically extended the Western [*Eastern*] trimester solution to the entire country in 1992 by a vote of 357 to 283. But when 248 conservative deputies appealed, the Constitutional Court reaffirmed the primacy of protecting "unborn life" and rendered a Solomonic verdict, declaring abortion "illegal but free from punishment." Instead of insisting on

[59] Katarina Belwe, "Frauenpolitische Aspekte der Arbeitsmarktentwicklung in Ost- und Westdeutschland," *DIW-Wochenbericht* 31 (1991): 421 ff. See also Birgit Bütow and Heidi Stecker, eds., *EigenArtige Ostfrauen. Frauenemanzipation in der DDR und den neuen Bundesländern* (Bielefeld, 1994).

[60] Cordula Kahlau, *Aufbruch. Frauenbewegung in der DDR* (Munich, 1990); Christina Schenk, "Der Politikbegriff von ostdeutschen Frauen am Beispiel des UFV," in *Eigen–Artige Ostfrauen*, 285 ff.; Young, *Triumph of the Fatherland*, 80 ff.

prosecution, it suggested mandatory counseling as a prerequisite for termination. The revised law of 1995 only preserved medical and criminal indications, added a requirement for an "open-ended" consultation with a recognized center for all other cases, and limited reimbursement of costs to the truly needy. This complicated compromise restricted earlier Eastern practice and denied women the right to control their bodies, but it decriminalized abortion and sought instead to encourage childbearing. It satisfied no one—but it appears to work reasonably well in practice.[61]

The transformation of the workplace after 1990 was a second area in which many Eastern women experienced the unification process as a loss. The collapse of the uncompetitive Eastern industries dramatically increased female unemployment in the new states, eventually reducing the number of working women to about two-thirds, the same level as in the West. Moreover, the distribution of female occupations also converged on the Western pattern, only somewhat reducing the higher gender segregation in the East. During the process of conversion, men's jobs in the East became even more male, but more men also entered previously female jobs, and women continued to cluster in relatively few occupations, such as secretaries, salesgirls, and so on. While the shift from physical labor in freight and transportation to white collar jobs might have been welcome, the underdeveloped service sector could not absorb enough female newcomers.[62] Although some talented individuals benefited from the new market opportunities, for most working women the process of displacement and reorientation created much unexpected anxiety.

In the area of citizenship and participation, the unification process has brought more visible gains. Although the activists of the UFV joined the Communist successor party PDS, the access of East German women to decision-making has improved according to measurable indicators such as legislative prominence, visibility in the media, and control of the debate on women's issues. As a result, the courts and the legislative process are beginning to recognize the importance of reproductive work, gradually increasing pension amounts for time spent in caring for children. The inclusion of an equal rights clause in

[61] Mushaben, Lennox, and Giles, "Women, Men and Unification," 158 ff. Cf. Myra Marx Ferree, "The Gendering of Governance and the Governance of Gender: Abortion Politics in Germany and in the US," paper at gender conference in Chapel Hill, September 1999.

[62] Heike Trappe and Rachel Rosenfeld, "Occupational Sex Segregation in East and West Germany, 1980s and 1998," paper at gender conference in Chapel Hill, September 1999. See also Irene Dölling, "Verliererinnen und Gewinnerinnen. Frauen in Ostdeutschland," *Potsdamer Universitäts-Zeitung*, October 1999, 13.

the Amsterdam Treaty has also given the European Court of Justice a legal basis for injecting Anglo-American conceptions of individual equality into judgments on women's issues, decreasing discriminatory practices.[63] By becoming part of the more pluralist politics of the Federal Republic, Eastern women have not just lost certain welfare supports but have also gained possibilities for pursuing a more individualized version of equality. The changes in the German "gender order" during the last decade of the twentieth century therefore appear to go into contradictory directions.

Gendering the Nation

The regime ruptures of twentieth-century Germany have produced a wide range of contradictory definitions of womanhood. The authoritarian paternalism of the Empire favored maternal homemakers, but the voluntary motherhood of the Weimar Republic created a liberated "new woman," while the racist backlash of the Third Reich returned to the ideal of the prolific Aryan mother. In the postwar period, socialist egalitarianism promoted capable female workers whereas democratic efforts to restore motherhood prized fashionable consumers, and both were in turn challenged by an individualized feminism that propagated self-confident career women. While the Right tended to essentialize motherhood and domesticity as female destiny, the liberal middle stressed personal choice and individual rights and the Left generally preferred equality supplemented by welfare supports. Which linkages do these constructions of gender roles suggest between conceptions of the social order and notions of nationhood?[64]

A popular cliché associates the societal dominance of paternalism with the political prevalence of an aggressive nationalism, reducing women by and large to the role of victim. If one ignores its Latin origin and its original reference to a territorial state,[65] the term *Vaterland* can

---

[63] Young, *Triumph of the Fatherland*, 202 ff.; Joyce Mushaben, "*Mütterurteile contra Vaterstaat*: Reconfiguring Maternal Welfare Rights in Germany and in the US," as well as Jytte Klausen, "German Women and Citizenship: Between Familialism and Liberalism," papers at gender conference in Chapel Hill, September 1999.

[64] Yuval-Davis, *Gender and Nation*, 22 ff., concentrates on reproduction, culture, citizenship, and war. Cf. Mechtild Rumpf, "Staatsgewalt, Nationalismus und Geschlechterverhältnis," in Frauen und Geschichte Baden-Württemberg, eds., *Frauen und Nation* (Tübingen, 1996), 12–29; and Geoff Eley and Ronald Suny, eds., *Becoming National* (New York, 1996), 260 ff.

[65] *Langenscheidts Enzyklopädisches Wörterbuch*, Part II, Deutsch-Englisch (Berlin 1975), 1647. See Todd Berryman, "The Rhetoric of Liberation: German Patriotism and Nationalism Against Napoleon, 1812–1814" (M.A. thesis, Chapel Hill, 1999).

for instance be construed as denoting a male nationalizing project.[66] On the surface the very male-centeredness of their nationalist rhetoric suggests interpreting the authoritarian Empire and the aggressive Third Reich as misogynist creations, while treating democratic or socialist regimes as paragons of female rights. Moreover, certain versions of manhood, such as feudal codes of honor or militaristic sentiments, are closely associated with conceptions of the state that are anchored in national prestige and social militarism.[67] In nationalist propaganda, women served as important objects of symbolic signification, representing literary images of *Kultur* and embodying the entire nation in statues of Germania.[68] Finally, homophobic prejudice has also been an essential element of most nationalist definitions of German identity.[69]

The contest over reproduction shows, nonetheless, that women gradually succeeded in asserting their wishes in family planning against pressures to ensure the perpetuation of the nation. Maternalist appeals to collective responsibility fed on natalist concerns for waning strength due to the declining birthrates as well as on eugenic fears about genetic decadence due to the reproduction of the hereditarily ill, the insane, and the criminal. But individualist arguments for choice could draw on democratic efforts to extend notions of civil rights to women, enabling them to make their own decisions about their bodies. In actual practice, both discourses nonetheless tended to intermingle because the Weimar welfare state introduced an element of voluntary motherhood, while the postwar gains for choice were buffered by the continuation of maternal benefits. After the Nazis' selective pro- and antinatalism had discredited collective compulsion by dictating both birthing and killing, the tenor of the postwar debate shifted from the primacy of maternalist arguments to a greater recognition of the importance of individual rights. The long struggle for abortion rights demonstrates an increasing insistence on female self-assertion.[70]

In the realm of work, women also slowly escaped the traditional role as mothers and established claims for independent, albeit still unequal

---

[66] Koonz, *Mothers in the Fatherland*; and Young, *Triumph of the Fatherland* use this cliche in their titles.

[67] Ute Frevert, *Men of Honor: A Social and Cultural History of the Duel* (Cambridge, 1995). See also Karen Hagemann, *"Männlicher Mut und teutsche Ehre"* (Padernborn, 2002).

[68] Reagin, *German Women's Movement*, passim, as well as her new project on the idealization of the *Hausfrau* as part of Imperial German identity. See also Patricia Herminghouse and Magda Mueller, "Looking for Germania," in *Gender and Germanness*, 1–8.

[69] George L. Mosse, *Nationalism and Sexuality: Middle Class Morality and Sexual Norms in Modern Europe* (Madison, 1985).

[70] Ann Taylor Allen, "'Das Recht des Kindes, seine Eltern zu wählen.' Eugenik und Frauenbewegung in Deutschland und Großbritannien, 1900–1933," in the forthcoming volume edited by Juliane Jacobi, Meike Baader, and Sabine Andresen.

careers. The imperial idealization of the bourgeois *Hausfrau* as mistress of the domestic sphere left the public world of employment to men, although it was understood that proletarian women had to work.[71] Energetic reformers, however, succeeded in subverting this gendered division of labor by an extension of such "motherly pursuits" as teaching, nursing, and social work into the public realm, first through charity but eventually for pay. The manpower demands of the world wars also propelled countless women into the workforce to make up for the male draft by "manning" assembly lines in munitions factories or tending the wounded. Ultimately, structural changes in the economy, such as the rise of white-collar occupations of secretary and salesgirl, overrode the chauvinist labor policies that sought to shield men from female competitors by restricting the latter to their maternal roles. Although often struggling to reconcile family duties with careers, women succeeded in slowly expanding their working roles, albeit largely in subordinate capacities.[72]

Overcoming male resistance, the women's movement also gained greater space for female participation in the public sphere. Already during the Empire, a minority of activists, not content with their control of servants, children, and social relations, ventured out of the home by using the rhetoric of maternalism for protecting motherhood, increasing work opportunities, and forming their own organizations.[73] In the Weimar Republic the granting of full civil rights established a competitive women's politics that ranged across the entire ideological spectrum and that achieved some welfare reforms. The Nazis quickly reversed these advances since they were only willing to tolerate female mobilization in inferior and acclamatory roles. Since women's initiatives in the GDR were soon reined in, while traditional organizations reemerged in the FRG, it took the cultural revolution of the 1960s to spark a new, grassroots feminism that insisted on complete control over reproduction, equality in the workplace, and citizenship in the public realm. Though gender issues were involved in the struggle between the Right and the Left, the competition over women's support served successively to enlarge the scope of female politics.[74]

---

[71] Bonnie Smith, *Ladies of the Leisure Class: The Bourgeoises of Northern France in the 19th Century* (Princeton, 1981). See also Canning, *Languages of Labor*, 324 ff.

[72] Heineman, "The Hour of the Woman," 354 ff.; and Konrad H. Jarausch, *The Unfree Professions: German Lawyers, Teachers and Engineers, 1900–1950* (Oxford, 1990), 40 ff, 80 ff., 125 ff., 172 ff.

[73] For one forerunner, see Stanley Zucker, *Kathinka Zitz-Halein and Female Civic Activism in Mid-Nineteenth Century Germany* (Carbondale, 1991).

[74] Nave-Herz, *Geschichte der Frauenbewegung*, 123 ff.

These hard-won gains indicate that clichés of Germany as "fatherland" oversimplify the complex relationship between gender and nation by neglecting the agency of women. In the nation-building project, women played an essential role as accomplices: By telling stories and singing songs, mothers transmitted national culture to their children; by working in patriotic associations or field hospitals, many women strengthened popular morale in wartime; by manning soup-kitchens and volunteering for charitable agencies, bourgeois women labored to reduce social tensions in the nation.[75] In drawing middle-class boundaries against the lower orders, women also often took a lead: By setting standards of cleanliness, decency, and frugality, they spread bourgeois values throughout the population; by determining the suitability of social acquaintances, they made decisions on respectability; and by selecting marriage partners for their children, they helped transmit property.[76] Finally, in the project of widening the circle of political participation, women were also centrally important in establishing many of the voluntary organizations that made up the network of civil society. It is no accident that female leaders are prominent in most reform causes, seeking to remedy gross social abuses.[77]

The possibilities for some female agency under paternalist regimes and the persistence of versions of maternalism in leftist governments suggest ironic paradoxes in the actual experiences of women. Around the turn of the twentieth century, ideological prescriptions and legal codes such as the BGB undoubtedly privileged the pater familias at home and made manhood a prerequisite of active citizenship in the public realm. But the German record in the subsequent decades also reveals a paradoxical interaction of maternalism and egalitarianism in redefining womanhood, which, despite many setbacks, moved along a trajectory of increasing women's control over their bodies, chances for work, and public participation across the different regimes. Such piecemeal advances may seem insufficient by current standards of individualized equality and autonomous feminism that emphasize how much still needs to be done. But when viewed from the perspective of women's daily struggle to combine family with work, these hard-won changes

---

[75] Kaplan, *Making of the Jewish Middle Class*, 41 ff; Hong, *Welfare, Modernity and the Weimar State*, 141 ff.

[76] Cf. the essays by Ursula Vogel and Ute Gerhard in Jürgen Kocka, ed., *Bürgertum im 19. Jahrhundert. Deutschland im europäischen Vergleich* vol. 1(Munich, 1988), 406–68 to Dolores Augustine, *Patricians and Parvenus: Wealth and High Society in Wilhelmine Germany* (Oxford, 1994), 122 ff.

[77] Hong, *Welfare, Modernity and the Weimar State*, 141 ff.

did slowly improve the quality of female lives through strengthening protections for difference while enlarging chances for equality.[78]

Yet the potential contribution of a gender perspective to broadening conceptions of the German past remains somewhat incomplete. Activists like the formidable Alice Schwarzer, who in 1975 wrote the famous treatise *Der kleine Unterschied*, have much reason to be satisfied with what has been achieved in the past quarter-century. In the meantime, the history of women has largely been rescued from oblivion; the ugly discrimination suffered by females in the past has been incontrovertibly documented; and many signal achievements of the women's movement have been acknowledged.[79] But these successes have been gained at the price of locating the new specialty of women's history largely outside established disciplines to provide a sheltered space. To escape such marginalization, it is necessary to reintegrate the gender perspective more strongly into concurrent discussions on political loyalty, conceptions of power, experiences of migration, or constructions of national identity. Perhaps the renewed emphasis on female agency will provide an opportunity to bring into sharper focus the paradoxical contributions of women to the troubled course of German history in general.[80]

[78] Gisela Bock, "Gleichheit und Differenz in der NS Rassenpolitik," *Geschichte und Gesellschaft* 19 (1993): 277–310; and Ann Taylor Allen, "Feminist Movements in the US and Germany: A Comparative Perspective, 1848–1933," in Michael Geyer and Manfred Berg, eds., *Cultures of Rights* (Cambridge, UK, 2002).

[79] Alice Schwarzer, "'Die gläserne Wand'. Siege und Niederlagen der Frauen im Kampf gegen die Männerherrschaft," *Der Spiegel* (2000) no. 41: 80–84; Ute Gerhard, "Mehr als einhundert Jahre Frauenbewegung. Tradition und Unerledigtes," *Ariadne* (2000) no. 37–8: 14–21.

[80] See also the report on the conference "'Blickwechsel' Frauen- und Geschlechtergeschichte—Allgemeine Geschichte. Bilanzen und Perspektiven," at Stuttgart, 24–26 September 2000 on H-Soz-Kult.

10

In Pursuit of Happiness: Consumption, Mass Culture, and Consumerism

Much as cataclysmic violence forged the short twentieth century, a revolution of consumption marked its *longue durée*. At the end of the century, the consumer, as opposed to the soldier, had emerged as the most readily recognized subject of twentieth-century history, the allure of mobility and abundance replacing the fascination with firepower. Mass consumption is increasingly presented as the destiny of German history, its refuge and redemption. The emergence of a consumer-oriented society is becoming the narrative of the age.[1]

Throughout the twentieth century, most intellectuals in Europe and the United States have tenaciously held the opposite view. They felt

[1] Alon Confino and Rudy Koshar. "Regimes of Consumer Culture: New Narratives in Twentieth-Century German History," *German History* 19 (2001): 135–61. Both authors are careful to speak of narratives, but the practitioners of the grand literature of consumption rather think of the consumer society as an alternative and equivalent of industrial society. Brief and useful summaries are Peter N. Stearns, "Stages of Consumerism: Recent Work on the Issues of Periodization," *Journal of Modern History* 69 (1997): 102–117; Craig Clunas, "Modernity Global and Local: Consumption and the Rise of the West," *American Historical Review* 104 (1999): 1497–511; and Daniel Miller, "Consumption as the Vanguard of History: A Polemic by Way of an Introduction," in Daniel Miller, ed., *Acknowledging Consumption: A Review of New Studies* (London, 1995), 1–57.

that there had to be more to life than going to the supermarket or to Mallorca. They rejected reckless commodification, commercialization, and standardization, which they associated with the rise of "the masses."[2] But the fact of the matter is that the twentieth century ended, at least as far as Germany is concerned, neither with a bang nor a whimper, but, genuinely, with a consumer revolution. That is, the inhabitants of the German Democratic Republic chose to join those of the Federal Republic because they wanted to partake in the liberties that the citizens of the latter state so fully enjoyed. This remark is commonly made tongue-in-cheek, as if it implied an illegitimate and improper longing. But inasmuch as GDR citizens went straight to the market, this act rather displayed a mature recognition, honed both by a socialist education and western television, that "choice and credit" are intrinsic elements of those liberties and have possibly become their most tangible everyday expression for most citizens.[3] Of course, by the same token these avid shoppers could and should have known that lack of credit meant "social death" and that upon arrival in the West it took money to be a person.[4] The secret of citizenship, in any case, is "getting and spending" in the large and small dramas of everyday choice and their public display on television as the school of the consumer nation. These dramas articulate that ever larger numbers of people stake "a real portion of their personal identities and their quest for meaning—even their emotional satisfaction—on the search for and acquisition of goods" and in this process "make" society in acts of consumption.[5] This fortuitous concatenation of choice and credit in the mass act of consumption remade German history.

Because of their peculiar stake in shaping individual and collective identities and meanings, consumers are not simply a fact of life to be acknowledged as a matter of course but are historical subjects endowed with what social scientists call "agency."[6] Both common sense and high theory tell us that consumers are acting under all kinds of constraints and conceits. Yet, however much consumers may be fooled in the desire for and the act of consumption, they make things happen with vast and unanticipated consequences. They make their own his-

---

[2] John Carey, *The Intellectuals and the Masses: Pride and Prejudice among the Literary Intelligentsia 1880–1939* (Boston, 1992); Michael Ermarth, "Heidegger on Americanism: Ruinanz and the End of Modernity," *Modernism/modernity* 7 (2000): 379–400.

[3] John Benson, *The Rise of Consumer Society in Britain, 1880–1980* (London, 1994), 4.

[4] See the wonderful case study on eighteenth-century Leipzig by Robert Beachy, "Bankruptcy and Social Death: The Influence of Credit-Based Commerce on Cultural and Political Values," *Zeitsprünge. Forschungen zur frühen Neuzeit* 4 (2000): 329–43.

[5] Stearns, "Stages of Consumerism," 105.

[6] William H. Sewell, "A Theory of Structure: Duality, Agency, and Transformation," *American Journal of Sociology* 98 (1992): 1–29.

tory, as it were, and thus take on a role that in other ages was ascribed to elites or to great men. The idea of the consumer as sovereign is quite often invoked as an ironic gesture, but it should not be that way. Whether consumers actually liberate themselves in the act of consumption may be open to doubt, but the impact of consumption is, for all intents and purposes, huge.

The problem is that there are so many small and smallest acts of consumption, so many things to be consumed, so dazzling an array of conveying the meaning of goods, so elaborate a machinery to get them to the consumer, and so intricate a debate over the nature of consumer desire, that in the end we lose sight of what consuming subjects actually do and what they effect. Even seasoned historians confess that the notion of consumption currently in use is exceedingly polymorphous. It refers to, among others, terms such as commodification, spectatorship, commercial exchanges, and social welfare as well as to acts that involve the desire for and sale, purchase, and use of durable and non-durable goods, collective services, and images.[7] The concept of a consumer society is, if anything, even broader, encompassing the availability of an ample range of goods for a multiplicity of consumers, a system of mass media that allows for the collective attribution of meaning to objects, the differentiation of a world of objects into discrete spheres of taste, fashion, or style in which these objects and their meaning are appreciated and used as markers of distinction, and not the least a wholesale shift in the self-definition of society from production to consumption, from work to leisure, and, one might add, from producing destruction to creating waste.[8] What we encounter here is what one German historian calls a "quasi-totality."[9] It is easy to see how one can get absorbed in this paradigm, much as previous historians have been caught in equally totalizing technologies of production and destruction.

The salient question, however, is how consumers as the new sovereigns in their republic of choice and risk shaped and transformed German history in the course of the twentieth century. The German historian's temptation lies in reading the consumer revolution of the late twentieth century back in time and thus producing a history of the

[7] Victoria de Grazia, "Changing Consumption Regimes," in Victoria de Grazia and Ellen Furlough, eds., *The Sex of Things: Gender and Consumption in Historical Perspective* (Berkeley, 1996), 11–24.

[8] John Brewer and Roy Porter, eds., *Consumption and the World of Goods* (London, 1993), 1–15.

[9] This totality even non-plusses Hannes Siegrist, "Konsum, Kultur und Gesellschaft im modernen Europa," in Hannes Siegrist, Hartmut Kaelble and Jürgen Kocka, eds., *Europäische Konsumgeschichte. Zur Gesellschafts- und Kulturgeschichte des Konsums (18. bis 20. Jahrhundert)* (Frankfurt, 1997), 13–48, here 17.

fortuitous rise of a consumer society from small and impoverished beginnings to exuberant endings, from slow carriage-like cars to fast and
sleek ones, from dreams to reality. The act and event of consumption,
once mushed up and compacted into the historical skin of consumer
society, easily turns into a new teleology of history in which conspicu-
ous origins, the much touted "consumer revolution" of eighteenth-century Britain or nineteenth-century France, lead to Germany's "arrival
in the West" after many trials and tribulations.[10]

This history, the cultural historians' attempt at a master narrative,
does not capture the intricate architecture of an emergent consumer
society. This society was put together at different moments in time
from different materials and under changing circumstances. British
historians have pointed to the "orgy of spending" in mid-eighteenth
century as a consumer revolution.[11] The loud pleasures of Britain contrast quite sharply with the high civility and sensuous decorum of
urban Parisian life—by no means limited to a small elite, but emulated
by large segments of the populations—with its department stores and
taste professionals.[12] The latter contrasts with both the gaudy side of
the American consumer revolution and with the more familiar homogenizing couplet of all-gray and all-flat mass-production and mass-consumption.[13] None of this prepares for the mass-cultural frenzy of Berlin. If German historians have recently concluded that the rise of
consumption in the 1950s has nothing to do with any of the above and
surely not with Americanization, they reinforce the curious incongruity of what structurally appears to be the same phenomenon.[14] High
consumption, it seems, occurs in streaks, spurts, and reiterations, at

[10] Neil McKendrick, "Commercialization and the Economy," in Neil McKendrick,
John Brewer, and J. H. Plumb, eds., *The Birth of Consumer Society: The Commercialization
of Eighteenth-Century England* (London, 1982), 9–194, here 9–33: "The Consumer Revolution of Eighteenth-Century England"; Rosalind H. Williams, *Dream Worlds: Mass Consumption in Late Nineteenth-Century France* (Berkeley, 1982); and Axel Schildt, *Ankunft im
Westen. Ein Essay zur Erfolgsgeschichte der Bundesrepublik* (Frankfurt am Main, 1999).

[11] McKedrick, Brewer, and Plumb, *Birth of Consumer Society*, 9–33.

[12] In addition to Williams, *Dream Worlds*, see Leora Auslander, *Taste and Power: Fur-
nishing Modern France* (Berkeley, 1996); and Marie Louise Roberts, "Samson and Delilah
Revisited: The Politics of Women's Fashions in 1920s France," *American Historical Review*
98 (1993): 657–84.

[13] Jean-Christoph Agnew, "Coming Up for Air: Consumer Culture in Historical Per-
spective," in John Brewer and Roy Porter, eds., *Consumption and the World of Goods* (Lon-
don, 1993), 19–39; Jackson Lears, *Fables of Abundance: A Cultural History of Advertising in
America* (New York, 1994); Susan Strasser, Charles McGovern, and Matthias Judt, eds.
Getting and Spending: European and American Consumer Societies in the Twentieth Century
(New York, 1998).

[14] Axel Schildt, *Moderne Zeiten: Freizeit, Massenmedien und "Zeitgeist" in der Bundesrepublik der 50er Jahre* (Hamburg, 1995), 398–423.

different places, as orgies and cool calculations, but not really in an evolving history. While we may usefully create concepts such as a "consumer society," it does not pay to think of them as being created in a continuous process or even cut from the same cloth.[15] Instead, we find quick and intense spurts of consumption on the one hand and slow-downs and even collapses on the other.

We take measure of the architecture of German consumer society from three discrete vantage points, each one with its own temporal matrix. First, we look at a revolution of consumption that, oddly, most twentieth-century consumer-society historians and theorists tend to shun, assuming it over and done with when they begin—the revolution in food consumption.[16] In the long view, of course, they are right: The recurring scarcities and food riots have become a matter of the more distant past or far-away places.[17] But at close range, we still encounter moments of intense and general hunger and, indeed, starvation in the twentieth century that matter intensely in the making of German consumer society. Hunger and starvation generally retained a lurking presence in an otherwise bounteous "world of goods"—although attempts to put them together remain rare.[18] For German history, the linkage of hunger and affluence both as reality and as mentality—and of one's own affluence and other peoples' hunger—is imperative, because one cannot be understood without the other. For the longest time, German dreams of consumption and consumer society were born from the nightmares of hunger and want.[19]

Second, historians rightly point to the late twentieth century as the moment of a consumer revolution in Germany, but find it difficult to establish a genealogy of this moment of transformation. It takes a leap of imagination to compare late twentieth-century consumer society with its precursor, the Wilhelmine worlds of high consumption and luxury on the one hand and of its generous household budgets of the working-class on the other. When and where these episodes of high consumption burst onto the scene, however, they radically challenge the way that society constitutes itself. They transform nations. The problem is how we can conceive of these mutations engendered by

[15] What can be done is demonstrated quite ably by Ariane Stihler, *Die Entstehung des modernen Konsums. Darstellung und Erklärungsansätze* (Berlin, 1998).

[16] Sidney Mintz, "The Changing Roles of Food in the Study of Consumption," in *Consumption and the World of Goods*, 261–73.

[17] Wilhelm Abel, *Agricultural Fluctuations in Europe from the Thirteenth to the Twentieth Centuries*, trans. Olive Ordish (New York, 1980).

[18] Mike Davis, *Late Victorian Holocausts: El Niño Famines and the Making of the Third World* (London, 2001).

[19] Michael Wildt, *Am Beginn der "Konsumgesellschaft". Mangelerfahrung, Lebenshaltung, Wohlstandshoffnung in Westdeutschland in den fünziger Jahren* (Hamburg, 1994).

consumption. Moreover, what is the relation between a Germany created from the spirit of consumption and the other Germanys, created
from the spirit of production or destruction? It is charming to think, as
some historians do, that rock 'n' roll may have had something to do
with the emergence of a new Germany, which is to say that German
identity and destiny really could be had for a song and dance.[20] But
the question is how we get from one to the other.

For the most part, though, historians have focused on quite different
issues. They have focused on the high aspirations, dreams, and utopias
of a coming age of mass-culture, so brilliantly observed and foretold
by Siegfried Kracauer in his Weimar writings.[21] At the same time they
attempt to wrest some sense of a mass-consumer society from times
that are not generally known for their high spirited consumption. To
be sure, actual consumption in the 1930s, 1940s, and 1950s cannot be
underestimated, but the striking thing about this period, between the
1910s and the 1950s is not its world of commodities but the explosive
expansion and the extraordinary investment into controlling mass culture or, if one so wishes, the mass consumption of culture. The intensity of these conflicts merits attention, all the more since Weimar, the
Third Reich, and East and West Germany created radically contrary
regimes of consumption. Actual mass consumption in Germany began
to flourish when consumers emerged from these regulatory regimes.

Thus, we have three quite different stories of consumption, all
spliced into the course of twentieth-century German history—two
brief, but sharp spasms of extreme hunger, a protracted period of intense struggles over regimes of mass consumption and leisure, and
streaks of high consumerism at the beginning and the end of the century. If taken together, these otherwise dissimilar and discontinuous
moments suggest, at the very least, the centrality of consumption for
public and private life, which is not fully reflected in history and historiography.[22] The force of social, political, and cultural struggles over
consumption suggests, moreover, that there is something to the claim
that the act of consumption and the norms and values that came with
it transformed society. While this argument may seem self-evident
from the vantage point of the late twentieth century, it is a very tall
claim to make in view of the German powers of production and destruction. But it is not, as we shall see, a frivolous claim.

[20] Uta G. Poiger, *Jazz, Rock, and Rebels: Cold War Politics and American Culture in a Divided Germany* (Berkeley, 2000).
[21] See especially Siegfried Kracauer, *The Mass Ornament: Weimar Essays*, trans. Thomas
Y. Levin (Cambridge, Mass., 1995). Susan Buck-Morss, *Dreamworld and Catastrophe: The
Passing of Mass Utopia in East and West* (Cambridge, Mass., 2000).
[22] Confino and Koshar, "Regimes of Consumer Culture."

Freedom from Want and the
German Order of Things

During the second half of the nineteenth century, a revolution of consumption began to take shape that came full circle during the second half of the twentieth century. Scientific and industrial innovations in food production ushered in an age of plenty that attained an impossible dream—freedom from the most elemental want, that is, want of food.[23] The abundance of food most succinctly characterizes the breakthrough and eventual assurance of mass welfare in the industrial world. In this welfare of the "little people" we may discern moments and memories—and also, projections and utopias—of the idea of happiness of the many, a tangible sense of well-being and security, the very foundation on which modern consumer society is built. Food consumption, in turn, mirrored the general conditions of the emergent consumer society, for the selection, preparation, and consumption of food has traditionally been a source of pleasure, status, and the identity of communities.[24] Only when food was subsumed into a grander world of goods and services and became one among many commodities do we reach the apex of the consumer revolution.[25]

Yet throughout the first half of the twentieth century hunger and indeed starvation remained a profound social reality.[26] While hunger was never fully eradicated as a condition affecting the urban and rural poor, it became a general calamity at the end and in the aftermath of the two grand wars, between 1915 and 1923 and between 1944 and 1953, affecting a vast majority of Germans and reaching its nadir be-

---

[23] Hans Jürgen Teuteberg and Günter Wiegelmann, eds., *Der Wandel der Nahrungsgewohnheiten unter dem Einfluss der Industrialisierung* (Göttingen, 1972); Wilhelm Abel, *Massenarmut und Hungerkrisen im vorindustriellen Europa. Versuch einer Synopse* (Hamburg, 1974); and Daniel Roche, *Histoire des choses banales: Naissance de la consommation dans les sociétés traditionelles (XVIIe–XIXe siècle)* (Paris, 1997).

[24] Alois Wierlacher, Gerhard Neumann, and Hans Jürgen Teuteberg, eds., *Kulturthema Essen. Ansichten und Problemfelder* (Berlin, 1993); Hans Jürgen Teuteberg, Gerhard Neumann, and Alois Wierlacher, eds., *Essen und kulturelle Identität. Europäische Perspektiven* (Berlin, 1997).

[25] Hans Jürgen Teuteberg, "Der Verzehr von Nahrungsmitteln in Deutschland pro Kopf und Jahr seit Beginn der Industrialisierung (1850–1975)," *Archiv für Sozialgeschichte* 29 (1979): 331–88.

[26] Alf Lüdtke, "Hunger in der Großen Depression: Hungererfahrung und Hungerpolitik am Ende der Weimarer Republik," *Archiv für Sozialgeschichte* 27 (1987): 145–76, is a noteworthy exception. We are much better informed about the nineteenth century. See Christoph Sachsse and Florian Tennstedt, *Geschichte der Armenfürsorge in Deutschland. Vom Spätmittelalter bis zum Ersten Weltkrieg* (Stuttgart, 1980); and Norbert Preußer, *Not macht erfinderisch. Überlebensstrategien der Armutsbevölkerung seit 1807* (Munich, 1989).

tween 1917–1919 and 1946–1948. These are short time-spans in a person's life and in the history of a century, all the more since during those years actual conditions varied according to seasons and vagaries of distribution. But in moments of subsistence crises, time stretches forever and the body's memory of deprivation never ceases. In terms of conditioning attitudes and experience, these moments had a lasting impact. The "dream of having enough to eat"—without, one should add, letting other people starve—profoundly shaped the order of things in Germany.[27]

Hunger and famine conditions tend to be woven into a heavy blanket of incomprehension and forgetting on the one hand and denial and justification on the other. Consider the much debated question of whether domestic food production, plus minimal imports, could have fed hungry Germans in World War I. This debate is inseparable from the issue of the Allied blockade, which lasted into July 1919 and was set up with both the intent to undercut German food supply and the more dubious strategic aim of starving Germany into submission.[28] The strategy did not work. If Germans starved these food scarcities are, nonetheless, now commonly attributed to a horrendously inefficient German requisitioning and distribution system.[29] Starvation conditions, inasmuch as they existed, were the result both of bad politics and of food panics, or so it seems.[30] This is quite a different story if compared to German claims that castigated the illegality of British starvation warfare and made the Lords of the Admiralty into deranged baby-killers and genocidal maniacs.[31]

None of this debate, however, captures the reality of the German food crisis.[32] Starting with 1916/17 and peaking in 1918/19, famine-

[27] Michael Wildt, *Der Traum vom Sattwerden. Hunger und Protest, Schwarzmarkt und Selbsthilfe in Hamburg 1945–1948* (Hamburg, 1986).

[28] Avner Offer, *The First World War: An Agrarian Interpretation* (New York, 1990).

[29] Robert G. Moeller, *German Peasants and Agrarian Politics, 1914–1924: The Rhineland and Westphalia* (Chapel Hill, 1986).

[30] Belinda J. Davis, *Home Fires Burning: Food, Politics, and Everyday Life in World War I Berlin* (Chapel Hill, 2000).

[31] Werner Schäffer, *Krieg gegen Frauen und Kinder. Englands Hungerblockade gegen Deutschland, 1914–1920* (Berlin, 1940); Ernst von Kiezell, *Weltkrieg und Bevölkerungspolitik* (Munich, 1941)

[32] Anne Roerkohl, *Hungerblockade und Heimatfront. Die kommunale Lebensmittelversorgung in Westfalen während des Ersten Weltkrieges* (Stuttgart, 1991) and her more general essay, "Die Lebensmittelversorgung während des Ersten Weltkrieges im Spannungsfeld kommunaler und staatlicher Maßnahmen," in Hans Jürgen Teuteberg, ed., *Durchbruch zum modernen Massenkonsum. Lebensmittelmärkte und Lebensmittelqualität im Städtewachstum des Industriezeitalters* (Münster, 1991), 309–70. See also Gunther Mai, " 'Wenn der Mensch Hunger hat, hört alles auf'. Wirtschaftliche und soziale Ausgangsbedingungen der Weimarer Republik," in Werner Abelshauser, ed., *Die Weimarer Republik als Wohlfahrts-*

like conditions spread through most urban and industrial areas like the Ruhr, Berlin, and Silesia. Episodes of extreme scarcity occurred sporadically for significant social groups throughout the entire period between 1915 and 1923. These extremely severe conditions were the result of a multiplicity of factors, which include the severing of Germany from the international distribution system, the serious decline of German agricultural production in the latter parts and the aftermath of the war, notorious inequalities in distribution, major blunders of agricultural officials (for instance, the famous slaughter of pigs in 1915), and major transportation crises.[33] Yet despite wide-spread starvation, few people actually starved to death. There was enough food, in one sense, because there were always ways to stretch meager resources—legally or illegally, through self-provisioning, the black market, or theft.[34] More significantly, the much maligned communal provisioning system did provide for the most basic needs—thin as the soup from soup kitchens and "stretched" as ersatz bread were. Communal services maintained a floor that roughly coincided with what nutritional scientists had identified as *Existenzminimum*—one of the quintessential contributions of German nutritional science to the revolution in consumption.[35] What poor relief provided was not enough to live on but too much to die for—which is why the significantly rising mortality among civilians in 1918/19 was due to hunger-related diseases and illnesses (as well as to the influenza pandemic) rather than to outright starvation.[36]

Conditions after 1945 were, if anything, worse, but the effect was much the same.[37] Again, with the exception of the Eastern territories,

---

staat. *Zum Verhältnis von Wirtschafts- und Sozialpolitik in der Industriegesellschaft* (Stuttgart, 1987), 33–62 Lothar Burchardt, "The Impact of the War Economy on the Civilian Population of Germany during the First and the Second World Wars," in Wilhelm Deist, ed., *The German Military in the Age of Total War* (Leamington Spa, 1985), 111–36.

[33] Joe Lee, "German Administrators and Agriculture during the First World War," in Jay M. Winter, ed., *War and Economic Development* (Cambridge,UK, 1975).

[34] Martin H. Geyer, *Verkehrte Welt. Revolution, Inflation und Moderne, München 1914–1924* (Göttingen, 1998), 167–204

[35] See Dana Simmons, "The Minimal Frenchmen: Defining Standards of Living in France, 1850–1958," (Ph.D. dissertation, University of Chicago, forthcoming), with an excursus on the German *Existenzminimum*.

[36] The same argument can be made for the milk supply for babies, which was sufficient (in part because of the dramatic decline in the birth rate), although older children apparently suffered grievously. It seems that Vienna may have been the one city where this minimum floor could not be provided. Maureen Healy, "Vienna Falling: Total War and Everyday Life, 1914–1918" (Ph.D. dissertation, Chicago, 1999).

[37] We are quite well informed about the conditions after 1945. See Karl-Heinz Rothenberger, *Die Hungerjahre nach dem Zweiten Weltkrieg. Ernährungs- und Landwirtschaft in Rheinland-Pfalz, 1945–1950* (Boppard, 1980); Gabriele Stüber, *Der Kampf gegen den Hunger*

famine-like conditions rarely lead to death.[38] Food supplies reached a nadir between late 1946 and mid-1948. In contrast to 1918/19, it became a national calamity and, although the countryside still fared better than the towns and cities, rural areas were also affected because of the massive influx of evacuees and refugees.[39] Conditions in early 1947 were devastating, with mass starvation an omnipresent reality. Still, the basic and now centralized provisioning system continued to operate and covered even the lowest ranks in the rationing system in a, just barely, minimal way.[40] But this time, it was not the rationing system that provided the *Existenzminimum*. If Germans survived, it was the result of the philanthropy of the victors, including the Russians.[41] While Germans were panicked by fantasies about the Allies starving the nation to death, they were in fact saved by the Allies.[42]

The provisioning efforts of the Allies, meager as they may have appeared in the face of calamity, stood in sharp contrast to the deliberate starvation politics on the part of the Germans (and Austrians) in both world wars. In World War I, the war between armies turned into a war of starvation against the civilian population in the Russian military zone, in Austrian-occupied Serbia, and in northeastern Europe, occupied by the German Army (*Oberost*).[43] A harsh requisitioning system was made worse by massive plunder and pillage, which was exacerbated by a multi-front civil war. What in 1918 could be observed as random, though pervasive acts of German pillage and extortion became a systematic and deliberate strategy of denuding entire areas of all foodstuffs and of destroying and degrading land, water, and facilities.[44] The result was famine and mass death deliberately induced by German action. In this, the situation in eastern Europe and Russia also

---

1945–1950. Die Ernährungslage in der britischen Zone Deutschlands, insbesondere in Schleswig-Holstein und Hamburg (Neumünster, 1984); Günter J. Trittel, *Hunger und Politik. Ernährungskrise in der Bizone, 1945–1949* (Frankfurt, 1990); Michael Wildt, *Der Traum vom Sattwerden: Hunger und Protest, Schwarzmarkt und Selbsthilfe in Hamburg 1945–1948* (Hamburg, 1986); and Rainer Gries, *Die Rationen-Gesellschaft. Versorgungskampf und Vergleichsmentalität. Leipzig, München und Köln nach dem Kriege* (Münster, 1991).

[38] Ruth Kibelka, *Ostpreußens Schicksalsjahre 1944–1948* (Berlin, 2000).

[39] Stübner, *Kampf gegen den Hunger*; and Rothenberger, *Hungerjahre*.

[40] Rainer Gries, *Die Rationen-Gesellschaft. Versorgungskampf und Vergleichsmentalität: Leipzig, München und Köln nach dem Kriege* (Münster, 1991).

[41] John E. Farquharson, *The Western Allies and the Politics of Food: Agrarian Management in Postwar Germany* (Leamington Spa, 1985).

[42] To my knowledge, there is no good study on these starvation fantasies.

[43] Vejas G. Liulevicius, *War Land on the Eastern Front: Culture, National Identity and German Occupation in World War I* (Cambridge, Mass., 2000). See also Jonathan Gumz, "The Habsburg Occupation of Serbia, 1915–1918 " (Ph.D. dissertation, Chicago, forthcoming).

[44] Christian Gerlach, *Krieg, Ernährung, Völkermord. Forschungen zur deutschen Vernichtungspolitik im Zweiten Weltkrieg* (Hamburg, 1998); and Gustavo Conti and Horst Gies,

differed significantly from the widespread famine conditions in European overseas empires.[45] These catastrophic situations worldwide do not diminish the very real hunger in Germany, but they highlight the privilege of German mass-survival despite calamity.

The debates on the extent of food scarcities in Germany have overshadowed the discussion of the architecture of the rationing system that circumscribed access to food, as well as the political and social imaginary that at once informed it and was formed by it. German ideas of a consumer society were profoundly shaped by this imaginary, as a brief survey of the consumer in the rationing system, food production, and marketing suggests.

The rationing regime was rather more comprehensive and total in World War II and its aftermath than in World War I.[46] It was always complemented (less so in World War II than in World War I) by access to the open market and, for that matter, the illegal black market. In fact, most historians agree that the rationing system, to guarantee survival, required poor-relief and philanthropy, the black-market, and a scratching, clawing, and prostituting system of self-help.[47] But inasmuch as the rationing system established basic access to food, it shaped a regime of inclusions and exclusions and a system of social stratification that overturned nineteenth-century, bourgeois notions of privilege and status in German society.[48]

The unequivocal winners of rationing were all those who never had to enter the system. These were above all the so-called self-suppliers who lived mostly in rural areas, deepening the division and mutual suspicion between city and countryside.[49] "Bourgeois" wealth still mattered, inasmuch as the independently wealthy, among them the large and small war profiteers, could afford black-market prices. It is abundantly evident, however, that the truly privileged were large organizations, especially the armed forces and industrial corporations. The armed forces obtained a far greater share of foodstuffs and supplies than was their due, and large corporations established an extensive

Brot, Butter, Kanonen. Die Ernährungswirtschaft in Deutschland unter der Diktatur Hitlers (Berlin, 1997).

[45] Paul H. Kratoska, ed., *Food Supplies and the Japanese Occupation in South-East Asia* (New York, 1998); and Arup Maharatna, *The Demography of Famines: An Indian Historical Perspective* (Delhi, 1996); John Iliffe, *Famine in Zimbabwe, 1890–1960* (Gweru, 1990).

[46] The best study on the subject is Gries, *Rationen-Gesellschaft*.

[47] Geyer, *Verkehrte Welt*; Willi A. Boelcke, *Der Schwarzmarkt 1945–1948. Vom Überleben nach dem Kriege* (Braunschweig, 1986); and Wildt, *Traum vom Sattwerden*.

[48] Martin H. Geyer, "Teuerungsproteste, Konsumentenpolitik und soziale Gerechtigkeit während der Inflation," *Archiv für Sozialgeschichte* 30 (1990): 181–215.

[49] Benjamin Ziemann, *Front und Heimat. Ländliche Kriegserfahrung im südlichen Bayern* (Essen, 1997).

system of storage for provisioning either their canteens or their workers directly. In World War I, the discrepancy between institutional consumers and non-self-supplying civilians was egregious.[50] In World War II, the gap seems to have diminished somewhat, but in the Third Reich one has to figure in the extensive food-hoards of NS organizations, such as the ones by *Gauleiter* as the regional defense officials.[51] In any case, privileged access to food and consumer commodities accrued with corporate and military power. It profited clients, workers, and soldiers, and maintained the old-style good life for elites such as officers and managers.[52]

On the other side were all those who were thrown out of the system, but who were not self-suppliers. In World War I these were mostly people who were institutionalized. Among the best known cases were patients in mental asylums, but general hospitals and other institutions, such as prisons, appear to have been affected as well.[53] Among these groups we find an extraordinarily high mortality rate, attributable, at least in part, to a system of triage that condemned to death those who were considered incurable or incorrigible. The institutional nature of this politics of starvation and its subsequent rationalization as the elimination of "life not worth living" are rightly seen as the threshold toward a deliberate politics of annihilation in World War II.[54] In the Third Reich, we find this regime refined into a science of administered differentiation that allotted various outcast groups a negative minimum graded to the point of deliberate starvation to death.[55] This world of the excluded was the opposite of the world of corporate provisioning as the main source of relative well-being.

In between "haves" and "have-nots" we find the vast majority of (non-self-supplying) consumers. In the mind of one of the most promi-

[50] N. P. Howard, "The Social and Political Consequences of the Allied Food Blockade of Germany, 1918–19," *German History* 11 (1993): 161–88.

[51] Corni, *Brot, Butter, Kanonen*, 555–82.

[52] As a result, food protests, particularly in the Navy, resembled the meat and beer protests of the prewar period and were curiously anachronistic. But so were the dining habits in the officer messes in the rear and on ships. The privileges of the armed forces preserved older conflicts in which wealth and status (rather than survival) were at issue.

[53] References are scattered throughout Roerkohl, *Hungerblockade*. See also Michael Burleigh, *Death and Deliverance: "Euthanasia" in Germany ca. 1900–1945* (New York, 1994).

[54] Karl Binding and Alfred Hoche, *Die Freigabe der Vernichtung lebensunwerten Lebens. Ihr Maß und ihre Form* (Leipzig, 1920), translated by Walter E. Wright, Patrick G. Derr, and Robert Salomon as *Permitting the Destruction of Unworthy Life: Its Extent and Form* (Terre Haute, Ind., 1992).

[55] Herbert Obenaus, "Hunger und Überleben in den nationalsozialistischen Konzentrationslagern (1938–1945)," in Manfred Gailus and Heinrich Volkmann, eds., *Der Kampf um das tägliche Brot. Nahrungsmangel, Versorgungspolitik und Protest 1770–1990* (Opladen,

nent postwar German sociologists, Helmut Schelsky, this group of average consumers, *Normalverbraucher* as they were labeled in World War II and its aftermath, was the well-spring of an undifferentiated middle-class society in Germany.[56] This theory is as wrong as it is revealing. The fact that consumers were made into a distinct social group in the context of rationing is, of course, worth our attention because it suggests that the state, as opposed to the market, established the "consumer" as a discrete population. The irony is, however, that this consumer formed an underclass of "inferior means" consisting of non-working housewives, children, the handicapped, the sick, and the old.[57] The mere consumers with their "graveyard ration card" were at the bottom of a tiered system of supplementary provisioning that unequivocally favored those who worked.[58] While this system of division was still quite underdeveloped in World War I and while the GDR adopted its own, Soviet-inspired system (which honored function in the labor process rather than physical labor and, hence, privileged a labor aristocracy), the basic fact of the matter is that the rationing system privileged the producing society over the non-producing one (with mothers in the former group), and, with the exception of the GDR, physical labor over function. While inegalitarian and grossly anachronistic in its emphasis on physical labor, this rationing society was so readily championed as the new middle-class society because of its bias against inherited wealth and meritocracy and in favor of the working man, *Otto Normalverbraucher*. This was not exactly a leveled consumer society, but rather the *Volksgemeinschaft* that Germans had come to envision as a homogeneous totality. It is ironic to contemplate that the Soviet Union brought back intelligence and function, that is, meritocracy, into this system but proved incapable of delivering the goods.[59] In any case, when East German workers struck in 1953, they did not challenge the system of rationing but revolted against the inability of the GDR to live up to their vision of the *Volk*.[60] In this, the 1953 uprising against the GDR regime resembles the strikes

---

1994), 361–76. The differentiation is captured remarkably well in Boris Shub, *Starvation over Europe (Made in Germany): A Documented Record 1943* (New York, 1943).

[56] Helmut Schelsky, "Die Bedeutung des Schichtungsbegriffes für die Analyse der gegenwärtigen deutschen Gesellschaft [1953]," in Helmut Schelsky, ed., *Auf der Suche nach Wirklichkeit* (Düsseldorf, 1965), 331–36.

[57] Davis, *Home Fires Burning*, 48–75, 237–38.

[58] Gries, *Rationen-Gesellschaft*, 93–106

[59] Kaminsky, *Wohlstand, Schönheit, Glück*, 15–35.

[60] Katherine Pence, " 'You as Woman Will Understand': Consumption, Gender and the Relationship between State and Citizenry in the GDR's Crisis of 17. June 1953," *German History* 19 (2001): 218–52.

against the Wilhelmine regime in 1917/18. Both were strikes in which the state was challenged to supply food for quality labor. Contrary to Schelsky, this exchange was hierarchical rather than egalitarian, but it was considered just.

The imperative of food provisioning also emerged as the main force in the reorganization of food production. Seen from a late nineteenth-century vantage point, the future of Germany lay with an increasingly sophisticated and differentiated as well as progressively globalized division of labor. Food production and marketing were among the main promoters of globalization.[61] This bright and shiny future, however, did not happen. Instead, we find a turn to self-sufficiency, accompanied by the rationalization and industrialization in domestic agriculture and food-production—so that at the end of the twentieth century the European Community had the most highly developed factory-style food system anywhere in the world.[62]

This turn to self-sufficiency was initiated by agricultural interests against the vehement protests of consumer advocates.[63] Nonetheless, it was completed by consumers turning to self-sufficiency in the wake of World War I, a position which was re-ascertained in the post–World War II "market order."[64] This latter (West German) order placed a premium on the stability and sustainability of domestic food supply for the "average consumer" at affordable, if distinctly above world-market

---

[61] Gertrud Helling, *Nahrungsmittel—Produktion und Weltaußenhandel seit Anfang des 19. Jahrhunderts* (Berlin, 1977).

[62] Paul Brassley, *Agricultural Economics and the CAP: An Introduction* (Oxford, 1997).

[63] The problem was that self-sufficiency at affordable prices was only to be had at the cost of relentless rationalization and industrialization that transformed the German countryside, albeit in different ways in East and West, more radically than anything the German lands had seen since the agricultural revolution in the late eighteenth and early nineteenth centuries. To forestall these radical consequences of self-sufficiency, the German farm lobby (and particularly estate owners) instead sided with the nationalists, who had ever since the late nineteenth century waged a relentless campaign for expanding living space because they feared that available land could not sustain the German population and that globalization made Germany vulnerable. They instead envisioned the preservation of agriculture, both as economic and political force, and of a rural German way of life through imperial expansion, settlement, and the consolidation of a vast rural hinterland in the East. See Hans Rosenberg, *Grosse Depression und Bismarckzeit* (Berlin, 1967); Jens Flemming, *Landwirtschaftliche Interessen und Demokratie. Ländliche Gesellschaft, Agrarverbände und Staat 1890–1925* (Bonn, 1978); and Hans Erich Volkmann, "Landwirtschaft und Ernährung in Hitlers Deutschland 1939–1945," *Militärgeschichtliche Mitteilungen* 35 (1984): 9–74.

[64] Christoph Nonn, "Vom Konsumentenprotest zum Konsens. Lebensmittelverbraucher und Agrarpolitik in Deutschland 1900–1955," in Hartmut Berghoff, ed., *Konsumpolitik. Die Regulierung des privaten Verbrauchs im 20. Jahrhundert* (Göttingen, 1999), 23–45.

prices. It was deliberately set against the anarchy and fluctuations of global commodity markets. While West Germany expanded into the Common Market, with its French and Italian agricultural hinterlands and its Dutch food factories, the GDR attempted to achieve the same end with rather more mixed results in Eastern Europe.[65] In both cases, the vision of a global division of labor that consumer advocates had favored at the turn of the last century disappeared never to return. The brief famine-like episodes had left their indelible trace. The quest for order and stability of food supplies, the profound distrust of international markets beyond government control—these are the foundation on which the postwar German commodity order was built. It is—and this is the effect of hunger—more of an "order" than a "market," and the consumers have been willing to swallow all manner of dysfunctions, such as butter mountains, milk lakes, and fruit spoilage, because their experience suggested (or did so until the BSE scandal in the new millennium) better to be safe with the state than sorry with unregulated markets. The German order of things, at least as far as agricultural commodities are concerned, has come to rest on the foundations of a closed system.

The distrust of markets found its main outlet in distribution and retailing. In view of the late-blooming love for farmers' markets, artisan producer-retailers, and fruit vendors, it is worth remembering how ready consumers were to trash these shops, literally and metaphorically. Historians of World War I, especially, relate extraordinary stories about the abuse heaped on retailers as vile, price-gouging shop-keepers and venomous market-women.[66] There was no love lost between consumers and retailers. What consumers objected to was the principle of a market economy as unreliable and untrustworthy, for catering to those with money rather than need and thus reinforcing instead of abolishing non-work-related social hierarchies.[67] In the wake of World War I, with markets partially restored, the situation got worse rather than better. Protests of panicked consumers escalated into self-help riots that catapulted Germany into a "war" over food, with farmers

---

[65] Ulrich Kluge, *Vierzig Jahre Agrarpolitik in der Bundesrepublik Deutschland* (Hamburg, 1989); and Arnd Bauerkämper, "Junkerland in Bauernhand?" in his *Durchführung, Auswirkungen und Stellenwert der Bodenreform in der Sowjetischen Besatzungszone* (Stuttgart, 1996), 78–102.

[66] Davis, *Home Fires Burning*; and Martin H. Geyer, "Teuerungsproteste, Konsumentenpolitik und soziale Gerechtigkeit während der Inflation," *Archiv für Sozialgeschichte* 30 (1990): 181–215.

[67] On the development of the retail market, see Uwe Spiekermann, *Basis der Konsumgesellschaft. Entstehung und Entwicklung des modernen Kleinhandels in Deutschland 1850–1914* (Munich, 1999).

arming posses and vigilante groups, and hordes of consumers pillaging hapless farms and shops. The reintroduction of the market led into a crisis of the state.[68]

In view of these circumstances it is surprising that some historians would consider the robust activities of getting what it takes to survive by whatever means in the post–World War II world of black markets and self-help as the German "curriculum for the postwar" market-oriented consumer-society.[69] Occasionally, it seems, even historians can get caught slumming, especially if Fassbinder's Maria Braun (Hanna Schygula) can be imagined as going to the market with them.[70] Still, the question is when and where Germans learned to trust the market. Despite its allure as the wild and wicked origin of consumer society, the black market world of self-help was not the solution. Nor did the tiny minority of German officials who vigorously argued for marketization, foremost Ludwig Ehrhard, change the mind of the Germans, even after the huge "hunger marches" with their demand for Allied provisioning had died down.[71] The surprise effect of the currency reform—shops full with goods—has often been described as the turning point, but it rather opened up a gap between the haves and the have-nots and, thus, encouraged a return to the idea that markets were for the wealthy.[72] On the other hand, the American "Raisin Bombers" that supplied Berlin are usually underestimated in their symbolic, as opposed to material, significance. They symbolized what the German "average consumer" had wanted ever since 1916—not a market culture, but a potent authority to guarantee subsistence. The Americans did something the Germans had never been able to achieve: They took away the deep insecurity over consumption. In actual fact, the Marshall Plan, the currency reform, and the emergent market order of West Germany achieved this end, but it took a long time for emotions to

---

[68] Gerald D. Feldman, *The Great Disorder: Politics, Economics, and Society in the German Inflation, 1914–1924* (New York, 1993).

[69] Lutz Niethammer, "Privat-Wirtschaft. Erinnerungsfragmente einer anderen Umerziehung," in Lutz Niethammer, ed., *'Hinterher merkt man, daß es richtig war, daß es schiefgegangen ist'. Nachkriegserfahrungen im Ruhrgebiet* (Berlin; Bonn, 1983), 17–105. Michael Wildt, "Hunger, Schwarzmarkt und Rationen—der heimliche Lehrplan der Nachkriegszeit," in Detlef J. K. Peukert, ed., *Improvisierter Neubeginn. Hamburg 1943–1953* (Hamburg, 1989), 46–55.

[70] Rainer Werner Fassbinder, dir., "Die Ehe der Maria Braun" [The Marriage of Maria Braun], Germany, 1978, color, 102m.

[71] Christoph Kleßmann and Peter Friedemann, *Streiks und Hungermärsche im Ruhrgebiet 1946–1948* (Frankfurt, 1977); and Paul Erker *Ernährungskrise und Nachkriegsgesellschaft. Bauern und Arbeiterschaft in Bayern 1943–1953* (Stuttgart, 1990), esp. 348–59, 391–404.

[72] Paul Erker, "Hunger und sozialer Konflikt in der Nachkriegszeit," *Der Kampf um das tägliche Brot. Nahrungsmangel, Versorgungspolitik und Protest 1770–1990*, 392–408.

catch up with actuality. The realization that markets would provide consumer goods, that retailers actually wanted to sell them, and that artisans might offer services for good money, took a very long time to sink in. The idea of markets as just, providing access to commodities for a vast majority of people; as equal, ratifying the exchange of commodities for labor rather than for inherited wealth and status; and above all as reliable, supplying necessities at affordable prices for the masses—all this came as a genuine "miracle" to unbelieving Germans.

Still, habits and suspicions died hard. If West Germans came to trust the market, if they moved on from satisfying their hunger to consumer durables, their suspicion of commodities faded even more slowly than their distrust in the market. The main obstacle to the emergence of a consumer society was the resilient fear of being cheated by commodities, and that cheap goods were junk. The clearest expression of this search for quality goods—an intriguing analogue to "quality work"—came with the efflorescence of a culture of brand names that were the main beneficiaries of the postwar consumer boom.[73] German commodity culture favored such brands because they guaranteed predictable value (at a higher price), and the emergent mass consumer of the 1950s and 1960s wanted nothing more than security and predictability.[74] They came to buy what they knew and, at least initially, expected it to last for an eternity. Quality was everything. It was not until this idea went out the window in the 1970s that the German consumer revolution could truly start.

This is the moment to return to the mid-nineteenth-century revolution of consumption to see what became of it. In a way, the historiography suggests a telling answer. The latter started out with the "transformation of consumption habits under the impact of industrialization" (1972), segued into "Eating and Cultural Identity" (1997), and ends, for the time being, with "Eating and Quality of Life."[75] This sequence reflects a revolution in taste and desire and a discovery of pleasure that was going on subterraneously throughout the long twentieth century but took off only in the 1960s and 1970s to remake German identity—

---

[73] Wildt, *Vom kleinen Wohlstand*, 149–63; Griess, *Rationen-Gesellschaft*, 323–35; and the forthcoming magnum opus by Victoria de Grazia, *An All-Consuming Power: How American Market Culture Won over European Commercial Civilization*, especially the chapter "Big Brand Goods: How Marketing Dispossessed the Old Market Place" (presented at Modern European History Workshop, University of Chicago).

[74] Hans Braun,"Das Streben nach 'Sicherheit' in den 50er Jahren. Soziale und politische Ursachen und Erscheinungsweisen," *Archiv für Sozialgeschichte* 18 (1978): 279–306.

[75] Teuteberg, *Wandel der Nahrungswohnheiten*, Teuteberg, *Essen und kulturelle Indentität*, Gerhard Neumann, Alois Wierlacher, and A. Wild, eds., *Essen und Lebensqualität. Natur- und Kulturwissenschaften im Gespräch* (Frankfurt am Main, 2001).

literally so, because only now regional differences in consumption gave way to a new national and transnational (and increasingly status-based) variety of foods.[76] How truly radical this change was can be judged by the fact that even (some) Italians and French taste-makers have now come to warm up to the idea of Germany as a gourmet nation. Rumor has it, moreover, that even in Berlin one can finally eat well.[77] More importantly, however, the average consumer has developed a taste for variety and the new, and the supermarkets, once sites for the cheap or functional and always the predictable commodity, now cater to these desires. Even mass-chains nowadays sell novelty and adventure.

This late twentieth-century regime of taste and pleasure has come a long way from the days of hunger and want. But it is even farther away from what Germans had craved when a consumer culture appeared within their reach at the beginning of the twentieth century. What we encounter here is a revolution of experience and expectations that overthrew very deeply held ideas about the reliable order of things in a just society that was anchored in the dire memories of want and privation.

German Dream Time: Mass Culture Between Public Spectacle and Domesticity

In view of the late-twentieth-century experience we might be inclined at this point "to go shopping" in order to find the emergent German consumer and trace the origins of German consumer society. Yet, despite a dazzling world of commodities, the way to consumer society led—in Germany more so than in other advanced industrial countries—through the remaking of older forms of popular culture as well as elements of high culture into mass culture. The mass consumption of culture or, if one so wishes, of cultural products, reached its apogee between the 1910s and the 1950s, folding into the mass-consumption

[76] Michael Wildt, "Abschied von der 'Freßwelle' oder die Pluralisierung des Geschmacks. Essen in der Bundesrepublik Deutschland der fünfziger Jahre," *Kulturthema Essen*, 211–225; an abbreviated English version appeared as "Plurality of Taste: Food and Consumption in West Germany during the 1950s," *History Workshop Journal* 39 (1995): 23–41. Uwe Spiekermann, "Regionale Verzehrsunterschiede als Problem der Wirtschafts- und Sozialgeschichte im Deutschen Reich," *Essen und kulturelle Identität*, 247–82.

[77] Wolfgang Protzner, ed., *Vom Hungerwinter zum kulinarischen Schlaraffenland. Aspekte einer Kulturgeschichte des Essens in der Bundesrepublik Deutschland* (Wiesbaden, 1987).

of commodities and an emergent consumer society in West Germany in the 1960s, with the East Germans following suit in the 1970s.[78]

The rise of mass culture is most commonly associated with the advent of the mass media and their technologies—the rotary printing press, cinema, radio, and television—which, in overcoming the boundaries of place and time, are said to have created the conditions for a mass existence beyond class, gender, and regional (confessional and ethnic) divisions.[79] The rise of mass culture is further connected with new forms of mass entertainment, such as dancing, revues, soccer, racing, or athletics, which had the dual capacity of accommodating people as participants and spectators, although mass audiences became the prime target.[80] As a third element we can list the gamut of more private activities that cultivate the body and the soul—mass-tourism (including hiking and an elaborate spa culture), but also the many forms and techniques of body culture (gymnastics, swimming, skiing, nudism, yoga) that gained a scattered, but distinctly "mass" following.[81]

Explorations in all these fields suggest that commercial forms of mass culture, and especially the mass media, were expanding in leaps and bounds since the turn of the century, superceding older forms of plebeian and folk culture and industrializing, as it were, nineteenth-century popular culture.[82] Nonetheless, historians are hard-pressed in assessing the place and the impact of mass culture in German life. Given historians' disregard for the phenomena themselves, we do not get a good sense of how mass culture might possibly have structured and shaped experience.[83] More surprisingly, only a few historians have set their sight on the massive contestations that make the very idea of

[78] Kaspar Maase, *Grenzenloses Vergnügen. Der Aufstieg der Massenkultur 1850–1970* (Frankfurt, 1997).

[79] Axel Schildt, "Das Jahrhundert der Massenmedien. Ansichten zu einer künftigen Geschichte der Öffentlichkeit," *Geschichte und Gesellschaft* 27 (2001): 177–206. Bernd Weisbrod, "Medien als symbolische Form der Massengesellschaft. Die medialen Bedingungen von Öffentlichkeit im 20. Jahrhundert," *Historische Anthropologie* 9 (2001): 270–83.

[80] See, for example, Christian Schär, *Der Schlager und seine Tänze im Deutschland der 20er Jahre. Sozialgeschichtliche Aspekte zum Wandel in der Musik- und Tanzkultur* (Zurich, 1991); and Christiane Eisenberg, "Massensport in der Weimarer Republik. Ein statistischer Überblick," *Archiv für Sozialgeschichte* 33 (1993): 137–77.

[81] Christine Keitz, "Die Anfänge des modernen Massentourismus in der Weimarer Republik," *Archiv für Sozialgeschichte* 33 (1993): 179–209; and Ernst Gerhard Eder, "Sonnenanbeter und Wasserratten. Körperkultur und Freiluftbadbewegung in Wiens Donaulandschaft 1900–1933," *Archiv für Sozialgeschichte* 33 (1993): 245–74.

[82] Wolfgang König, *Geschichte der Konsumgesellschaft* (Stuttgart, 2000), 332–86.

[83] Miriam Hansen, *Babel and Babylon: Spectatorship in American Silent Film* (Cambridge, Mass., 1991), is a good example.

mass culture, let alone their practice, so embattled.[84] It should not surprise that there will always be those who consider the "consumption
of culture" as uncouth, if not altogether blasphemous.[85] This would
seem all the more the case in a world in which *Kultur* as the founding
discourse of the nation is set against a world of commerce, industry,
and technology.[86] But what is at stake with mass culture is not only
people's claiming knowledge or making merry, but people's claiming,
for themselves, the necessary time and the discretionary money to fab-
ricate their own way of life, and cultural entrepreneurs' providing the
tools and the means to that end.

When Germans talk about mass culture or consumer society, they
refer to neither of the two but speak instead of *Freizeit* and *Freizeitgesellschaft*. "Free time," literally, is what the Germans were after, and free
time is what mass culture and, eventually, mass consumption came to
occupy.[87] Mass culture was inextricably embroiled in making free time
into the field of activities in which people become what they are (or,
in any case, have the time to dream who they might want to be). We
need not engage here in the academic labors, fascinating as they are,
of identifying the getting and spending of one's time (much as the getting and spending of one's wage) as a feature of labor in the industrial
age, in contradistinction to leisure as a privilege (*Musse* in German)
associated with power and wealth.[88] Nor need we reiterate the history
of free time: While industrial labor relentlessly encroached on people's
time, and reduced and mechanized natural or sacred time, it also produced on its own a surplus of time and money thanks to technologies
of mass-production and the rationalization of labor processes, commonly summed up under the somewhat misleading headers of Ford-

---

[84] Adelheid von Saldern, "Überfremdungsängste. Gegen die Amerikanisierung der
deutschen Kultur in den zwanziger Jahren," in Alf Lüdtke, Inge Marßolek, and Adelheid
von Saldern, eds., *Amerikanisierung. Traum und Alptraum im Deutschland des 20. Jahrhunderts* (Stuttgart, 1993), 213–44.

[85] Leo Lowenthal, "Historical Perspectives on Popular Culture," in Bernard Rosenberg
and David Manning White, eds., *The Popular Arts in America* (New York, 1957), 46–58.
Ann Bermingham, "Introduction: The Consumption of Culture: Image, Object, Text," in
Ann Bermingham and John Brewer, eds., *The Consumption of Culture: Image, Object, Text,
1600–1800* (London, 1995), 1–20.

[86] Georg Jäger, "Der Kampf gegen Schmutz und Schund. Die Reaktion der Gebildeten
auf die Unterhaltungsindustrie," *Archiv für die Geschichte des Buchwesens* 31 (1988): 163–
91.

[87] Arnold Sywottek, "Freizeit und Freizeitgestaltung—ein Problem der Gesellschaftsgeschichte," *Archiv für Sozialgeschichte* 33 (1993): 1–20.

[88] Aleida Assmann, *Arbeit am nationalen Gedächtnis. Eine kurze Geschichte der deutschen
Bildungsidee* (Frankfurt am Main, 1993).

ism and Taylorism.[89] Free time, in short, is the product of the industrial age. The notion of a *Freizeitgesellschaft* (leisure society) on the other hand is usually reserved for a situation in which work no longer is the central pivot around which societies organize and hence is usually identified with the arrival of a post-industrial age in the 1960s or1970s.

The quest for free time was a much embattled issue. In the first instance, it had to be wrested away from powerful adversaries reluctant to grant it—the eight-hour day and paid vacation (gained, lost, and regained) being the heroic expression of this battle in the 1920s, and with the free Saturday, the further reduction of work-hours, and the extension of paid vacation to twenty-eight or more working days, marking the arrival of the miracle years in the late 1950s.[90] The question of homemaking as work was never actually resolved, although household appliances and services promised release time.[91] The actual time gained in this fashion, however, was not infrequently reinvested into servicing the needs of leisure-time activities with the effect that women got caught one way or the other. Inasmuch as free time was gained, it instantly became the subject of yet another contestation over who would control or occupy its use.[92] Here, the challenge of mass culture, as an ever more prominent option for spending one's free time, proved crucial. Indeed, free time and mass culture became so closely associated that they could appear to be one and the same thing, at least in the heyday of mass culture between the 1920s and1950s.

The signal importance of the confrontation over the uses of mass culture becomes instantly evident if we pause and reflect that Germany has not really had *one* mass culture but went through no less than four distinct mass cultural regimes in a mere forty years, between the 1920s and the 1950s, not counting the occupation forces—modernist, nationalist, socialist, and Christian-Catholic. Each one of these regimes articulated its own mass cultural design. They differed not just in terms of their message but also in terms of their visual, aural, and textual composition as well as the role they were meant to play in reconfiguring

---

[89] Mary Nolan, *Visions of Modernity: American Business and the Modernization of Germany* (New York, 1994).

[90] Michael Schneider, *Streit um Arbeitszeit. Geschichte des Kampfes um Arbeitszeitverkürzung* (Cologne, 1984); and Udo Achtern, *". . . denn was uns fehlt ist die Zeit. Geschichte des Arbeitsfreien Wochenendes* (Cologne, 1988).

[91] Gisela Bock and Pat Thane, eds., *Maternity and Gender Policies: Women and the Rise of the European Welfare States, 1880s–1950s* (London, 1995).

[92] Adelheid von Saldern, "Massenfreizeitkultur im Visier. Ein Beitrag zu den Deutungs- und Einwirkungsversuchen während der Weimarer Republik," *Archiv für Sozialgeschichte* 33 (1993): 21–58.

society. To be sure, continuities and crossovers linked them, much as there was a continuous history of importations (often associated with Americanization), but it would be foolish to presume that mass culture was continuous just because the media market expanded and contracted in a single arc between the 1910s and the 1950s.[93]

What was schemed and designed was not some abstract concept of mass culture but the way that people used their free time. Hence, we should not lose sight of the stubborn insistence on part of the masses, who were the object of these mass-cultural schemes, that their free time was nobody's business but their own and that they could use it as they wished. People, it seems, found their own paths through the maze of mass-cultural activities and picked and chose as they saw fit. At this point, it is still quite difficult to tell which elements of mass culture diverse social groups picked for themselves and what they made of them. What we do know is that "the masses" were the most persistent and vociferous advocates of consuming culture. Notwithstanding the massive political stakes in people's free time, they set the stage for mass culture by investing their own free time—and in case of doubt, they invested it into their own, no longer so private and intimate dream-time.

Sometimes the mass consumption of culture was simply a matter of distraction offered by an expanding culture industry. But at other times it held out the hope that, at least in their free time, people could be whatever they wanted to be. This dream time gained an extraordinary valence even in the absence of a genuine commodity culture. It held out the hope and the expectation for a world full of opportunity and chance. It was most successful at selling dreams of a future life. Mass culture proved to be most powerful when these dream worlds interacted with reality and when real life provided the opportunity to live up to one's dreams. All four regimes offered this opportunity, but it was, as we shall see, only adopted twice. As far as the study of German mass culture is concerned, it is quite curious that the regimes of mass culture that most appealed to mass-culture theory should be the ones the Germans did not particularly care for.

"Weimar culture" is an extreme case for the substantive power of mass-cultural dream time. It is one of the most successful mass-cultural phenomena of the twentieth century, veritably "the visual embodiment of the modern per se."[94] Yet historians have a difficult time finding this "Weimar" (or, in actual fact, Berlin) mass culture in the Weimar Republic. Initially, it seemed to have a presence, above all, in

---

[93] Wildt, "Das Jahrhundert der Massenmedien."

[94] Janet Ward, *Weimar Surfaces: Urban Visual Culture in 1920s Germany* (Berkeley, 2001), 7.

the fierce resistance against it.[95] If one tries to think of an actually existing Weimar mass culture, an ebullient proletarian culture or even the Catholic revival were far better candidates.[96] Motorcycle races out in the country, the beginnings of a mostly local tourism, and the sports and dance crazes (but not necessarily the Charleston) would also figure prominently. And yet Weimar culture is remembered not for these mass-cultural events in a lower case but for the programmatic dreams of a privileged, urban *beau monde* to create a society liberated from the shackles of authority and social constraint. Actually, what is remembered are the stand-ins for its intents—the artificial-silk-stockinged legs, for example, of Marlene Dietrich, the Breuer chairs, the Bauhaus wares, "Mackie Messer" and other assorted songs, the Comedian Harmonists, Berlin as metropolis.[97] This mass-culture promised a different kind of reality. Weimar culture thrived because its dreams had the ability to worm their way into public consciousness even when there was no commensurate reality. But therein lies the true challenge of mass culture.

It took effort to produce this dream-text. It was designed and propagated as a distinctly modern style of life (what Max Weber aptly called *Lebensführung*). What made Weimar culture so prominent, so generally recognized, and so hated among its enemies, is this artifice of style and the universal desires this style fostered. The proponents of this style were journalists, often came from professions such as architecture, psychology, and business management, or moved from high art into script writing, film making, design, and advertising.[98] They included quite an unusual number of women among them. They formed a stratum of "applied intellectuals," who, in show-casing their cultural wares, typically designed the future for their product and, with it, a style of life. In promoting this kind of mass culture, they created a distinct and instantly recognizable German future—a future, moreover, that could be moved, as the many exiles among them would soon discover. Like so much else in Weimar Germany, this culture proved short-lived, precarious, unstable, and reversible. But its promoters and sponsors invested

[95] Dieter Mayer, *Linksbürgerliches Denken. Untersuchungen zur Kunsttheorie, Gesellschaftsauffassung und Kulturpolitik in der Weimarer Republik (1919–1924)* (Munich, 1961).

[96] Dieter Langewiesche, "Politik—Gesellschaft—Kultur. Zur Problematik von Arbeiterkultur und kulturellen Arbeitsorganisationen in Deutschland nach dem Ersten Weltkrieg," *Archiv für Sozialgeschichte* 22 (1982): 359–402.

[97] Manfred Smuda, ed., *Die Großstadt als "Text"* (Munich, 1992). Needless to say that Marlene Dietrich only appeared in one film during the Weimar Republic, *Blue Angel. Der blaue Engel*, dir. Josef von Sternburg (Germany, 1930), b/w, 108 m.

[98] Anton Kaes, Martin Jay, and Edward Dimendberg, eds., *The Weimar Source Book*. (Berkeley, 1994).

an inchoate reality with an instant memory of modernity that haunted its opponents and was a source of pleasure for its advocates, even before it had quite arrived and long after it was gone.

In designing a mass-cultural style, the designers of Weimar culture deliberately turned German society into a mass-cultural project, for much as they designed their own wares for cultural consumption, their main claim to fame is that they quite literally gave shape and meaning to a cultural revolution that came with the commercialization of popular culture and the spectacularization of everyday objects and activities. They remade quotidian life into a cultural artifice and sold it as mass-cultural dream. Thus, in focusing on urban spaces of communication such as train stations, hotel lobbies, subway stations, and, above all, the new sites of mass entertainment—cinema palaces, sports arenas, dance halls, and the like—as well as the commercial streets and passageways with their electric signs, they remade them into spaces of unfettered circulation and communication that facilitated, or so it was suggested, a new fluidity and mobility, a world of (chance) encounters that transcended a divisive society. In reporting on cinema as mass entertainment, they championed the case for social masquerade and sexual confusion as the new form of subjectivity.[99] In the quest for functional bodies, in urban architecture and modern design, much as in body culture, they saw articulated the labors of mechanical precision—whether it was in the mass-ornaments of gymnasts, the "functional kitchen" that rationalized the movements of housewives, the rigorous regimes of an exercise culture (the latter more for men than for women), or the chorus lines of such girl troops as the Tiller Girls.[100] Where the opponents of mass culture saw a monotony of repetition, its proponents raved over the exquisite (second) nature of a particularly fine-tuned and hygienic body, a fashion (clothes, perfumes) that signaled and revealed it, and an environment that, quite literally, engendered a modern style of life.[101]

The benefits and miseries of such stylized existence were exemplified in the countless reflections on its most prominent inhabitants—young saleswomen and white-color workers. As masks and figures,

[99] Miriam Hansen, "America, Paris, the Alps: Kracauer (and Benjamin) on Cinema and Modernity," in Leo Charney and Vanessa Schwartz, ed., *Cinema and the Invention of Modern Life* (Berkeley, 1995), 362–402.

[100] Patrice Petro, "Perceptions of Difference: Woman as Spectator and Spectacle," in Katharina von Ankum, ed., *Women in the Metropolis: Gender and Modernity in Weimar Culture* (Berkeley, 1997), 41–66.

[101] Peter Fritzsche, "Landscape of Danger, Landscape of Design: Crisis and Modernism in Weimar Germany," in Thomas W. Kniesche and Stephen Brockmann, ed., *Dancing on the Volcano: Essays on the Culture of the Weimar Republic* (New York, 1994), 29–46.

clerks and girls shattered conventions and customs—even if they did nothing of this sort in real life.[102] The fantasy stuck. The peculiar power of the "girl," more formidably expressed in the (grown-up) "new woman," derived from (the spectacle of) the willful orchestration of sexuality and of gender.[103] The figure of the clerk explored the class-troubles, the confusion of origins and identities.[104] Both cases involved a great deal of fantastic projection. Both the "new woman" and the "clerk" were willful creations, designed to demonstrate that with quotidian life in the city elevated to the standard of modern times, old boundaries of class and gender, power and sexuality must fall to give way for a "modern" society.[105] The reality of such figures was ephemeral in the Weimar Republic, but the desire for experimentation, the will to explore and explode boundaries of pre-determined existence was not. If the cult of quotidian life was still the exception in Weimar, it would become the norm after another war. Forty years later, the Beatles would become the quintessential expression of an *Angestellten-kultur*, the *Girl-Kult* was dressed up by Mary Quant, and the Weimar clerk was fictionalized in James Bond, the difference being that they were British mass-cultural icons that entered Germany under the moniker of Americanization.

This shift of Weimar aspirations to England is above all a consequence of the Nazi pursuit of mass culture. Because the Nazis so vigorously opposed Weimar culture, it was thought that they must have disavowed mass culture altogether. But the Nazis instead engaged in what one might call reverse engineering, reacting against the fictitious and real design of a liberatory mass culture, which they denounced as American, in building their own. They set out to model their mass culture in contrast and opposition to what they branded as depraved, inferior, and Jewish culture. The Third Reich sponsored a great deal of mass-cultural activity.[106] We have to contend with the unsavory reality that cinema, radio, and other forms of mass entertainment (revues, dancing, sports) all reached peak audience numbers during the first

---

[102] Atina Grossmann, "Girlkultur or Thoroughly Rationalized Female: A New Woman in Weimar Germany," in Judith Friedlander, ed., *Women in Culture and Politics: A Century of Change* (Bloomington, 1986); and Katharina Sykora, "Die Neue Frau: Ein Alltags-mythos der zwanziger Jahre," in Katharina Sykora, ed., *Die Neue Frau* (Berlin, 1993), 9–24.

[103] Petra Bock, "Zwischen den Zeiten. Neue Frauen und die Weimarer Republik," in Petra Bock and Katja Koblitz, eds., *Neue Frauen zwischen den Zeiten* (Berlin, 1995).

[104] Siegfried Kracauer, "Die Angestellten. Aus dem neuesten Deutschland," in Siegfried Kracauer, ed., *Schriften I* (Frankfurt, 1978), 205–304.

[105] Irmgard Keun, *Das Kunstseidene Mädchen* [1932] (Munich, 1991).

[106] Peter Reichel, *Der schöne Schein des Dritten Reiches. Faszination und Gewalt des Faschismus* (Frankfurt, 1994).

years of war.[107] Thus the years between 1938 and 1943, rather than those between 1924 and 1929, emerge as the high point for an entire range of mass cultural activities. The years in which the Nazis turned toward global and genocidal war were also the golden age of German mass culture. These were the days of grand and popular films and radio plays, memorable soccer games, all manner of public entertainment (among them the trend-setting *Bunte Abend*, a form of revue and quiz show that had become the craze in the 1930s), and an astounding efflorescence of mental and physical self-improvement regimes.[108] Then again, war and mass culture go hand-in-hand everywhere. It would have been surprising if the Nazis had not joined the bandwagon. The real question concerning mass culture is what the Nazis made of this connection.

The regime of mass culture deployed by the Nazis was not of one piece. But once the competing institutions and agencies and the sheer proliferation of activities is accounted for, we can discern three guiding principles. First, Nazi mass-cultural activism promoted a culture of work and reproduction (which is a rather more dubious claim to be made for Weimar culture). Its intent was unabashedly productivist— to increase efficiency whether at home in the kitchen or in child-care, or at work in industry and (albeit less so) in agriculture.[109] Ideology articulated this quest for efficiency in making quality labor and racially pure motherhood a service to the *Volk*.[110] The "aestheticization of labor" such as the oft-caricatured campaign for "a springtime in the factory" (initiated by Albert Speer, who wanted to have new glass facades, flower beds, lawns, and, above all, immaculately clean factories) were among the most publicized efforts to retool.[111] Home and family improvement schemes—new cookbooks, hygiene lessons, home economics, and maternal and child care—fit the same pattern.[112] Mass culture in the Third Reich first and foremost aimed at making individual needs

[107] Adelheid von Saldern, ed. *Radiozeiten. Herrschaft, Alltag, Gesellschaft (1924–1960)* (Potsdam, 1999); Bernd Drewniak, *Der deutsche Film, 1938–1945. Eine Gesamtübersicht* (Düsseldorf, 1987); and Eric Rentschler, *The Ministry of Illusion: Nazi Cinema and Its Afterlife* (Cambridge, Mass., 1996).

[108] Michael Maaß, *Freizeitgestaltung und kulturelles Leben in Nürnberg 1930–1945. Eine Studie zu Alltag und Herrschaftsausübung im Nationalsozialismus* (Nuremberg, 1994).

[109] Carola Sachse et. al., ed., *Angst, Belohnung, Zucht und Ordnung. Herrschaftsmechanismen im Nationalsozialismus* (Opladen, 1982).

[110] Nancy R. Reagin, "Marktordnung and Autarkic Housekeeping: Housewives and Private Consumption under the Four Year Plan, 1936–1939," *German History* 19 (2001): 162–84.

[111] Anson G. Rabinbach, "The Aesthetics of Production in the Third Reich," *Journal of Contemporary History* 11 (1976): 43–74.

[112] Lisa Pine, *Nazi Family Policy* (Oxford, 1997).

and desires part of a collective experience that it set out to orchestrate and validate. If Weimar culture presented the Tiller Girls, Nazi mass culture turned labor into a mass ornament. The orchestration of work and reproduction served the enhancement of racial collectivity—and in this we find the essence of the Nazi mass-cultural regime.

Second, after some initial hesitation mass culture was geared toward the pursuit of enjoyment. The "Strength through Joy" organization of the German Labor Front became a veritable supermarket for mass-addressed fun and games.[113] However, it orchestrated enjoyment with a twist. Typically, its activities were supervised and its events closely monitored. One purpose of such collective activity may just have been surveillance, but the altogether more important one was to foster enjoyment as a collective rather than individual experience. Enjoyment was not simply presented as mass spectacle but advertised as spectacle of the masses—Leni Riefenstahl blazing the trail for this mass ornamentation of fun and games. The media and the arts, controlled by the Propaganda Ministry, served very much the same purpose. They deserve attention not only for being the most powerful and, as far as one can gauge, the most consequential catalysts of mass culture in the Third Reich, but also because they were instrumental in articulating and orchestrating the nation. Radio and cinema (aided by advertisement and propaganda) created instant national community in two ways. On one hand, they had the effect of generating a national habitus of listening and viewing in one's free time. On the other, they generated (and were set up to that end) a nation conscious of itself—literally so in instigating an awareness of the nation as a collective aural and visual space.[114] The Nazi elites undoubtedly had uplifting visions for this radio- and cinema-nation. Hitler speeches, Furtwängler directing Beethoven's Ninth Symphony, grand marches, and the peculiar, documentary rhetoric of Nazi weekly newsreels fit their expectations. The masses most definitely discovered themselves as *Volk* in the public intimacy of the *Wunschkonzert* and the melodramatic pathos of the movies. In both ways, mass culture and mass entertainment produced the nation as an intimate, instantly present media-body.[115]

---

[113] Wolfhard Buchholz, "Die Nationalsozialistische Gemeinschaft 'Kraft durch Freude'. Freizeitgestaltung und Arbeiterschaft im Dritten Reich" (Dr. phil., Munich, 1976); Carola Sachse, "Freizeit zwischen Betrieb und Volksgemeinschaft. Betriebliche Freizeitpolitik im Nationalsozialismus," *Archiv für Sozialgeschichte* 33 (1993): 305–28.

[114] Inge Marßolek, "Radio in Deutschland 1923–1960," *Geschichte und Gesellschaft* 27: 207–39; Georg Seesslen, *Natural born Nazi. Faschismus in der populären Kultur* (Berlin, 1996 [2001]), 207–39.

[115] David Bathrick. "Making a National Family with the Help of Radio: The Nazi "Wunschkonzert"," *Modernism/modernity* 4 (1997): 115–127; Inge Marßolek, " 'Aus dem

The third element of the mass-cultural configuration of the Third Reich must remain more tentative and speculative. Much has been made of the promise of mass-enjoyment as a form of wish-projection. The subscription campaign for the Volkswagen is perhaps the best known case, but the extensive building and settlement schemes and, even more so, the promise of high mobility and mass tourism across imperial spaces, roads, and rail networks have attracted some attention.[116] We need concern ourselves neither with whether these plans and visions were real or sham nor with their tendency to cast the masses as rapt audiences in spectacles of the nation, as for example in the project for *Germania*, the reconstruction of Berlin after victory, or as pilgrims as is the case for the designs of Death Castles (*Totenburgen*) along the imperial border. Enough spectacular mass enjoyment was built into all these plans to make them more than mere monuments. Yet they were designed as vast sites of memory, not of modernity, but of death and victory. This kind of spectacle followed neither the functional rationale of Speer's "Beauty of Work" nor the politics of distraction in "Strength through Joy" but rather an economy of sacrifice and death. In this, we can discover a more general principle. Mass mobility and mass enjoyment, together with an entire world of mass-cultural goods, were to be gifts, facilitated by the invisible labor of invisible workers, that gave presence to a racial past of heroic death after victory. While the surfeit of enjoyment in Nazi mass culture was meant to distract from the war, the future of the Nazi mass-cultural project depended on it. Enjoyment was the gift for killing.[117]

This victory culture disappeared with the collapse of the Nazi regime. But the taste and sound, the sensory habitus of Nazi mass culture did not go away. The mass-cultural mindset of the Nazi years lingered on in both Germanys far into the postwar years. This phenomenon is still largely terra incognita, but more or less incidental comments suggest that a mass-cultural imagery, a distinct 1940s sound, and, above all, a sense of camaraderie, joviality, and banter were deeply shaped by Nazi mass culture.[118] If the mass-articulation of *Gemütlichkeit* has become so much of an exchangeable national genre (with the stereotypi-

Volk, für das Volk'. Die Inszenierung der 'Volksgemeinschaft' im und durch das Radio," in Inge Marßolek and Adelheid von Saldern, eds., *Radiozeiten. Herrschaft, Alltag, Gesellschaft (1924–1960)* (Potsdam, 1999), 123–38.

[116] Hasso Spode, "'Der deutsche Arbeiter reist.' Massentourismus im Dritten Reich," in Gerhard Huck, ed., *Sozialgeschichte der Freizeit* (Wuppertal, 1980), 281–306.

[117] Deborah Dwork and Robert Jan van Pelt, *Auschwitz 1270 to the Present* (New York, 1996), make this argument for the plans concerning the after history of the Auschwitz death camp.

[118] Ute Keuler, *Häberle und Pfleiderer. Zur Geschichte, Machart und Funktion einer populären Unterhaltungsreihe* (Tübingen, 1992).

cal regional inflection in which Hamburg provided the singing sailor, Bavaria the brass bands, and the Rhineland mass routines such as *Schunkeln*); if mass dances did become so prominent and so highly ritualized phenomenon (of slow and fast dances and an elaborate dance floor-etiquette); if there emerged a national melodramatic pathos, a type of German stand-up comic, a routine of skits, a combination of the jolly and sentimental, a rhythm for every emotion—if all this was instantly present, though perhaps not well understood, it is because these things became everyday business in the Third Reich.[119] The Nazis managed to bring together a budding popular culture, often regional and ethnic in origin, and a spectacular urban culture and combined them into national mass-cultural events that shaped sensory expectations as much as routines of enjoyment. In this sense we can speak of Nazi mass culture as a habitus—unselfconscious among contemporaries perhaps, but sufficiently in evidence to drive a younger, postwar generation of baby-boomers into paroxysms of rage and alienation.[120]

Only if we consider both the radical modernism of the Weimar experiment with mass culture and the attractions of Nazi mass culture can we begin to make sense of the postwar years. The Allies attempted to break the power of interwar dream worlds with a determination that, in the face of a still hegemonic Nazi mass culture, may seem less of a misguided venture than often thought.[121] Likewise, both the West and the East German governments desperately tried to step off the mass-cultural accelerator. Intellectuals on both sides attempted to fend off, yet once again, a mass culture of distraction. They hoped to chain it to sound principles of social order and sought to protect German society from the chaos of a modern, secular, American world. The masses continued to flock to the movies, crave entertainment, and hold out for better times. But the sheen was gone from mass-cultural abandon. Nobody cared for the spectacular confusions of gender and class in Weimar culture. Nobody was interested in the grandiose schemes of mass-enjoyment of the Nazi years. The vast majority of Germans wanted security, the basic necessities of life—and, yes, the *Wunschkonzert*, too, though less as an expression of the national presence than as private leisure time.

All things not being equal, the East German regime had a heavier burden to carry entering the postwar years, but stood a better chance

---

[119] Inge Marßolek, "Vertraute Töne und Unerhörtes. Radio und Gedächtnis im Nachkriegsdeutschland," in Elisabeth Domansky and Harald Wezel, eds., *Eine offene Geschichte. Über kommunikative Tradierung der nationalsozialistischen Vergangenheit* (Tübingen, 1999), 145–72.

[120] Georg Seesslen, *Tanz den Adolf Hitler. Faschismus in der populären Kultur* (Berlin, 1994) and his *Natural Born Nazi*.

[121] Gabriele Clemens, ed., *Kulturpolitik im besetzten Deutschland 1945–1949* (Stuttgart, 1994).

than the West to wean the German masses from the Nazi course of mass destruction and mass distraction. Of course, the perennial distrust of Communist functionaries, a reflection both of their Stalinism and their refugee experience, dampened any initiative.[122] But the SED could draw on quite extraordinary assets. The socialist culture movement had reached its apogee during the Weimar Republic when it linked up with the general mass cultural excitement of those years. Compared with "Weimar culture" it may well be considered the more popular and more gregarious version of mass culture.[123] Much of this movement had been either destroyed or taken over by the Nazis, but there was every reason to believe that this tradition could be revived and regenerated. Typically, the newly founded DEFA studio almost instantly produced a number of outstanding films, such as Wolfgang Staudte's *The Murderers Are Among Us* (1946).[124] Also, the humanist-progressive intelligentsia returned to East Germany from exile, attracted by the antifascism of the SED, which they saw exemplified in a pedagogic ideal that sought to link popular culture and the arts.[125] They wagered that masses could be weaned from both fascist tastes and the cheap thrills of capitalist entertainment with a new culture for the masses. They were more than eager to prove that the popular desire for enjoyment could be satisfied without abandoning artistic traditions. None of these hopeful expectations, however, is easily recognized in the emerging SED politics of mass culture, which, in no time at all, used up the accumulated cultural capital of the socialist movement and alienated the masses whom it so desperately tried to attract.

The historical and political debate on mass culture and, for that matter, on consumption in the GDR has almost exclusively focused on the nature and degree of regime control on one hand and the self-assertion of recipients and consumers of mass culture on the other.[126] The results of many of these studies are predictable: Control was far from total. There were always ways around the dictates of the regime for both producers and consumers, although the game was difficult and, at times, dangerous. Still, writers, film makers, dramatists, and artists

[122] Jeffrey Herf, *Divided Memory: The Nazi Past in the Two Germanys* (Cambridge, Mass., 1997).

[123] Adelheid von Saldern and Dietrich Mühlberg, "Kontinuität und Wandel der Arbeiterkultur," *Mitteilungen aus der Kulturwissenschaftlichen Forschung* 30 (1992): 226–59.

[124] Seán Allan, "DEFA: An Historical Overview," in Seán Allan and John Sandford, eds., *DEFA: East German Cinema, 1946–1992* (New York, 1999).

[125] David Pike, *The Politics of Culture in Soviet-Occupied Germany, 1945–1949* (Stanford, 1992).

[126] Simone Barck, Christoph Classen, and Thomas Heimann. "The Fettered Media: Controlling Public Debate," in Konrad H. Jarausch, ed., *Dictatorship as Experience: Towards a Socio-Cultural History of the GDR* (New York, 1999), 213–39.

were testing the limits of the permissible.[127] The consumers, of course, could always resort to Western radio and television. But they also lambasted the purveyors of culture (including the officially accepted artists) in petitions and letter campaigns, created their own subcultures (as for example in the irrepressible waves of youth culture), or pieced together their own leisure time activities, shielding them against the intrusions of the state and using what the state had to offer toward their own ends. Important as these testimonies of an indomitable spirit of self-assertion are—and as much as we may want to characterize the GDR as a society of "cunning hunters and gatherers" of enjoyment as much as for consumer goods—they tend to elide what is so intriguing about the GDR in the first place.[128] Here we encounter a state that deliberately set out to remake and, in fact, to create a nation on the principles of mass mobilization in industry, in defense, and in culture.[129] And yet this state was scared into paralysis by the mobility of desires and wants it unleashed in the process and ended up spending ever greater efforts controlling and containing and, one must surmise, to simply fathom what its very own empowerment of the masses had kicked off.

Perhaps the most telling features of this failed project is the disappearance of the mass-cultural activism of the early years behind a bureaucratic screen of "mass organizations" and the stifling of the socialist-humanist revival in attacks against modernism and cosmopolitanism. The former indicates the regime's insecurities in the face of mass mobilization.[130] By the mid-1950s, the entire civic life—work place, home, and free time—was enmeshed in a thicket of organizations.[131] These organizations soaked up the entire public sphere of mass activities so that nothing much was left of the initial mass-cultural initiatives and their utopian pathos. By the same token, the pedagogic impulse not simply to reeducate, but to open up new horizons, to bring the German and the world's cultural heritage to underprivileged

---

[127] Among others, see Tom Biburger, *Sprengsätze. "Der Lohndrücker" von Heiner Müller und der 17. Juni 1953* (Berlin, 1995).

[128] Ina Merkel, "Der aufhaltsame Aufstieg in die Konsumgesellschaft," in Neue Gesellschaft für bildende Kunst, ed., *Wunderwirtschaft. DDR-Konsumkultur in den 60er Jahren* (Cologne, 1996), 8–20.

[129] See the comparative perspective in Stephen Kotkin, "Modern Times: The Soviet Union and the Interwar Conjuncture," *Kritika: Explorations in Russian and Eurasian History* 2 (2001): 111–64.

[130] Peter Hübner, "Zur Rolle der 'Massenorganisationen' im Alltag des DDR-Bürgers," in Enquete-Kommission Aufarbeitung von Geschichte und Folgen der SED Diktatur in Deutschland, ed., *Machtstrukturen und Entscheidungsmechanismen im SED-Staat und die Frage der Verantwortung*, vol. II/3 (Baden-Baden, 1995), 1723–69.

[131] Detlef Pollack,"Das Ende einer Organisationsgesellschaft. Systemtheoretische Überlegungen zum gesellschaftlichen Umbruch in der DDR," *Zeitschrift für Soziologie* 19 (1990): 292–307.

groups, and to create a new culture beyond class divisions, did not lack its enthusiasts either—and not just among elites as cynics might argue.[132] But the effects of such pedagogic idealism consisted not only of the muzzling of the media and a rigid surveillance of the arts, but also of an all-round pedagogic overkill in which teaching and preaching replaced enjoyment.

The most significant example of the contradiction and tensions in building a socialist mass culture came at the end of the 1950s, at the moment when the GDR was emerging from a decade of extreme scarcities and violent Sovietization. The GDR was poised to enter a new era, building more high-tech industries and providing more abundant goods. This was also the moment to generate a less abrasive and more popular culture and to foster a culture of and for the masses in which they could find themselves. In the most famous experiments of this kind, the *Bitterfelder Weg* (1958–64), artists were to exchange roles with workers—with workers and artists creating a culture of work and everyday-life experience.[133] Neither side got from the other what they wanted. Artists were stymied, workers did not find themselves represented, and the functionaries were aghast about workers and authors finding quotidian life dismal and dysfunctional. In actual fact, quite a fascinating literature and cinematic oeuvre did emerge, but the entire effort was cut short when the SED regime abandoned its own initiative in a drastic and dramatic purge that spelled the end of any and all attempts to create a socialist mass culture.[134]

The high drama of these purges has somewhat overshadowed the fact that the masses who supposedly were the agents and recipients of this mass-cultural initiative created their own culture. With improved circumstances, they developed a robust appetite for commodities with which they occupied their free time—new furniture, kitchen equipment, clothes, country cottages, and Schreber gardens.[135] If anything, they could be found establishing their own network of commodity exchanges (among which tickets for sought-after cultural events or books figured quite prominently), debated at great length such issues as fash-

---

[132] Ingeborg Muenzen-Koenen, ed., *Literarisches Leben in der DDR 1945–1960. Literaturkonzepte und Leseprogramme* (Berlin [GDR], 1979).

[133] Marc D. Silberman, *Literature of the Working World: A Study of the Industrial Novel in East Germany* (Bern, 1976); and Günther Rüther,. *"Greif zur Feder, Kumpel". Schriftsteller, Literatur und Politik in der DDR 1949–1990* (Düsseldorf, 1991).

[134] Günter Agde, ed., *Kahlschlag. Das 11. Plenum des ZK der SED 1965. Studien und Dokumente* (Berlin, 1991).

[135] Gerlinde Irmscher, "'Arbeitsfrei mit Küßchen drauf'," in Neue Gesellschaft für bildende Kunst, ed., *Wunderwirtschaft. DDR-Konsumkultur in den 60er Jahren* (Cologne, 1996), 37–47.

ion versus durability, sensible standards of well-being versus luxury, the continuing need for qualification (as a prerequisite for upward mobility) versus the desire for leisure, and appropriate versus inappropriate forms of mass culture.[136] Among the latter, the British pop invasion no doubt figured prominently (especially when it came to long hair and short skirts), as did the rather more overtly sexual dating behavior of teenagers and its consequences in the form of unwanted pregnancies and abortions.[137]

The SED regime did battle with all these signs of permissiveness. Ubiquitous and repressive as it was, however, its entire huge apparatus of mass culture and surveillance also became oddly irrelevant. It was singularly incompetent in organizing and providing meaning for the quotidian life, which it so desperately attempted to orchestrate. The masses in turn proved to be cunning consumers who put together their own everyday culture. If their world was for the most part work oriented, it nonetheless became increasingly defined by the creative appropriation of goods. Not by chance did the terrain of the everyday in the GDR emerge as the greatest surprise to historians and perhaps as the most cherished memory of a state and a mass-cultural project that have otherwise disappeared.[138] If "Weimar culture" cathected memory onto mass design, GDR popular culture created an unmistakable and memorable style of everyday culture that epitomized happiness for the masses. Alas, the SED regime exhausted itself in attempting to deliver goods that were never quite good enough and in satisfying the robust appetite of the East German consumer nation.

The similarity and difference of East Germany in relationship to West Germany and the latter's difference from preceding regimes of mass culture become instantly evident in a statement that the very young, but highly opinionated Jürgen Habermas made in 1956. He saw free time being taken over by "consumption-time" and clearly did not consider this a good thing.[139] He made mass culture the particular target of his ire, but mass culture was fast disappearing in a world of commodities. Habermas captured, albeit disapprovingly, the transition

---

[136] Dietrich Mühlberg,"Überlegungen zu einer Kulturgeschichte der DDR," in Hartmut Kaelble, Jürgen Kocka, and Hartmut Zwahr, eds., *Sozialgeschichte der DDR* (Stuttgart, 1994), 62–94.

[137] Dorothee Wierling, "Die Jugend als innerer Feind. Konflikte in der Erziehungsdiktatur der sechziger Jahre" in Hartmut Kaelble, Jürgen Kocka, and Hartmut Zwahr, eds., *Sozialgeschichte der DDR* (Stuttgart, 1994), 404–25; and Poiger, *Jazz, Rock, and Rebels*.

[138] Dokumentationszentrum Alltagskultur der DDR e.V., ed. *Fortschritt, Norm und Eigensinn. Erkundungen im Alltag der DDR* (Berlin, 2000).

[139] Jürgen Habermas, "Notizen zum Verhältnis von Kultur und Konsum," *Merkur* 10 (1956): 212–228, here 216.

from a regime of mass-cultural dreams into a consumer society . This dynamic West German process in the 1950s was, by all accounts, one of the most consequential processes of modernization of German society, changing the taste, the mores, and the habitus, the bonds of belonging and the relations among people.[140]

West German intellectuals set the tone for the reception of this process. For the first time since the 1920s, public comment about the state of culture was captured again by Mandarin academics and literati.[141] The latter held that a further advance of mass culture could not but destroy the foundations of a West German spiritual recovery—interpreted less as a recovery from war and fascism than from modernity—which they considered possible within the context of an autonomous *Kultur* led by elite groups who served as moral arbiters for the nation. Their overriding concern was the power of a technological age to level a hierarchy of tastes, to homogenize society, and to alienate the individual from himself in a machine-dominated culture.[142] The regulation of mass culture, a veritable moral police vis-à-vis the masses and the preservation of an authentic realm of the spirit, often identified with nature and *Heimat*, emerged as the Mandarins' main solutions. This rhetoric derives from the archive of cultural pessimism that dates back to the turn of the century and had accompanied the rise of popular and mass culture. Still, this was the 1950s, and it was striking how supremely unconcerned these jeremiads were about the formation of a mass-cultural taste in the Third Reich and how singularly they focused on the main antagonist of the interwar years: *Amerika*. Mass culture was identified with—and condemned as—markets, media, and technology, rather than with the state cult of regulated distraction or pedagogic uplift. They were antitotalitarian to be sure, but the object of their curious antitotalitarianism was the United States.[143]

The Mandarins wanted regulation and moral policing as their own prerogative—and got it. In a political culture that aimed at "as much freedom as possible and as little regulation as necessary" and in which even the price of bread was deregulated, the regulatory overkill in the mass media sector is striking.[144] Although the print media faced a

---

[140] Axel Schildt and Arnold Sywottek, eds., *Modernisierung im Wiederaufbau. Die westdeutsche Gesellschaft der 50er Jahre* (Bonn, 1993).

[141] Axel Schildt, *Zwischen Abendland und Amerika. Studien zur westdeutschen Ideenlandschaft der 50er Jahre* (Munich, 1999).

[142] Michael Ermarth, "Heidegger on Americanism: Ruinanz and the End of Modernity," *Modernism/modernity* 7 (2000): 379–400.

[143] Konrad H. Jarausch and Hannes Siegrist, eds., *Amerikanisierung und Sowjetisierung in Deutschland 1945–1970* (Frankfurt, 1997).

[144] Harm G. Schröter, "Konsumpolitik und 'soziale Marktwirtschaft'. Die Koexistenz liberalisierter und regulierter Verbrauchsgütermärkte in der Bundesrepublik der 1950er

highly competitive market, especially after the Allied license system was abolished, they instantly developed an elaborate regime of self-censorship.[145] Radio and television were public corporations with carefully selected boards of supervision that encompassed the main political parties and "mass organizations" (such as the church and the trade unions). The tendency toward organizing the mass media as a way of controlling them was surely not a prerogative of the East. Mass organizations flourished even in the Western media—with the religious denominations, women, farmers, high culture, and *Heimat* culture, although not the trade unions and youth, all getting their slice of the pie. But regulation had a curious effect that ran quite counter to the Mandarins' good intentions. It consolidated the mass cultural taste as it had developed in the 1930s and 1940s with an emphasis on what the Germans inimitably call *Unterhaltungsmusik* (entertainment music), radio-plays and skits and other domesticated forms of distraction.[146] With the decline of the radio and cinema in the late 1950s, public television became the enduring refuge of this particularly German cultivation of distraction.[147] The real-life effect of moral policing consisted not in some moral uplift or a more spiritual culture but in the consolidation of a distinctly German mass-cultural taste. Every opinion poll confirms that this is what the *Volk* wanted—and got, despite the intellectuals' cultivation of the spirit.

Despite its survival on television, however, this mass-cultural holdover did not prevail. Already by the late 1950s and surely by the mid-1960s it came under sustained attack, and by the mid-1970s had disappeared into a plurality of consumer tastes and orientations. Given the significance of this development, which put German culture beyond the interwar mass-cultural configuration, and given the simultaneous failure of the GDR to develop a socialist alternative, the difficulty in mapping this transition is puzzling. Most commonly, it is attributed to a cultural revolution set in motion by the student rebellion of the 1960s.[148] But this account is as much the figment of an intellectual elite as that of 1950s intellectuals about mass culture.[149] It reflects the same

Jahre," in Hartmut Berghoff, ed., *Konsumpolitik. Die Regulierung des privaten Verbrauchs im 20. Jahrhundert* (Göttingen, 1999), 113–33, here 113.

[145] Ottfried Jarren, "Medien und Kommunikation in den fünziger Jahren," in Axel Schildt and Arnold Sywottek, eds., *Modernisierung im Wiederaufbau. Die westdeutsche Gesellschaft der 50er Jahre* (Bonn, 1993), 433–38.

[146] Schildt, *Moderne Zeiten*, 209–305.

[147] Siegfried Zielinski, *Audiovisions: Cinema and Television as Entr'actes in History* (Amsterdam, 1999).

[148] Gerd Koenen, *Das rote Jahrzehnt. Unsere kleine deutsche Kulturrevolution 1967–1977* (Cologne, 2001).

[149] Axel Schildt, Detlef Siegfried, and Karl Christian Lammers, eds., *Dynamische Zeiten. Die 60er Jahre in den beiden deutschen Gesellschaften* (Hamburg, 2000).

ambition of moral guidance and misses out on the curious travels on the twisted road from interwar mass culture to postwar consumer culture that used American culture as its lodestar.

Two distinct groups used American mass culture to set themselves against what they considered an oppressive German taste. First, predominantly but not exclusively proletarian youth groups, who emerged out of war-time and postwar gangs, developed their own flamboyant urban culture of free time whose signatures were hard rock, hyper-feminine women, fast motorcycles (with scooters emerging as the upscale "Mod" alternative), rambunctious concerts, and hangouts at street corners and in public spaces.[150] Simultaneously, we find an upwardly mobile group of mostly young professionals who adopted what they made into an American high culture—cool jazz, authentic black music, Southern literature, and American college and university culture.[151] Needless to say, there were a few lounge lizards and rat-pack fans among them, although they are surprisingly difficult to identify amid all the serious high-cultural ambition for a more spiritual America.

Both groups were quintessentially "Fifties" and disappeared in the transition into consumer society. Their basic posture, however, was of immense consequence. American culture (or what they made of it) served exceptionally well their rebellion against the mass taste of the 1940s. Their America, however, as progressive and wild as it was, was still exceedingly remote and exotic and in this sense no different from the *Amerika* of the Mandarins. This changed only when and where the real United States developed into a transnational commercial culture. The situation was prefigured by American cinema, which conquered the German markets in the wake of both wars—but the second time around wiped out what was left of the film culture of the 1930s and 1940s within a mere ten years, although mass-cultural tastes really only changed in the 1970s. In fact, the stubborn survival of a "German taste" is a striking, if not well understood aspect of the eventual transition into a full-fledged consumer society in West Germany.[152] On a much grander scale, the same happened with a music-centered youth culture. Youth had been notoriously neglected by German radio with the

---

[150] Kaspar Maase, *BRAVO Amerika. Erkundungen zur Jugendkultur der Bundesrepublik in den fünfziger Jahren* (Hamburg, 1992); and Thomas Grotum, *Die Halbstarken. Zur Geschichte einer Jugendkultur der 50er Jahre* (Frankfurt, 1994).

[151] Axel Schildt, "Die USA als 'Kulturnation'. Zur Bedeutung der Amerikahäuser in den 1950er Jahren," in *Amerikanisierung*, 257–69.

[152] Thomas J. Saunders, *Hollywood in Berlin: American Cinema and Weimar Germany* (Berkeley, 1994). For television, see Irmela Schneider, *Amerikanische Einstellung. Deutsches Fernsehen und US-amerikanische Produktionen* (Heidelberg, 1992).

effect that an emergent youth culture simply abandoned it—turning to jukeboxes or (the upscale) gramophone and listening to commercial stations such as Radio Luxemburg or Europe 1 and, above all, the American Forces Network. By the mid-1960s, an uninhibitedly commercialized youth culture was taking over and effectively breaking the monopoly of German mass-cultural taste.[153] Because America continued to be so utterly strange, if tantalizingly fascinating (we may think of Bob Dylan, the Byrds, Country Joe and the Fish, or the outrageous violence of Sam Peckinpah's movies), a much more germane cohort of British teenagers did much of the Americanizing or, in actual fact, "whitened" black rhythm and blues. The antidote to 1940s mass culture, in any case, was commercial entertainment, and the latter capitalized (quite literally) on the experience of black America. Whatever the "red republic" of student protesters accomplished, this was the cultural revolution of 1960s Germany. Notwithstanding this commercial revolution, a distinctly "German rhythm"—it was (and is) effectively the German variety of country music—persisted in radio and television and on the dance-floor, even if the latter was increasingly relegated to the realm of the uncool and politically incorrect.

A second agent of West Germany's transition into consumer culture is better known for what the cultural authorities wanted to do with her than for what she accomplished. The German *Hausfrau* and, more so, the many unmarried *Fräulein*, were supposedly the repositories of good values, the inexhaustible source of love and support for a much-damaged mankind, and the custodians of domesticity and clean living, in addition to being a good housekeeper and a caring mother for her many children. This is what political and cultural rhetoric expected of women.[154] With virtuous women tending the home, the wild desires of mass culture would most assuredly be domesticated. Ironically, the 1950s pundits, in one way, got what they wanted. Domesticity shredded any grandiose vestige of public (mass) culture. Reliably, Habermas also spoke out against a "regression into nuclear-family group-egotism."[155] He was right about the egotism, but like his more conservative colleagues, he did not notice the lustful gleam in the eyes of women

[153] Detlef Siegfried, "Vom Teenager zur Pop-Revolution. Politisierungstendenzen in der westdeutschen Jugendkultur 1959 bis 1968," in Schildt, Siegfried, and Lammers, eds., *Dynamische Zeiten*, 582–623.

[154] Robert Moeller, *Protecting Motherhood: Women and the Family in the Politics of Postwar Germany* (Berkeley, 1993).

[155] The quotations are from Axel Schildt, "Freizeit, Konsum und Häuslichkeit in der 'Wiederaufbau'-Gesellschaft. Zur Modernisierung von Lebensstilen in der Bundesrepublik Deutschland in den 1950er Jahren," in Siegrist, Kaelble, and Kocka, eds., *Europäische Konsumgeschichte*, 327–48, here 335.

looking into an overflowing refrigerator, their penchant for listening
to entertainment radio (and consistently asking for more), such bad
habits as smoking and drinking, the desire to look their best, and not
just on Sundays, their wish to have a new kitchen and a bath and a
house and a garden and a stone terrace for garden furniture, and, not
least, to be free and take off whether it was on vacation or in the bed-
room. If Touropa provided the means for the former, Beate Uhse and
Oswald Kolle eventually did so for the latter.[156] Domesticity turned out
not at all the way it was meant to be. It promised homeliness, but delivered a frenzy of consumption—in the late 1950s and early 1960s, not
quite yet the play of desire and choice that consumer theorists envisioned consumption to be, but wave upon wave of excessive satisfaction of want and need for food, clothing, furniture, and mobility as
well as for light, air, and every "thing" that promised enjoyment. A
new commercial culture of credit and risk, which women embraced
far more than men, made sure that these things could be had without
calumny. Housewives firmly anchored the social market economy in
the everyday and thus "must be viewed as the bearers of a specifically
feminine form of historical agency."[157] They produced the Federal Republic as a consumer society and held it in motion with their relentless
drive, increasingly orchestrated by advertising, to upscale more simple
wants and to refine more ordinary desires, whether it was with strips
of red peppers and olives on sandwiches or with their own bodies.

The odd thing is that this commercialization of consumption in the
service of domesticity snapped the Germans out of their interwar, Weimar, and Nazi mass-cultural spectacles and propelled them into the
miracle world of a consumer society.

Happiness and Its Discontents

While not perfect, de Grazia's definition of a consumer culture as a
"society-wide structure of meaning and feeling organized primarily
around the acts of purchase" is the most useful one we have.[158] This
peculiar market- and mass-commodity-centered social order emerged

[156] Ute Frevert, "Umbruch der Geschlechterverhältnisse? Die 60er Jahre als geschlecht-
erpolitischer Experimentierraum," in *Dynamische Zeiten*, 642–60. Elizabeth Heineman,
"From the Weimar Reformers to the West German Sex Wave" (paper presented at the
American Historical Association, 2002, San Francisco).

[157] Erica Carter, *How German Is She? Postwar West German Reconstruction and the Consuming Woman* (Ann Arbor, 1997), 7.

[158] Victoria de Grazia and Ellen Furlough, eds. *The Sex of Things: Gender and Consumption in Historical Perspective* (Berkeley, 1996), 7.

late in Germany. To be sure, even in the absence of a consumer society, Germans did not languish in a world without goods. As we have seen, there were moments of extreme scarcity, but mass consumption clearly existed, if we understand it as "the extension of goods to a wide range of individuals who participated, though at quantitatively and qualitatively different levels, in the social world of commodities."[159] The way from mass consumption to a consumer society, however, was anything but straightforward. Contrary to what we may think or wish, more consumption by more people did not equal consumer society. Quite to the contrary, throughout the first half of the 1920s it looked as if the former would prevent the latter—and there is every indication that this is what a good part of the German population considered right.

In terms of consumption-extravaganza, the Wilhelmine turn-of the-century culture is difficult to beat, with a veritable cult of objects among its well-to-do urbanites. We may think of the opulent fabrics and the exquisite detail of men's and women's clothes, the sinuous curves and rich materials of *Jugendstil* design, or the craze for jewelry and accessories such as shoes, gloves, furs, hats, or canes, and the mind-popping fetishism they engendered. Neither should one disregard the things that made up the trousseaus of marriageable young women in rural society or, for that matter, the sturdy elegance of Sunday clothes of working men. Still, household budgets indicate clearly demarcated and, indeed, segregated spending patterns.[160] We may even think of the little Weimar shop girl dressing up as *garçonne* and wearing Shalimar (the favorite "oriental" perfume) as a variation of this theme, although the latter would mean pushing the definition of mass consumption, because the girl with short-cropped hair (the *Bubikopf*) and in a pant-suit with her feminine perfume clearly made herself into what she wanted to be in the act of consumption.[161] Still, one could as well treat this behavior as a peculiarly urban, insular mode of consumption in a world of largely segregated consumption patterns.

The point is that mass consumption, even when and where it improved in quality and quantity, as in the Wilhelmine period, remained overwhelmingly tied to and reinforced pre-configured class milieus that were differentiated according to gender and age as well as to region and confession. Indeed, there is every indication that with growing consumption these markers of difference rather increased than decreased. People simply ate more of what they knew best, and neither

---

[159] Ibid., 143.

[160] Klaus Tenfelde, "Klassenspezifische Konsummuster im Deutschen Kaiserreich," in *Europäische Konsumgeschichte*, 245–66.

[161] Sabine Hake, "In the Mirror of Fashion," in *Women in the Metropolis*, 185–201.

Weimar nutritionists nor Nazi dietitians could convince them otherwise.[162] They bought more of the same and spent the surplus, if there
were any, for little luxuries—extra candy, a special dress, new and
fancy shoes, better cutlery for Sunday. The situation is aptly captured
in the notion of estate-like barriers of consumption (*konsumständische
Barrieren*).[163] Well into the middle of the twentieth century, quantitatively and qualitatively ample consumption served the purpose of
maintaining and reinforcing pre-existing social boundaries rather than
dissolving them. Indeed, given the flux on the labor market and the
changing nature of occupations (for example, the rise of white collar
work), consumption rather reinforced social boundaries that otherwise
were disappearing—and, notwithstanding "Weimar culture," consumption patterns during the Weimar Republic rather seem to under-
line this point. Typically, the emerging German automobile industry
produced cars as luxury items and its advertisements featured unat-
tainable splendor, designed not to attract the masses but to keep them
away from these trophy commodities at a moment long after Henry
Ford had begun to produce his Model T.[164] Hence, the idea that an expansive regime of mass consumption, repeatedly promised and often
reneged throughout the first half of the twentieth century, eventually
begot the consumer society of the Federal Republic is not convincing.[165]

How, then, did consumer society appear on the German scene?
While insufficient as an explanation, the rather sudden descent of a
number of large appliances onto households ruined by war cannot
possibly be underestimated. The arrival of electric stoves, refrigerators,
washing machines, television, flushing toilets, indoor plumbing, new
kitchens, and electrical gadgets, all this in a mere fifteen years, was an
overwhelming experience.[166] The phenomenal rise of detergents as the
new miracle weapon not simply against dirty laundry but against the
drudgery and hard labor of a washing day, as well as the mass-avail-
ability of synthetics as over- and underwear and, more generally, as a
new way of dressing (the disappearance of aprons, and the advent of
long pants for boys, light fabrics for girls, and eventually the mini,

---

[162] Uwe Spiekermann, "Regionale Verzehrsunterschiede als Problem der Wirtschafts-
und Sozialgeschichte im Deutschen Reich," in Hans Jürgen Teuteberg, Gerhard Neumann, and Alois Wierlacher, eds., *Essen und kulturelle Identität. Europäische Perspektiven*
(Berlin, 1997), 247–82.

[163] Tenfelde, "Klassenspezifischer Konsum."

[164] Wolfgang Sachs, *For Love of the Automobile: Looking Back into the History of Our Desires*, trans. Don Reneau (Berkeley, 1992).

[165] Confino and Koshar, "Regimes of Consumer Culture."

[166] Arne Andersen, *Der Traum vom guten Leben. Alltags- und Konsumgeschichte vom
Wirtschaftswunder bis heute* (Frankfurt, 1997).

which made its debut as a dress rather than a skirt) made a modern lady-like and gentlemanly lifestyle attainable by the masses. Not least, the simpler indicators of affluence, first the ample supply of cigarettes and chocolates and eventually an ever more elaborate array of goods to please the senses, gave growing wealth a tangible expression. Add to this the new home and the new car as the truly big-ticket items for which an entire nation worked with singular determination, and even then the intensity of the sudden love-affair of postwar Germans and their commodities is difficult to convey.[167]

Germans turned into champions of consumption with much the same obsession that they attended to work. They rationalized their frenzy for commodities with the needs of households that had to be built from scratch. While older studies pointed to the miracle of Ludwig Erhard's market economy as the mainspring of the commodity bonanza that found its "natural" consumers in a country impoverished by war, newer research points to the orchestration of desire through advertisement. Once the proclivity is overcome to counter with an emphasis on indigenous sources of commodity culture the Mandarins' argument that all of this was a conspiracy of *Amerika*, the adaptation and acculturation of American influence will also become more visible.[168] But this said, the trickling down of appliances into ever more households, while changing a way of life, did not by itself generate a consumer society. These commodities loosened taste barriers and even "fabricated a new liberation theology of individual happiness and consumer comfort," as Paul Betts argues convincingly.[169] But to produce a consumer society, the prefigured tiers of consumption and inherited patterns of household-budgeting had to give way to lifestyles and lifestyle milieus. This was a rather more treacherous process, and is the cultural revolution that a generation of rebellious students claimed for itself.

Several aspects of this development are worth noting. First, rampant consumption generated a common culture of commodities that found their home in newly up-scale department stores.[170] For one, it led to an upward leveling of class boundaries—as, for example, the much

---

[167] See Schildt, *Moderne Zeiten*; and Hanna Schissler, ed. *The Miracle Years: A Cultural History of West Germany 1949–1968* (Princeton, 2001).

[168] Anselm Doering-Manteuffel, "Dimensionen von Amerikanisierung in der deutschen Gesellschaft," *Archiv für Sozialgeschichte* 35 (1995): 35–70. Volker Berghahn, *America and the Intellectual Cold Wars in Europe: Shepard Stone between Philanthropy, Academy, and Diplomacy* (Princeton, 2001).

[169] Paul Betts, "The Nierentisch Nemesis: Organic Design as West German Pop Culture," *German History* 19 (2001): 185–217, here 209.

[170] König, *Geschichte der Konsumgesellschaft*, 91–107.

touted, more lady-like appearance especially of young women in their Courrège dresses and little white boots, even when and where they vamped the lady with an extra-short hemline. For another, rampant consumption dissolved slowly but surely the rural-urban division as one of the most persistent divides in German society, which also meant that it brought the more traditional Catholic milieus into the realm of consumer society. When finally rural and urban folks came to agree on casual apparel as their preferred mode of dress, mass consumption had reached its apogee. Disposable income was spent on similar kinds of commodities, following a mass taste rather than classes of consumption. Second, work or, more significantly, vocation (*Beruf*), declined as a social marker.[171] That is, while the intensity of work and work discipline significantly increased (not the least as a result of compacted work hours) and while status ascriptions retained their significance (although the habit of adding professional titles to the name eventually decreased), they no longer defined social identities, at least not to the same extent that they did at the beginning of the century—which is to say that even a Herr Professor had to be a *Mensch* and conform to certain codes of behavior and appearance in order to be somebody in society. Most definitely, the sons of miners or, for that matter, farmers or such artisans as bakers would not automatically be expected to enter the same trade. While money was not everything, even the more vaunted vocations became but a source of income which, in defining levels of consumption and life styles, established one's social place. With vocation receding as a social factor that constituted barriers of class and taste, there was no longer a self-evident limit to establishing identities in the act of consumption.

These hard social indicators are complemented by more intangible or, in any case, less well-articulated factors of which two seem to be more relevant in the (West) German context than elsewhere. The first is best captured in the cumulatively changing nature of experience. Given the stakes of the interwar debate on "experience," it is rather difficult to get an appreciation of the very tangible dislocation of this first-hand knowledge of the world in the aftermath of World War II. Without discounting a mostly theoretical argument about the impact of the mass media on sense-perception and the replacement of primary forms of experience by mass-mediated ones, the more practical, postwar German considerations have to do with the fact that for a good

---

[171] Friedrich H. Tenbruck, "Alltagsnormen und Lebensgefühle in der Bundesrepublik," in Richard Löwenthal and Hans-Peter Schwarz, eds., *Die Zweite Republik. 25 Jahre Bundesrepublik Deutschland—eine Bilanz* (Stuttgart, 1974), 288–310.

part of the German population, past experience was no guide for the present because of the tremendous shake-up of the population at the end and in the wake of the war and the subsequent mobility of people.[172] This decline of primary and inherited experience was reinforced, on one hand, by the decimation of a middle generation in war, which set the young against the old with their very different prewar and postwar horizons of experience, and, on the other, by the quite deliberate dissimulation strategies of the Hitler Youth generation to unlearn their socialization and forget their experience as a survival strategy in the postwar world. In either case, the desire for the new and the readiness to abandon the old, which we tend to associate with a working consumer society, emerged in the German context as a sociocultural mechanism to rid oneself of the past. One of the more tangible expressions of this came in the late 1950s and early 1960s, when older Germans began to throw out left and right their old furniture, which they had treasured only a while ago as transgenerational inheritance. It is only befitting that other and many younger people bought up the same furniture to acquire the sheen of a past they did not have. But this typically is the kind of operation that marked the transition into consumer society, the emergence of a vintage industry.

The second factor was most clearly expressed in the relativization of inherited ways of life. This phenomenon is most commonly associated with the strikingly sudden disappearance of older milieus, as for example a distinctly proletarian or, for that matter, Catholic culture.[173] More generally, it may be associated with the devaluation of all kinds of nationalist, socialist, Catholic, or liberal legitimation strategies that had given these discrete ways of life a certain sense of decorum and righteousness. With less of an ideological cocoon to shelter and justify "the way things have always been," the changing horizon of information and communication, because of the mass media and a new mobility, could more easily facilitate a culture of, quite frequently envious, comparison, and processes of acculturation and adjustment that came to be associated with the new and splendiferous commodity explosion. But this captures the process only very incompletely. An entire universe of moral certainties, invested by the authority of the state, the church, and the educated elite, and, in smaller towns, the control of

---

[172] See chapter 7.

[173] Josef Mooser, *Arbeiterleben in Deutschland 1900–1970. Klassenlagen, Kultur und Politik* (Frankfurt, 1984); and Benjamin Ziemann, "Der deutsche Katholizismus im späten 19. und 20. Jahrhundert. Forschungstendenzen auf dem Weg zu sozialgeschichtlicher Fundierung und Erweiterung," *Archiv für Sozialgeschichte* 40 (2000): 402–22.

notables, crumbled in the face of invidious comparison—and all that was left, although there was much of it, was a world of goods with which to negotiate exactly the way one ought to live. This is the moment when Weberian *Lebensführung* turned into a search for a lifestyle that would capture, consolidate, and orient individual existence.[174]

What matters in all of this is the shift from commodity culture to consumer society. The imperative of the 1950s was, as the saying went, "to build a new existence"—and in this, most everyone tacitly acknowledged that commodities were not just satisfying needs, but were also a way of anchoring one's life. But what the avid consumers got was more than they had bargained for. Rather than getting more of what they had always wanted or what previous regimes had promised, and rather than shoring up and recreating inherited ways of life, they were catapulted into a world in which the act of getting and spending, the consumption of commodities, replaced and substituted for inherited ways of life. The majority of Germans wanted to satisfy their needs and wants, but they got a society in which needs and wants proved unlimited and in which the very act of consumption defined who and what you were in a society-wide structure of meaning and feeling organized primarily around the act of getting and spending. This kind of culture was usually associated with *Amerika*, but now it was homegrown with various and sundry American commodities and experiences (such as they were afforded by the new entertainment culture) sprinkled in.

Much as this process was driven by an economy of wants and desires, it was always also a contested arena for the reconfiguration of a society that was shattered by war and had lost its orientation. Hence the extraordinary combination of self-serving satisfaction and deep disappointment among the first generation of postwar consumers who got what they wanted and yet had hopelessly lost their bearing, clinging desperately to anachronistic pre-consumer standards and values served up lovingly on television in soap operas—some of them, like famous *Familie Hesselbach*, tongue-in-cheek, some of them, like the *Schwarzwaldklinik*, with the fake pathos of yesteryear. Hence the trouble with the family in the 1960s and 1970s. Family had just begun to settle in the late 1950s, only to fall apart in a grand way. The much-vaunted family proved exceedingly fragile in the face of conflict between generations and between genders, which all had their source in struggles

---

[174] Hans-Peter Müller, *Sozialstruktur und Lebensstile. Der neuer theoretische Diskurs über soziale Ungleichheit* (Frankfurt am Main, 1992); and Gerhard Schulze, *Die Erlebnisgesellschaft. Kultursoziologie der Gegenwart* (Frankfurt, 1992).

over the ways that people wanted or felt they had to live their lives and spend their free time. Hence, also, the otherwise inscrutable rage and anxiety of a generation of young consumers who turned against the idea of consumer society even as they lived it like nobody else in Europe. Part of the problem was, of course, the claim of the young and rebellious that they should lead society and define the meaning of things, and that they should be paid back in respect for their own relative deprivation in relation to the professional and working classes. But the major part was a very distinct despair over the vast dislocation of values, customs, and norms seemingly only enhanced by consumer society and, at the same time, the very anxiety about the magnitude of experimentation over all aspects of life, in which parents, tradition, ideology, and religion were no guidance at all and in which meaning and feeling, the ways of ordering one's life, had indeed become a matter of consuming desire.

It is difficult to escape the paradox that while so much German public debate was bent on arresting this process, the process itself gathered strength in the midst of such adversity, often advanced by the very same people who so adamantly opposed it. We may think here not only of the Adenauer governments during he 1950s, which, while advancing a restoration of vested authority in public and private life, effectively paved the way for an age of mass consumption. The student and youth movements of the 1960s and 1970s repeated the pattern. In challenging consumer society, they emerged as its most profligate consumers. This contradiction is not least exhibited in the West German trademark of humanism and efficiency—evident on one hand in the work of a designer like Jill Sanders and on the other in "Saturday Night Live" spoofs of black-clad, high-strung, and endlessly brainy German lifestyle consumers in New York—that characterized the post-national cosmopolitanism of West German society.[175] These tensions and contradictions are a product of the remaking of values and norms for which consumer society has become both cause and effect. This was not always the case, not even in postwar Germany. And it was never true for East Germany.[176] But the very fact that consumer society was ushered in as a way of rebuilding society in the wake of the war, makes plausible that postwar (West) Germans became more dependent on consumerism in providing meaning and orientation than most any other nation.

---

[175] Ronald Ingelhart, *The Silent Revolution: Changing Values and Political Styles among Western Publics* (Princeton, 1977).

[176] Ina Merkel, *Utopie und Bedürfnis. Die Geschichte der Konsumkultur in der DDR* (Cologne, 1999).

Consumer society, whatever else its merits and pathologies, established the market of meanings and feelings in which the moral universe of a shattered German society was remade. Inasmuch as the open experimentation and, in hindsight, often unfathomable follies and rages of consumption have created a society that has remade itself into a plural and altogether cosmopolitan nation, German history in the second half of the twentieth century has indeed had a happy ending.

PART III

LOOKING BACK
AT THE TWENTIETH
CENTURY

11

Survival in Catastrophe:
Mending Broken
Memories

Many older Germans feel an almost obsessive need to talk about their personal past, especially to a friendly listener from abroad. With little prodding, grizzled men having a beer in a pub will regale a stranger with wartime anecdotes, mostly told as adventure stories from World War II, since those who witnessed the First have largely passed away. Similarly, elderly women enjoying coffee and cake will tell horrifying tales of long nights in air raid shelters, scrounging for food during the postwar period, and desperate efforts to hold their families together despite daunting odds.[1] Presented with much animation, these unstoppable recitals of dire scenes from decades ago contrast oddly with the security and prosperity of present-day surroundings, echoing instead the trials and tribulations of youth. Wordy as they tend to be, the accounts are nonetheless full of strange silences, and differ remarkably from the official histories of German development produced by politicians, journalists, and scholars.

---

[1] Marc Fisher, *After the Wall: Germany, the Germans and the Burdens of History* (New York, 1995); and Jane Kramer, *The Politics of Memory: Looking for Germany in the New Germany* (New York, 1996).

In contrast to the success narratives after 1945, German life histories of the first half of the twentieth century tend to be cast in the trope of "survival stories." Whether they are presented in free-flowing conversations, controlled oral histories, simple and refined autobiographies, or fictionalized accounts such as the novels of Christine Brückner,[2] these recollections do mention such personal events as birth, graduation, first job, marriage, building of a house, and so on. But these stepping stones are usually overshadowed by references to such outside dangers as wars and revolutions, inflation and depression, flight and expulsion—in short, by existential threats that needed to be overcome. Much like Dickensian novels, these tales of triumph over adversity are replete with references to those who did not make it, and the authors take pride in coping, in muddling through, in making do during adverse circumstances. Although an outside questioner might want to hear the stories of perpetrators, these accounts suggest that the lives of the older generations derived much of their meaning from an incessant struggle merely to survive.[3]

The retelling of individual life stories points to a growing intellectual fascination with "memory" as a form of collective coping with postmodern uncertainties. Through workshop, journal, and book titles, the term has become somewhat inflated, including everything from personal recollections to shared heritage practices and collective invocations of tradition.[4] Although welcome, this attention to the presence of the past runs the risk of considering unreflected memory, especially when amplified by gripping media pictures, as more authoritative than the results of scholarly research.[5] In the German context, such a culturalist perspective has been somewhat slower to develop, although the recent heightening of Holocaust sensibility has also created a veritable

[2] Christine Brückner, *Jauche und Levkoien* (Frankfurt, 1975). Better known is Walter Kempowski's multi-volume "chronicle of the German middle class," starting with *Tadellöser und Wolff* (Hamburg, 1978 ff.).

[3] Compare Lutz Niethammer, ed., *"Hinterher merkt man, daß es richtig war, daß es schiefgegangen ist." Nachkriegserinnerungen im Ruhrgebiet* (Berlin, 1983), 259, to Omer Bartov, *Murder in Our Midst: The Holocaust, Industrial Killing and Representation* (New York, 1996), 89 ff.

[4] Alon Confino, "Collective Memory and Cultural History: Problems of Method," *American Historical Review* 102 (1997): 1386–1403; and David Crew, "Remembering German Pasts: Memory in German History, 1871–1989," *Central European History* 33 (2000): 217–34.

[5] Konrad H. Jarausch and Martin Sabrow, eds., *Verletztes Gedächtnis. Erinnerungskultur und Zeitgeschichte im Konflikt* (Frankfurt, 2002); James E. Young, *Formen des Erinnerns. Gedenkstätten des Holocaust* (Vienna, 1997); Dominick LaCapra, *History and Memory after Auschwitz* (Ithaca, 1998).

"memory industry" that treats remembrance as a moral imperative.[6] The discrepancy between positive public pictures and critical academic studies of dictatorship suggests that for Germany the question turns less on the invocation of tradition than on the transmission of individual recollections that do not always agree with what is officially presented as "history."[7]

The elusive process through which personal remembrances turn into public memory therefore requires a more systematic discussion. The reflections by Maurice Halbwachs and Jacques Le Goff indicate that because most incidents are forgotten, those that are retained are the result of repeated retelling, making individual recollection a social act.[8] By being relived in communication rituals, such as family holidays, veterans' meetings, or church socials, these personal experiences gradually blend into group recollections, coalescing into figures of remembrance for those who shared a similar fate. Such collective representations finally tend to interact with competing recollections in the public realm, vying to have their version accepted as binding for the national community to obtain material and political benefits. Interacting with scholarly research, intellectual critiques, and political guidance, these exchanges of individual accounts and group remembrances create a memory culture with remarkably independent ideas about the past. The German language establishes a similar distinction between personal recollection (*Erinnerung*) and public memory (*Gedächtnis*).[9]

The social constitution of memory suggests a narratological approach that would treat individual tales as stories, asking about their emplotment to unlock their meaning. It also implies a sociological effort to discern the points of intersection among personal memories to analyze their transformation into figures of remembrance for different groups. Finally, it encourages cultural questions about the formation and shape of a public memory culture, analyzing its political signification. How do different individuals recall their own trajectories within

[6] Alf Lüdtke, " 'Coming to Terms with the Past': Illusions of Remembering, Ways of Forgetting Nazism in West Germany," *Journal of Modern History* 65 (1993): 542 ff.; and Ulrich Speck, "Wenn Dracula flattert. Geschichte, Erinnerung, Wahrheit—ein Kongreß in Wien," *Frankfurter Rundschau*, 14 March 2001.

[7] Werner Weidenfeld, ed., *Geschichtsbewußtsein der Deutschen. Materialien zur Spurensuche einer Nation* (Cologne, 1987); and Elisabeth Noelle-Neumann, *Demoskopische Geschichtsstunden. Vom Wartesaal der Geschichte zur Deutschen Einheit* (Zurich, 1991).

[8] Maurice Halbwachs, *Les Cadres sociaux de la mémoire*, reprint (New York, 1975), 273 ff.; and Jacques Le Goff, *History and Memory* (New York, 1992), 97 ff.

[9] Marie Claire Lavabre, *Le Fil rouge. Sociologie de la mémoire communiste* (Paris, 1994); and Aleida Assmann and Ute Frevert, *Geschichtsvergessenheit—Geschichtsversessenheit. Vom Umgang mit deutschen Vergangenheiten nach 1945* (Stuttgart, 1999).

the larger cataclysms? Which shared recollections have become so powerful as to create collective images that constitute group identities? Finally, what kind of public memory culture emerges from these contests, especially when popular recollections conflict with intellectual efforts to impose critical versions for didactic purposes?[10] Instead of stressing what the Germans ought to have done, this perspective might help explain how they actually experienced their self-induced catastrophes and afterward managed to live with the terrible burden of their memories.

Survival Stories

In contrast to the pervasive success orientation of American self-representations, which mention setbacks only as challenges to be overcome, German life histories that cover the first half of the twentieth century are mainly cast as survival narratives.[11] Even the copious memoir literature of famous persons, be they political leaders, such as Chancellor Kurt Kiesinger, or cultural icons, such as Stefan Heym, contains harrowing experiences.[12] The oral histories conducted by Lutz Niethammer in the Ruhr Basin, as well as in East Germany during the 1970s and 1980s, provide an even stronger picture of popular suffering, literally using the term *Überleben* in many accounts: In the summer of 1945, one interviewee remembered, "we hugged one another, we had left [the war] behind, once more we had escaped" with our lives.[13] A constant struggle for survival also informs the thousands of autobiographies collected by the novelist Walter Kempowski as material for his collages, since their authors are ordinary people who responded to newspaper ads soliciting their life stories.[14]

A rather untutored example of this leitmotif is my uncle's retelling of the life stories of a Berlin family, written after his retirement in the early 1960s. Untrained as a historian, Bruno Jarausch was a trade-

---

[10] Mary Fulbrook, *German National Identity After the Holocaust* (London, 1999), chap. 6.

[11] John Bart Gerald, ed., *Survival Prose: An Anthology of New Writing* (Indianapolis, 1971); and Kathryn Rhett, ed., *Survival Stories: Memoirs of Crisis* (New York, 1997).

[12] Kurt-Georg Kiesinger, *Dunkle und helle Jahre. Erinnerungen 1904–1958* (Stuttgart, 1989) in contrast to Stefan Heym, *Nachruf*, 2nd ed. (Munich, 1988).

[13] Lutz Niethammer, ed., *"Die Jahre weiß man nicht, wo man sie heute hinsetzen soll."* *Faschismuserfahrungen im Ruhrgebiet* (Berlin, 1983), 7 ff., vol. 1 of his oral history of the working class at the Ruhr.

[14] For his documentary novels, Walter Kempowski collected several thousand manuscript autobiographies. See *Das Echolot. Ein kollektives Tagebuch Januar und Februar 1943*, vol. 1 (Munich 1993).

school teacher with a vivid interest in the past, who set out to trace the development of his clan from its Silesian roots, first documented in 1704, to its later transplantation to the German capital. This text is based upon parish records, wills and deeds, other official documents, personal letters, some diary entries, snippets from local histories, and his exceptional recall. It presents a rich and multi-dimensional account, looking back not just at one life but at the fate of a kin group through some of the vicissitudes of the twentieth century. The tone is direct but not without irony, musing about the unexpected twists and turns of a fortune that started out in a fairly promising fashion only to result in multiple disasters and partial redemptions.[15] Since the Jarausch history is too long to reproduce in its entirety, a brief digest of the most important life events of key protagonists will have to suffice.

The narrative begins in the Silesian village of Michelwitz from which Hugo Jarausch (my grandfather) moved to the German capital Berlin in 1891 to set up a grocery store. The family's growing prosperity was threatened by World War I, forcing both sons to serve at the front. During the Weimar Republic the older brother became a trade-school instructor while the younger brother obtained his Ph.D. with a dissertation on the Icelandic sagas. But the father died during the Depression, forcing the sale of the store. During the Third Reich, both boys started their teaching careers and got married, and the younger one had a son. In World War II, the younger brother was killed at the Russian front, but the older one survived. The widow avoided the allied bombs that destroyed her apartment by moving to the Bavarian countryside. Returning from a POW camp after two years and working on a farm for several more, the older brother finally managed to return to Berlin to rejoin his wife. The young mother struggled to support her infant by teaching in private girls schools until getting a public appointment in the Rhenish city of Krefeld in 1951. After the death of the grandmother, in a retirement home, it was the late 1950s before a semblance of normalcy returned to these shattered lives.

Although these intertwined stories are not typical in all details (there is no flight from the East), their outlines indicate a succession of experiences that can be generalized to a considerable degree. Repeated allusions to "good times" followed by "terrible times," suggest that ordinary lives followed a cyclical pattern that contrasted positive memories of collective advancement with negative recollections of widespread suffering. The good times consisted of the late Empire, the middle years of the Weimar Republic, the period of peace of the Third

---

[15] Bruno Jarausch, "Erinnerungen in einer schlesisch-märkischen Familie" (MS, Berlin, 1960), in the author's possession.

Reich, and then the postwar recovery starting in the mid-1950s. The bad times were the years from the middle of World War I to the end of inflation (1916–23), from the Great Depression to the early Third Reich (1929–35), from the middle of World War II to the currency reform (1942–48/53), and, perhaps, even part of the 1990s, especially in the East.[16] Governed by criteria such as work, food, and housing, this everyday chronology is rather different from the official history of regime changes in 1918, 1933, 1945, and 1989, suggesting that what matters most to people is not high politics but the changing quality of their lives.

Bruno Jarausch's story focuses on moments of crisis rather than on periods of normalcy, since he considered the former memorable and the latter ordinary. While he devotes considerable space to personal events such as marriages and jobs, and even describes vacations in detail, the narrative emphasizes the interruptions resulting from war and economic threats since they wreaked havoc with carefully thought out life plans. In these dramatic instances, history seems to have directly intervened in ordered lives, changing the conditions of existence and forcing individuals to adapt or perish. The hapless people caught up in such events can describe them, but they do not really question their own responsibility for them.[17] Instead, these life histories tend to be told in a reactive fashion, representing individual biographies as subject to irrational forces beyond one's control, which allows individuals the role of merely coping, trying to muddle through, or hoodwinking fate. The recollections of ordinary people, therefore, present a succession of fragmented scenes and portray a past that is incoherent, unstable, and incomprehensible.

Such preoccupation with survival creates a mental horizon fixated on a single individual, stripping away social proprieties and viewing life as a Darwinian struggle. Most stories are told in the first person and describe the fight of one atomized individual against a hostile world, reflecting elemental responses to real necessities and serving as self-justification for the egotistical behavior needed to preserve one's own existence. Sometimes the "I" is expanded to the "we" of a nuclear family or an immediate support community, ignoring its multiple strains in an idealized recollection of mutual aid in extreme circumstances.[18] These tales of endurance center on the various strategies that

[16] Ulrich Herbert, " 'Die guten und die schlechten Zeiten.' Überlegungen zur diachronen Analyse lebensgeschichtlicher Interviews," *Faschismuserfahrungen*, 67–96.

[17] Wartime letters of Konrad Jarausch to his wife and brother, 1939–1942, in the author's possession.

[18] Lutz Niethammer, "Privat-Wirtschaft. Erinnerungsfragmente einer anderen Umerziehung," *Nachkriegserfahrungen*, 39, 69.

made it possible for the narrator to succeed. Beyond repeated references to outright luck, the accounts suggest as dominant responses a withdrawal into a private world and a distrust of political involvement. There is a strong hortatory undertone in these remembrances that recommends to the younger generation strategies of hard work, personal connections, and partial collaboration as guarantor for future success.[19]

Many survival stories are openly gendered, with male narratives celebrating physical exploits, personal daring during wartime, or professional achievements during peacetime.[20] In contrast, female accounts tend to be cast as stories of self-sacrifice and personal privation so as to hold their families together, centering on the care of children, husband, or parents.[21] Generational differences also loom large in recollections because the same event can have different implications for distinctive age groups. While the younger Konrad might safely fantasize about heroic deeds during the early years of World War I, the older Bruno remained skeptical since he had to face the mortal dangers of combat.[22] Subtle distinctions of social class also surface in popular retelling as an important influence on the chances of staying alive through the catastrophes. Workers' accounts tend to focus on the harsh struggle with unemployment or starvation, while middle-class narratives instead revolve around the destruction of a family business, the decline of professional status, or the loss of ancestral lands.[23]

Stories of persecution due to race, national origin, and political involvement offer an even more dramatic plot but are only rarely encountered in popular narratives. Since Nazi discrimination and genocide silenced Jewish citizens and most survivors dispersed to other countries, their recollections have entered German memories only in exceptional cases.[24] Similarly, the horrendous tales of western or Slavic

[19] Margot Schmidt, "Krieg der Männer—Chance der Frauen? Der Einzug von Frauen in die Büros der Thyssen AG," *Faschismuserfahrungen*, 198. See Lutz Niethammer, *Die Volkseigene Erfahrung. Eine Archäologie des Lebens in der Industrieprovinz der DDR* (Berlin, 1991), 157, 630.

[20] Niethammer, *Faschismuserfahrungen*, 163, 267; as well as Niethammer, *Volkseigene Erfahrung*, 100 ff.

[21] Niethammer, *Volkseigene Erfahrung*, 136 ff.; and Lisa Heinemann, "The Hour of the Woman: Memories of Germany's 'Crisis Years' and West German National Identity," *American Historical Review* 101 (1996): 354 ff.

[22] Peter Loewenberg on the Nazi youth cohort in *Decoding the Past: The Psychological Approach* (New York, 1983).

[23] Michael Hayse, "Recasting the West German Elites: Higher Civil Servants, Business Leaders and Physicians in Hessen, 1945–1955" (Ph.D. dissertation, Chapel Hill, 1994).

[24] For exceptions, see Inge Deutschkron, *Ich trug den gelben Stern* (Cologne, 1983); and Marcel Reich-Ranicki, *Mein Leben* (Frankfurt, 2000).

slave laborers' suffering during the world wars have largely been externalized because most are written in languages other than German.[25]
In contrast, memories of antifascist resisters have been canonized by
the Left in the form of secular martyr stories that highlight admirable
moral commitment in the face of overwhelming odds. The Right has
had a more difficult time accepting the legacy of the bourgeois resistance because the elite members of the *Widerstand* could be charged
with treason to the war effort.[26] Instead of denouncing such repression,
the recollections of the majority tend to recall isolated incidents of persecution as cautionary tales, motivating a retreat from politics to ensure personal survival in repressive regimes.

Narratives about the East German dictatorship follow a similar out-
line, although in a more moderate fashion, as they recount a Schwej-
kian muddling through by complicity with and subversion of authority. The autobiography of the writer Günter de Bruyn, for instance,
shows how a single, albeit patient, individual could cope with a powerful and irrational system, achieving a semblance of a normal life
under rather abnormal circumstances. His stories also portray a struggle against a hostile world full of ideological demands, political
threats, and everyday frustrations, and emphasize implicit opposition
to rather than explicit agreement with the SED regime. Nonetheless,
such tales are less extreme because the GDR was not as life threatening,
the Stasi was more subtle in its methods of repression, and the longer
life span of Communist rule required greater adaptation. At least in
theory, the Marxist-Leninist ideology was also more humane than the
racial fantasies of the Nazis, making collaboration more understand-
able.[27] GDR accounts therefore extend the survival trope into the second half of the century, blending it with some elements of their own
success narrative.

The representation of individual experiences as survival stories suggests a strenuous, but rather limited effort to make sense of seemingly
nonsensical events. This trope provides a clear thematic focus that determines the relevance of different incidents and creates a simple, yet
flexible plot line capable of integrating a variety of dramatic scenes
into a memorable narrative. At the same time, this perspective indicates the failure of ideological explanations, which focus on nation or

---

[25] Ulrich Herbert, *Fremdarbeiter. Politik und Praxis des 'Ausländer-Einsatzes' in der Kriegswirtschaft des Dritten Reiches* (Berlin, 1986).

[26] Jürgen Danyel, *Die geteilte Vergangenheit. Zum Umgang mit Nationalsozialismus und
Widerstand in beiden deutschen Staaten* (Berlin, 1995); Peter Steinbach, " 'Stachel im Fleisch
der deutschen Nachkriegsgesellschaft.' Die Deutschen und der Widerstand," *Aus Politik
und Zeitgeschichte* 24 (1994): 3–14.

[27] Günter de Bruyn, *Vierzig Jahre. Ein Lebensbericht* (Frankfurt, 1996).

class, in providing transpersonal meaning to the confusing succession of events. The primary emphasis on muddling through represents individual actions as mere responses to larger, uncontrollable forces and thereby evades the question of personal responsibility for the catastrophes. Finally, the stress on survival—on overcoming enormous obstacles and restoring a semblance of order to individual lives—provides a source of pride that permeated the postwar years. This framing of popular recollections is not just an inevitable result of the disconcerting events themselves, but an individualized attempt to order memories in a particular way.

Figures of Remembrance

Before turning into long-range "cultural memory," shared individual stories pass through a stage of collective remembrance that fixes them into a figurative pattern. This intermediary level, slighted in Jan Assmann's typology, involves the recollection of certain defining events that affect large groups and shape their identity through a specific way of being preserved. By being narrated in a particular, stylized form, diverse personal fates are gradually combined into collective experiences that can be invoked for emotional solidarity, material gain, and the like.[28] But depending upon the perspective of the group to which one belongs, the traumas of the Third Reich and the SED regime have left distinctive traces, although differing in substantive recollection and interpretative connotation. The incompatibility of such partial accounts has led to conflicts among competing versions of an event that vie with one another for control over the memory of the larger community. Once established, many of these figures of remembrance tend to assume a life of their own, passing on to new generations like secondhand smoke.

The shock of the world wars burned into German recollections a succession of catastrophic images that in turn came to dominate collective remembrances. The middle-class history of the Jarausch family portrays the Wilhelmian period as *die gute alte Zeit*, the good old days of order and prosperity in which even working-class resentment against patriarchal exploitation affirmed its basic stability. World War I ruptured that security for soldiers like Bruno Jarausch, who vividly described the *Fronterlebnis* of fighting in the trenches, even if their con-

---

[28] Halbwachs, *Les Cadres sociaux de la mémoire*, 273 ff.; and Jan Assman, "Kollektives Gedächtnis und kulturelle Identität," in Jan Assman and Tonio Hölscher, eds., *Kultur und Gedächtnis* (Frankfurt, 1988), 9–19.

structions ranged from a rightist sense of male bonding to a leftist interpretation of the pointlessness of war. As the first total war, it pulled civilians into the vortex of suffering, for instance, in the *Kohlrü-* ~~*Stock*~~ *benwinter* of 1917 with its starvation induced by the British blockade, which some women denounced as the height of folly, but others saw as a triumph of "the will to persevere."[29] Finally, the defeat of the Kaiser's armies sparked the "bread and peace" revolution of 1918, which both founded the Weimar Republic and spawned the rightist myth of a *Dolchstoß* by the Left that was supposed to have stabbed the victorious German army in the back.

One construction that proved capable of subsuming such differences was the reference to a community of fate, a *Schicksalsgemeinschaft* that bound all of its members together in shared suffering. Conjuring pictures of wheelbarrows full of worthless money or people standing in endless bread lines, recollections of the hyperinflation of 1923 and the Great Depression of 1929 were uniformly negative since even those who profited from the twin disasters were loath to admit it in public. Similarly, Bruno Jarausch's description of the Third Reich as an overpowering fate indicates individual helplessness and sidesteps the issue of personal agency, which might have raised uncomfortable questions of guilt by collaboration with the Nazis. Fatalistic representations of World War II as an affliction from above made it possible to tell various individual tales, all of which shared the basic framework of a fate that remained inexplicable in the final analysis. Echoing Hitler's references to "providence," this self-view turned the racist *Volksgemeinschaft* into a different kind of community of suffering.[30]

This selective perception accounts for the prevalence of the victimization perspective in German recollections of wartime and postwar chaos. Although Konrad Jarausch's letters describe his anguish over the mass death of Russian POWs, his brother's history does not mention his own participation in military killing, racial genocide, or slave labor, showing little sympathy for the pain inflicted upon others.[31] Instead, collective memories accentuate German suffering in the fierce struggle on the Eastern Front against the Red Army, the helpless subjection to Allied saturation bombing of cities like Dresden at home, or the desperate flight from the East to escape the expected and real re-

[29] Jürgen Kocka, *Klassengesellschaft im Krieg 1914–1918* (Göttingen, 1973).

[30] Frank Trommler, "The Historical Invention and Modern Reinvention of Two National Identities," in Norbert Finzsch and Dietmar Schirmer, eds., *Identity and Intolerance: Nationalism, Racism and Xenophobia in Germany and the US* (Cambridge, 1998), 21–42.

[31] See the controversy about the Wehrmachtsausstellung in Munich on H-German, summer 1996. See also Hamburger Institut für Sozialforschung, *Verbrechen der Wehrmacht. Dimensionen des Vernichtungskrieges* (Hamburg, 2001).

venge of the Red Army. Since they affected the majority, the hunger and cold of the severe winter of 1946–47 seem to have left deeper traces in collective remembrances than either the disappearance of the Jews from the neighborhood or the slave labor of Polish POWs.[32] In a sense, these recollections point out that racial war was terrible for everyone, but they elide the crucial distinction between perpetrators, bystanders, and victims.

The example of the expulsion from the East at the end of World War II illustrates how some group experiences come to assume a definitive shape and relevance beyond those immediately concerned. While voluntarily fleeing the Red Army or being forcefully expelled from their ancestral homes, over twelve million women, children, elderly people, and a few noncombatant men severely suffered in trekking hundreds of kilometers to the west, being plundered and raped, and starving and freezing during the winter. When they arrived at last in camps or with relatives, many poured out their traumatic experiences to sympathetic listeners who had been prepared by Goebbels's propaganda for such tales of horror. Often, the refugees also talked to one another about what had happened, seeking solace in shared suffering. To obtain public help, refugees organized into groups whose spokesmen recounted their terrible fate in a stylized form, and the FRG government supported an oral history project to document their plight and support claims for a return to their homeland. Although in the East the subject of *Umsiedler* remained taboo, in the West the cumulative process of social retelling and media broadcasting combined millions of disparate recollections into one common memory of the *Vertreibung*.[33]

When they reach the postwar era, German life histories, nonetheless, shift imperceptibly from accounts of suffering to celebrations of successful rebuilding, economic revival, and political rebirth that create more positive images. The arduous task of physical reconstruction has come to be symbolized by the *Trümmerfrauen*, hard-working women who cleared the rubble from the bombed cities and salvaged the bricks to build new houses for decimated families. In the West, economic recovery is celebrated by tales of the currency reform, Ludwig Erhard's gamble on replacing the worthless Rentenmark with the new deutsche Mark, which overnight filled the shelves of stores with consumer goods and jump-started the economic miracle. In the East, the *Auf-*

---

[32] Robert Moeller, *War Stories: The Search for a Usable Past in the Federal Republic of Germany* (Berkeley, 2001).

[33] Theodor Schieder, ed., *Dokumentation der Verteibung der Deutschen aus Ostmitteleuropa*, 5 vols. (Bonn, 1954–1961); and Elisabeth Horst, "The Expulsion of the Germans from the East and the Creation of Memory, 1944–1960" (M.A. thesis, Chapel Hill, 1994).

baugeneration points with much pride to such Socialist projects as the construction of its own steel industry in the newly built city of Eisen-hüttenstadt.[34] Compared to the exciting purchase of the first car, whether VW beetle or Trabi, political events, such as the founding of the rival successor states, seem to have left fewer memories. In presenting positive accounts of restoring normalcy, narrators are in effect praising their own achievement of recovery.

In the West, it took the youth revolt of 1968 to challenge representations of victimization or success and to create a set of alternative recollections. The Marxist, anarchist, and radical democratic rebellion of postwar children bridled at their parents' evasions regarding complicity with the Third Reich and tried to invoke the heroic example of the antifascist resistance as a base for reforming society. At the same time the young rejected the complacency of the consumer mentality by pointing to the hypocrisy of the Vietnam War, the capitalist degradation of the environment, and the paternalist domination of women. The heady experience of solidarity in the New Social Movements of the 1970s created a set of emancipatory countermemories based on participation in peace marches, antinuclear protests, and sexual provocations. During the 1980s, the older generation and more conservative youths, led by Chancellor Helmut Kohl, tried to undo this "cultural revolution" to restore the satisfaction with postwar success. In this ideological confrontation, supporters gradually enlarged the minor events of the youth revolt into a veritable generational myth of 1968 to rouse its partisans and scare its detractors.[35]

In the East, it was the unexpected collapse of Communism and the subsequent rush to German unity that overthrew the postwar memory regime. During the exhilarating autumn of 1989, the contradictory mixture of official claims to progress and personal recollections of intimidation no longer held a restive population in check. Ordinary East Germans rejected the habit of acquiescence to authority, while intellectuals, like Christa Wolf, repudiated the Communists' instrumentalization of antifascism as justification for their new dictatorship. The mass exodus, democratic awakening, and reformist agitation in the SED demonstrated that the regime had lost its moral legitimacy and that people were ready to reclaim their independence. Rich in memorable moments, dramatic events from the Leipzig demonstra-

[34] See Rosemarie Beier, ed., *Aufbau West—Aufbau Ost. Die Planstädte Wolfsburg and Eisen-hüttenstadt in der Nachkriegszeit* (Berlin, 1997), catalogue of a Deutsches Historisches Museum exhibition.

[35] Arthur Marwick, *The Sixties: Cultural Revolution in Britain, France, Italy and the United States, c. 1958–c.1974* (Oxford, 1998).

tions to the fall of the Wall have created new recollections of popular empowerment through protest and self-determination, suggesting involvement rather than compliance. But because of the subsequent "unification crisis," many East Germans have started to feel nostalgic for lost security, while Westerners grumble about the material cost of unification, once again reviving memories of victimization.[36]

These upheavals of 1968 and 1989 have produced intriguing individual stories and inspiring group anecdotes but have so far failed to coalesce into new narratives of democratization.[37] Literary portrayals indicate their rich resonance for the activists of the 1960s and the dissidents of the1980s, but for the uninvolved majorities, the events appear to remain contested because of their ambivalent consequences. Perhaps the temporal distance is still too short, and the participants too young, to surround these struggles with the golden glow of youth remembered by age. Perhaps the peaceful character of the demonstrations and the gradual character of the ensuing changes have prevented their collective invocation as basis of later canonization, although the fall of the Wall ought to have been dramatic enough. Perhaps the effect of the democratic challenges on individual lives was also less drastic than the suffering during depression and war, keeping them from being etched into public memory in the same way. Finally, the collapse of Communism may have blocked their acceptance, since it revived the survival cum victimization trope as representation of the second German dictatorship.

Through all these changes, three fundamental perspectives, defined by a group's relation to the events in question, have remained rather persistent. First, there are the victims, whose numbers seem to have miraculously increased over time. Although only few camp inmates or resistance members survived to tell their tales after 1945, a media-created Holocaust recollection of Nazi atrocities against the Jews has come to dominate the official memory culture and the self-consciousness of the intellectuals.[38] In contrast, the recollection of GDR victims is focused on the less drastic Soviet special camps, the later Stasi high security prisons, the expulsion of dissenters to the West, and the police chicanery against opposition members. Although some sites, like Bu-

---

[36] Daniela Dahn, *Westwärts und nicht vergessen. Vom Unbehagen in der Einheit* (Berlin, 1996); and Hans Misselwitz, *Nicht länger mit dem Gesicht nach Westen. Das neue Selbstbewußtsein der Ostdeutschen* (Bonn, 1996).

[37] Konrad H. Jarausch, "1968 and 1989: Caesuras, Comparisons, and Connections," in Carole Fink, Philipp Gassert, and Detlev Junker, eds., *"1968": World Transformed* (Cambridge, 1988).

[38] Bernd Giesen, *Intellectuals and the German Nation* (Cambridge, 1998); and Mariam Niraumand, *The Americanization of the Holocaust* (Berlin, 1995).

chenwald, are contested, in both cases the preservation of the legacy of suffering serves as a core of identity for victims and as a legal basis for restitution claims. Regarding the Third Reich, however, the minority of the persecuted has succeeded in dominating historical recollections, while victims' organizations are still struggling to impose their harsh view of the SED regime upon the memory culture of the FRG.[39]

Second, there are the perpetrators, who have tended to be less vocal in presenting their own versions of the past. Since many of the chief culprits were imprisoned or committed suicide, the Third Reich is recalled in guilt-ridden conversion accounts such as the successful Speer memoirs, and only recently has a whole spate of Hitler Youth books dared to show more positive recollections. Since the substance of Nazi war and genocide cannot be defended in public, apologias of the Hitler regime tend to emphasize the good aspects of a bad cause, for instance, the decline in unemployment or the building of the Autobahn.[40] In contrast, representatives of the defunct GDR, like Hans Modrow, have an easier time in explaining their altruistic motives since the socialist utopia is not such a fundamental rupture with the Enlightenment traditions of the West. Even if there are also some self-incriminations, the majority of the East German memoirs instead stresses the bad implementation of a basically good idea. Blaming an imperfect realization allows such groups as the PDS to cling to the socialist idea and to hope that it will work out better the next time.[41]

Finally, the perspective of the majority of the population is that of collaborators who often claim to have been only bystanders, but who in fact abetted the dictatorial regimes. Regarding the Third Reich, a whole series of excuses has emerged to explain personal complicity, beginning with doing one's duty to being a patriot to not being able to foresee the bitter end. Nonetheless, such public events as the Wehrmacht exhibition, documenting the atrocities committed by the regular army, have made it more difficult for ordinary people to disassociate themselves from the horrors of the Nazi regime.[42] Regarding the GDR, it has once again been easy to plead that one led a normal life within the niches of the regime, withdrew into a private realm, and made only minimal concessions to the SED. Moreover, references to the illusion of the East being the "better Germany," that is, the humanitarian and

---

[39] *Spuren Suchen und Erinnern. Gedenkstätten für die Opfer politischer Gewaltherrschaft in Sachsen* (Leipzig, 1996).

[40] Albert Speer, *Inside the Third Reich: Memoirs* (New York, 1970).

[41] Günter Schabowski, *Der Absturz* (Berlin, 1991); and Hans Modrow, *Ich wollte ein anderes Deutschland* (Berlin, 1998).

[42] Hamburger Institut für Sozialforschung, ed., *Vernichtungskrieg. Verbrechen der Wehrmacht 1941 bis 1944. Ausstellungskatalog* (Hamburg 1997).

socially progressive ideology of Socialism, can be invoked to motivate a degree of collusion with the Party's demands.[43] Split into victim, perpetrator, and bystander perspectives, group accounts are replete with contending recollections which highlight different lessons that refuse to produce a coherent sense of the past.

Public Memory Culture

When projected into the public arena, the competing individual stories and collective recollections lead to the creation of a memory culture that defines how a country deals with its own past. In this debate about the meaning of earlier events, the print and electronic media select certain dramatic images and voices, amplify their intensity, and broadcast their messages to a wider audience that wants to be entertained and have its sentiments reinforced rather than challenged. Nonetheless, historians attempt to present scholarly reconstructions of the record that sometimes conflict with popular versions, but their more sophisticated accounts tend to reach fewer readers and sometimes pursue interpretative agendas of their own. Finally, politicians also tend to invoke symbols from the past, refer to collective experiences, and promote their own, often rather one-sided, lessons to mobilize their followers. In the German case, the complex interaction that formed a public memory, dominated by the legacy of the Third Reich, is referred to by the somewhat awkward term *Vergangenheitsbewältigung*.[44]

The most immediate memory problem after World War II was the uncertainty of how to deal with the fallen soldiers after the second, even greater defeat. While the Allied occupiers made sure that their own heroes were remembered appropriately, German graves were spread all over the continent, often unmarked and in countries deeply resentful of Nazi atrocities. The dismantling of the Wehrmacht and the initial prohibition against veterans' organizations removed the military basis for a memorialization of the dead soldiers, leaving the task to civilian authorities. But millions of families needed to find a public way to address their bereavement, which had become more painful because it had lost its overarching national purpose. The results were pragmatic and piecemeal solutions, such as a *Kriegsgräberfürsorge*, that

[43] Stefan Wolle, *Die Heile Welt der Diktatur. Alltag und Herrschaft in der DDR, 1971–1989* (Berlin, 1998).

[44] Charles S. Maier, *The Unmasterable Past: History, Holocaust and German National Identity* (Cambridge, 1988); and Peter Reichel, *Vergangenheitsbewältigung in Deutschland* (Munich, 2001).

attempted to catalogue and maintain graves, oversee the simple addition of names to existing memorial tablets in churches, and lobby for the introduction of a *Volkstrauertag*, a national day of mourning that dwelt on personal sacrifice in a generally apolitical way.[45] Unlike in France, public monuments to fallen soldiers of World War II are rare in Germany.

Initially, the suffering of victims of German aggression and atrocities did not weigh with similar intensity on the public conscience. When occupation soldiers forced the local population to view the shocking evidence of killing in liberated camps like Buchenwald, many tended to look away, claiming not to have known anything about these atrocities. Allied insistence on reeducation and denazification added an element of confrontation, exemplified by the denunciation of the Nuremberg trials as "victor's justice," that made it possible for Germans to close ranks with the *Persilscheine*, the whitewashing of one's Nazi past. Preoccupied with its own struggle for survival, the populace abandoned its initial soul searching, preferring to ignore the collaborators and repress these troubling memories in order to get on with their personal lives. Returned émigrés and antifascists, who insisted on a more thorough accounting, quickly found themselves isolated and surrounded with an unbreachable wall of silence.[46] As a result, many of the sites of persecution, once they were no longer used as DP or refugee camps, went untended for years.

In the divided country, only critical minorities were willing openly to confront the terrible memories of Nazi crimes. Claiming the mantle of the antifascist resistance, the SED held the traditional elites culpable, expropriating Junkers and capitalists, and denouncing professors and journalists as accomplices of the Third Reich. This resolute distancing from the past provided a clear break, but its economic reductionism exculpated scores of ordinary *Mitläufer* by heaping all guilt upon the bourgeoisie and externalizing it to the Federal Republic. In the West, such intellectuals as the writers of Gruppe 47, such Protestant clergymen as Martin Niemöller, and such philosophers as Karl Jaspers, raised the issue of German guilt. Leading statesmen—for instance, Konrad Adenauer, Theodor Heuss, and Kurt Schumacher—also condemned the atrocities but tended to limit responsibility to the Nazi leadership, the SS, or SA, rather than implicating industrialists or gen-

---

[45] Sabine Behrenbeck, *Der Kult um die toten Helden. Nationalsozialistische Mythen, Riten und Symbole 1923–1945* (Cologne, 1996); and Klaus Naumann, *Nachkrieg in Deutschland* (Hamburg, 2001).

[46] Harold Marcuse, *Legacies of Dachau: The Uses and Abuses of a Concentration Camp, 1933–2000* (Cambridge, 2001). See Frank Stern, *Im Anfang war Auschwitz. Antisemitismus und Philosemitismus im deutschen Nachkrieg* (Gerlingen, 1991).

erals. Nonetheless, the FRG accepted its collective responsibility and negotiated restitution payments to Israel and the Jewish community to regain international respectability.[47]

In both successor states, the majority of the population, nonetheless, obdurately clung to its own, more favorable, memories of the Third Reich. Well into the 1950s, the public, in opinion surveys, considered National Socialism a good idea badly carried out, and strong minorities continued to call Hitler a great statesman. Hence, "the politics of the past" helped integrate former Nazis into the economy or the civil service, and ritualistic references of contrition regarding German atrocities were met with a deafening silence. More candid private conversations used evasive phrases like "antipartisan retaliation," painted the Nazis as an aberration, and recalled the full employment and public order of the Third Reich, apparently untouched by the critical efforts of professional historians in the new Institute of Contemporary History. While such openly neo-Nazi parties as the Sozialistische Reichspartei were forbidden in the West, the SED insisted on forming a neo-nationalist party, the NDPD, to integrate former Nazis into its regime.[48] In general, the Cold War hastened public forgetting since it projected guilt onto the other side by painting it as totalitarian or neofascist.

To legitimize their competing systems, the GDR and FRG gradually developed contrasting memory cultures out of a shared experience. The East German version claimed "progressive" traditions of the labor movement and humanist intellectuals, erecting monuments not just to the liberating Red Army, but also to Marx and Engels and such Communist leaders as Teddy Thälmann. The historical exhibition in the Zeughaus in the heart of Berlin represented the past as a glorious struggle for emancipation, culminating in the inevitable advance of the East German state. West German self-understanding had a more difficult time in recovering submerged democratic traditions of the 1848 revolution, restoring Christian legacies, or reconnecting to achievements of high culture. The exhibition on German history, housed in the Reichstag building on the western side of the Wall, sought to raise questions about liberal aspirations as well as illiberal setbacks in a more nuanced understanding of the past.[49] This difference in self-

---

[47] Jeffrey Herf, *Divided Memory: The Nazi Past in the Two Germanys* (Cambridge, 1997); and Niethammer, *Faschismuserfahrungen*, 209 ff., 213ff.

[48] Richard and Anna Merrit, *Public Opinion in Occupied Germany: The OMGUS Surveys, 1945–1949* (Urbana, 1970); and Norbert Frei, *Vergangenheitspolitik. Die Anfänge der Bundesrepublik und die NS-Vergangenheit* (München, 1996).

[49] Deutscher Bundestag, ed., *Fragen an die Deutsche Geschichte. Ideen, Konzepte und Entwicklungen von 1800 bis zur Gegenwart*, 17th ed. (Bonn, 1993).

representations was compounded by the growing distinction in respective life experiences in the East and the West.

Only when many perpetrators were starting to pass away in the 1960s and 1970s did critical approaches to the German past begin to make real headway with the populace. In the East, the arrival of a generation that had been brought up on antifascist rhetoric helped distance the public from a past that could no longer be discussed in personal terms, thereby effacing contrary memories. It took exceptional writers like Christa Wolf to raise the issue of individual complicity.[50] In the West, the creation of the special prosecutors office in Ludwigsburg, the Eichmann trial in Jerusalem, as well as the subsequent Auschwitz case in Frankfurt, raised the question of personal responsibility. Authors like Rolf Hochhut and Günter Grass encouraged rebellious youths to ask embarrassing questions about the wartime behavior of their fathers, while media representation, such as the American television series on the Holocaust, helped create a greater awareness of Jewish suffering. The hiring of a new cohort of critical history teachers also made the subject of the Third Reich a more central part of the curriculum, and the critical work of contemporary historians helped explode popular myths.[51]

During the 1980s, East and West Germans, nevertheless, showed a curious hunger for a usable past that would assuage some of the pangs of suppressed guilt. In the GDR the narrowness of the Marxist tradition encouraged the search for broader legacies that would include the partial rehabilitation of proscribed figures like Martin Luther, Frederic the Great, or even Otto von Bismarck. Beneath the blanket of ideological uniformity, the public began to rediscover its different regional roots in Prussian or Saxon heritage.[52] In the West, hundreds of thousands of people flocked to exhibitions of the glories of the medieval Hohenstaufen emperors, the splendid Roman remains in the Rhine valley, and the like. But when neoconservative historians like Ernst Nolte or Andreas Hillgruber began to question the self-critical version of the German past in print, progressive intellectuals, led by the formidable Jürgen Habermas, unleashed a *Historikerstreit* that rejected such apolo-

---

[50] Christa Wolf, *Kindheitsmuster* (Darmstadt, 1976).

[51] Axel Schildt, Detlef Siegfried, and Karl-Christian Lammers, eds., *Dynamische Zeiten. Die 60er Jahre in den beiden deutschen Gesellschaften* (Hamburg, 2000); and Peter Krause, "Die Rezeption des Eichmann-Prozesses in der deutschen Presse" (Ph.D. dissertation, Berlin, 1999).

[52] Helmut Meier and Walter Schmidt, eds., *Erbe und Tradition in der DDR. Die Diskussion der Historiker* (Berlin, 1988).

getic revisionism.[53] While scholarship and the media became ever more vigorous in denouncing German guilt, public sentiment continued to long for a less problematic version of the past.

Conflict between personal memories, collective representations, and public memorialization tended to come to a head during various ill-fated anniversaries of German history. How should the fiftieth return of the Nazi seizure of power, the unleashing of World War II, or the defeat of the Wehrmacht be commemorated in public? Under the glare of international observation, politicians would utter predictable phrases of regret, make symbolic gestures of contrition, or convene scholarly conferences, while older TV viewers recalled the event quite differently. When the East and the West officially celebrated the end of the Third Reich as "liberation," many surviving participants remembered a crushing defeat and the beginning of their own suffering, hardly a cause for joy. It took until 1985 for President Richard von Weizsäcker to engage this difference candidly when he argued that both meanings of 1945 were causally related and inextricably intertwined. Ten years later, personal memories poured into the media in a veritable flood, providing a forum for discussing the link between the suffering of victims and perpetrators.[54]

German unification added another layer of complications to this embattled memory culture by superimposing Western structures upon different Eastern patterns. In some ways this was a positive development since the *verordnete Antifaschismus* of the GDR went only skin deep, while the reluctant confrontation with the past in the FRG created a more personal sense of responsibility. In other ways, this uneven conflation of antagonistic memory regimes has also caused considerable difficulties since many East Germans felt robbed of their past when Lenin statutes were toppled unceremoniously and streets were suddenly renamed.[55] The collapse of the second German dictatorship did not just efface Party emblems or shut down factories but left a welter of confusing personal memories among the Eastern population, ranging all the way from repression to normalcy, while the disappear-

[53] Richard Evans, *In Hitler's Shadow: West German Historians and the Attempt to Escape from the Nazi Past* (New York, 1989); and Peter Baldwin, *Reworking the Past: Hitler, the Holocaust and the Historians' Debate* (Boston, 1990).

[54] Dagmar Barnouw, *Germany 1945: Views of War and Violence* (Berkeley, 1996); and Geoffrey Giles, ed., *Stunde Null: The End and the Beginning Fifty Years Ago* (Washington, D.C., 1997).

[55] Helga Welsch, Andreas Pickel, and Dorothy Rosenberg, "East and West German Identites: United and Divided?" in Konrad H. Jarausch, ed., *After Unity: Reconfiguring German Identities* (Providence, 1997), 103 ff.

ance of items of material culture inspired a pervasive sense of loss. Since more positive recollections did not fit into the Western indictment of the GDR as a totalitarian system, they surfaced in a strange form of nostalgia, sometimes called *Ostalgie*, for an East that never existed in this form.[56]

No wonder the Germans have had a hard time settling on acceptable national holidays. While the Second Empire proudly celebrated its victory over France in Sedans's Day, the Weimar Republic failed to create a democratic holiday, while the Third Reich combined tradition with innovation in the Führer's birthday as well as May 1 as Labor Day. The GDR compelled its citizens to commemorate the liberation by the Soviets on May 7, as well as its own founding on October 7; and the FRG had trouble making June 17, the date of the East Berlin uprising, a popular day of German unity. Since the negative meanings of November 9, such as the outbreak of the 1918 revolution, Hitler's beer hall putsch, or the anti-Semitic pogrom of 1938, overwhelmed the joyful memory of the fall of the Wall, the enlarged Federal Republic ultimately settled upon October 3, the day of the formal accession of the five new states as new national holiday. This somewhat artificial solution bypasses other controversial dates like January 27, the day of the liberation of Auschwitz, or June 20, the date of the resistance putsch against Hitler in 1944.[57]

The result of such efforts to cope with German catastrophes is an insecure memory culture full of taboos and given to controversy. When accepting the publishers' peace prize in October 1998, the novelist Martin Walser introspectively probed his own resentment against "the instrumentalization of our shame for present purposes." His somewhat opaque speech culminated in the warning: "Auschwitz is not suited to serve as a routinized threat, a means of intimidation that can be used at any time, be it as a moral club or as an exercise in duty." Stung by this provocation, Ignatz Bubis, the liberal head of the Central Council of Jews in Germany, denounced this conclusion as "latent anti-Semitism" and the speaker as "an intellectual fire-bug." The ensuing media uproar pitted "normalizers," like Karl-Heinz Bohrer, who argued that pride was a prerequisite for feeling shame, against critics who insisted on the undiminished "weight of the crimes." By reen-

[56] Jürgen Kocka, "A Common View of a Divided Past? Historical Consciousness in West Germany and East Germany," *The Third Charlemagne Lecture* (London, 1997). See also Dietrich Mühlberg, "Vom langsamen Wandel der Erinnerung an die DDR," in *Verletztes Gedächtnis*.

[57] Edgar Wolfrum, *Geschichtspolitik in der Bundesrepublik Deutschland. Der Weg zur bundesrepublikanischen Erinnerung 1948–1990* (Darmstadt, 1999).

acting earlier controversies, this storm signaled how far the Berlin Republic still was from a "new normalcy" since the old ghosts refused to go away.[58]

Mending Broken Memories

In contrast to the affirmative recollections of their neighbors, most German memories of the twentieth century are extraordinarily negative. Pierre Nora's somewhat nostalgic conception of French *lieux de mémoire* that collectively constitute a positive sense of nationhood could not simply be transposed across the Rhine because too many German places instead conjured up problematic aspects of the past.[59] Apparently without qualms, the British can still celebrate the daring exploits of their discoverers, the grandiose visions of their empire-builders, and the heroism of resisting the Blitz over London. Even after the failure of the Soviet experiment, the Russians take much pride in their victory over Hitler's aggression in the "Great Fatherland's War," which cemented their hegemony over East Central Europe and justified their superpower status for a half-century. Forgetting their collaboration, the smaller European countries continue to recall their spirited resistance against Nazi domination.[60] Yet what could Germans remember positively from their troubled record, especially in the twentieth century?

To counteract such a "lack of memory," Friedrich Meinecke suggested that Germans ought to recall the richness of an earlier past, full of stellar cultural accomplishments.[61] In a physical sense, this positive legacy was embodied in the soaring cathedrals, the imposing castles, and the impressive city-halls, which represented proud moments in stone to be guarded and rebuilt by historic preservation. In an emotional sense, the mixture of pleasing landscapes and towns, customs

---

[58] Martin Walser, "Erfahrungen beim Verfassen einer Sonntagsrede," *Börsenblatt des deutschen Buchhandels* 82 (13 October 1998), 17–24. "Moral verjährt nicht" interview with Ignatz Bubis, *Der Spiegel* (1998) no. 49. See Karl-Heinz Bohrer, "Schuldkultur oder Schamkultur," *Neue Züricher Zeitung*, 12/13 December 1998.

[59] Etienne François and Hagen Schulze, eds., *Deutsche Erinnerungsorte*, 3 vols. (Munich, 2001); Jürgen Danyel, "Unwirtliche Gegenden und abgelegene Orte. Der Nationalsozialismus und die deutsche Teilung als Herausforderung einer Geschichte der deutschen 'Erinnerungsorte'," *Geschichte und Gesellschaft* 24 (1998): 463–75.

[60] Anrei S. Markovits and Simon Reich, *The German Predicament: Memory and Power in the New Europe* (Cornell, 1997), 34–41.

[61] Karl Heinz Bohrer, "Erinnerungslosigkeit. Ein Defizit der gesellschaftskritischen Intelligenz," *Frankfurter Rundschau*, 16 June 2001.

and dialect, provided a sense of rootedness that informed the peculiarly German cult of *Heimat*, a magic homeland that ranges all the way from local place to the entire nation. In a cultural sense, the celebration of creative geniuses in literature, music, or philosophy by the likes of Goethe, Beethoven, or Kant supported a national tradition of expressive and reflexive *Kultur* that could compare with any other.[62] But on closer inspection, this heritage seems protean and contradictory, changing dramatically in the confrontation with modernity and containing many seeds of its own destruction. Recaptured in splendid exhibitions, older legacies might illustrate signal achievements, but they can hardly serve as a firm anchor for positive memories.

The multiple gaps and odd silences in personal narratives suggest that the catastrophes of the twentieth century have ruptured beyond repair any affirmative relationship to the past. The Jarausch family history demonstrates that well-laid life plans might be drastically altered from one day to the next by uncontrollable outside forces such as war, hyperinflation, or economic depression. When brothers or husbands died before their time, spouses were scattered, apartments or possessions destroyed, and careers ruptured, a threatening history appeared to teach "a survival ideology."[63] Since perpetrators tend to remain silent and victims have been generally externalized, the dominant group recollections of the bystanders do not revolve around German crimes but rather center around their own suffering during bombing, expulsion, and hunger. This tendency toward retrospective self-victimization may be offensive to survivors because it blocks compassion, but the highlighting of the terrible consequences of aggression and repression may also provide some psychological barrier against their repetition.[64] German memories, therefore, rarely address the Holocaust directly but rather focus on more general nightmares of dangers that might suddenly recur and shatter one's existence.

An astounding transformation has, nonetheless, turned the recollections of a persecuted minority into the official public memory during the last half-century. After the war, only a small group of survivors,

---

[62] Rudy Koshar, *Germany's Transient Pasts: Preservation and National Memory in the Twentieth Century* (Chapel Hill, 1998); and Alon Confino, *The Nation as a Local Metaphor: Württemberg, Imperial Germany and National Memory, 1871–1918* (Chapel Hill, 1997).

[63] Lutz Niethammer, "Biographie und Biokratie," *Mitteilungen aus der kulturwissenschaftlichen Forschung* (Festschrift für Dietrich Mühlberg) 37 (1996): 370–87, and *Volkseigene Erfahrung*, 254.

[64] Peter Steinbach, "Die Vergegenwärtigung von Vergangenem. Zum Spannungsverhältnis zwischen individueller Erinnerung und öffentlichem Gedenken," *Aus Politik und Zeitgeschichte* (1997) no. 3: 3–13

regime opponents, critical intellectuals, and religious leaders insisted on accepting responsibility for Nazi crimes. Outside pressure from occupying countries undoubtedly helped support such a rethinking of the past, but the majority of the population rather preferred to cover its own complicity with merciful silence. Although the Cold War confrontation of antifascism and antitotalitarianism complicated matters, by the 1960s a series of dramatic court cases, literary accusations, and media productions began to change public perceptions.[65] The generational revolt against the fathers and the more critical teaching in the schools eventually succeeded both in overriding the oral testimony of family members and in creating a virtual identification with strange victims. Although the collapse of Communism doubled the burden of a dictatorial past, the repeated contestations over responsibility have ultimately succeeded in replacing the apologetic recollections with a more self-critical public memory.[66]

How could such a fundamental reversal of attitudes toward the past occur? Hermann Lübbe's argument, that collective silence aided the material rebuilding and reintegration of collaborators into a society, might have a point for the postwar period. But in the long run, willful forgetting risked the creation of, in Ralph Giordano's words, "a second guilt" because it simply hid the skeletons in the closet.[67] Liberal leaders like Theodor Heuss, progressive intellectuals like the Mitscherlichs, and critical scholars like Karl-Dietrich Bracher, therefore, called for a therapeutic "working-through," an open discussion about responsibility for Nazi crimes.[68] Their appeals have been heeded by religiously inspired groups such as Aktion Sühnezeichen, which brought young Germans together with their neighbors to care for the graves of World War II soldiers. In such unlikely places as the Bavarian city of Passau, everyday historians also uncovered irritating proof of the ubiquity of collaboration, incarceration, and annihilation.[69] Gradually such mounting evidence made even reluctant Germans realize that they

[65] Contrast Frei, *Vergangenheitspolitik*, 7 ff., with Manfred Kittel, *Die Legende von der "Zweiten Schuld". Vergangenheitsbewältigung in der Ära Adenauer* (Frankfurt, 1993).

[66] Konrad H. Jarausch, "A Double Burden: The 'Doppelte Vergangenheitsbewältigung' of the Germans," in Jörn Leonhard, ed., *Ten Years of German Unification: Transfer, Transformation, Incorporation?* (Birmingham, 2001).

[67] Hermann Lübbe, "Verdrängung: Über ein Verhältnis zur deutschen Vergangenheit," *Der Monat* 2 (1979): 55–65; and Ralph Giordano, *Die Zweite Schuld. Oder von der Last ein Deutscher zu sein* (Hamburg, 1987).

[68] Alexander Mitscherlich and Margarete Mitscherlich, *Die Unfähigkeit zu trauern. Grundlagen kollektiven Verhaltens* (Munich, 1967).

[69] Anja Rosmus-Weniger, *Widerstand und Verfolgung am Beispiel Passaus 1933–1939* (Passau, 1983).

could only live with their haunting memories if they related their personal fate to larger processes and accepted responsibility for those whom they hurt along the way.

The symbolic form that this mending of memories might take, nonetheless, remains hotly contested since it needs not only to console but also to irritate. The Bitburg disaster of Kohl's and Reagan's attempt to memorialize Allied and German soldiers, which turned out also to include SS graves, shows how far from settled such issues are.[70] The memorial of the Neue Wache that transformed a Prussian guardhouse and GDR military monument into a site of commemoration for all victims of war and repression has proven more successful since the enlarged pieta by Käthe Kollwitz represents a general human theme of a mother caring for a dead son.[71] The proposal of a citizens' group, headed by Lea Rosh, to create a central Holocaust memorial in Berlin took a decade of controversy before the Bundestag finally decided to construct 2,700 concrete pillars, rather than one simple column, near the Brandenburg Gate, inscribed in Hebrew with the Biblical injunction against killing.[72] The intense conflicts over form and content or memorialization indicate that neither politics nor art can offer simple solutions for healing memories that are as broken as those of the Germans and their victims.

The conflicting stories of perpetrators, bystanders, and victims may never be brought into complete harmony since they represent widely different experiences that are interconnected only by the infliction of suffering. Instead of requiring frantic efforts to produce a single, authoritative narrative, these divergent memories challenge historians to reflect more systematically on the effect of their own experiences when constructing accounts of the past.[73] The fracturing of individual recollections implies that it might be more useful to understand the development of this catastrophic century as a series of life-threatening ruptures that set in motion desperate efforts to survive and to return to normalcy. Rather than being suppressed as partisan simplifications, the contending group versions ought to stimulate a rethinking of the German past, one that accepts its fundamental fragmentation but that

---

[70] Fulbrook, *German National Identity*, chapter 4.

[71] Konrad H. Jarausch, Hinrich C. Seeba, and David P. Conradt, "The Presence of the Past: Culture, Opinion and Identity in Germany," in *After Unity*, 25 ff.

[72] Brian Ladd, *The Ghosts of Berlin: Confronting German History in the Urban Landscape* (Chicago, 1997).

[73] See Peter Fritzsche, "Kollektives Gedächtnis und deutsche Identität nach dem Zweiten Weltkrieg," and Y. Michal Bodemann, "Vom Prozeß in Jerusalem zum Kniefall in Warschau und weiter," in *Verletztes Gedächtnis*.

also looks for points of intersection between different experiences. As a way to greater tolerance in public memory, the novelist Walter Kempowski suggests that the living ought to pay more attention to the fading voices of the dying or the dead: "Listening might make it possible for us finally to get along with each other."[74]

[74] Kempowski, *Echolot*, 7.

12

The Century as History:
Between Cataclysm
and Civility

Educated Germans crossed the threshold into the twentieth century with optimistic expectations. "Another life is struggling to emerge from time: The old departs—and the new strives to be born," a literary magazine welcomed the *Jahrhundertwende* in January 1900. Similarly, the liberal philosopher Theobald Ziegler viewed "the veiled future, full of hope and longing," while thinking about "the land of our children with some concern." When reviewing the course of the nineteenth century, Germans could take much pride in the achievement of national unification, "the joining in one people" that triggered a turn from idealism to a "growing realism" in dealing with the world. In science, technology, and industry there were no doubts about "massive progress." Though worried about the Left's exploitation of social strife, the propagation of a Nietzschean individualism, and the projection of a new idol of "power," Ziegler faced the future with quiet confidence. Like most Germans who wrote their visions of the coming century into a "golden book," he was convinced "that our nation is generally healthy."[1]

---

[1] Joseph Lauff, "Jahrhundertwende," *Velhagen und Klasings Monatshefte* 14 (1899) no. 5: 1 ff; Theobald Ziegler, "Auf der Schwelle des neuen Jahrhunderts," *Neue Rundschau*

A hundred years later at the end of the millennium, reality had trumped such positive predictions in drastically negative ways. To be sure, the titles of a year-long *Spiegel* retrospective, seeking to mirror the twentieth century, indicated much breathtaking progress—the exploration of space, the decoding of genetic secrets, the discovery of new energies, the advances of medical treatment, and the spread of electronic mass communication. But they pointed even more strongly to such shocking developments as the creation of world empires, the rise of communist or fascist dictatorships, the economic crises of capitalism, the unparalleled killings of the world wars and the Holocaust, and the bouts of ethnic cleansing—in short, to an unimaginable increase in human suffering. The tenor of these essays suggested that improvements in daily lives produced by emancipation movements, the welfare state, or the emergence of popular culture were overshadowed by the nightmare legacy of death and destruction.[2] In retrospect, the progressive and barbarous aspects of the century seem to be inextricably intertwined.

This fundamental ambivalence is best captured by personal scrapbooks and individual stories that offer a kaleidoscope of images and memories. Charles Stewart's and Peter Fritzsche's effort at "imagining the twentieth century" therefore poses as "inescapably autobiographical," covering both public events and private lives. Striking individual snapshots, such as babies in nurseries, women in bathing suits lighting up cigarettes, or unemployed migrant laborers, are juxtaposed with conventional pictures of soldiers marching off to war in 1914, a nuclear mushroom cloud, a toppled Lenin statue, and the like. Such collages reduce the century to a collection of multiple images to be cited, contrasted, or superimposed at will, bereft of any logic.[3] In *My Century* the Nobel-Prize-winning writer Günter Grass provides a literary analogue of annual calendar pages, based on single short stories that range from an eyewitness account of the Boxer Rebellion to a description of a six-day bicycle race. The sometimes amusing, sometimes touching scenes

---

11 (1900): 1–17. See Frank Möller, "Aufbruch ins 20. Jahrhundert. Gegenwartserfahrungen und Zukunftserwartungen der wilhelminischen Elite zur Saekularwende 1900," *Geschichte in Wissenschaft und Unterricht* 50 (1999): 730–39.

[2] "Hausmitteilung. Betr. Augstein, 20. Jahrhundert" and "Am Ende des Millenniums," *Der Spiegel* (1998) no. 45: 3 ff. See also Joachim Fest, "Das Böse als reale Macht. Hitlers noch immer verleugnetes Vermächtnis," *Der Spiegel* (1999) no. 43: 182 ff.

[3] Charles C. Stewart and Peter Fritzsche, eds., *Imagining the Twentieth Century: Exploring the Odd Passages and Side Doors of Our Collective Memory* (Urbana, 1997). See also the coffee table book of the National Geographic Society, ed., *National Geographic Eyewitness to the 20th Century* (New York, 1998), 49 ff., which calls 1910 "the women's decade," never mind World War One or the Russian revolutions!

reveal the writer's social-democratic sympathies for the underdog, peaceful cooperation, and so on.[4] But such clever photomontages and evocative capsule stories only highlight that the century as a whole has left a rather troubling and confusing legacy.

Historians, therefore, have had much difficulty in trying to put the recent past into a systematic perspective. The presentation of an ordered sequence of events in college textbooks that begins with imperialism and ends with the Cold War tends to dissolve in confusion in the last third of the century.[5] The readings, proposed by such individual scholars as Robert Conquest, suffer from privileging a particular concern, such as the failure of Marxism.[6] For instance, the American revisionist Gabriel Kolko has characterized the period as a "century of war" marked by international and internal military strife initiated largely by the West.[7] The French liberal thinker François Furet has fastened upon the triangular clash of Communist, Fascist, and democratic ideologies among intellectuals, a theme reiterated by the British Balkan historian Mark Mazower.[8] The German-Jewish critic Dan Diner has sought "to understand the century" from an East European perspective to explain how the worldwide civil war between the ideologies could turn into German ethnic cleansing and genocide.[9] No wonder that editors of essay collections have given up any attempt to systematize and instead include as many different themes as possible in the hope that some of them will resonate with their readers.[10]

How can anyone make better sense of a century marked by its very excesses, riven by contradictions, and known for its inherent disorder? A useful starting point might be the very discrepancy between the sanguine expectations and grave disappointments in the first half of the twentieth century since the reasons for which subsequent events escaped the prognostications of the contemporaries need to be explained. Such an approach would resist the temptation to reorder the confusion

    [4] Günter Grass, *Mein Jahrhundert* (Göttingen, 1999). Typically enough, the book has no preface or introduction to justify the selections and does not even have jacket copy.

    [5] Compare Chester V. Easum, *Half Century of Conflict* (New York, 1952), with Robert O. Paxton, *Europe in the Twentieth Century*, 3rd ed. (Fort Worth, 1997).

    [6] Robert Conquest, *Reflections on a Ravaged Century* (New York, 1999).

    [7] Daniel Kolko, *Das Jahrhundert der Kriege* (Frankfurt, 1999).

    [8] François Furet, *The Passing of an Illusion: The Idea of Communism in the Twentieth Century* (Chicago, 1999); and Mark Mazower, *Dark Continent: Europe's Twentieth Century* (London, 1998).

    [9] Dan Diner, *Das Jahrhundert verstehen. Eine universalhistorische Deutung* (Munich, 1999). Unfortunately, the book's chronology breaks off in 1957, thereby failing to address the second half of the century.

    [10] Michael Howard and William Roger Louis, eds., *The Oxford History of the Twentieth Century* (New York, 1998).

into a new narrative that would be limited by physical location and ideological commitment. Hence, the following reflections will begin with some conceptual issues, such as periodization, that ought to be resolved before any interpretation can be attempted. Without trying to extract a single meaning from multiple events, they will seek to take seriously their manifest disorder evident in the instability of space and time, and ponder the ironies of the double reversal of their trajectories. In trying to define the German role, these musings will depart from the usual procedure of a forward-moving narration and instead look back at the perplexing century.

Conceptualizing the Century

Centuries are merely calendrical artifacts, devices for labeling an expanse of time that exceeds the span of a usual human life. Although the educated started to think in centuries only around 1800, the public seems to have an insatiable desire for treating chronological shorthand as reality, especially when garnished by a colorful adjective such as "golden" or "terrible."[11] Wary of reifications, historians instead tend to use centuries as a "relatively 'neutral' chronological framework," suggesting that a multitude of developments are contained within the same timeframe to indicate their contemporaneity and interrelatedness. But what is actually associated with any given hundred years depends upon the analyst's geographical focus, thematic interest, or ideological preoccupation, making this unit of time a screen upon which any number of different themes can be projected as long as they coincide temporally.[12] Although constrained by the chronology of actual events, such a constructivist perspective implies that no self-evident lessons can be drawn from the twentieth century, but that its twisted course suggests contradictory readings.[13]

Dating the beginning or end of a century is therefore not predetermined but must be the result of analytical decisions. Since 1900 was not a particularly memorable year, historians have been uncertain when to start, some commencing with the apogee of imperialism in the 1890s and others delaying until the outbreak of World War I. The terminal

[11] Manfred Jakubowski-Thiessen et al., eds., *Jahrhundertwenden. Endzeit- und Zukunftsvorstellungen vom 15. bis zum 20. Jahrhundert* (Göttingen, 1999).

[12] Clive Pointing, *Progress and Barbarism: The World in the Twentieth Century* (London, 1998), 3 ff.

[13] Peter Jennings and Todd Brewster, *The Century* (New York, 1999). Chronicles are the simplest form of presentation since they claim only to compile "facts" without making any conscious arrangement.

date also remains somewhat in doubt, as the collapse of Communism in 1989/91 marks an important dividing line, but the new Balkan wars extend into the 1990s. In the context of German politics, the fall of Bismarck in 1890 might indicate a more important caesura than the appointment of Bülow ten years later, while the reunification of the two successor states in 1990 might serve as a better end point than the later move of the government to Berlin. If one wants to stress the legacy of the nineteenth century, its successor can start only in 1914, and if one prefers to focus on the collapse of the Soviet Union, the period will end in 1991, making, indeed, for a "short twentieth century."[14] But if one looks to important shifts in government instead, one could also argue for a time period from 1890 to 1999, creating a much longer century.

Similarly contested is the internal periodization of the twentieth century, breaking it down into smaller units according to important turning points. It must be remembered that the notion of a "caesura" is merely an analytical device to distinguish time periods according to some intervening event that results in a difference in character. On a global scale, economic historians have argued for the Great Depression of 1929 and the Oil Shock of 1973 as the key markers of the past century.[15] In a more limited German sense, there has been general agreement on the importance of the creation of the Weimar Republic in 1918, the Nazi seizure of power in 1933, and the end of German sovereignty in 1945. But for the postwar period, the subdivisions are much less certain since the establishment of separate states in 1949, the building of the Wall in 1961, the social-liberal coalition in the West in 1969, and the fall of Ulbricht in 1972 in the East seem of lesser significance.[16] As a more comprehensive alternative, one might argue for the importance of the "cultural revolution" of 1968 as a generational and social watershed. While there is a consensus on the reunification date of 1990 as a caesura, only time will tell whether 1999 will really mark the beginning of a "Berlin Republic."[17]

A second set of issues concerns the failure of leading master narratives to offer a coherent account of developments in the twentieth cen-

[14] David Blackbourn, *The Long Nineteenth Century: A History of Germany, 1780–1918* (New York, 1998).

[15] Pointing, *Progress and Barbarism*, 4 ff.

[16] Klaus Tenfelde, "1914 bis 1989—Einheit der Epoche," *Aus Politik und Zeitgeschichte* (1991) no. 40: 3–11; Werner Müller, "Doppelte Zeitgeschichte, Periodisierungsprobleme der Geschichte der Bundesrepublik und der DDR," *Deutschland Archiv* 29 (1996): 552–59; and Wolfgang Schieder, "Deutsche Umbrüche: 1918, 1933, 1945, 1989," *Alexander von Humboldt Stiftung Magazin*, no. 73 (1999): 11–24.

[17] Karl-Dietrich Bracher, "Zeitgeschichtliche Anmerkungen zum 'Zeitenbruch' von 1989/90," *Neue Züricher Zeitung*, 20 January 1991; and Konrad H. Jarausch, "1968 and

tury. The traditional form of a national storyline deals with the internal competition of various groups for power, and the external struggle for recognition, influence, or ascendancy. For Germany, the leading textbooks of Volker Berghahn and Mary Fulbrook focus on the implications of the multiple regime changes at home as well as on the territorial consequences of the successive world wars abroad. For the postwar period such an approach has to tell the story of a divided nation and explain the reasons for its eventual reunification.[18] The emphasis on politics presents identifiable actors and derives unmistakable lessons, but such an approach leaves out most of what concerns ordinary people's lives—for instance, the introduction of such items as the wristwatch, TV, bras, zippers, jeans, and running shoes. Moreover, because of the untold suffering of the wars and the Holocaust, the German case cannot be represented as a success story—it instead tends to be narrated as a negative example in which an excess of nationalism almost destroyed nation and state.[19]

The Marxist counternarrative is hardly more successful in presenting a convincing interpretation of the twentieth century. This perspective pays particular attention to the cycles of economic development, the social class struggle, the global competition of imperialism, and the resultant wars. In *Age of Extremes* the accomplished British scholar Eric Hobsbawm proposes the conception of a "short century" from 1914 to 1991 that was overshadowed by its catastrophic beginning, followed by a "golden age" during the Cold War, and concluded with a renewed crisis toward the end. Some parts of his structural argument can well explain major developments such as the Great Depression and decolonization, but other aspects such as the bloody record of Stalinism in the Soviet Union are treated too lightly. At the same time Hobsbawm has difficulties explaining the unforeseen collapse of Communism at the end of the century, which contradicts the historical optimism inherent in the Marxist vision.[20] Perceptive East German historians realized

---

1989: Caesuras, Comparisons, and Connections," in Carole Fink, Philipp Gassert, and Detlef Junker, eds., *1968: The World Transformed* (Cambridge, 1998), 461 ff.

[18] Volker R. Berghahn, *Modern Germany: Society, Economy and Politics in the Twentieth Century* (Cambridge, 1982); and Mary Fulbrook, *The Divided Nation: A History of Germany, 1918–1990* (Oxford, 1992). See also Christoph Kleßmann, Hans Misselwitz, and Günter Wichert, eds., *Deutsche Vergangenheiten—Eine gemeinsame Herausforderung* (Berlin, 1999).

[19] Eberhard Jäckel, *Das deutsche Jahrhundert. Eine historische Bilanz* (Stuttgart, 1996), 337 ff. See also "Schneller, freier, jugendlicher. Frauen in Hosen, Jugendkult, und der ständige Blick auf die Uhr—ein Rückblick auf das 20. Jahrhundert," *Der Tagesspiegel* 4 December 1999.

[20] Eric Hobsbawm, *The Age of Extremes: A History of the World, 1914–1991* (London, 1994). For a trenchant critique, comparing Hobsbawm to Furet, see Manfred Hettling, "Der Mythos des 20. Jahrhunderts," *Saeculum* 49 (1998): 327–45.

toward the end of the GDR that their approach was unable to offer a convincing explanation of Hitler's rise to power and of the racist dimension of the Holocaust.[21]

The modernization focus has turned out to be equally problematic since the catastrophes of the century have called the very substance of modernity into question. Visions of progress in democratic government, popular prosperity, social equality, and cultural creativity still populate Anglo-American textbooks, as if modernity had not revealed a terrifying face by new methods of domination and clever machines for mass killing.[22] The liberal representation of the German case as a deviation from civilized western norms has in retrospect become problematic since the Anglo-American exemplars have not always lived up to their own standards and the Germans could claim that they followed many of the same tendencies as others, only in a somewhat more extreme form. It remains to be seen whether Hans-Ulrich Wehler can bring off his magisterial effort to offer a coherent interpretation of twentieth-century German history from a modernization perspective.[23] Skeptics might wonder whether the German problem might have been not a lack of modernity, but, rather, its excess in certain areas such as warfare and scientific racism.

A final set of issues concerns the evaluation of the basic trajectory of development throughout the twentieth century. As indicated above, many contemporaries hoped the ineluctable march of progress would bring a better life for everyone. Countless indicators seemed to herald advancement, such as the lengthening life span, produced by improved nutrition, sanitation, and better medical treatment. Journals of the educated classes were replete with celebrations of new discoveries that promised to lift the veil from natural processes and make the world intelligible to human reason. There was an undeniable spread of wealth from the elite downward to the middle classes, eventually reaching, through collective bargaining, even the hard-pressed members of the proletariat and affording them some moments of leisure. There were countless technological advances like the automobile, enshrined in the newly founded Deutsche Museum in Munich, that promised to make daily life easier while overcoming distance through rapid communica-

---

[21] Rolf Badstübner, Vom "Reich" zum doppelten Deutschland. Gesellschaft und Politik im Umbruch (Berlin, 1999).

[22] Theodore S. Hamerow, The Birth of a New Europe: State and Society in the Nineteenth Century (Chapel Hill, 1983); and Roderick Phillips, Society, State and Nation in Twentieth Century Europe (Upper Saddle River, N.J., 1996).

[23] Christian Graf von Krockow, Die Deutschen in ihrem Jahrhundert 1890–1990 (Hamburg, 1990), presents a popularized version of the Sonderweg thesis. Hans–Ulrich Wehler has yet to finish the twentieth century volume of his impressive German social history.

tion and travel.[24] No wonder that the notion of "progress" became a fundamental frame of reference for the twentieth century.

The actual experiences in the succeeding decades, nonetheless, belied this expectation and suggested a new age of barbarism instead. Did not the twentieth century witness more killing than any previous age, during ethnic clashes, world wars, class conflicts, and racial genocide? Were not the modern dictatorships much more efficient in their repression of individuals, regimentation of society, and incarceration of presumed enemies than older authoritarian regimes? Was there not endless exploitation and discrimination according to social class, gender, and race, which increased human misery rather than diminishing suffering? Much of twentieth-century thought was, therefore, taken up with reflecting on this disappointment, trying to explain how the enormous potential for good could turn into its very opposite. Especially in Germany, notions of inevitable human progress became difficult to sustain, and the educated often succumbed to cultural pessimism of the Right or the Left. The debate is still inconclusive on whether these appalling developments should be construed as regrettable backsliding on the way upward or whether they were in some fundamental sense a product of modernity itself.[25]

Deciding on periodization, narrative focus, and trajectory ultimately depends upon the criteria used for selection among a confusing variety of choices. The broad-ranging Berlin retrospective on twentieth-century art illustrates that such standards are not contained in the events themselves, but result from analytical perspectives of the observer, the so-called *Blickachsen*, that focus on certain stylistic or cultural preferences. Some scholars might fasten upon the novelty of developments, thinking especially about technological innovations and material advances. Other observers would instead emphasize the duration of certain tendencies, ignoring short-term changes for more long-term transformations. Yet other commentators might look to the effect that certain incidents had upon the subsequent course of events, merely highlighting those that had repercussions down the line. Instead of struggling to impose a single interpretation, scholars might do well to heed Manfred Hettling's injunction and open their views to a "plurality of 'stories' " that might ultimately constitute twentieth century history.[26]

---

[24] Möller, "Aufbruch ins 20. Jahrhundert," 730 ff. See Eve M. Duffy, "Representing Science and Technology: Politics and Display at the Deutsches Museum" (Ph.D. dissertation, Chapel Hill, 2002).

[25] Zygmunt Bauman, *Modernity and the Holocaust* (Ithaca, 1989); and Hans Maier, ed., *Die modernen politischen Religionen* (Frankfurt, 2000).

[26] Peter-Klaus Schuster, "Das XX. Jahrhundert—Ein Jahrhundert Kunst in Deutschland," introduction to the exhibition catalogue (Berlin, 1999); and Hettling, "Mythos des kurzen 20. Jahrhunderts," 344–45.

Uncertainties of Space
and Time

The disjuncture between expectations at the beginning of the century
and its eventual outcome, the contrast of degradation, starvation, and
annihilation on the one hand and of utter privilege, wealth, and consumption on the other, are too egregious to be fitted into a conventional narrative. Scholars would like history to progress smoothly
across extreme contortions while audiences expect a retrofitted predictability. But the twentieth-century experience suggests that space ex-
pands and contracts precipitously, time twists and bends dramatically,
and political regimes do not follow one another as if they were a succession of kings. The course of history shifted not just once, but three,
four, or five times. Key events remade life not only in one nation, but
in a continent. They decided who was German and who was not, who
in Europe would survive and who would perish. In the end, things
did not even out. The nation that has emerged at the end of the century
is a long way from the one that started it. However much one might
prune this past, its trajectory veers off at odd angles, suggesting that
uncertainty might be the principle of twentieth-century history rather
than an abnormality to be explained away.

A simple look at a succession of maps, in 1914, 1918, 1923, 1939, 1941,
1945, 1949, 1961, and 1990 illustrates that German territory has varied
wildly. Although historians may inquire into the causes of these fluctuations, they rarely explore the persistence of territorial change and
its consequences. The expectation of a constant German territory
clashes with the reality of continually changing, radically expanding
and contracting borders. What is elided here is the action of border-
making, which, if one takes the maps at face value, appears as one of
the German and, for that matter, central and eastern European preoccupations of the century.[27] To be sure, we have come to understand
quite a bit about ethnic struggles or even cooperation in border regions, but we know little about what this conflict over territory actually entailed for the participants, the nation at large, and the international community.[28] It is important to note, therefore, that the very
thing—the "container nation"—that postwar historians have come to

[27] Alexander Demandt, ed., *Deutsche Grenzen in der Geschichte* (Munich, 1990); and
Klaus Zernack, *Preußen, Deutschland, Polen. Aufsätze zur Geschichte der deutsch-polnischen
Beziehungen* (Berlin, 1991).

[28] William W. Hagen, *Germans, Poles and Jews: The Nationalities Conflict in the Prussian
East, 1772–1914* (Chicago, 1980). See also Till van Rahden, *Juden und andere Breslauer* (Göttingen, 2000).

take for granted proved extremely volatile and subject to recurrent, deliberate, and emotionally highly charged action. Both geopolitical struggles and their prerequisite, the emotional investment in territory, are of interest here.

Consider further, on the basis of the 1918 and 1942 maps, that German presence cut deeply into Poland, the Baltic states, Belarus, the Ukraine, and Russia among others—and to such an extent that their recent histories become inexplicable without the fact of German intrusion. Does this mean that Belarus should become a part of German history and vice versa? This suggests not only that German territoriality expanded and contracted in rapid succession, but that German space overlaid others and was, in turn, overlaid by others. Much has been said about "westernization" and "sovietization" in recent years,[29] but the physical presence of huge armies, the dependence on security, indeed, the sovereignty of patron-states, and, not least, the interpenetration of markets, particularly in the second half of the century, are the most striking elements of this process. The history of territorial overlay is a two-way street in which presence rather than influence matters. As a result, separate histories become inextricably linked, even if only one side remembers the fact. Belarus in 1942 is one example.[30] Berlin in 1962 is another.[31] Territorial overlay is, in any case, a persistent, if rescindable reality of twentieth-century history and quite contrary to what German territory is imagined to be—a stable entity.

The renowned philosopher Karl Popper provides a further example of the uncertainty of spatial definitions of Germanness. In actual fact, Popper was Austrian born, but Austria, of its own free will, was part of Germany when he launched the career that brought him global fame—in Christchurch, New Zealand.[32] Popper's life story and intellectual project are, undoubtedly, German or, in any case, central European—and if not, do they belong to New Zealand? They do, because without the hospitality of New Zealand, Karl Popper would not be what he became. The same could be said of all the major and minor intellectual figures who could write because they escaped annihilation

[29] Konrad H. Jarausch and Hannes Siegrist, eds., *Amerikanisierung und Sowjetisierung in Deutschland 1945–1970* (Frankfurt, 1997); and Anselm Doering-Manteuffel, *Wie westlich sind die Deutschen? Amerikanisierung und Westernisierung im 20. Jahrhundert* (Göttingen, 1999).

[30] Christian Gerlach, *Kalkulierte Morde. Die deutsche Wirtschafts- und Vernichtungspolitik in Weissrussland 1941 bis 1944* (Hamburg, 1999).

[31] Marc Trachtenberg, *A Constructed Peace: The Making of the European Settlement 1945–1963* (Princeton, 1999).

[32] Malachi H. Hacohen, *Karl Popper, the Formative Years 1902–1945: The Politics and Philosophy in Interwar Vienna* (New York, 2000).

by flight. Even if this tiny class of intellectuals might be an exception, there are all those others who began their lives somewhere between Königsberg and Freiburg, but who ended up in the United States, Australia, or Israel, most of them against their own will. Do they have to exhibit patriotism in exile to be acknowledged as part of a violently fractured German space?[33]

Equally, if differently troublesome, is the case of another ethnic minority, one that first was moved to Alma Ata to end up in Lahr or Pforzheim. These *Volksdeutsche* are a fragment of a much wider German-speaking population, mostly in eastern Europe, some of whom are readily acknowledged as Germans, while others (Yiddish speaking Jews) were not. Since the fate of these populations was a persistent concern throughout the twentieth century, and they were subject to such extreme action, one might expect that they would emerge as central protagonists in a German history with all the contradictory impulses this entails, but they did not. Instead, they were made to disappear at the margins, swallowed up by a fiction of spatial identity. Wherever we turn, the space of German history is beyond the control and the power exerted on German territory.

Since its spatial extent stretched and shrank, the commonsense notion of a stable German "territory" turns out to be problematic. Rather than being a self-evident and, moreover, coeval foundation, space is subject to recurrent action that alters it time and again. The hard facts are that the territory of German history is local and global (in the case of the Jewish expellee) and global and local (in the case of the Berlin crises of 1948 and 1961), and that Germany is implicated very directly in the history of Belarus and can be invoked in New Zealand. Therefore, the first and most important conclusion to be drawn is that German territoriality has been uncertain because its changing shape did not follow a predictable path of development. It would be foolish, however, to think that these oscillations were arbitrary, and it would be repugnant to consider them without their consequences. They are frequent enough to cause one to think of the nation-state that has come to prevail in historiography as a fiction of security and stability worth studying in its own right, but it ought not to be made into the cornerstone of history.

The question of experienced time is no less problematic. The reality of disrupted chronology haunts twentieth-century German history from one end to the other. Despite the best efforts of historians soberly

[33] Friedrich Wilhelm Graf, "Tagtraum vom Bürgerhumanismus. Aus Liebe zum Vaterland. Die Geschichtsbilder des deutschen Juden Hans Baron," *Frankfurter Allgemeine Zeitung*, 24 June 2000.

to write about earlier eras, past and present blend into and are set against each other. The time sequence of twentieth-century German history does not progress smoothly. Neither does it follow a rail track—not even a multi-rail track—of imagined progress. Rather, it breaks the bounds of chronological history with its extraordinary reversals and interventions. Moreover, it is rife with exorbitant fictions of beginnings and ends, ranging from the expectations of an apocalypse before World War I to the expectations of a third world war and more real ecological disasters during the 1980s.[34] These fictions bespeak the issue of time, raising philosophical and historical questions about its relativity and incongruity.[35]

How does time become "real"—that is, embodied in actors and actions—in twentieth-century German history? When considering ordinary life histories, which have a self-evident continuity beyond the fluctuations of political maps, we immediately encounter as the signature of the century the very precariousness of life because of human intervention rather than the relentlessness of nature. Mass death and genocide make it a story of absence and disappearance, of lives not lived, of lives threatened and endangered, and of lives haunted by death long after the threat to survival was gone. At times, loss and endangerment were so stark a reality that they threatened to overshadow all other aspects of life. If there was something like a collective experience, it was the encounter with mass death, with irretrievable loss. As a national experience, this encounter was irredeemably divided along the lines of action—it was murder and sacrifice.[36] This division cannot be undone. It is the tear that rips through the fabric of twentieth-century time.

Since it is the living who remember the dead, the lines of their lives establish the closest thing to continuity that twentieth-century German history has. The fact itself is striking and may account for the turn to and fascination with family and everyday life histories that run across the markings of recurrent upheavals. That so fickle and short a thing as a life history should be one of the most durable entities is an indica-

---

[34] Klaus Vondung, *Die Apokalypse in Deutschland* (Munich, 1988); and Klaus Scherpe, "Dramatisierung und Entdramatisierung des Untergangs—zum ästhetischen Bewußtsein von Moderne und Postmoderne," in Klaus Vondung and Andreas Huyssen, eds., *Postmoderne. Zeichen eines kulturellen Wandels* (Reinbek, 1986), 270–301.

[35] Günter Dux, *Die Logik der Weltbilder. Sinnbilder im Wandel der Geschichte* (Frankfurt, 1982).

[36] Andreas Hillgruber, *Zweierlei Untergang. Die Zerschlagung des Deutschen Reiches und das Ende des europäischen Judentums* (Berlin, 1986). Although Hillgruber's equation of the two deserved to come under attack, the outrage against it does not mend that tear in German history.

tion of what kind of century it has been. Hence, it is not quite by chance that such histories often enough resemble scrapbooks, the most apt medium of recalling "disrupted lives" because they freeze-frame what would otherwise become lost time.[37] The latter is a suitable metaphor for the peculiar experience of time in twentieth-century Germany: People live on but lose their time not just once, but several times over.

Much has been made of former Nazis, such as "Fritz K.," who ended up as a honored citizens of the Federal Republic.[38] His life history is surely more typical than that of Ruth B., who was born in Tel Aviv (1923) and came to Darmstadt in 1947 to help rebuild the new Germany—and succeeded.[39] Apparently, Fritz K. never made any bones about his having been a Nazi (much as the exceptional Ruth B. never left any doubt that she was German, born of Jewish parents). But in each of these cases, which are separated by the chasm of the Holocaust (which claimed Ruth B.'s parents, who had returned to German-speaking Prague), labors of adjustment and acts of transition were required, even though neither of the two disavowed their respective past. Their adjustments started from radically opposed points of experience: In 1942 Ruth B. was stuck in London as a seamstress, her parents incarcerated in Terezin, while Fritz K. was roaming the length and width of Greater Germany. These are labors redefined by time, making its abstract progression real—and they made Ruth B. and the Federal Republic a winner, whereas Fritz K., despite wealth and prestige, turned out to be a loser.

Although no amount of history can undo the contrary effect of events on these two lives, both life histories had in common a split in direction that inadvertently separated them from their past. Apologetic claims to the contrary, there was, to be sure, no tabula rasa, no "zero hour," no new beginning.[40] But there was no simple continuity either, although each protagonist embraced his or her respective past. Not only did they end up in times they never thought they would experience, but the new experience changed them irrevocably, even if it appears that Fritz K. had to be dragged into the present and never really felt at home there,

[37] Gay Becker, *Disrupted Lives: How People Create Meaning in a Chaotic World* (Berkeley, 1997).

[38] Hartmut Berghoff, and Cornelia Rauh-Kühne, *Fritz K. Ein deutsches Leben im zwanzigsten Jahrhundert* (Stuttgart, 2000).

[39] There is no biography of Ruth B. The discussion is based on Michael Geyer's personal recollections.

[40] Gerd Trampe, ed., *Die Stunde Null. Erinnerungen an Untergang und Anfang* (Stuttgart, 1995); and Geoffrey Giles, ed., *Stunde Null: The End and the Beginning Fifty Years Ago* (Washington, D.C., 1997).

much in contrast to Ruth B., who thereby surprised her far-flung relatives and friends. Following German life histories—including those who were German at one point and those who would become German at another—through the twentieth century gives the lie to a linear progression of time. Time is what people make of their experience under changing and, often enough, involuntary circumstances.

Because conditions changed so dramatically and repeatedly, one of the main preoccupations of people consisted of transforming from one person into another, changing appearance, shedding memories with each new era—and contesting the truthfulness of the changes made. In hindsight, all these personae of one person or family and, for that matter, of the nation can be found assembled in photo albums or artfully rendered in vignettes of the century.[41] They are the source of quiet puzzlement and, not infrequently, of shocking discovery. While the scandal of hidden pasts still preoccupies the debate, the terrifying experience of seeing oneself as some other persona, as a stranger, is "memory in the face of loss, personal recollection in the face of public eventfulness."[42] This widespread sense of *temps perdus* pervades the German experience of the twentieth century.

The rewriting of curricula vitae has tended to be an eminently political process: There were socialists who started as imperialists, monarchists who became republicans, fascists who turned into Bolsheviks and Bolsheviks who ended up as fascists, communists who grew into democrats and vice versa. And there were those special cases like the *Germanist* Schneider/Schwerte, president of the Technical University at Aachen, who abandoned his SS uniform together with his name in 1945 to become an upright citizen of the FRG. He was so upright that he proceeded to remarry his inadvertently widowed wife.[43] The uproar about the reverse case, a Swiss man—although he vehemently denies the charge—becoming a Lithuanian child survivor of the Holocaust, may serve as a further example of the same phenomenon.[44] Finally, in the emergent Berlin Republic an entire industry has begun to reconvert émigrés, such as Marlene Dietrich, into German patriots, replete with a German officer as a love object—a truly "foreign affair."[45] Whether

---

[41] Günter Grass, *My Century*, trans. Michael Henry Heim (New York, 1999).

[42] Stewart and Fritzsche, eds. *Imagining the Twentieth Century*, 3.

[43] Ludwig Jäger, *Seitenwechsel. Der Fall Schneider/Schwerte und die Diskretion der Germanistik* (Munich, 1998); and Claus Leggewie, *Von Schneider zu Schwerte. Das eigentümliche Leben eines Mannes, der aus der Geschichte lernen wollte* (Munich, 1998).

[44] Binjamin Wilkomirski, *Fragments: Memories of a Wartime Childhood*, trans. Carol Brown Janeway (New York, 1996).

[45] Steven Bach, *Marlene Dietrich: Life and Legend* (New York, 1992).

as personal gesture or as collective phenomenon, past, present, and future were persistently at odds and in need of repeated renegotiation. One might well think of this activity as the quintessential German pursuit of identity in the twentieth century.

Because experience and memory were so closely intertwined with regime changes, policing time became a German preoccupation. The clash between Republicans and Monarchists offers a first glimpse of the hostile encounter over memory and experience. The Nazis were obsessed with their political enemies and with racial genealogy: The danger of non-Aryans "passing" for Germans, the notorious difficulty of distinguishing Aryans from others, was a source of intense concern.[46] By the same token, the East German regime was haunted by the fear of converts and renegades, "wreckers" whose former class position made them untrustworthy allies and, more likely, inadvertent enemies.[47] West Germany had its own convulsions when the outing of old Nazis began in earnest in the 1970s, since seemingly upright democrats were revealed to be former fascists and murderers—or suspect for concealing the positions they held in the Third Reich.[48] The talk about *Wendehälse* (turncoats) in the wake of unification highlights the persistence of distrust of arriving in yet another regime of memory and experience.

In the progression of twentieth-century German histories, each new present undercut the preceding one and its respective trajectories into the future. Each new incarnation of the nation set itself up against the preceding one—a process that began with the Wilhelmine Empire's (1890–1918) distancing itself from the Bismarckian Reich and that found its latest instantiation in the so-called Berlin Republic, juxtaposed against the old Federal Republic. Time and again belying people's expectations, the actual course of events proved the idea of a continuous history in twentieth-century Germany to be a fantasy. Hence, we ought to ask what happens when time does not proceed chronologically but in spurts of experience and memory under shifting circumstances and as a result of deliberate intervention—when events escape the control of contemporaries, making one wonder what human agency makes them do so with such frequency. We may leave it to philosophers to decide whether uncertainty is a human condition. The point here is that disrupted time and fractured space are the predomi-

[46] Götz Aly, Peter Chroust, and Christian Pross, *Cleansing the Fatherland: Nazi Medicine and Racial Hygiene* (Baltimore, 1994).

[47] Mary Fulbrook, *Anatomy of a Dictatorship: Inside the GDR, 1949–1989* (Oxford, 1995).

[48] For the infamous Filbinger case (a former naval judge who became prime minister of Baden-Württemberg, although he had issued numerous death sentences at the end of the war), see Ralf Hochhut, *Die Juristen. Drei Akte für sieben Spieler* (Reinbeck, 1979).

nant, twentieth-century German experience and, hence, the condition to be understood.

Perhaps an extraordinary literary achievement can suggest how such a history might be written. In *Jahrestage*, Uwe Johnson's epic novel of twentieth-century Germany, actions and events ineluctably intrude to alter the course of people, communities, and entire nations.[49] The main character, Gesine Cresspahl, moves through the debris of pasts and presents in East and West Germany, Europe, and the United States over the course of the recollection written down in diary form between August 1967 and August 1968 for her daughter Mary, born in Düsseldorf and raised in New York City. Gently portrayed by the author as a thinking woman within a world beyond her control, Gesine Cresspahl is sifting through her incongruous worlds of experience and through the slices of a disrupted history. Mrs. Cresspahl is "produced" by the events of the century, but with cunning and courage she not only manages her own life (and that of her daughter, although Mary more often motions her mother to make sense) but also sorts out German history by pondering the myriad of experiences that have affected her presence as a German employee in a New York bank.[50] Johnson's novel is unsurpassed as a densely packed account of the disrupted times and fractured spaces that constitute German experiences in the past century.

Not only the narrative technique of switching space and layering time, but also Johnson's philosophical understanding of the course of events, could suggest a solution. At the very end of the novel, Gesine Cresspahl meets her old English teacher from Jerichow/Mecklenburg, Herr Kliefoth, who reminds his former student of her father's view of the world: "*Geschichte ist ein Entwurf.*" The phrase may well be translated into English as "History is a construction," which would well suit the carpenter Heinrich Cresspahl.[51] Herr Kliefoth refers to it to suggest that history is a net (or matrix) thrown over unpredictable events to locate them in an unstable space and an uncertain time. Although this is a not a popular approach among practicing scholars,[52] Reinhart Koselleck comes close to suggesting a similar approach to the writing of history in the modern age.[53] It is, in any case, a principle that one might use to reassemble the confusing debris of twentieth-century German

---

[49] Uwe Johnson, *Jahrestage*, 4 vols. (Frankfurt/Main, 1970–1983)

[50] Bernd Neumann, *Uwe Johnson* (Hamburg, 1994), 654–55.

[51] Johnson, *Jahrestage*, 4: 1891.

[52] Jean Leduc, *Les historiens et les temps: conceptions, problématiques, écritures* (Paris, 1999).

[53] Reinhard Koselleck and Wolf-Dieter Stempel, eds., *Geschichte. Ereignis und Erzählung* (Munich, 1973), and *Futures Past: On the Semantics of Historical Time*, trans. Keith Tribe (Cambridge, UK, 1985).

history. If Walter Scott's linear narrative provided a model for nine-teenth-century history, Uwe Johnson's fragmented multilocal and cross-temporal narrations might perform a similar function for the twentieth century.

The Double Reversal

Contrary to the claims of the master narratives, no single story line of development can adequately capture the confusing crosscurrents of central Europe during the twentieth century. For instance, the founding catastrophe of World War I set in motion further cataclysms such as the Great Depression, which in turn led to World War II, culminating in the unparalleled bureaucratic and industrial project of racial killing of the Holocaust. But for all its rhetorical bluster, the Cold War confrontation did not lead to World War Three, bringing instead an unprecedented prosperity to the West and eventually even helping to overthrow the Communist competitor in the East.[54] How do these incongruous events relate to one another, in what way can one explain the connection between the negative and the positive developments? At the risk of some oversimplification, one reading that recognizes the complexity of tangled developments might conceptualize the century as an unstoppable descent into bloody cataclysm followed by a gradual but ultimately successful return of a greater degree of civility.

A striking example of this trajectory is the drastic betrayal of the initially liberating promise of nationalism. The effort of liberal thinkers and businessmen to break out of the petty confines of parochialism spawned a powerful national movement that sought to unify German speakers (and some others) in the 1848 revolution. But the failure of the effort from below allowed Otto von Bismarck to harness national aspirations to the Prussian state, conquering territories in three victorious wars and cajoling the remaining princes into founding the Second Empire in 1871. Instead of developing into a satiated power and a constitutional state, this national-dynastic hybrid turned restless and aggressive, wishing to participate in imperial conquest and seeking to homogenize its citizenry linguistically, religiously, and racially. The bloody story of World War I and II needs no retelling to illustrate the pathological development of radical nationalism into National Socialism. What began as a cosmopolitan aspiration for self-determination

---

[54] See Roland N. Stromberg, *Europe in the Twentieth Century,* 4th ed. (Upper Saddle River, N.J., 1997); and James Wilkinson and H. Stuart Hughes, *Contemporary Europe: A History,* 9th ed. (Upper Saddle River, N.J., 1998).

ended up in a hegemonic frenzy of killing, surely a chilling inversion of the original aims.[55]

Another instance of disappointed hopes is the deflection of the drive for political participation and civil rights into its very opposite, modern dictatorship. The protest movement against Prince Metternich's reaction advocated popular self-government, whether in a moderate constitutional fashion or in a more radical democratic vein. But the compromise with the Hohenzollern crown left the liberal agenda unfinished so that the transition from notable to mass politics at around 1900 not only strengthened the forces of progress but also allowed reactionary and racist currents to acquire a mass base. Ironically, it was the excess of democracy in the Weimar Republic, such as the proportional franchise, that allowed the extremist movements of the Nazis and the Communists to topple the unloved system that defend itself too weakly.[56] The result was a "majority dictatorship" of the Right that reduced political participation to ritualized acclamation by abolishing civil rights, suppressing any critics of the regime, and instituting a cult of authoritarian leadership. Similarly, the explicitly antifacist rule of the SED also resorted to a "minority dictatorship," perpetuating unfreedom in the name of social progress.[57]

Yet another aspect of the reversal from confidence to gloom is the sudden end of popular prosperity and the return of grinding mass poverty. It took decades for the hunger riots and sweatshop protests of the mid-nineteenth century to be overcome by internal and external migration, large-scale industrialization, and labor agitation for a living wage. By the turn of the twentieth century the economist Karl Helfferich could, without fear of contradiction, talk in glowing terms about rising "popular prosperity" as the hallmark of the Second Reich.[58] But the shocks of the blockade-induced famine, the melting away of savings in the German hyperinflation, and the unemployed workers' struggle for survival during the Great Depression, ruptured this expectation of secure material progress. Even the return of some prosperity

---

[55] Compare Matthew Levinger, *Enlightened Nationalism: The Transformation of Prussian Political Culture, 1806–1848* (New York, 2000), to Eric Johnson, *The Nazi Terror: Gestapo, Jews and Ordinary Germans* (New York, 1999).

[56] Compare Jonathan Sperber, *Rhineland Radicals: The Democratic Movement and the Revolution of 1848–1849* (Princeton, 1991), to Donna Harsch, *German Social Democracy and the Rise of Nazism* (Chapel Hill, 1993).

[57] Martin Sabrow, "Der Konkurs der Konsensdiktatur. Überlegungen zum inneren Zerfall der DDR aus kulturgeschichtlicher Perspektive," in Martin Sabrow and Konrad H. Jarausch, eds., *Weg in den Untergang. Der innere Zerfall der DDR* (Göttingen, 1999), 83–116.

[58] Karl Helfferich, *Deutschlands Volkswohlstand 1888–1913* (Berlin, 1913).

during the peaceful years of the Third Reich turned out to be but a prelude for another plunge into homelessness, hunger, and despair for millions of Germans, triggered by the Nazis' defeat and lasting into the postwar years.[59] Once again an apparently justified hope was bitterly betrayed by the course of events in mid-century.

Even the social struggle for greater equality seems to fit into the same pattern of broken promises and unexpected calamity. Bourgeois observers around the turn of the century applauded the attempt of the lower classes to better themselves through further education, improved sanitation, better eating habits, and the like. Although still operating with paternalistic and familial assumptions, the women's movement also seemed to be making strides in the late Empire, gaining the vote with the Weimar constitution. But the hopeful tendencies of expanding welfare coverage to new groups foundered on the fiscal limitations of the Republic.[60] In contrast, Nazi egalitarianism turned lethal for all those excluded from the *Volksgemeinschaft*, ranging from political opponents to biological or racial inferiors, and produced a negative equality of suffering during the final years of the war. Similarly, the Communist project of social revolution abolished the remnants of the old elites and leveled the vast majority down into shared hunger and poverty, while privileging a new nomenclatura.[61] The liberation of women to labor in war production or in state-owned factories was not exactly the equality that its promoters had in mind.

Finally, the widespread faith in science and technology that was a large part of the optimism of 1900 was also cruelly disappointed half a century later. Were not the imperial German universities the model of the world and its technical colleges the envy of other nations? After all, new medical cures suggested the unending progress of *Wissenschaft*, while industrial spin-offs in metallurgy, electronics, and chemistry were fuelling the great prewar boom, and provided some of the weapons to fight the Great War.[62] The participation of the professoriate in wartime propaganda already raised some questions and the

[59] Gerald D. Feldman, *The Great Disorder: Politics, Economics and Society in the German Inflation, 1914–1923* (New York, 1993); and Harold James, *The German Slump: Politics and Economics, 1924–1936* (Oxford, 1986).

[60] David Crew, *Germans on Welfare: From Weimar to Hitler* (New York, 1998); and Young–Sun Hong, *Welfare, Modernity and the Weimar State, 1919–1933* (Princeton, 1998).

[61] David Schoenbaum, *Hitler's Social Revolution: Class and Status in Nazi Germany, 1933–1939* (Garden City, N.Y., 1966); and Konrad H. Jarausch, "Die gescheiterte Gegengesellschaft. Überlegungen zu einer Sozialgeschichte der DDR," *Archiv für Sozialgeschichte* 39 (1999): 1–17.

[62] Konrad H. Jarausch, "The Universities: An American View," in Jack R. Dukes and Joachim Remak, eds., *Another Germany: A Reconsideration of the Imperial Era* (Boulder, 1988), 181–206.

plight of science funding during the Weimar Republic was widely commented upon. But it was the expulsion of leading scientists by the Nazis that cut short scientific innovation, while the dedication of technology to rearmament deflected progress from consumer goods. The voluntary collaboration of historians or geographers with Nazi plans for conquest, the involvement of the medical community in racial experiments, and the contribution of engineers to ever more efficient killing machines (including the crematoria of the KZs) reversed benevolent perceptions of science and technology.[63] The tangible symbol of their destructive power logically became the nuclear bomb.

In these exemplary cases, but also in a multitude of other areas, originally positive developments curiously mutated into negative directions, leading Europe into an unprecedented cataclysm by mid-century. By reinforcing one another, seemingly independent developments in different sectors of human activity combined into a negative spiral that produced an unimaginable calamity. The photographs of charred landscapes, shocking film clips of hollow-eyed survivors, and chilling eyewitness descriptions of destroyed cities, monuments, and houses, dramatize the degree of self-destruction. In virtually every measurable indicator, from the available amount of food per capita to the number of children born, the period between 1944 and 1947 marks the bottom of the twentieth century. The only people who appear to have prospered were those who gained from the plight of others, for instance, blackmarketeers.[64] A key challenge for historians is, therefore, the explanation of the initial reversal from the great expectations in 1900 that led to the descent of an entire continent into the abyss less than five decades later.

Surprisingly enough, war-torn Europe did not remain a charred continent, inhabited by a shrinking and dispirited population living on the land—as some dire predictions envisaged. Instead, the destruction and suffering of 1945 functioned as a psychological shock, galvanizing a defeated populace into a laborious effort at reconstruction. Though it was not exactly a "zero hour," the total defeat also smashed some prior prejudices and initiated a lengthy, often private process of reconsideration of earlier experiences that allowed a gradual learning of new kinds of values and new patterns of behavior. Despite their flaws, the strenuous efforts of the occupying powers to denazify and reedu-

[63] Michael Burleigh, *The Racial State: Germany, 1933–1945* (Cambridge, UK, 1991); and Ulrich Herbert, ed., *National Socialist Extermination Policies: Contemporary German Perspectives and Controversies* (New York, 2000).

[64] Brian R. Mitchell, *International Historical Statistics: Europe 1750–1993*, 4th ed. (London, 1998).

cate their charges played a major role in this rehabilitation project. But there were also many antifascist Germans who had survived persecution and now stepped forward to remake the remnants of a nation in a more democratic and socialist fashion. Because it was both a defeat and liberation, the year 1945 came to function as the fulcrum around which developments once again turned—this time, however, into a more benign direction.[65]

The first example of the reversal toward civility is the fundamental discrediting of nationalism that eventually made West Germany into something like a "post-national democracy."[66] The loss of sovereignty transformed the country from a subject to an object of international politics, depriving the old elites of any chance to continue their hegemonic dreams. Its disastrous consequences—for instance, the loss of eastern territories and the division of the rest—inspired intellectuals to repudiate nationalism, even though many wanted to preserve some remnant of unity. Moreover, the integration of the Western successor state into NATO and the EEC as well as the incorporation of the Eastern rival into the Warsaw Pact embedded German politics into the wider context of Cold War blocs. The gradual westernization of the Federal Republic eased the skepticism of its western allies, while the subsequent *Ostpolitik* removed the historical fears of its eastern neighbors, thereby restoring some freedom of action. Through these steps the new elites learned that a civilian, multilateral, and economic policy would bring better results than would nationalist blustering.[67] The reward for learning this lesson was their partners' permission for eventual reunification, as long as it was buffered by further European integration.

Similarly, it was the dreadful experience of double dictatorship that ultimately turned a skeptical populace in a democratic direction. In the West, the resumption of politics began at the grassroots level to activate older traditions of self-government and culminated in the adoption of a new constitution, called the Basic Law, to avoid Weimar's mistakes. In the East the initial phase of an antifascist people's democracy quickly evolved into a second dictatorship when the SED failed to gain the expected approval at the polls. No doubt, the Cold War confrontation perpetuated authoritarian patterns, evident both in the style of

[65] Christoph Kleßmann, "Befreiung durch Zerstörung—Das Jahr 1945 in der deutschen Geschichte," *Schriftenreihe der Niedersächsischen Landeszentrale für politische Bildung*, no. 12 (Hanover, 1995).

[66] Term from Karl-Dietrich Bracher, *Wendezeiten der Geschichte. Historisch-politische Essays 1987–1992* (Stuttgart, 1992); and Konrad H. Jarausch, "Die Postnationale Nation. Zum Identitätswandel der Deutschen 1945–1995," *Historicum* (Spring 1995): 30–35.

[67] Christian Hacke, *Weltmacht wider Willen. Die Außenpolitik der Bundesrepublik Deutschland*, rev. ed. (Frankfurt, 1993).

Adenauer's chancellor democracy and in the personality cult of Walter Ulbricht. But with the generational revolt in 1968, the formal democratization of the West grew into an inner acceptance of democratic values and behavior patterns, especially among a significant segment of the young. It took two more decades for a sizable democratic opposition to coalesce in the East, which eventually succeeded in overthrowing the Communist rulers.[68] Far from easy or automatic, this complicated process nevertheless rooted democracy firmly in German politics.

The material transformation of a destroyed country into a prosperous and efficient society was no less startling, even if the East continued to lag behind. The initial removal of the rubble and rebuilding of housing and transportation lines was as much a physical necessity as a psychological balm, which allowed those with abused feelings to recover some sense of pride through evident accomplishment. The story of Ludwig Erhard's neoliberal currency reform and subsequent Economic Miracle has been told so often that it has become part of western folklore—but its outlines are nonetheless generally accurate. In the East the revival took a decade longer, and the economy, hampered by Russian reparations as well as by central planning, only reached levels that were impressive by comparison with its eastern neighbors. The return of prosperity allowed a new mass consumerism to develop in the FRG that made previously exclusive goods available to most of the population, a development followed on a more modest plane in the GDR. The Western currency, the deutsche Mark, came to represent the new wealth that East Germans rushed to join and other Europeans wanted to share, albeit in its Euro guise.[69]

The trauma of enforced equality also led to a rethinking of equal opportunity as a foundation for greater individualism in lifestyles. Already during the end of the war, the Nazi-imposed "community of fate" began to break up since some people survived the bombing and fighting unscathed while others lost their possessions, were taken prisoner, or were forced to flee their homes. The FRG responded by constructing a Social Market Economy that wedded a restored capitalism to an ever more extensive welfare state that reduced income disparities by taxation and protected citizens against most life hazards. The GDR sought to impose even greater equality with a social revolution that dispossessed landowners, industrialists, and businessmen, while sup-

---

[68] Axel Schildt, *Ankunft im Westen. Ein Essay zur Erfolgsgeschichte der Bundesrepublik* (Frankfurt, 1999).

[69] Anthony J. Nicholls, *Freedom with Responsibility: The Social Market Economy in Germany, 1948–1963* (Oxford, 1994); and Hannes Siegrist, ed., *Europäische Konsumgeschichte. Zur Gesellschafts- und Kulturgeschichte des Konsums, 18. bis 20. Jahrhundert* (Frankfurt, 1997).

porting basic foods, housing, and transportation for all—thereby bank-
rupting the stumbling planned economy.[70] In the FRG, the New Social
Movements of the 1970s revived feminism and slowly brought legal
gains for gender equality, while the post-material shift of the younger
generation led to a visible individualization of lifestyles. In the East, it
took a decade longer for different subcultures to develop that eventually eroded the nominal equality.

Finally, scientific and technological development also moved back
toward civilian pursuits, such as improving people's health and life-
experiences. With defeat, captured scientists and engineers were
shipped to the United States or the Soviet Union, and Germans were
forbidden to develop those nuclear, biological, and chemical (ABC)
weapons, deemed most destructive in a nuclear age. Because the rebuilding of scientific institutes took time and émigré scholars were reluctant to return to the devastated country, it was difficult to catch up
to international developments. But the Max Planck, Fraunhofer, and
other Western institutes soon regained the first rank of research, while
the bloated East German Academy remained more provincial behind
the Iron Curtain. As a result of losses and restrictions, the FRG came
to specialize in medium high technology, such as machine tools and
cars, while the GDR sought to compensate for its lack of materials by
improvising.[71] Gradual public realization of the involvement of science
and technology in the Holocaust led to intense ethical scrutiny of the
consequences of research for society, for instance, in genetic experimentation. The strength of the ecology movement and the success of
the Green Party at the polls are indicators of such moral sensitivity.

Even though many developments remained contested, their combined result has been the recovery of a surprising degree of civility in
Germany. For example, the *Spiegel* Affair showed that the constitutional guarantees of civil rights were strong, while the Federal Supreme Court often took lawmakers to task when their bills violated
legal norms.[72] Another indication is the demilitarization of society,
which has created a provision for alternate service in hospitals or old-
age homes that is chosen by almost the same number of young men
as regular military duty.[73] Yet another aspect is the antiauthoritarian

[70] Hans Günter Hockerts, ed., *Drei Wege deutscher Sozialstaatlichkeit. NS-Diktatur, Bundesrepublik und DDR im Vergleich* (Munich, 1998).

[71] Mitchell G. Ash, ed., *German Universities Past and Future: Crisis or Renewal?* (New
York, 1997).

[72] David Schoenbaum, *The Spiegel Affair* (New York, 1968).

[73] *Entmilitarisierung und Aufrüstung in Westdeutschland 1945–1956* (Herford, 1983); and
Jörg Hillmann and John Zimmermann, eds., *Kriegsende 1945 in Deutschland* (Munich,
2002).

shift of the late 1960s rebellion, which eroded traditional obeisance to authority and created an entire generation suspicious of government action, such as invasion of privacy and the like.[74] Similarly, "protection of life" has become a nonpartisan icon, so much so that the principle has made it rather difficult to achieve some kind of compromise in abortion questions.[75] Although xenophobia continues to erupt in ugly incidents, the vast majority of the population condemns antiforeigner violence and is gradually warming up to a form of multiculturalism.[76] Surely these are momentous changes in politics and society.

Across their stark differences, the two halves of the twentieth century were, therefore, linked through a collective process of learning that set out to avoid the repetition of the preceding catastrophes. The staggering amount of cruelty and killing in the two world wars led both to a revulsion against such barbarity and to a concerted effort to regain the momentum for human progress that had beckoned at the beginning of the century. Part of the rethinking involved a chastening of notions of human nature that began to recognize the human capacity for evil and sought to construct international and domestic systems in such a way as to prevent it from gaining the upper hand. The adoption of democratic forms of government and of a modified version of capitalist production after 1945 owed more to the drastic failures of dictatorship and to a pragmatic search for safeguards against potential relapses than to an idealistic quest for new departures.[77] The more positive course of the second half of the century can be understood as a testimony to a conscious intellectual attempt to come to terms with the horrors of the first decades, since its indubitable achievements were propelled by earlier ghosts.

The German Role

Within the confusing pattern of the twentieth century, the special role played by the Germans continues to be quite controversial. For the American intellectual critic Fritz Stern, "this could have become the German century" since "at the beginning of this century Germany was

[74] Martin Greiffenhagen and Sylvia Greiffenhagen, *Ein schwieriges Vaterland. Zur politischen Kultur im vereinigten Deutschland* (Munich, 1993).

[75] Joyce Mushaben, Geoffrey Giles, and Sara Lennox, "Women, Men and Unification: Gender Politics and the Abortion Struggle Since 1989," in Konrad H. Jarausch, ed., *After Unity: Reconfiguring German Identities* (New York, 1997), 137 ff.

[76] Klaus J. Bade, ed., *Die Multikulturelle Herausforderung. Menschen über Grenzen, Grenzen über Menschen* (Munich, 1996).

[77] Axel Schildt, *Zwischen Abendland und Amerika* (Munich, 1999).

the country in dynamic ascent."[78] The German political historian Eberhard Jäckel has gone even further and flatly asserted that "it *was* the
German century." He considered this designation appropriate because
"no other country burned its stamp so deeply upon Europe and the
world in the twentieth century as did Germany." Berlin's policy was
central in the outbreak and conduct of World War I, and even more
importantly, "under Hitler and in World War II, especially due to the
crime of the century, the murder of the European Jews." According to
Jäckel, the second half of the century continued to be dominated by
the aftereffects of these terrible developments, and "even at its end
Germany occupies an exceptional place in the memory of the nations
because of these events." In searching for a broader explanation of the
Holocaust, Dan Diner also ultimately came back to Hitler as the key
figure of the century.[79]

These claims to German importance curiously echo an older *Sonderbewußtsein* of the early 1900s that was predicated upon the superiority
of the Second Reich. Instead of worrying about the tenuous compromises between crown and parliament, German academics had celebrated the complicated system of the semiconstitutional Bismarckian
state as a creative reconciliation of the principles of authority and participation that would provide strength in the international arena. At
home they could point to such impressive indicators as the renown of
science and technology, the rapid gains in economic production and
prosperity, the spread of urban reform, and the perfection of the welfare state. Abroad they could take pride in the progress of trade, the
acquisition of colonies, and the reputation of the military. Around the
turn of the century, skeptics might mock a certain bourgeois provin-
cialism and blinkered self-righteousness, but in many ways Germany
had become a model of stability and progress not just for its Scandina-
vian neighbors, but also for visitors from defeated enemies like France
and interested neutrals like the United States.[80]

The argument for the centrality of Germany in the twentieth century,
however, rests more persuasively on the deleterious effects of Berlin's
policies upon European developments. Taking William II's exaggerated sense of self-importance at face value, many contemporaries
blamed the Kaiser for World War I, overlooking the complicated mixture of defensive intent and offensive style that characterized Berlin's
policy in the July crisis. As leader of the Central Powers, the German

---

[78] Fritz Stern, *Verspielte Grösse. Essays zur deutschen Geschichte* (Munich, 1996).

[79] Jäckel, *Das deutsche Jahrhundert*, 7 ff; and Diner, *Ein Jahrhundert verstehen*, 135 ff. See
also Hobsbawm, *Age of Extremes*, 21 ff;

[80] Helga Grebing, *Der "deutsche Sonderweg" in Europa 1806–1945* (Stuttgart, 1986).

Reich became the key enemy of Entente propaganda, thereby having to take the blame for all the suffering.[81] The even more terrible repetition of aggression and conquest under Hitler's aegis, which went far beyond anything that might be justified in terms of national self-determination, confirmed the worst fears of German designs for hegemony. Finally, the brutality of Nazi occupation, territorial restructuring, slave labor, ethnic cleansing, and racial annihilation has made the concept of the Holocaust synonymous with absolute evil. This negative perspective, which sees ordinary men as willing helpers in Nazi crimes, most strongly supports the claim to German exceptionalism in the twentieth century.[82]

Although inspiring a necessary soul-searching, this emphasis on the extraordinary role of the Germans nonetheless appears somewhat exaggerated in retrospect. Comparative genocide studies have begun to put German crimes into a broader context, for instance by contrasting the horrific colonial massacre of the Hereros to similar mass killings by other imperialist powers.[83] Moreover, Dan Diner correctly locates the origins of the practice of "ethnic cleansing" and forced population transfers in the Greco-Turkish struggles after World War I, which seem to have influenced Nazi thinking.[84] The controversial *Black Book of Communism* also puts the total figure of victims of the class struggle under Stalin and other leftist dictators considerably higher than the blood toll exacted by Hitler.[85] Such comparisons help to establish the general dimensions of a murderous century marked by unimaginable cruelties in both civil conflicts and international wars. Within a general pattern of killing, the Holocaust becomes somewhat less surprising, even if it retains its uniqueness as deliberate, state-directed, bureaucratic, industrial genocide of racially defined victims.[86]

The thesis of negative German exceptionalism, moreover, tends to ignore much of the international development of the second half of

[81] Konrad H. Jarausch, "The Illusion of Limited War: Chancellor Bethmann Hollweg's Calculated Risk, July 1914," *Central European History* 2 (1969): 48–76. See also Roger Chickering, *Imperial Germany and the Great War, 1914–1918* (Cambridge, 1998).

[82] Most notably Daniel J. Goldhagen, *Hitler's Willing Executioners: Ordinary Germans and the Holocaust* (New York, 1996).

[83] See the forthcoming study by Isabel Hull, "Military Culture and 'Final Solutions' in Imperial Germany" (working title).

[84] Diner, *Das Jahrhundert verstehen*, 79 ff. See also Norman Naimark, *Fires of Hatred: Ethnic Cleansing in Twentieth Century Europe* (Cambridge, Mass., 2001).

[85] Stephane Courtois et al., eds, *The Black Book of Communism: Crimes, Terror, Repression* (Cambridge, Mass., 1999). See also the forthcoming study of racial killing in the Soviet Union by Eric Weitz.

[86] Christopher Browning, *The Path to Genocide: Essays on Launching the Final Solution* (Cambridge, UK, 1995).

the twentieth century. While the aftershocks of German aggression and genocide were felt for decades, the superpower contest of the Cold War was not a German creation—instead, Central Europe was divided by the Iron Curtain, turning at best into an important area of military confrontation and diplomatic crisis. The two successor states might have played a disproportionate role in their respective blocs as showcases of competing ideologies and as stepping stones to control Europe through reunification, but despite their successful economic recovery, the FRG and the GDR were never powerful enough to dictate postwar developments in the same manner as earlier German regimes. Even if it helped cement the ideological polarization of Europe until *Ostpolitik* began to soften the ideological divide between the East and the West, the German problem hardly dominated the second half of the twentieth century to the same degree as it did the first.[87]

Such a Eurocentric focus also drastically underestimates those global trends in which the Germans played only a subsidiary role. For instance, the Wilhelmian fling with imperialism, though intense, was ended by the loss of the colonies in Versailles, redirecting Hitler's attempts at territorial conquest to contiguous European territory. Therefore, German racist phobias focused primarily upon other whites, declaring Jews and Slavs inferior while targeting blacks or other races to a lesser degree. Despite Germany's far-flung trading interests, the impulses toward globalization instead originated in imperial Britain or the United States, with its dynamic capitalism and investment in high technology. Even if Weimar modernism somewhat pointed the way, most developments associated with the rise of "popular culture" became more closely connected with "Americanization" of music or film. While German scientists laid some of the initial groundwork, the development of the nuclear bomb, the exploration of space, and the breaking of the genetic code instead took place in the United States or the Soviet Union.[88] Since the Germans were only peripherally involved in many worldwide aspects of recent history, it hardly makes sense to label the entire century with their name.

A less essentialist approach would see Germany, instead, as a site of an unusual accumulation of some general problems of modernity. Virtually all modernizing trends, from abortion reform to abstract expressionism, also swept through central Europe, where they impinged

---

[87] David Calleo, *The German Problem Reconsidered: Germany and the World Order, 1870 to the Present* (Cambridge, 1978).

[88] Charles Bright and Michael Geyer, "World History in a Global Age," *American Historical Review* 100 (1995), 1034–60; and Stefan Immerfall, ed., *Territoriality in the Globalizing Society: One Place or None?* (Berlin 1998).

upon an unsettled, still somewhat traditional society and, therefore, produced more backlash than elsewhere. Movements in favor of nationalism, eugenics, paternalism, or anti-Semitism were not particularly German inventions, but they encountered a more receptive audience in a country that was unsure of both its domestic arrangements and its place in the international order. Instead of stressing the continuities of an unchanging German national character, it might be more productive to ask why certain cross-national developments led to particularly dangerous consequences in central Europe.[89] To the degree that this calamity was part of a more universal crisis, Friedrich Meinecke might have been right in arguing that historians would have "to broaden the question concerning the German catastrophe to encompass the fate of the occident."[90]

In the final analysis, the important, but limited impact of Germany on the twentieth century was profoundly ambivalent, transforming itself from the civil to the catastrophic and back. Undoubtedly, the Germans were central participants in World War I and under the Nazi regime bore the ultimate responsibility for World War II, as well as for the horrors of the Holocaust. These unspeakable crimes have tarnished the German name and will continue to darken the historical record. But after 1945 West German leaders also helped spearhead the drive toward European integration and contributed with their *Ostpolitik* to ending the Cold War, while the East German people finally breached the Wall and hastened the collapse of Communism in the Soviet bloc. These postwar actions are evidence of a profound learning process that has sought to prevent the recurrence of catastrophes by constructive policies, designed to create more positive possibilities for the future.[91] Even the skeptical *New York Times* sees signs of a benign transformation of Germany into "a peaceful, prosperous nation surrounded by allies in the heart of Europe, and not a troubling powder keg." Though "the German problem is no more," the painful memories will continue to linger for a long time to come.[92]

[89] Michael Geyer, "Germany, or, The Twentieth Century as History," *South Atlantic Quarterly* 96 (1997), 663–702.

[90] Friedrich Meinecke, *Die deutsche Katastrophe* (Wiesbaden, 1946), 9.

[91] In contrast to the pessimism of Joachim Fest, "Das Böse als reale Macht. Hitlers noch immer verleugnetes Vermächtnis," Timothy Garton Ash, "Europa—ein einmaliges Modell," is more upbeat about the meaning of the century. *Der Spiegel* (1999) no. 43: 181 ff.

[92] "One Germany," *New York Times*, 9 October 2000.

Index